JOHN BRACKEN: A POLITICAL BIOGRAPHY

John Bracken, 1943 (© Karsh, Ottawa)

JOHN KENDLE

John Bracken:
A Political Biography

UNIVERSITY OF TORONTO PRESS

Toronto Buffalo London

© University of Toronto Press 1979
Toronto Buffalo London
Printed in Canada

Canadian Cataloguing in Publication Data

Kendle, John Edward, 1937-
John Bracken
Bibliography: p.
Includes index.
ISBN 0-8020-5439-0

1. Bracken, John, 1883-1969. 2. Politicians – Canada – Biography.
3. Progressive Conservative Party (Canada) – History. 4. Manitoba – Politics
and government – 1922-1958.*

FC3375.1.B73K35   971.27'02'0924   C79-094237-2
F1063.B73K35

For Judy, John, Andrew, and Nancy

Contents

Illustrations

Preface

This is a political biography of John Bracken, premier of Manitoba from July 1922 until January 1943 and leader of the Progressive Conservative party from December 1942 until October 1948. Although every effort has been made to present a rounded view of Bracken, the loss of his personal papers in the Winnipeg flood of 1950 and the lack of any substantial private material in the Bracken Papers in Winnipeg and Ottawa have necessitated an emphasis on his public career.

Even that task has not been as straightforward as one would have wished. The Bracken collection in the Provincial Archives of Manitoba contains no material for the first eighteen months of his premiership and none for the last three years. Moreover, the 300 boxes of material that rest in Winnipeg and Ottawa contain virtually nothing of substance by Bracken himself. All letters or memoranda by Bracken of value for this biography would fill no more than two slim file boxes. It has therefore been necessary to turn to the public record – legislative debates and newspapers – to interviews, and to other private manuscript collections in order to provide a reliable account of his political career. Even so, the workings of his mind, his philosophic stance, and the degree of his involvement in certain issues are still unclear and can only be surmised.

The major emphasis of the book is on Bracken's years as premier of Manitoba. No historian of Manitoba can venture far without realizing the enormous debt he owes to the work of W.L. Morton. His perceptive and sensitive study of the province, *Manitoba: A History*, is a clear and reliable guide to Manitoba's development, and this writer was constantly aware of Morton's sureness of touch and the soundness of his conclusions. However, apart from Morton, historians have been woefully negligent of Manitoba's history, particularly of the decades following the first war. The work of Murray Donnelly and Tom Peterson stands out in a bleak landscape of neglected themes. There are no monographic studies of the province's political, economic, or social development and only recently have honours and graduate students begun to explore the post-1919 period in a systematic fashion.

Owing to the lack of basic monographic work it has been necessary for me to deal with some issues at greater length than might otherwise have been the case. It is hoped that the book will contribute to the general understanding of Manitoba during the inter-war years. Nevertheless, this is a biography and I have explored and emphasized those problems and themes that were of greatest interest and concern to Bracken. In doing so I have reflected on the attitudes and ideas of his colleagues and of Manitobans generally but the book should not be confused with a general history of Manitoba for the 1920s and 1930s. That still remains to be written.

In preparing this book I have accumulated numerous debts. With a special thanks to John Bovey, Barry Hyman, Gilbert-Louis Comeault, and Betty Blight of the Provincial Archives of Manitoba, I am grateful to the librarians and staff of the Manitoba Legislative Library, the Public Archives of Canada, the National Library, the Saskatchewan Archives (located in both Regina and Saskatoon), the University of Saskatchewan Archives, Queen's University Archives, the Department of Agriculture (Ottawa), the University of Manitoba, and the University of Guelph. The Ontario Ministry of Education and the Leeds and Grenville County Board of Education provided valuable information about schools and education in the 1890s. The Hon. Jack Pickersgill and Professor Blair Neatby gave me generous access to those portions of the King Papers and King Diary that were still closed. The Progressive Conservative party and the New Democratic party permitted me to examine the records for the 1940s of the Progressive Conservatives and the CCF. Mrs Ralph Maybank allowed me to look at her husband's papers in the Provincial Archives of Manitoba; Mrs H.W. Winkler permitted me to examine the Howard Winkler Papers in the PAM; and Professor Norman Ward kindly forwarded copies of material in the Gardiner Papers.

I am particularly indebted to all the people who either allowed me to interview them or wrote lengthy letters recounting memories of Bracken. A full list is included in the Note on Sources but I wish to record my gratitude to Mrs Gladys Wilson, Bracken's sister, who willingly recalled their childhood days in Seeley's Bay during a lengthy interview in 1974 and who subsequently replied promptly and fully to my many queries. Douglas Campbell, former premier of Manitoba and a member of the Bracken party for the full twenty years; Locksley McNeill, Bracken's former secretary; Dick Bell; and Mel Jack were all generous with their time. I also wish to express my thanks to the Bracken family, particularly to Bruce Bracken, who, while showing a constant interest in my work, have never intruded and have never attempted to influence my conclusions or interpretations.

My typist Diane Walton has greatly lightened my task and deserves a special commendation for quickly transcribing my all but illegible drafts into clear type-script. I am also very grateful to Rosemary Shipton for her excellent editorial advice. My research and typing costs have been eased by the support of the Bracken Biography Fund at the University of Manitoba, the Canada Council, and the University of Manitoba Research Fund. The book has been published with the help of a grant from the Social Science Federation of Canada, using funds provided by the Social Sciences and Humanities Research Council of Canada, and a grant to University of Toronto Press from the A.W. Mellon Foundation.

My greatest debt is to Judy for listening patiently and critically to my ideas and for strengthening my resolve, and to my children John, Andrew, and Nancy for putting up with an often distracted father.

JK
Winnipeg
7 January 1978

Bracken revisits his birthplace, July 1943

Gertrude, John (standing), Manfred, and Gladys in 1889

with A.C. Cameron,
double sculls winners
1904

On the porch at Seeley's Bay, 1908
rear Ephraim, John, Alberta; *middle* Alice, Gertrude, Mary Bracken
(grandmother), Manfred; *front* Erma, Gladys

Alice Bruce as John first met her

Alice Bruce

professor of
field husbandry
c 1910

Premier Bracken in 1927

Bracken's first cabinet, August 1922

with Stuart Garson in 1942

TOP John, Gordon, Alice, Bruce, Doug, George in the early war years

Farm picnic, July 1944

OPPOSITE, TOP Delegates' farewell to the leader, PC convention 1948

Football finals
Toronto, 1943

with M.J. Coldwell and
Louis St Laurent at the
UN in 1946

box-car commissioner, Fort Garry Hotel, 1958

JOHN BRACKEN: A POLITICAL BIOGRAPHY

Abbreviations

BSA Bachelor of Scientific Agriculture
BP Bracken Papers
CLDL Canadian Labour Defence League
CCF Cooperative Commonwealth Federation
H of C House of Commons
HBMS Hudson Bay Mining and Smelting Company
ILP Independent Labour Party
IDB Industrial Development Board
MAC Manitoba Agricultural College
MWUC Mine Workers Union of Canada
NRMA National Resources Mobilization Act
OAC Ontario Agricultural College
PAC Public Archives of Canada
PAM Provincial Archives of Manitoba
SAB (R) Saskatchewan Archives Board (Regina)
SAB (S) Saskatchewan Archives Board (Saskatoon)
UFM United Farmers of Manitoba
U Sask A (S) University of Saskatchewan Archives (Saskatoon)
WEC Winnipeg Electric Company
WUL Workers' Unity League

1

Early years

John Bracken was born at Ellisville, Leeds County, Ontario, on Friday, 22 June 1883, the first child of Ephraim and Alberta (Gilbert) Bracken. The area is a beautiful part of Canada, a pocket of fertile lowland surrounded by ragged granite outcroppings lying just thirteen miles north of Gananoque, where the St Lawrence widens to embrace the Thousand Islands, and some twenty miles north-east of Kingston. Nearby, about three miles to the north and west, lies Seeley's Bay – a small village and farming community nestling beside a tranquil sheet of water that forms a part of the Rideau Canal system connecting Kingston with Ottawa, Canada's capital. It was here in the quiet and attractive dairy country of Eastern Ontario that John Bracken spent his youth.

The Brackens were of Scottish, Irish, and English stock. They had come by way of Scotland and northern Ireland to New York state in the late eighteenth century and had finally settled in the Mohawk valley at Sangerfield (just south of Utica). Shortly after the end of the War of 1812, Ephraim's grandfather, John Bracken, his young wife, Margaret (Warren), and their new-born son, William, decided to follow Margaret's father to Upper Canada. John bought land in the Seeley's Bay and Ellisville areas and proceeded to carve a living out of the wilderness and to raise a family. He had just begun to establish himself on a secure footing when he died unexpectedly in February 1831, leaving a pregnant wife and four young children. The new baby was a boy and was named John in memory of his father. With the help of her eldest son, William, now fourteen, Margaret continued to run the farm and raise her family.

When John was old enough, he took charge of the Ellisville property while William remained at Seeley's Bay. By the 1860s John had some 400 acres of rambling woodland and rock-strewn pastureland at Ellisville. In the mid-fifties John married Mary Maloney who, at the age of thirteen, had come from southern Ireland during the famine. After her marriage Mary became a convert from

Catholicism to Methodism and raised her family in that faith. She and her husband helped build the Olivet Methodist church that still stands at the junction of the Ellisville Road and Highway 32 to Gananoque.

John and Mary Bracken had three daughters, Elizabeth, Jennie, and Emma, and three sons, William, Ephraim, and George. Ephraim, the second son, was born in 1858. He and his brothers and sisters grew up in Ellisville and were educated at the one-room school about a mile down the road. As soon as they could, the boys helped on the farm and with the log-cutting that helped subsidize farm incomes in the region. By the late seventies the Brackens, with a flourishing dairy farm, were one of the most prosperous and respected families in the communities of Seeley's Bay and Ellisville. Handsome, well-muscled young men, the Bracken boys made many a heart flutter at local picnics and winter dances. It was not long before Ephraim was increasingly seen in the company of Alberta Gilbert, the slim attractive daughter of a well-to-do carriage-shop owner in Seeley's Bay. The young couple were married on 28 July 1881 and went to live in a small log cabin on the Bracken property on the Ellisville road about one-quarter of a mile from the main house. Here in their tiny home Alberta gave birth to her first child on 22 June 1883. The proud parents named him John after his great-grandfather who had settled the family roots in British North America.[1]

Ephraim and Alberta did not stay long in the log cabin. They spent the winter at the Bracken farm and then moved into a fine red brick house just down the road that had been built for them by Ephraim's father. Here they settled for the next five years and Ephraim continued to work on the Bracken land. It was a peaceful and happy time for them. Three more children were born during those years in Ellisville – Manfred (1885), Gertrude (1886), and Gladys (1888) – and the house soon echoed with the noise and laughter of the four youngsters. By 1888-9 John Bracken was a sturdy five-year old who every morning trudged off down the Ellisville road to the small one-room school that his father had attended. Independent and full of high spirits, he was already spending a great deal of time outdoors racing across the fields with his dog, collecting eggs, or learning to take his first stumbling steps on borrowed over-size skates on nearby frozen ponds. Yet there was another side to the coltish youngster. A photograph of the four children taken in 1889 shows him standing ram-rod straight, in the centre but slightly apart from the others. He is unsmiling, his head is erect, his jawline and mouth are firm, and his eyes look straight at you and through you. At six John Bracken is obviously determined, with a strong sense of responsibility and not entirely free of the tension so induced.

In 1889 Ephraim moved his family to Seeley's Bay where he purchased the dairy farm belonging to William Richardson. It was a flourishing 240 acres close to the Rideau and was reputed to have some of the best land in the community.

The farm house was built of red brick and was tall and stately, easily one of the finer homes in the area. It was here that John Bracken grew into manhood and it was Seeley's Bay that he always considered home.

As John grew older he began helping with the milking and the ploughing and the various chores and repairs around the place. These added duties should not suggest that John grew into a sober-sided youth. Far from it. He was serious when he had to be, but he had a devilish, irreverent side to his character and there was reputed to be no greater tease or prankster in Seeley's Bay. Wherever there was mischief afoot, young John Bracken was sure to be a part of it, if not the instigator.

During those years much of his exuberant energy was poured into sports in which he quickly and easily excelled. Organized sports were little known in those days, certainly not in Seeley's Bay, but this did not prevent the local youngsters from playing 'shinney' – a very rough game – on the frozen Rideau and baseball, soccer, and rugby in an informal but highly competitive atmosphere against the other small towns in the area. In his teens John was well-known throughout Leeds county as an excellent athlete. As his sister Gladys put it: 'He was tops in everything.' The sport he most enjoyed was cycling, which was highly popular in the nineties. He would go anywhere within a reasonable distance to race, propelling his clumsy heavy machine over the rough Leeds County roads to get to the starting line on time, afterwards turning back to Seeley's Bay to sleep before the early chores at 5:00 AM. He and his cycling friend Joe McElroy usually won or finished up among the leaders, so the long rides home in the late evening twilight were often pleasurable reflective journeys. John owed his success to the enormous driving power in his hard, heavily muscled legs. Almost fifty years later, in the early 1940s, old-timers could still vividly recall those bike races and the powerful, furiously pedalling 'Johnny' Bracken.[2]

There were also quieter if no less enjoyable diversions from chores and school work. He liked nothing better than to get a pan of apples, grab the latest *Family Herald and Weekly Star*, lie on the couch, and read and munch away. Every Sunday afternoon in the summer he passed either at the local swimming hole, 'the Point,' at the western end of Seeley's Bay, with his cousin Frank Bracken and the other village youngsters or by himself pushing his old flat-bottomed raft up and down the Rideau bordering the farm. And many a treasured evening or afternoon was spent off on his own quietly climbing trees and collecting and blowing bird's eggs to add to his rapidly growing collection. By the time he was fifteen he had boxes of them all neatly catalogued and stacked in his room.[3]

The Brackens were a close-knit family. John, his brothers, and three sisters – Erma (1898) had been born since the move to Seeley's Bay – were brought up in a stern but kindly household. All the youngsters were expected from an early age

to help out around the house and all were influenced by the deep religious convictions of their mother. A Methodist and a devout churchgoer, Alberta Bracken
was a firm stabilizing influence in the home who brought up her children to be
temperate and respectful with a strong sense of duty, responsibility, and loyalty.
By comparison with her more emotional, out-going husband, Alberta was a gentle
woman, no less firm-minded, but sensitive to her childrens' various needs and
considerate of natural childish rambunctiousness. In later life John was to say
that his mother was the greatest woman he ever knew and it is certainly clear that
the two were very close. She appreciated the abilities and ambitions of her handsome and powerful first-born and encouraged him in all he ever wanted to do.
Some said that John was spoiled; more likely it was an astute mother giving her
son the authority and leeway she knew he had the common-sense not to abuse.
As for John, he had a way with his tiny mother. When she tried to admonish him,
he would often just pick her up, hold her aloft, and then sit her down on a chair.
Her annoyance usually turned to laughter.[4]

Since the family's move to Seeley's Bay, John had attended the local two-room
school a short distance down the road from the farm. He was a good student who
always had his work done and was curious about what the class ahead of him was
doing. If given the chance he would probably have moved quickly and easily
ahead of his age group. His home environment was a supportive one for a youngster who liked to study and wanted to read. Alberta often did private tutoring
for the children in the area and the house had an abundance of books, magazines,
and journals lying about. In addition, all the children became thoroughly familiar
with the Bible. John often surprised his friends and his own children in later life
with his biblical knowledge.

Little is known about Bracken's years at either the Ellisville or Seeley's Bay
schools. The records for Ellisville only go back to 1898 and those for Seeley's
Bay to 1924.[5] But the Seeley's Bay school was in Leeds No 1 school district where
it was the practice for students to assemble at Newboro, about twenty miles
north of Seeley's Bay, to try the Public School Leaving examination. Thus, shortly
before his fourteenth birthday, John Bracken sat down in the school house at
Newboro to attempt his first major academic hurdle. In the event, he did quite
well, placing fifth out of forty in the Newboro area and about half-way down the
list for the district.[6]

There was little doubt that John would go on to high school. He wanted to
continue – already he was thinking of a law or medical career – and although he
could be ill-spared from the farm his parents, unlike many of their contemporaries,
recognized the value of a good education. But no high school existed in Seeley's
Bay nor anywhere nearby. In the late nineteenth century small villages found it
difficult to maintain high schools and to pay the teachers' salaries. As a result,

many farm children were unable to continue their education because of the problems of distance and transportation. Only if his parents could afford to pay board and room in town would a child go to high school. Fortunately, John's parents could afford the expense and in September 1897 he enrolled at the Brockville Collegiate to begin his matriculation studies.

When John alighted from the Brockville and Westport train at the Brockville station that autumn it marked the beginning of his first lengthy absence from home and the security of the family setting. It is unlikely that John, mature beyond his fourteen years, proved as prone to home-sickness as many have been in similar instances. Nevertheless, it required a major adjustment from the village youngster who suddenly found himself living in the county seat with over 8000 others. Unfortunately, we know little about that year in Brockville. None of the school records have survived and *The Brockville Times*, although conscientious about most local matters, is unrevealing about the activities of a single first-year high school student.[7]

Apparently, John made frequent trips back to Seeley's Bay for fresh clothes and good home cooking, and family lore has it that he spent more time than he should have in improving his rugby and hockey skills in a variety of pick-up games around Brockville. Certainly, his results in the first set of examinations that December suggested either a poor psychological adjustment to the move or too much time away from the books and on the sports field. In Form II, John Bracken finished in Class IV out of four classes.[8] It was not an auspicious beginning for a youngster of whom so much had been expected and who had expected better of himself.

On his return to the Collegiate after Christmas, John undoubtedly buckled down to work, chastened by his poor showing. That summer he had to sit Part I of his junior matriculation examination. Only if he passed would he be able to go on to Form III and the final segment of his Junior Leaving Standing. He must have been nervous as he looked over the examination sheets that July, but he had worked hard since Christmas and had played hockey only as a means of relaxing from his studies, so he settled down to his answers with reasonable confidence. As soon as the exams were over he returned to Seeley's Bay to help his father with the farm. As the date drew closer for the results to be published, John anxiously scanned the papers. Finally, on 15 August 1898 *The Brockville Times* listed the successful candidates. At first glance John could not find his name in the junior matriculation list. Obviously, he had missed it. He went through the list more slowly. He still could not find his name. Gradually the truth sank in. He had failed.[9]

In those days students were advised not to appeal until they had had an opportunity to talk over the results with their headmaster. But John never spoke with the headmaster of Brockville Collegiate. He accepted the fact that he had failed and saw no point in pursuing the issue. If he could not pass then he should not go back. He decided to give up his professional ambitions and to stay on the farm. Although acutely embarrassed by his failure he still had confidence in his farming and managerial abilities. He asked his father if he could manage the farm and Ephraim agreed. Neither he nor Alberta said one word of criticism to their eldest son, but Alberta must have agonized at how her son felt now that his dreams and plans had been dashed while John must have writhed at the distress he had caused his parents, particularly his mother.[10]

John's failure at Brockville Collegiate was a rude shock but he was determined not to mope about it or to rationalize it. Instead, he threw his energies into the farm and concentrated on making it the best in the county. The next four years were formative ones for John Bracken. The coltish prankster gradually became more subdued and serious-minded as the bulk of the decisions fell to him. After 1900, when Ephraim was elected a reeve for Leeds County and was often away at Brockville or on cattle drives, John virtually ran the farm unaided and unadvised by his father. He was helped enormously during these years by his younger brother Manfred who was a hard worker, 'a real hustler,'[11] but it was always John who gave the lead. He made the decisions and issued the orders. There was never any question who was in charge.

Ephraim had a number of farm journals scattered about the house and the bulletins of the Ontario Agricultural College had been regularly deposited at the door. He never paid them much attention, not because he scorned the advice of scientific agriculture but because he never seemed to have the time, nor perhaps the education, to absorb the material. As a youngster, John had often picked up the pamphlets and glanced quickly through them. Now that he was in charge he began to read avidly and soon journals, bulletins, and, where possible, books on agricultural matters flowed steadily into the house. As much as he could, he attempted to put into practice what he read and he experimented with new techniques and new machinery. The fields were enlarged and sown to clover, a crop rotation system was introduced, buildings and fences were repaired, and the dairy herd improved.[12] Shortly after the turn of the century he and Manfred acquired the first milk-machine in the area, thus relieving themselves and their hired hands of some of the more laborious farm work. Despite innovations of this kind it was still a hard life: up at 4:30 AM, 5 if they slept in, and in bed by 9:00 PM, if they were lucky, seven days a week.

As a result of the tough work and good farm food, John grew during these years from a strong youngster into a powerful, well-muscled young man, slightly over middle height with soft, curly brown hair, deep set eyes, firm strong mouth, and punishing grip. He continued to play rugby and hockey whenever he could and, of course, could always be lured away to race his bicycle, but these moments became fewer as he grew older and after 1900 he was not as flexible with his time. He spent most of his spare moments with his family. They went on occasional trips to Gananoque, or Jones Falls, or Brockville for picnics or shopping but rarely attended local dances. The Brackens were a strong temperance family and John was brought up to shun the evils of drink. When he was fifteen he took the pledge and the following year some local wags elected him Worthy Patriarch of the Sons of Temperance. But John viewed his commitment seriously and it was many years before he could be persuaded to have the occasional glass of beer.

The time spent with his family meant that John had few close outside friends. His natural reserve and self-sufficiency reflected the home environment. The family apparently did not talk a great deal. Gladys later wondered if they had talked enough. They were never critical within the family and seldom of others but this meant they were never really open with one another. Thoughts were kept to oneself and reflective, philosophical ruminations were a rarity. Even politics did not arouse family emotions. Although Ephraim had put on his Sunday best and driven his buggy twenty miles to Kingston one hot June day in 1891 for the funeral of Sir John A. Macdonald, he was not a fervent party man. He, like his brothers and father before him, usually voted Conservative but there were never lengthy discussions around the table about federal or provincial politics. The most John heard were the comments his father would make after 1900 about the problems facing the United Counties Council and the need for more money for road-building or bridge repair in Leeds and Grenville.

It was thus a quiet, closed-in world that John Bracken grew up in. Happy, reasonably prosperous, and well-respected, Ephraim and Alberta brought their children up to be sober, responsible, hard-working, and careful with money. These temperate virtues were reinforced by the utilitarian, pragmatic approach to the solution of problems demanded by farm life.

In 1901, after three years back in Seeley's Bay, John thought he might become a better farmer if he could take the two-year associate course in agriculture offered by the Ontario Agricultural College at Guelph. It was the custom in those days for the United Counties Council of Leeds and Grenville to encourage education in agriculture by recommending each year two young men from the counties to the Agricultural College. Since matriculation standing was not required for admission to the associate course, John was eligible. He submitted his application in the spring of 1901, and at the meeting of the Council on 19 June he was selected as one of the two students.[13] John was undoubtedly delighted but pressure of work on the farm and the prolonged absences of his father delayed his departure for Guelph until the following year. John left Seeley's Bay for Guelph in the autumn of 1902, the envy of his brothers and sisters and with the blessing of his parents.[14]

The young man who registered at the Ontario Agricultural College on 13 September was a self-assured, rather quiet, nineteen year old. Mature for his years, he was accustomed to assuming responsibility and taking the lead. He was friendly and easy enough to get on with but had about him an air of quiet firmness that belied easy contradiction. He was determined to do well and redeem, at least in his own eyes, his earlier failure at Brockville Collegiate.[15]

The Ontario Agricultural College and Experimental Farm had been founded in 1874 and by the time Bracken arrived it had gained a strong hold on the confidence of the farming community and was recognized as one of the best equipped colleges and well managed farms on the continent. It had an efficient staff of professors and lecturers and yearly attendance had increased steadily - about 300 enrolled in September 1902. A high proportion of its graduates remained in agricultural work or associated activities.[16]

Bracken settled easily and happily into the college. Anxious to do well in his studies, he buckled down to work immediately and was soon absorbed by the essays in English, the various problems of physics and maths, and the agricultural duties and experiments. He approached his work with a zeal and a tenacity that he had not shown in his Brockville days. There would be no repetition of that searing experience if he could help it. Despite his determination to do well, Bracken did not avoid other aspects of college life. He took an active part in YMCA work and entered with zest into the various sporting activities available to the students. The difference was that this time he resolved to keep everything in perspective.

During his first year Bracken took part in the annual athletic championship, played inter-year hockey, and, of course, turned out for the college rugby team. In the autumn of 1902 the OAC was playing in the junior series of the Ontario Rugby Football Union which was using rules placing a heavy emphasis on constant scrimmaging and thus on strength rather than on mobility, speed, and technique. It was a style of play suited to the husky, well-muscled farm boys who lacked the experience and training for a faster more sophisticated game. Finesse was certainly not a significant part of Bracken's initial play. Basically unskilled but powerfully equipped for the role of half-back, he ran over rather than around most of his opponents. His sons recall him chuckling in later life at his memories of those early games at Guelph. Hardened and toughened from farm work, Bracken and his OAC team-mates found most of their opponents that year easy pickings. But true to his nature Bracken did not rest content with simple physical superiority. He knew the game demanded more subtlety and technique, so he quickly became a student of it and a kicker of considerable skill. By the end of his first season he was not only a more accomplished player but had become a leader on the field and was the obvious choice for captain the next year.[17]

Bracken's performance in the classroom was even more rewarding and satisfying than on the sports field. He worked steadily in the library and soon impressed his teachers with his methodical, orderly mind.[18] In the Christmas examinations he stood first among the freshmen and made the honours list in every subject.[19] In the final exams in April 1903 he not only came first overall but also stood first in all four examination categories: English and Mathematics, the Physical Sciences, the Biological Sciences, and Agriculture. He thus won all four available scholarships, but as he was only able to hold one he opted for the agricultural award. It was a splendid performance for one who had been away from school work and studying for so long. Whatever had gone wrong at Brockville had obviously been overcome by 1903.[20]

His success indicated how removed he now was from the exuberant prankster of his youth. Although that side of him was never to be completely submerged it was now tempered by a more controlled, determined nature. His Brockville experience and the responsibilities of the farm had matured and subdued him. He was more reticent, less willing to give way to his emotions, and convinced of the virtues of thrift, responsibility, and hard work. He could so easily have been priggish or conceited with it all, but apparently he was not. A little arrogant at times, perhaps, a little aloof to outsiders; but friendly and respectful to those who knew him. He did not, however, let anyone get too close; he formed no strong personal attachments at the college. Considerate and polite but rather reserved, Jack, as his fellow students called him, remained slightly apart from the crowd who liked, admired, and esteemed him nevertheless.[21]

Bracken spent a pleasant summer running the farm and relaxing with his family and friends at Seeley's Bay but by September he was eager to return to Guelph. It would be his final year and he wanted to make the most of it. Once the rugby season had ended he buckled down to his books and experiments with additional vigour. As the April exams drew nearer he must have regretted that they would mark the end of his stay at OAC. He had enjoyed himself immensely in Guelph and had found the programme refreshing and stimulating. More than once he must have wondered what subjects he needed to make up at the matriculation level in order to be able to remain at OAC for two more years and obtain the degree of Bachelor of Scientific Agriculture. As it happened his professors had been wondering the same thing and they advised him to return to Brockville Collegiate at the end of the term, find out what had to be done, and wrote the necessary exams that summer.

Bracken decided to follow their advice and in late April he and his younger sister Gladys, who was to attend the collegiate the following autumn, were ushered into the office of the new principal, Mr Alec Mowat. Bracken explained his problem and the old records were discovered and dusted off. After examining them closely Mr Mowat apologetically told an astonished John Bracken that he had not failed his junior matriculation in 1898. In fact, he had done quite well and there was no need for make-up exams. It had all been a ghastly clerical error. Bracken's name had been wrongly omitted from the published list.[22]

This was a truly extraordinary turn of events and Bracken would have had every reason to feel aggrieved. But six years had passed since his departure from Brockville and his dreams of a legal or medical career had faded long ago. If he ever felt anger or remorse he never revealed it to his family and rarely drew attention to the error in later life. What he felt more than anything else was relief and joy that he would be able to return to the OAC to complete the requirements for the BSA degree. He hurried back to Seeley's Bay to let Ephraim and Alberta know the good news. It was not long before neighbourhood gossip had made it common knowledge that young 'Johnny' Bracken had not failed after all. Shortly after his return to the farm Bracken learned that in his recent exams he had again stood first overall and had been awarded the Governor General's Medal for general proficiency in second year.[23]

He returned to Guelph that autumn in a relaxed and confident mood and his last two years at OAC were happy and eventful ones. He continued to do well in all his academic work and topped his class in the spring examinations in 1905 and again half-way through his final year. In addition to his accomplishments in the classroom 'Jack' captained the small OAC team that won the Spoor Trophy in the stock-judging competition at the Chicago Fat Stock Show in December 1905[24] and remained active in sports. He continued to excel in the annual field day, was outstanding in gymnastics, and regularly played hockey. But his first love remained football, and much of his energy and administrative talent went into trying to improve the game at the college. Bracken captained the team in both 1904 and 1905. His ability as a player was summed up by *The O.A.C. Review* at the end of his final season: ' ... in after years when the talk turns to football, Jack Bracken's name will be brought into the conversation, his phenomenal runs will be discussed and the fact that he was the back-bone of the team during his college career will be remembered. The beau-ideal of a football player in build, he would have been the star player in much faster company than has been his lot to play with, and it is fairly certain that he would have been welcome on the varsity campus. This is Bracken's last year of football and the College team will miss his presence as a player very keenly.'[25] Bracken also served as a highly successful president of the Athletic Association during his final year, and his executive was considered 'the most progressive body' to have administered athletics at OAC. During its year in office a trainer had been hired, the gym refitted, a foundation laid for a permanent hockey rink, and the constitution revised.[26] It was a credit to Bracken's administrative ability and to his well-marked talent for getting others to co-operate and work under his direction.

The year ended with his classmates selecting him as the recipient of the college medal as 'the best all-round man' in the graduating class. In applauding the choice, *The O.A.C. Review* noted that 'From the first day of his freshmanship to the day of his graduation, Bracken has always been foremost in everything contributing to the welfare of the student body.' *The Review* wished him 'heartiest congratulations and God-speed in his future work.'[27]

John Bracken graduated from the OAC in the spring of 1906 with the degree of Bachelor of Scientific Agriculture. The previous four years had been happy and successful ones. He had received a good basic education at Guelph which, coupled with his own conscientious and thorough-going approach to problems, already deeply ingrained, was to stand him in good stead in the future. His successes on the sports field and in committee had drawn-out and honed his talents as a sensible, shrewd manager of men. In fact, if any one character trait was dominant it was shrewdness. Bracken would carefully analyse a problem, weigh and assess the variables, and decide whether action or patience would result in the best solution. It was a habit acquired on the farm at Seeley's Bay but his OAC years permanently entrenched it.

Bracken had enjoyed his years at OAC and considered the experience of college life one that should never be squandered by those who had the opportunity to attend. In a retrospective article written almost a year after his departure he jotted down some advice for future collegians. He advised them to choose their friends well, for while early upbringing was important it was crucial that a young man have 'the companionship of strong, upright, broad-minded men' at that moment in their lives. Similarly, while college discipline was necessary and important, self-discipline was the true mark of a man. College life, wrote Bracken, would often test the discipline within the man. One must constantly exercise one's will-power: 'For just as training increases the strength of the muscle and exercise the acuteness of the senses, so training and exercise combined, develop in the man a will power capable of mastering his feelings and holding them within bounds. This is discipline; the saviour of despondent moments; the means by which we grow; the strength of strong men.' Bracken urged the students to be diligent and inquisitive in their studies because their eventual success and usefulness would depend on how closely they had listened. The future would probably not provide another opportunity for intensive learning. But he also advised them to take an active part in the various college organizations which could enrich the soul and broaden the horizons. He warned against negative criticism and urged a positive approach to the solution of problems. He pointed out how valuable participation in sports could be: 'It was in these contests that we learned the value of preparation and training for the conflict, and in no other place could it be learned so well. It was there that "pluck" and "stick-to-it-iveness" taught many a man lessons that will at some future time bear fruit. It was there we learned the value of combination, or working together as contrasted by individual grandstand work. It was there we learned how to take defeat like men and congratulate our more efficient competitor. It was there that organization was power.'[28] Much of Bracken's basic attitude to life was summed up in this article written when he was twenty-four. His beliefs were to change little over the next sixty years.

Bracken left Guelph and the OAC with conflicting feelings. He regretted severing his ties with one of the happiest periods of his life yet, at the same time, he was anxious to move on and to make use of his education. There was also a personal reason for his ambivalence. During his last years at OAC he had met and become deeply fond of Alice Wylie Bruce who had been working at the college as a typist since the death of her father, a local architect. John and Alice had spent many a happy week-end afternoon walking along Guelph's peaceful shady streets or chatting in the living-room of Mrs Bruce's home on Oxford Street. Nothing had been said publicly about their future but it was assumed by those who knew the quiet and reserved John Bracken that marriage was not far from his mind. Before that could be, however, John had to find a job and become established. In mid-May, with a heavy heart but with confidence about the future, Bracken left Guelph for Seeley's Bay.

2

The West and scientific agriculture

A few days after his return to Seeley's Bay, Bracken packed his bag once more, said good-bye to his family, and walked down to the wharf where he caught the *Rideau Queen* for Ottawa. He had been offered a job at $75 a month with the Dominion Seed Branch of the Department of Agriculture and was on his way to find out more about it.[1]

A dominion seed division had existed since 1899 and had been raised to the status of a branch in December 1904 on the reorganization of the office of the commissioner of agriculture and dairying. Since 1905 the work of the Seed Branch had been prosecuted along two main lines – commercial and educational. The commercial work involved the enforcement of the Seed Control Act of 1905, inspection of seed and seed crops, seed testing, seed trade investigation, and the distribution of reference collections of economic seeds. The educational work was designed to stimulate interest in the production and use of better seeds. The branch tried to maintain a vigorous educational propaganda by organizing and helping to run local seed fairs, provincial seed exhibitions, field crop competitions, and seed judging classes, and by distributing bulletins and illustrated works on farm weeds. In 1905 five men were appointed to represent the Seed Branch across the country, one of whom was responsible for both Manitoba and Saskatchewan. Early in 1906 it had been decided to divide the district and give each province a separate representative. Bracken had been singled out as the most promising OAC graduate and offered the Manitoba post.[2] By the end of May, with his new responsibilities clear in his mind, he left for the West.

It was an exciting time for a young man to arrive in western Canada. After years of slow growth the prairie population was mushrooming at a phenomenal rate as immigrants poured in from Europe, Great Britain, Ontario, and the United States, flooding the cities and towns of the prairies and scattering out onto the bald plains of the new provinces of Saskatchewan and Alberta or hugging the wood lots and river systems at the edge of the shield as it arched north and west from Manitoba through northern Alberta. As the settlers located their homesteads and settled in to carve a living from the land, those who had farmed before found the soil and moisture conditions and the length of the growing season far different from anything they had experienced previously in the moist and humid regions of Europe and eastern North America. New techniques, new seed, and additional knowledge would be required to make a profitable living. For those who had had no previous experience of farming – and there were many who had left the cosy familiarity of the slums of Glasgow, Liverpool, or London for a new life in Canada – the experience was even more shattering. If they survived the psychological impact of their new environment they would need all the expert advice they could obtain. But it was not only the newcomers who Bracken had come West to assist. Even the more settled farming communities of western and southwestern Manitoba needed to be reminded of good farming practices and the merits of clean seed or informed about the dangers of weeds and smut.

For a few days after his arrival in Winnipeg Bracken was briefed on his duties by James Murray who had been in charge of the Manitoba-Saskatchewan district the previous year. Murray had worked hard to inaugurate seed fairs and field competitions under the direction of the agricultural societies. The seed fair was considered central to the educational work of the Seed Branch and those organized by Murray had been among the first on the prairies. It would be Bracken's responsibility to continue Murray's pioneering work and, if possible, to extend it.

Much of Bracken's time in June 1906 was spent behind a desk organizing competitions in standing fields of seed wheat for later that summer and arranging seed fairs for the winter of 1906-7. It was his baptism in administrative work and he soon found that he not only liked it but was good at it. He succeeded in adding two more seed fairs to the twelve organized by Murray and again secured space for seed grain exhibits at the Brandon Winter Fair the following February. During July and August he travelled by train and buggy to various corners of the province inspecting the operations of farmers who made a specialty of growing and selecting seeds of cereal grains. In the early winter months much of his time was spent organizing and advertising the seed fairs that began in December.[3]

Despite the appalling weather in southern Manitoba that winter all the seed fairs were a resounding success and Bracken was widely congratulated for his organizational skill, his initiative, and his thoughtful approach to the problems of the Manitoba farmer. His speeches on proper seed selection were given close attention by his farm audiences and were considered 'splendid,' 'able,' 'brilliant,' and 'most interesting' by the rural and urban papers. His remarks often led to animated discussions that lasted throughout the evening. Undoubtedly there was a thirst for new and reliable information and Bracken's conscientious and understanding, yet firm, approach was appreciated. He praised exhibits handsomely when they deserved it but he was not afraid to point out failings and examples of shoddy practice. This frankness was respected and he soon became widely known in the farming community as an intelligent, forthright, and 'most enthusiastic official.'[4]

Bracken's reputation spread to Saskatchewan and early in 1907 he was asked to judge the cattle and hogs at the annual Stock Breeders' show in Regina, 20-22 March.[5] Here, for the first time, he met W.R. Motherwell, the minister of agriculture for Saskatchewan, who was in the process of organizing the Department of Agriculture in the new province. Without realizing it, Bracken was obviously being appraised during his stay in Regina and it was not long after his return to Winnipeg that Motherwell called at his office and asked him if he would be interested in becoming the new superintendent of fairs and institutes and secretary of the Saskatchewan Stock Breeders' Association. This was a highly flattering offer. Not only would it be a promotion but it would mean heavier and extensive responsibilities. It was a rare opportunity for a young man of twenty-three and a compliment to his hard work, enthusiasm, and organizational skills. Bracken accepted immediately and left for Regina in mid-May.[6]

Bracken had joined a department whose head believed implicitly in agricultural education in order to promote better farming methods.[7] In 1907 Motherwell was a vigorous, aggressive, imaginative man, at the height of his powers. He knew Saskatchewan's needs and was determined to fulfil them. Bracken had heard a good deal about Motherwell and closer acquaintance only confirmed the good reports. The young man was deeply influenced by Motherwell's aims and ideas and over the next decade he was to work energetically on their behalf.

Through the medium of lectures, bulletins, demonstrations, and farmers' institutes Motherwell hoped to spread current knowledge and practices throughout the province in order to ensure 'a sound and stable agriculture.' His department encouraged the employment of agricultural secretaries by rural municipalities and close co-operation with provincial and regional livestock and grain-growing associations. Although Motherwell was concerned about poor farming practices in the older districts, much of the educational programme was aimed at the thousands of new settlers who were flooding into the province. He was a strong promoter of agricultural societies as a means of getting the farmers together 'to discuss problems, hear speakers, sponsor competitions, and hold exhibitions or fairs.' It was thus a measure of Bracken's ability that he had been selected to run that crucial branch of Motherwell's department.[8]

Bracken arrived in Regina on 17 May 1907. He liked the city immediately and, after finding quarters in the new YMCA facing the park, he settled easily into his new surroundings. For the next two years he worked hard and conscientiously.

His work in Saskatchewan was a natural extension of his work in Manitoba for the Dominion Seed Branch. A good deal of it was administrative and organizational in character and he spent much of his time behind a desk.[9]

Bracken's working files reveal a methodical, well-organized civil servant who attended to the smallest detail. His letters were businesslike and to the point. There were no flattering remarks or rhetorical flourishes. If anything, he was perhaps a little too austere. He was willing to be firm and decisive even if the news he conveyed was unpalatable.[10]

In addition to his desk work, Bracken was expected to attend as many of the fairs as possible, participate on the lecture circuit, consult and advise institute officers, and ensure that the fairs were conforming to Motherwell's criteria. He took his responsibilities seriously and travelled widely throughout the province during the years 1907-9. He regularly took his turn on the lecture circuit speaking primarily on 'Features of Successful Grain Growing' and 'The Work of the Agricultural Society' and gave numerous demonstrations in judging beef cattle or draft horses.[11]

He soon became a familiar and respected figure on the Saskatchewan plains. A farmer himself, Bracken was most at ease when talking over agricultural problems with other farmers. He asked numerous questions about yields, preparation of the soil, and summer-fallowing and then would point out, firmly but kindly, how yields could be increased with different or improved methods. His strongest asset was that he did not talk down to his farm audience. No matter whether it was to a lone man in the middle of a field or a crowd of fifty in an overheated and stuffy townhall, Bracken spoke in a casual, friendly manner. His talks were laden, often densely packed, with information but they were worth listening to. They were based on a thorough knowledge of sound farm practices and the latest ideas about dry-land farming. He always gave the impression that he cared how each farmer did. More than once he would say, 'That land will produce forty bushels to the acre, or it will produce ten; the difference in production is you.' His intimate understanding of farm problems and his concerned but frank approach to their solution quickly earned him many friends in Saskatchewan and a deserved reputation elsewhere.[12]

Bracken soon discovered that his job did not confine him to Saskatchewan. In October 1907 he attended the convention of the American Association of Farmers' Institute Workers held in Washington, DC, where he read a paper on 'Institute Organizations and Methods' as found in Canada and the northwestern states.[13] The trip east gave him an opportunity to spend some time in Guelph with Alice whom he had not seen since a hurried visit earlier in the year. In September 1908 he was again back in eastern Canada, this time in charge of the Saskatchewan exhibit at the fall fair in Toronto. Once the fair was over he and Alice made a quick visit to Seeley's Bay to see the Bracken family and to tell them of their plans to be married the following summer.

An attractive family photograph taken about that time shows a relaxed and confident John Bracken. He is now twenty-five, handsome and obviously fit, and it is clear that the past two years in the West had been good to him. They had broadened his experience, widened his contacts with the agricultural world, and confirmed his abilities as an agricultural scientist.

Bracken was particularly busy during the winter of 1908-9 but he still found time to read the newspapers and listen to the animated gossip in the office. Ever since the passage of the University Act in 1907 debate had been raging in the province over the location of the University of Saskatchewan and the relationship to it of an Agricultural College. In January 1909 after an exhaustive discussion over many months and a special investigative trip to the United States, the University Senate approved President Walter Murray's recommendation that a College of Agriculture be organized as a constituent college of the University of Saskatchewan. It was a momentous decision. The university became the first in Canada to incorporate an agricultural college as an integral part of higher education. The decision meant the association, and not the unnatural divorce, of vocational, liberal arts, and scientific education, and led to important developments in the curriculum which were to be of lasting benefit to agricultural education. In April it was announced that Saskatoon had been selected as the location of the new University of Saskatchewan.[14]

Long before that decision was made Bracken knew that he would be intimately involved with the new institution. Shortly after the January meetings he was asked by his immediate superior, W.J. Rutherford, the deputy commissioner of agriculture, if he would be interested in joining the staff of the College of Agriculture as the professor in charge of extension work. Rutherford had already agreed to become dean and professor of animal husbandry and was prepared to support Bracken's application. Bracken must often have wondered if he would be asked to join the new college. Now that he had, he quickly agreed.[15] His appointment was announced in April and greeted with enthusiasm by the press which referred to him as 'an ideal official, courteous and prompt in the discharge of his duties, active in promoting in every way the interests of agriculture and possessed of excellent judgement and unquestioned ability.'[16]

Bracken and Rutherford were to take up their full-time duties the following year. In the interim they would remain with the Department of Agriculture but would be paid for advising the university's Board of Governors on the preparation of the Saskatoon site, the erection of buildings, and the selection of equipment and stock. For the time being, the exact nature of Bracken's duties were left undefined until a professor of field husbandry had been appointed.[17]

Bracken was delighted with his new job. It would mean less travelling and thus less time away from his new bride. Alice and John were married on his twenty-sixth birthday, 22 June, at her mother's home on Oxford Street in Guelph. It was a joyous moment for the young couple and marked the beginning of a long and happy life together.

John and Alice had barely arrived back in Regina when he was told by Rutherford that the two most obvious candidates for the professorship of field husbandry were well settled and unwilling to move. Murray and Rutherford wanted Bracken to take the job. Both believed him to be equal, if not superior, in ability to the other candidates and, if given the opportunity for study, easily capable of repairing any current deficiency in knowledge. The two men were prepared to recommend Bracken's transfer to the Department of Field Husbandry, as professor, at a salary of $2500 a year. It was a golden opportunity for Bracken and once he was assured that he could spend the winter months at various agricultural colleges in the United States he agreed to accept the new position.[18] In late October he and Alice left for the south and did not return to Saskatchewan until the following May.

During the winter of 1909–10 Bracken visited a number of agricultural colleges and attended a variety of conferences in the United States, finally settling after Christmas at the University of Illinois. He had soon discovered that his agronomy was rather 'rusted' after three years away from field work and the classroom but by the spring this problem had been repaired. He had been particularly attracted by the courses and experimental work at the Agricultural College at the Champaign campus of the University of Illinois. Years later members of the staff still remembered Bracken as a man who was always asking questions, constantly absorbing ideas and information. While at Champaign he was asked to lecture to undergraduates about western Canadian farm problems and he impressed his audience with his common sense and his practical approach. Bracken benefitted especially from his close observations during April and May of the techniques in field experimentation in use at Champaign. They were to influence his own work considerably over the next decade. By mid-May his studies were complete and he and Alice returned expectantly to Saskatchewan and to their new life in Saskatoon, a city of 12,000 situated on the banks of the South Saskatchewan River some 150 miles north-west of Regina.[19]

In 1910 the university still presented a bleak and forbidding prospect. It was located away from the centre of the city on the east side of the river where over 1300 acres had been set aside. There were no trees, just shrubs in the hollows and during the winter months the wind swept and howled uninterruptedly across the bald prairie and round the isolated buildings. Although the campus gradually took on a softer appearance with the sowing of lawns and the planting of trees, the new collegiate gothic structures still felt the full impact of the elements. After 1911 John and Alice lived on the campus and their early experiences must have been similar to those of Jean Murray, who still shudders as she remembers the ice-cold bedrooms and the frost on the plaster of the, as yet, uninsulated president's house.[20]

The next ten years were happy ones for the young couple. They were joined in the West in early 1910 by Ephraim, Alberta, Gertrude, Erma, and Manfred who homesteaded at Tessier only thirty miles south-west of Saskatoon. Ephraim and Manfred had grown tired of running the dairy farm on their own and like so many others in eastern Canada had decided to settle in the West, lured by the opportunities it appeared to offer. Gertrude soon moved into Saskatoon to teach music and in 1912 she was joined by Gladys, now married, who taught in the local school system. Most of the work on the farm was done by Manfred although John would slip away when he could to help with the plowing and relax from his college duties. John actually filed for a homestead at Tessier himself in June 1912 but was unable to work on his quarter-section and his entry was cancelled in 1913.[21]

It was reassuring to have John's parents nearby, for in December 1911 Alice gave birth to their first child, John Bruce Bracken. Bruce, as he was called, was soon joined by Doug (1913), Gordon (1916), and George (1918). Alice managed the additional work and responsibility in her even-tempered and efficient manner and shielded her husband from the bulk of the domestic chores. As Bruce and Doug grew older and more adventuresome they would roam at will around the university and the agricultural college. Active and mischievous youngsters, the older boys by 1920 could often be seen tearing around, and through, the shrubbery with George desperately striving to bring up the rear. They were soon referred to as 'regular limbs of satan.'[22]

Bracken worked harder during the decade in Saskatoon than he had ever done in his life. His first two years were spent preparing the experimental fields, helping to draft the initial curriculum, and assisting – as in the past – with seed fairs and stock-judging competitions. After the Agricultural College opened in October 1912 he was also responsible for lectures on crops and soils and for laboratory work in the BSA, associate, and short-course programmes offered at the college.

The demands on his time and energy became increasingly severe.[23] In addition to his teaching and administrative responsibilities Bracken continued to do a great deal of extension work and to write up the results of his crop and tillage experiments in the form of bulletins and pamphlets for distribution to farmers. He also wrote extensively for various farm newspapers and periodicals about better farm practices. He was constantly asked to speak about his experimental work at conventions and conferences in eastern Canada and the United States as well as in all three prairie provinces. By 1920 he was widely known and respected as a leading expert on dry-land farming.[24]

As early as 1915 it was evident that Bracken was working too hard and the first signs of strain and declining resilience that were to plague him later in life had begun to show. In the spring term of 1914 illness prevented him from completing his lectures on soils and forage crops and in the spring of 1915 he was confined to bed with a severe virus infection. Despite these warnings he continued to work extraordinarily long hours in the experimental fields, at his desk, and on the lecture and judging circuit.

The area of responsibility that absorbed most of his interest and energy and for which he was best known by agronomists was the research and experimentation he initiated on crop plants. Bracken was emphatic that farming was a business. To be successful it had to be profitable. In order that the farmer could conduct his business successfully he had to know 'the conditions that must be provided before plants can grow, the factors that militate against satisfactory growth and the means at man's disposal for controlling the factors that limit yields.'[25] He realized that the cost of production was only partly within the power of the farmer to control; nevertheless the main causes of failure were due to 'poor crops or poor management, either by the individual or the state.'[26] He saw his experimental work as a contribution to sensible and more profitable farming.

Bracken designed an experimental programme on a broad and comprehensive basis to yield reliable information about the best methods of producing cereals and forage crops. He was interested in the time, rate, and method of seeding, the relation of different methods of tillage to crop yields, and the best rotation of crops for the maintenance of soil conditions. He also experimented with foreign grains and showed a particular interest in alfalfa. It was to Bracken's credit that from the beginning he placed a heavy emphasis on work with a variety of forage crops when most people could think only of wheat, oats, and barley.[27] By 1916 Bracken had also succeeded in persuading the Saskatchewan government to fund a sub-station system in the province in order that testing could be done under a variety of soil and climatic conditions.[28]

Although later researchers found flaws in Bracken's work, claiming he did not plan his experimental layout so that a mathematical comparison of yields could be obtained, it would be invidious to judge his work by the standards of a later more scientific age. His research was being done before there had been any serious breakthrough in statistical work for experiments of that nature. Also his own education was not sufficient to allow him to do advanced agricultural work. It would have been difficult for anyone with the type of education acquired by Bracken at Guelph and his brief stint in the United States to undertake highly sophisticated research. What Bracken's work provided was a good deal of fundamental information about dry-land farming that could be passed on to the rural people. His was pioneering research and essential in its time.[29]

The extent of Bracken's responsibilities while in Saskatoon meant that he formed few close friends. His natural reserve was reinforced by his absorption in his work. He was polite and friendly but never gave the impression that he wished people to get too close. He kept his own counsel and generally went his own way. He was firm in his opinions, with a natural air of authority, and did not like to be challenged. By his mid-thirties he was well known and widely respected but there seemed a certain aloofness or hardness in his manner. Those who did get to know him soon realized that he had not lost his irreverent sense of humour nor his basic humility and friendliness but few got close enough to penetrate the facade.[30]

Bracken was at his most relaxed and congenial when out on the extension circuit talking with farmers or taking an active part in sport. His opportunities to play regularly while at Saskatoon were limited but he did manage to turn out for the occasional rugby and soccer games and even coached the Varsity rugby squad in 1919. Although he was now in his thirties his play revealed he had lost none of his essential skills or strength. In 1917 the student newspaper, *The Sheaf*, commented upon Bracken's 'accurate kicking,' and in describing how he had 'scored by a remarkable play, pulling several of his opponents along with him,' it indicated that Bracken was as powerful as ever, no doubt hardened by his long hours in the experimental fields. His toughness had been underlined the previous year when he and an opponent had a 'severe collision' during a soccer game resulting in the other player's retirement. Bracken had played to the end despite the loss of a few teeth.[31] In 1912 Bracken also took up the game of curling and, like so many thousands of others before and after, he was soon absorbed by its congenial but competitive atmosphere. He took naturally to the game and was soon skipping his own rink. He never became a contender for championship honours but he won his share of cups and prizes over the years. For the rest of his working life curling was to be his principal means of relaxation, far from the duties and vicissitudes of public office.

In early 1920 Bracken was offered the principalship of the Manitoba Agricultural College in succession to J.B. Reynolds, who was leaving to become president of the OAC. It was a highly attractive offer and one that Bracken accepted with alacrity. He had been happy at the University of Saskatchewan and had believed in the concept and role of agricultural education as defined by Motherwell and Murray. But he would soon be thirty-seven, he was ambitious, and he had a young family to support. The job in Manitoba would bring fresh challenges, added prestige, and additional income. The combination was too enticing to turn down.

Murray viewed Bracken's departure with regret and made every effort to keep him.[32] Both he and Rutherford saw Bracken's leaving as 'a distinct loss' to the University of Saskatchewan.[33]

After attending his last committee meeting and ensuring that his experimental programme for the summer was properly launched, Bracken and his family left for Winnipeg in June 1920. Bracken was, of course, quite familiar with Manitoba, having returned to it often over the years as a lecturer or judge. The province and its capital, Winnipeg, had grown considerably since Bracken had first come west in 1906. Thousands of immigrants had poured into the 'Gateway to the West,' settling in the north end of the city and adding a rich ethnic dimension to the dominant Anglo-Saxon culture. Thousands of others had pushed the agricultural frontier further north in central and western Manitoba, often homesteading on questionable sub-marginal land. Alice and John found Winnipeg a more interesting city than Saskatoon and they adjusted quickly to it. They soon settled into their new home on the college's Fort Garry campus located in a loop of the Red River about six miles south of down-town Winnipeg, and Bracken began to familiarize himself with his new job.

His chief project over the next two years was a major agricultural survey of the province. It grew out of Bracken's discovery that there was insufficient knowledge available of provincial farm life. He and his staff devised an extensive and intricate questionnaire that was taken personally to farmers in fifteen representative municipalities in the province by teams of researchers during the summer of 1921. It was a major undertaking that by early 1922 had been only partially completed. Bracken hoped that once all the results were written up a major research programme could be devised for the MAC staff.[34]

Bracken enjoyed his new responsibilities. In addition to the survey, he straightened out the accounting system, supervized the more efficient management of the college farm, took an active interest in sports, and showed considerable sympathy for individual student difficulties. His relationship with his staff was congenial although, as in Saskatoon, he kept himself slightly apart and was clearly a man of firm opinions, not easily swayed once his mind was made up.[35] He also continued to play an important part in farm organizations, for he was now widely known and deeply respected throughout Canada and the United States. His reputation was further enhanced by the publication of two books based on his numerous bulletins and pamphlets written while in Saskatchewan. *Crop Production in Western Canada* was published in 1920 and *Dry Farming in Western Canada* in 1921, and both remained basic texts for decades.

By 1922 John and Alice were happily established in Manitoba. Despite his busy schedule Bracken found that he had more time to himself now that he was not directly involved in experimental work. As a result, he was more relaxed than he had been for years. His sons remember him as freer and easier after the move to Manitoba and his fondness for practical jokes was more in evidence. At thirty-nine Bracken was at ease with himself and looking forward with pleasure to completing the agricultural survey and devising a research programme for the college.

3

Premier of Manitoba

Shortly after midnight on Friday, 21 July 1922, the phone rang in Bracken's house on the Fort Garry campus. Groggy, and annoyed at being awakened from a deep sleep, Bracken stumbled to the phone wondering who could be calling at such an hour. It turned out to be W.R. 'Billy' Clubb who in the provincial election three days earlier had won the Morris seat for the United Farmers of Manitoba. Clubb apologized for the lateness of the call and explained that he and the other twenty-three UFM members had been meeting all evening in an effort to decide who should lead their group in the legislature. Since the UFM had the most seats they would be obliged to form the government and their leader would become the premier of Manitoba. Clubb told Bracken that he was one of three candidates being considered. If he was interested the UFM group would like to see him at 10:00 AM in the basement of the Odd Fellows Hall on Kennedy Street.

Bracken was staggered by the message. He had never been actively involved in politics and had never indicated any interest in becoming so. Preoccupied with his responsibilities at the Agricultural College, he had not paid much attention to the election and had not taken the time to vote. He could not understand why the UFM members would turn to him. After asking Clubb a few questions and promising to attend the morning meeting, he hung up and told an astonished Alice the news.

Like most people in western Canada the Brackens were familiar with the political upheavals that had taken place in Manitoba in recent years. Only a few weeks earlier the Liberal government of T.C. Norris had resigned after being defeated on a vote of censure in the legislature. It had brought to an end two years of political muddle and legislative inaction during which the Liberals had struggled to govern with only twenty-one supporters in a fifty-five seat house.

The Liberals had come to power in 1915 in the aftermath of revelations that the Conservative administration of Sir Rodmond Roblin had been involved in fraud and corruption in the construction of the new Legislative Building. A sweeping electoral victory had given the Liberals a mandate for an impressive programme of advanced legislation. During the next five years Manitoba was the centre of reform activity in Canada. Temperance legislation was enacted; women were given equal voting rights; compulsory education was introduced; a Workmen's Compensation Act and a Minimum Wage measure were passed; a Bureau of Labour was established; cheaper money was made available to farmers by the Manitoba Farm Loans and Rural Credits Act; a public health nursing system was set up; an Industrial Conditions Act was passed; and Mothers' Allowance covering widowed dependent mothers, the first of its kind in Canada, was also introduced. Other equally progressive legislation followed and was complemented by major road building and public works programmes. It was an exciting and oftentimes refreshing period, but it was enormously costly.

At the end of their first term the Liberals had had deficits in three out of five years. To make matters worse a depression held the West in its grip. Agricultural prices had tumbled on the world market and urban unemployment was causing grave concern. Industrial unrest, running high since 1918, had resulted in the Winnipeg General Strike of 1919, severely isolating and dislocating the city. The western farmers, equally distressed by declining income, rising prices, and a 30 per cent increase in freight rates, had finally decided to enter the federal political arena in an effort to redress their grievances, and in January 1920 the Progressive party had been founded in Winnipeg.

Despite these ominous signs of dissatisfaction with the existing system, Norris had decided to contest the election of 1920 on his government's record. So confident were they of victory that the Liberals gave virtually no attention to constituency organization and were satisfied with minimal campaigning. The result had been a rude shock. The legislature had been splintered. Only twenty-one Liberals had been returned. The Conservatives had seven, Labour eleven, and Independents four. The greatest surprise was the success of the United Farmers of Manitoba who had elected twelve members.

The name United Farmers of Manitoba had only recently been adopted by the Manitoba Grain Growers' Association which had been founded back in 1903 in an effort to improve the economic condition of the western farmer by agitating for lower tariffs and reduced freight rates. Like its counterparts in other provinces, the Grain Growers' Association had remained studiously aloof from politics throughout its existence. Then, increasingly dissatisfied with the lack of interest and attention given the farmers' plight at the end of the war and stimulated by the victory of the United Farmers of Ontario in the recent Ontario election, the Manitoba farmers at their annual convention in January 1920 had not only recommended a change in name but had finally endorsed political activity. Distrustful of the mainline parties and generally suspicious of the party system, the farm candidates had advocated the principles of non-partisan politics – initiative, referendum, and recall. Their basic argument had been that farmers should elect farmers to represent farmers. The decision to run candidates in the 1920 election had been left to each UFM local. No overall leader was chosen, no common platform was devised, and the farm candidates had run more or less as individuals relying primarily on local assistance.

The situation had changed significantly by election day 1922. Although the farm candidates still had no leader and had not met as a group before the election, they did have a published and generally accepted platform which strongly favoured efficient, administrative, and non-partisan government. Moreover, they had an excellent organization based on the UFM locals. Never before had there existed in Manitoba such a committed and active grass-roots organization. As a result most observers thought the UFM had an excellent chance of victory. Certainly, the Winnipeg business community thought so. It had, with the assistance of certain of the farm leadership, such as George Chipman, the editor of the *Grain Growers' Guide*, and W.R. Wood, secretary of the UFM, formed the Winnipeg Progressive Association in May and had openly endorsed the UFM platform while itself calling for 'a strong, stable and efficient government which will realize the desire of the average citizen in town and country.'[1]

By Wednesday morning 19 July it was clear that the forecasts had been correct. The UFM had won twenty-four seats, the Liberals seven, the Conservatives six, the Socialists and Labour six, there were eight Independents, and it looked likely that the Progressive Association would elect one in Winnipeg. Three deferred elections in The Pas, Rupertsland, and Ethelbert were to be held in the autumn. As the largest group in the legislature the UFM would be obliged to form a government. Since the farmers had no recognized leader, their initial task would be to find one.

The farm group had met for the first time on Thursday, 20 July, at 8:00 PM, in the basement of the Odd Fellows Hall on Kennedy Street. The meeting had been convened by W.R. Wood and George Chipman who, after opening the proceedings, left. Since very few of the twenty-four farm MLAs knew each other, there was initial uncertainty about a chairman but Clifford Barclay from Springfield was finally chosen.

Barclay began proceedings by pointing out that although they did not have a majority they were the largest group and would be called on to form a government. They therefore had to choose a leader. Was there anyone present who thought he should be leader? No one volunteered. Would anyone present put forward someone else in the room? Again, no one spoke. Then, said Barclay, they would have to look outside. The group began considering possible candidates on the understanding that the individual finally selected should have their unanimous approval. Barclay allowed a general discussion but once a name encountered opposition it was temporarily dropped. Among the first to be mentioned was Thomas Crerar, the leader of the federal Progressive party. Norris, the outgoing premier, was also suggested; so were Bob Hoey, the Progressive MP for Springfield; Colin Burnell, the president of the UFM; Robert Forke, the Progressive MP for Brandon; W.R. Wood; and George Chipman. During the course of the discussion Clubb added Bracken's name to the list. Clubb had worked with Bracken the previous summer on a special committee to review the price of oil and gas to the farmer and had been much impressed by his extensive knowledge of Manitoba and his calm efficiency. By midnight only three names had not been eliminated – Crerar, Hoey, and Bracken. All three were phoned immediately although it was now after midnight. Crerar was asked to come by at 9:00 AM, Hoey at 9:30, and Bracken at 10:00.

John and Alice spent a restless night. Bracken's initial reaction was to say no to the sudden choice facing them. He considered himself totally unsuited for the job. He had no strong party allegiances, although if pressed he would probably have admitted to Liberal leanings. He had barely settled into his job at the Agricultural College and was looking forward to years of challenging work as its principal. If his thoughts ever strayed beyond the MAC they usually turned to the possibility, in ten years or so, of a university presidency or the directorship of a research institute. For the time being he was happy. He and Alice and the boys were now well-settled into their new life in Manitoba. To give it all up for politics had never entered his head. As the night passed he admitted he was intrigued by the challenge and possibilities that the premiership would offer, but by morning his common sense had reasserted itself. He left for downtown in a borrowed Model-T to thank the farmers for their offer and to refuse it.

When the UFM members reassembled at 9:00 AM Crerar was very friendly, wished them well, but said no. He was followed by Hoey who made a sympathetic speech, gave a lot of good advice, but also said no. Then it was Bracken's turn. He moved to the front of the room 'nervous as a boy saying his first piece at school.' He began badly and stumbled over his words. Seeing that some in the hot and stuffy room had taken off their coats, he did the same. This put him more at ease and for the next half-hour he talked with the farmers about the task facing them. He expressed sympathy for their movement at both the federal and provincial levels and wished them well in their efforts. But he pointed out that he thought he was better suited for the agricultural job for which he had been trained. He believed he could be of more assistance to the farmers by remaining at the MAC. With this he left.

Despite his refusal Bracken had made a considerable impact on the farmers with his straightforward manner and informed judgment. They had appreciated his understanding of their problems and his sound advice. According to Doug Campbell, the youthful, newly elected member from Lakeside, he appeared to have a sensible and non-political attitude and he talked their language. The group unanimously agreed that Bracken was the man they wanted. Bracken, however, proved difficult to persuade and it was not until their third meeting that day that he finally agreed to take the leadership of the group and thus the premiership of Manitoba.

Why did Bracken take the job? He had shown no previous interest in politics and such an abrupt change of course struck many, then and later, as surprising. There is no simple explanation. The answer probably lies in a combination of factors. It has to be remembered that although Bracken was a political neophyte without any apparent political ambition, he was aware of the tensions in the farming communities of western Canada. He had worked closely for ten years with Walter Scott's Liberal administration in Saskatchewan which had been highly sympathetic to the agrarian viewpoint, and, as with anyone who had talked continuously to western farmers and who regularly read the *Grain Growers' Guide*, he was familiar and sympathetic with the farmers' plight and with their nonpartisan activism. He was later to say that he had taken the premiership because he did not want to see the UFM fail. If they had been unable to find a suitable leader their efforts of the previous two years might have been for nought.

Certainly there was a strong appeal to his sense of duty. The third meeting between Bracken and the UFM delegation had taken place in Bracken's living room and Alice had been present throughout. Led by Clubb and Barclay, the delegation had emphasized that they needed strong leadership, that political experience was not essential – after all only eight of them had any experience of the legislature, and that only with a man such as Bracken as their leader, someone who was widely respected in the community, could they hope to bring Manitoba efficient and less costly government. Alice was impressed by the sincerity and candour of the delegation and she finally told her husband that the men had a good case and that if he decided to accept the offer she would support him.

The non-partisan nature of the task also appealed to him. He had always favoured co-operative effort, 'team play' as he called it, and he usually sought the best advice available, whatever the source, before reaching conclusions. Moreover, the delegation was stressing the need in Manitoba for a sound, efficient, and businesslike administration. Bracken believed he was capable of achieving that. He had been confronting and resolving such problems for the past sixteen years.

It should also be remembered that Bracken at thirty-nine was still a relatively young man at the height of his powers. He was ambitious and there lurked not far below the surface his lifelong love of challenge. It is clear that he was aware of the gamble involved in accepting the premiership. As he pointed out years later to an inquisitive reporter: 'I had the best job in the province, and they wanted me to take the worst one. On the one hand was a narrow, safe way to get through life. On the other was uncertainty.'[2] He accepted the position knowing that he would be required to work with greater intensity than ever before and hoping he would justify the confidence placed in him. At 5:20 PM on Friday, 21 July, it was made public that Manitoba had a new premier.[3]

The choice of Bracken as leader of the farm group and as premier of Manitoba was favourably received by everyone. His lack of political knowledge was not considered a handicap. As John Dafoe pointed out in his editorial in the *Manitoba Free Press* on 22 July: 'Professor Bracken is confronted with a business task, calling for powers of organisation, foresight, acumen and sagacity – the qualities of the administrator and business man. These qualities, judged by his record to date, Professor Bracken has ... A highly competent agricultural expert has been placed at the head of affairs in a province which is in its wealth-producing activities, primarily agricultural.'[4] The *Tribune*, the local Conservative paper, shared the *Free Press*'s satisfaction. Manitoba had got the type of man best suited to her needs. He was not a politician and he came to the premiership 'clean-handed and free-handed.'[5]

Bracken faced, however, a daunting situation. He was now leader of a party whose members he did not know and which did not have a majority in the House. The province was saddled with a large debt, with no sinking fund, and it was in the midst of a depression. Moreover, he did not have a seat in the House. In fact, he had never witnessed the opening or closing ceremony of a legislative session, and he had never made a political speech.

There was little time for reflection before Bracken must tackle the immediate task of selecting a cabinet. The composition of the cabinet had not been discussed during his initial meetings with the farmers. When he had asked the delegation for their views they had refused to discuss the selection and requested that Bracken act entirely on his own initiative even if it meant going outside party ranks to do it. Bracken had agreed although privately he realized he would need assistance. Over the next few days he relied heavily on the advice of Richard Craig, a prominent Winnipeg lawyer and former Conservative who had won on the Progressive ticket in Winnipeg. A person of considerable ability and widely respected, Craig early established himself as the strong man in Bracken's party and one of the premier's principal advisers and stalwart defenders over the next five years. Craig fully shared Bracken's deep commitment to a strong, stable, and non-partisan government based on honest and efficient administration.[6]

With these principles in mind the two men put together a small six-man cabinet which was sworn in on 8 August. Knowing that the most important task facing his government was the stabilization of the province's finances, Bracken had gone outside the elected group and chosen F.M. Black, the treasurer of the United Grain Growers, as the new provincial treasurer. Black, a dry dour Scotsman re-knowned for his frugality and efficiency, was a sound choice and an indication of the belt-tightening to come. As expected, Clubb was named minister of public works, while Craig took the crucial post of attorney-general. Duncan McLeod (Arthur) became provincial secretary and Neil Cameron (Minnedosa) took the agriculture portfolio. Bracken decided to look after the controversial education ministry himself.

The cabinet reflected the dominant interests in the province and answered the *Tribune*'s earlier plea for 'men of sound business judgement' whose passion for politics was 'an altogether minor consideration.'[7] It was essentially agrarian in nature and of British stock. The only one not identified with farming was Craig. Black had been with the United Grain Growers since 1917, while Clubb, McLeod, and Cameron were practising farmers and had obviously been chosen to represent the needs of the important farming communities of the province – the south, the southwest, and the west. There were no French-Canadian or Catholic mem-bers in the cabinet. Craig, Cameron, McLeod, and Bracken had been born in On-tario, Black in Scotland, and Clubb in Manitoba. All with the exception of Bracken, who had been raised a Methodist, were Presbyterians.[8] The only member of the new cabinet to have legislative experience was Clubb (1920–2), and that was but of brief duration. However, Craig had school-board and Cameron and McLeod municipal experience, while Black, of course, had considerable financial expertise. The cabinet was designed to meet the needs of good administration and to set at ease those who feared unnecessary changes. It was a conservative, sober, middle-aged group of respected citizens noted for their ability and effi-ciency in their professions, men of agreeable temperament and ease of manner.

All in all, the cabinet met with approval. The reduction of portfolios from seven to six was taken as evidence of Bracken's intention to effect economies where possible without affecting services. Bracken's assumption of the educa-tional portfolio was seen as a reassurance to the public that the system would stay essentially the same despite clamourings in some quarters for change. The cabi-net's inexperience of partisan politics was not seen as a major disadvantage. As the *Free Press* pointed out in an editorial entitled 'The New Government,' 'the prob-lems before them are purely administrative.'[9]

Having formed his cabinet, Bracken's next most pressing concern was to gain a seat in the legislature. From the start it looked as if the most logical place for him to run would be in the frontier constituency of The Pas. To allow Black to run there might risk defeat, for he was not a northerner nor a man identified with the mining needs of the area and he did not have the compensating prestige of the premier's office to off-set the criticism these deficiencies would generate. Black would run in Rupertsland, and the by-election there was set for 13 September. By the time Bracken left for The Pas on Wednesday, 30 August, to make campaign arrangements, Clubb, Cameron, and McLeod had all been re-elected unopposed in by-elections and Nicholas Hryhorczuk had been returned unopposed in Ethelbert.

The Pas constituency was a vast, sprawling area reaching from the Saskatchewan-Manitoba boundary to Hudson Bay. In all senses it was a frontier constituency, accessible only by rail and water, dependent on trapping, hunting, and mineral development. Although agricultural products were grown in the vicinity of The Pas, they were for the community itself rather than as a major source of income. The leading citizens of The Pas were conscious of their needs and of their vulnerability in a farm-dominated province. They were aware that if the interests of The Pas in particular and of the north generally were to be listened to seriously, then it would be necessary to have as their sitting MLA a man of influence with the government. By mid-August many were asking, why not John Bracken, the new premier of Manitoba?

Bracken and Craig arrived in The Pas early on 31 August. During the day Bracken met with the town council and with the executive of the Northland Association, an organization of local businessmen and prominent worthies, and that evening he spoke to a packed house at the Lyric Theatre.[10] It was Bracken's first political speech and on rising he said he was particularly anxious not to be misunderstood. He wanted to make it clear that he had not come to The Pas to foist himself on the constituency but rather to outline the policy of the government. He would consider it an honour to occupy the seat, but he had no intention of trying to bribe the electors by offering them special consideration for their problems. He assured his audience that whether the local electorate returned a private member or himself as their MLA the vast resources of northern Manitoba would not be neglected by his administration. His government firmly believed that if Manitoba was to have a great future it could not continue to rely solely on wheat. It would have to diversify its agricultural base and expand its industrial and mining activities. Knowing that there was a good deal of concern throughout the province about his government's stand on the issue of temperance, Bracken promised that it would be submitted to a referendum as soon as possible and if the results favoured a lifting of prohibition the government would enact legislation without delay. In concluding, he indicated that he would not be returning to Winnipeg the next day as planned but would be staying on a little longer to get additional information about the territory.[11]

Bracken's decision to stay on in The Pas was an astute one. He had quickly detected the anxious feelings in the constituency. For him to come and go in the space of two days would be an affront. It would be much more sensible to spend time in the area, meeting its citizens, and generally familiarizing himself with the problems and potential of the north. By mid-September when Bracken left The Pas his decision had proven a wise one. The Northland Association and the local branches of the UFM and the Independent Labour party had all endorsed him as their candidate. The main reason for the widespread support was the obvious one – the town needed a strong man as its representative, a man who would have influence with the government.[12] With these three important organizations behind him it would be difficult for Bracken to lose the election scheduled for 5 October.

In the midst of these important political developments Bracken was called to Winnipeg by a wire informing him that his father was dying. Ephraim had been in poor health since suffering a stroke in 1921. He had had a relapse a few weeks earlier while spending the summer with John and Alice. Bracken returned south immediately and was present when Ephraim died on 14 September. He made the long, sad journey back to Seeley's Bay with his father's body and attended the funeral service at the Olivet Methodist church which Ephraim had attended as a youngster and where he was buried in the family plot. After brief visits with relatives and friends in Ellisville and Seeley's Bay, Bracken returned to Manitoba.

By the time he arrived back in The Pas on 26 September the election was already in full swing. Bracken found that he had three opponents. Two of them, Dr P.C. Robertson, running as an Independent, and R.H. McNeill, running ironically as a government supporter, believed that a local man would be a better representative for the northern constituency than an outsider. His third opponent was Herman Finger, the first mayor of The Pas, who had been a member of the delegation which had made the bargain with the Roblin government in 1912 about the inclusion of The Pas in Manitoba. Certain commitments were made by the Roblin government which Finger maintained had not been upheld by the Norris administration. His sole purpose in running was to ensure that the present government fulfilled those obligations.[13]

Over the next nine days there was feverish activity in the constituency as the candidates and a number of outside speakers made last-ditch appeals to the electorate. Considerable efforts were made to capture the French vote, about 30 per cent of the total. P.A. Talbot (LaVerendrye), A.R. Boivin (Iberville), Albert Prefontaine (Carillon), and A.L. Beaubien, the federal MP for Provencher, all spoke and campaigned on Bracken's behalf while Joseph Bernier, the Independent member for St Boniface, spoke in support of Finger. Also, Nicholas Hryhorczuk, the UFM member for the neighbouring constituency of Ethelbert, addressed a meeting of some sixty Ukrainians on the weekend before Bracken's return. The most vitriolic speaker was Colonel Arthur Sullivan, a lawyer who had run as a Conservative in Winnipeg in the July election. He vigorously supported Herman Finger.[14]

Bracken took an active part. He replied to charges through interviews, made numerous public speeches, and could often be found in the midst of small groups in the stores or on the streetcorners. He made his final speech on Monday, 2 October, to an overflow audience at the Lyric Theatre. He was given a rousing reception as he walked to the platform. He said he would not deal with matters of general policy but would simply restate the government's aims as outlined a month ago: 'Our purpose, briefly stated, is to give to the province an honest, efficient and businesslike administration; to eliminate waste and cut down expenses to the lowest possible minimum consistent with efficient service; to develop all our natural resources as rapidly as our finances will permit; to endeavour to re-establish the faith of the people in public life and public officials.'[15] Turning to the liquor question, Bracken again promised, as he had throughout the campaign, that a referendum would be held as soon as possible after the next session of the legislature and legislation introduced accordingly. As for the settlement between the local community and the Liberal government of Toby Norris which had so preoccupied Herman Finger and was of deep concern to the town, Bracken said it was final and binding as it stood. The government was prepared to examine it on its merits, but it did not agree that the Norris government had either acted in bad faith or reneged. He concluded his first political campaign by reminding his audience that the government needed an extra seat in the interests of legislative stability. Thus a vote for him on 5 October was not a vote for John Bracken, 'it was a vote for The Pas, a vote for stable government, for moderate views, for the reduction of differences in race and creed, for a better understanding of the north by the south. It would be a vote against outside interference by people who did not understand local conditions.' It was a good, solid, hard-hitting speech that was greeted at the end by a storm of applause.

The result of the election was an overwhelming sweep for Bracken. He received 472, Finger 118, Robertson 71, and McNeill 38. The labor vote was virtually unanimous for Bracken and in Poll #2 where the vote was almost exclusively labor, French, and Ukrainian, Bracken received 129 out of the 156 votes cast. Only one poll did not report. The ballot box for Reid Lake was lost when a canoe overturned in a whirlpool on the Grassie River near the fourth portage. Anyway, 'most of the people at the post were out trapping, and only some half-dozen votes could have been recorded.' Nothing could have indicated more clearly the nature of the constituency.

Bracken was widely praised for his conduct throughout the campaign. In a frontier constituency like The Pas where sectional interests were high there were many temptations to cater to local prejudices and sympathies in order to draw votes, but as both the *Pas Herald and Mining News* and the *Lethbridge Herald* pointed out, Bracken had not pandered to sectionalism. 'He took a broad gauge view of the situation in abstaining from "playing politics" and bending himself to the issue of good government, not compromising himself, but letting it be known that it was for the legislature and not for himself to decide on policies.' The papers praised him for his straight-forward manner. A man without Bracken's strong convictions would have easily succumbed.[16]

Bracken stayed in the constituency another week cementing the ties that had grown since early September. On Thursday, 12 October, he entertained his election committee at a dinner at the Opasquai Hotel. About midnight he paid a short visit to the dance being held at the Community Hall. It was an enjoyable evening and a fitting end to Bracken's first venture into politics. The following afternoon the election special left for Winnipeg. Bracken was returning with twenty-eight seats in the fifty-five member house, a slim majority that would be lost when Talbot took the Speakership. Nevertheless, encouraged and satisfied by his victory in The Pas, he could now turn his full attention to the pressing needs of the province.

4

Brackenism

Bracken and his farm colleagues fully appreciated that the rejection of the Norris government by the electorate was a request for honest, efficient, businesslike administration and a departure from partisan political warfare.[1] Above all it was a demand for economic government. By the time Bracken turned his attention to financial problems in mid-October, the province was losing money at the rate of $3500 a day, a figure which the government later claimed had risen to $5000 a day by the end of the fiscal year. These were staggering sums, and drastic measures were essential if Manitoba was again to pay its way.

Bracken and his cabinet quickly decided on a dual programme of reduced expenditures and increased taxes. In an effort to cut the costs of government, Bracken ordered a streamlining of departmental business and a reduction in the civil service. By Christmas a number of civil servants had been dismissed and more followed in the New Year. In his February budget Black revealed the government's intention of raising $2,000,000 through a variety of taxes including an income tax, automobile licence fees, and a new gasoline tax and of providing a sinking fund for the gradual remission of the provincial debt.

The reaction of this concerted effort to keep expenditure within the revenue was generally favourable.at first although there was some concern in the civil service where employees were often left uncertain of their fate to the last minute.[2] The major criticism came from the Conservative opposition, the business community, and the *Tribune*. The Winnipeg newspaper found the budget 'profoundly disappointing.'[3] Rather than exploring avenues of economy and following them, the government had taken the easy way out and imposed taxes on everything in sight. The *Tribune* considered the provision of a sinking fund particularly 'reckless.' Overall the budget revealed a 'lack of courage in the financial administration of the province.'[4] It 'might have been evolved by a committee of school-boys.'[5]

Accusations of extravagent action were also hurled by the Conservative finan-

cial critic John Haig and by the Winnipeg business community who were appalled
at the impact new taxes might have on the continued development of the province.[6] The *Manitoba Free Press* shared none of these fears and scoffed at criticism: ' ... nothing much will be gained from talking buncombe. There is general
agreement that the budget should be balanced. The private credit of every individual and every institution in the province would suffer if Manitoba were to
keep on registering a deficit of a million a year.'[7]

Bracken could not have agreed more. He claimed, and quite justifiably, that
he and his ministers bore no responsibility for the poor financial state of the province. This was entirely due to the Norris administration. He pointed out that no
Manitoba government had ever taken office with a greater legacy of debt than
the present one. All the new government could do was attempt to rectify the situation and 'keep the expenditures within the revenue.' Rigid economy and both
new and increased taxes were necessary to achieve this. By late autumn 1923 the
government had cut expenses by $650,000 and Bracken was able to assure Mani-
tobans that with continued restraint and additional sources of revenue the government would be paying its way within a year.[8]

In the event, Bracken's prediction was realized. General improvement in the
international economy and a consequent rise in grain prices brought prosperity
back to the prairies in the mid-twenties. This boom, combined with fiscal caution
and added revenues from government liquor sales, enabled Bracken to announce
a surplus of $133,395, or $350 a day, in 1924. By 1926 this had risen to $600,388,
or $1600 a day.[9]

During the same period, 1922–6, the Bracken administration held the capital
debt increase to $4,552,000, compared to $40,008,000 for the period 1915–22.[10]
Since no sinking fund had been provided before 1923 the province faced a prolonged period of mounting debt, but from 1923, under the direction of Black
and Bracken, every new or refunding long-term issue contained provision for a
sinking fund of one-half per cent. By 1927 it was estimated that $219,000 per
year would be paid out of revenue for sinking fund purposes, increasing in time
to $400,000, which it was hoped would pay off the capital debts of the province
in fifty-three years from date of debenture issue. The accumulated deficit had
stood at $1,990,208 at the end of 1922. This was soon being paid off over a per-
iod of twenty years at an annual cost for interest and sinking fund of $160,000.
The Bracken government similarly reduced expenditures for capital purposes
from $14,517,261 in 1921 to $2,124,242 in 1926 and reduced the annual budget
from $10,771,387 in 1921 to $10,269,868 in 1926. As a result of this drastic
programme of cutbacks, Manitoba was the only province in Canada which decreased its expenditures between 1921 and 1926.

This did not mean that Bracken abandoned all the reforms and public projects initiated by the Norris administration but some changes did have to be made. In the area of public works the government was active in the construction and maintenance of trunk and market roads and it assisted municipalities and drainage districts in the maintenance of trunk drains. It also completed, but at a slower pace, various projects begun by the previous government, the most important being the Brandon and Selkirk mental hospitals, the School for the Deaf, and the grounds of the Legislative Building. The legislative vote in 1923 for these matters was $1,150,000 but there were no funds allotted in 1924, 1925, or 1926 and only $40,000 in 1927. Moreover, the various agencies and schemes designed to aid the farmers that had been introduced by Norris, particularly the Rural Credit societies, the Farm Loans Association, and the Winkler Cow Scheme, were either drastically reformed and put on a more businesslike basis or abandoned altogether.

By 1927 the credit of the province had been restored. In fact, Manitoba bonds were selling at a better price than those of Alberta and Saskatchewan. Bracken was proud of this financial record.[11] He never failed to point out in the late twenties that within three years of assuming office his government had put the province on a pay-as-you-go basis, had established a sinking fund, and had generally provided the type of businesslike operation that the people of Manitoba had demanded. An election pamphlet of 1927 attributed the financial record of Bracken's government to 'what may be accomplished when politics is divorced from the business affairs of the government.' It is more likely that it was the result of changes in the international economy and a remorselessly frugal husbanding of the province's revenues. No matter what group or party had been in office at that time it would have pursued the same policy. In all the emotional rhetoric from opposition groups and the strident declamations of the *Tribune*, not one hint of an alternative method of resolving Manitoba's economic ills was ever aired. Fawcett Taylor, the Conservative leader, and his two financial experts, John Haig and Sanford Evans, were always the most critical of Bracken. But they accused the premier of extravagence. Their main point was that if the Conservatives were in office they would be even more frugal.[12] At no time was it argued that the government should deliberately overspend and deficit finance. Not only was this an unknown economic doctrine at the time, but anything hinting of additional expenditures or of deliberately unbalanced budgets would have been an anathema to the public. Even the Conservatives were well aware of that.

Bracken's handling of the economic difficulties of the province reflected his pragmatic, businesslike, and non-partisan approach to the problems of government, a manner of conduct that was soon widely known as 'Brackenism' and that was to characterize his entire political career. He had made the purpose of his government clear in his first legislative speech on 22 January 1923. He had told a hushed chamber that 'We are not here to play politics or to represent a single class, but to get down to the serious business of giving this province an efficient government ... '[13] Bracken firmly believed that party politics such as existed during the Roblin era had no place in the running of the province. He thought that important issues should be examined on their merits and discussed objectively from a broad range of perspectives. They should not be dealt with cavalierly in a partisan manner, they were too important for that. His stance was in keeping with the 1922 UFM platform and properly reflected the attitudes of his rural and urban supporters; initially, however, it only added to the government's difficulties.

The twenty-seven government members who filed into the legislative chamber for the first time in January 1923 were woefully inexperienced. Only eight had been there before and none of them had been on the front benches. Throughout that session and for much of the next five years the farm group caucused more than any political group in Manitoba before or since. Those meetings were educational experiences for the new MLAs. They provided an opportunity for wide-ranging discussions and the voicing of contrary opinions. Bracken chaired the caucus with a very loose rein, with the result that many of the meetings became endurance tests and added to the difficulty of reaching clear decisions or finding common ground. Undoubtedly Bracken should have exercised tighter control but the farmers' resentment of centralized leadership made that difficult, certainly during the first often anarchic session. Gradually, however, the farm MLAs realized the need for greater co-operation and organization and by 1924 the Bracken group began to function more effectively as a unit. This was crucial to their survival, for their majority was always slim and it was often necessary for them to run from one committee room to another to save the day.[14]

During those early sessions of the House the farm MLAs provided easy pickings for the talented and rambunctious opposition benches. The splintering of the opposition vote in 1922 had meant that only the best of the Conservative, Liberal, and Labour members had been returned. Together they made formidable opponents for the new government. The commanding figure in the House was Toby Norris, the former premier. Widely respected and of dignified mien, he was an excellent debater and in his penetrating, remorseless fashion he continuously made life uncomfortable for the new government. Even more impressive was the front-bench trio of the Conservative party: Fawcett Taylor, Sanford Evans, and John Haig. Taylor, the leader, had a fine war record and was extremely popular. As a former mayor of Portage la Prairie and a lawyer to numerous farmers, Taylor understood rural and urban conditions equally well and used his knowledge to good effect in the House. He and Sanford Evans were two of the best-dressed men in the chamber and could often be seen in morning dress with black cutaway coats and serge trousers. Evans was the patrician of the House. Tall, good-looking, with a gracious manner, he was the epitome of a 'gentleman' and would not have been out of place in the House of Lords. His speciality was finance and every year from 1923 until his retirement in 1936 the government's budget was subjected to a ruthless and sometimes telling scrutiny. The roughest tongue in the House belonged to John Haig who, it was said, often opened his mouth only to go away and leave it running. Haig sat as one of the ten members for Winnipeg and was convinced of the necessity of having his name appear every day in both Winnipeg papers. Despite his verbosity, Haig was a tough opponent, quick to seize the advantage, and Bracken found him particularly difficult to deal with.

While not quite as colourful as the Conservatives, the Labour group had an equally impressive front bench. All were long-committed radicals or socialists and some had played a prominent part in the events surrounding the Winnipeg General Strike of 1919. John Queen, who had been jailed for a year for his involvement, never let an opportunity slip by to embarrass the government and his soft Scots burr must often have sounded more like a rasp to the sensitive ears of the farm group. S.J. Farmer and, until his health failed in 1923, Fred Dixon were both telling debaters. In their quiet, sincere fashion they provided an alternative perspective on the social and economic questions of the day and Bracken often found himself privately in agreement, particularly with Dixon for whom he had a deep respect. The fourth Labour front-bencher was William Ivens who shared with Haig a capacity for long-windedness. This trait made him unpopular in the chamber but not ineffective, for he was an able and honest man.

On the government side, Bracken, Clubb, and Black, all inexperienced debaters, took little part in the cut-and-thrust and relied heavily on Craig. He has been likened to Horatius at the bridge as he stood in the chamber, confident and dapper in his well-cut suit, fending off the questions and barbed remarks with his witty, incisive, and shrewd responses while behind him sat the silent ranks increasingly ready to vote as directed.[15]

The new government had drawn its support primarily from the farm community, particularly that segment in the Anglo-Saxon bastion of the southwest, and to a degree from the business community of Winnipeg, both of which had been anxious for a stable, businesslike administration. Despite these political debts and its considerable inexperience, the Bracken government was not controlled during those early uncertain years by either interest group. It attempted to serve both if possible but was always prepared to take a hard line with either if necessary. As a general frame of reference the government adopted the UFM platform of 1922, but the declining strength of the UFM in the mid-twenties and the farmers' continuing disinterest in the traditional mechanisms of power politics meant that the Bracken administration was never subjected to direct pressure from the UFM.[16] Despite this freedom, Bracken always remained sensitive to rural needs and every

January he and his colleagues attended the annual UFM convention. Generally the farmers were satisfied with the performance of the Bracken government, particularly its retrenchment programme which always had their support. After 1922 the UFM became increasingly disengaged from provincial politics and in 1928 abandoned political activity altogether.

Similarly, Bracken was never at the beck and call of the business community in Winnipeg. True, he would often meet with delegations from the Board of Trade and other business groups and in late 1923 he had a so-called 'secret meeting' with some Winnipeg businessmen at the Fort Garry Hotel in order to explain his government's tax legislation, but such gatherings were in keeping with his stated policy of listening to all forms of advice.[17] His close attention to proffered opinions did not mean that he was bound by them. In fact, many Winnipeg businessmen wished he had been. They thought the government's taxation policies potentially crippling to the economic development of the province. In the main, however, the business community, like the farmers, had little to complain about. The first Bracken administration provided the stable government they required.

During its initial year in office there were three major issues, apart from the economy, that demanded government attention – education, the Wheat Board, and the liquor referendum. True to his principles and to his mandate, Bracken chose to handle all three in a non-partisan manner.

He dealt first with the problem of provincial education. The state of education in Manitoba was causing considerable concern by late 1922. Costs had risen from $175,000 to $2,000,000 in the previous five years. Farmers in many municipalities were now unable to meet their school taxation,[18] and dozens of primary schools throughout the province were closed for lack of funds; higher education, at the university and the Agricultural College, was costing far more than many thought necessary. A few weeks after Bracken's victory at The Pas the government was searching for some means of lowering the excessive cost of maintaining and operating schools in Manitoba.

Unable to devise a quick and easy solution, Bracken decided to appoint a royal commission to survey educational conditions and requirements in the province and recommend the most efficient means of satisfying them. The announcement was made in the speech from the throne at the opening of the session in January 1923. Bracken persuaded his old friend, Dr Walter Murray, the president of the University of Saskatchewan, to be chairman. When the Murray Commission reported in 1924 it recommended special grants in low assessment districts, a minimum income for teachers, and larger school units. In his attached report on higher education Dr E.S. Learned of the Carnegie Foundation was very critical of the lack of support given the university and the Agricultural College, although he admired the way they had persevered under difficult conditions. He recommended the amalgamation of the two institutions on the Fort Garry site.[19]

Bracken was unable to implement most of the recommendations for financial reasons, but he did introduce legislation in 1924 ensuring that no schools would have to close for lack of funds and in 1924 the university and the Agricultural College were united, although not on one site until 1929. Bracken raised the grant fifteen cents a day for the second year of service by a teacher and twenty-five cents a day for subsequent years. This made Manitoba the first province to make a practical and definite attack on the problem of constantly changing teachers in the rural schools. By cutting the government grant in aid of transportation to schools from 50 to 40 per cent and reducing the university grant by $100,000, Bracken was able to spend more money on elementary education than in any previous year. This was commendable although it was unfortunate that it was achieved at a cost to higher education.[20]

Although a complex issue and one that generated considerable emotional response, the education problem in the province was relatively easily resolved. It involved no major political decisions and it did not endanger the government. That was not the case with the Wheat Board, a controversial question which threatened the life of the government. It was Bracken's first major test.

The national marketing of wheat had been a primary concern since the end of the war. In the summer of 1922 the Liberal government at Ottawa had passed an act creating a board with apparently satisfactory power to market wheat. The board was to come into existence on being granted certain concurrent enabling powers by any two western provinces. Both the Alberta and Saskatchewan governments had called special sessions and the necessary powers had been granted, but when individuals were approached to sit on the board they had refused, generally on the grounds that the 1922 legislation did not provide for sufficient control over the millers or the transportation system. The board therefore had not materialized.

Despite a reasonable marketing of the 1922 crop the spread between the price paid to the farmer at his shipping point and the price quoted on the Liverpool market – at this time approximately 95 cents and $1.38 per bushel respectively – had kept considerable interest alive in a permanent national wheat marketing system. Both Premier Greenfield of Alberta and Premier Dunning of Saskatchewan wanted Manitoba to co-operate with them in the establishment of a wheat board.[21] By early 1923 it was clear that the Bracken government would have to decide what its stand would be.

Initially Bracken was prepared to recommend to his caucus that wheat board legislation be introduced by the government, even though he personally favoured a co-operative selling agency and though he realized that Manitoba had less to gain and more to lose than Alberta and Saskatchewan through having an earlier harvest and being closer to the market. He knew that refusal to co-operate might damage the board's chances of success and harm the farmers further west. He said

he would go along with Alberta and Saskatchewan if they and the various farmers'
organizations on the prairies agreed 'to lay plans immediately in an endeavour to
develop a purely co-operative non-profit non-compulsory organization to handle
subsequent crops.'[22]

The Alberta and Saskatchewan governments and various farm organizations
were prepared to comply with Bracken's request but he did not introduce the
legislation right away. Although he had been quite confident in January that a
Wheat Board bill could be introduced with the backing of the government, by
March he was not so sure.[23] On 6 March Bracken announced in the legislature
that compulsory wheat marketing legislation would be introduced by the government, but when asked by Haig if it would be a government measure he would not
commit himself.[24] He knew by then that a split had developed in the government
caucus over the bill. It was this division that was holding up its presentation to
the legislature and threatening its ultimate fate. In the house as a whole about 30
per cent of the farmer members were against the bill and were putting up a stren-
uous battle against it in their caucuses. Some were opposed to the compulsory
features embodied in the legislation, others held out on the grounds that while it
might benefit Saskatchewan and Alberta with their later harvests and longer hauls
to market it would militate against the farmers of Manitoba.[25] In fact it had become obvious by mid-March that the Wheat Board bill would be defeated. The
only possible way to save it would be to append the fate of the government to it.[26]

In the event, Bracken finally introduced the Wheat Board bill in early April
but made it clear that the members of his own party were free to vote as they
liked; it was to be a house measure, not a government bill. Its defeat would not
be interpreted as a vote of censure. By the time the bill came forward for second
reading on 13 April the cabinet and government caucus were split and since the
opposition groups were almost solidly opposed to a compulsory wheat pool the
result seemed inevitable.[27]

Bracken attempted to defend the bill, moving second reading of it in a speech
of over two hours. In a professorial manner he gave his audience a comprehensive
and frank analysis of the merits and defects of a central marketing scheme. In
conclusion he recommended adoption of the bill, claiming that a centralized
marketing agency would probably do much better in marketing the western
crops than the existing system. A board would encourage better farming; it would
result in lowering the costs of production, transportation, and marketing; and it
would pave the way toward a voluntary co-operative centralized selling agency.
On concluding his speech near 11:00 PM Bracken sat down to a round of hearty
and appreciative applause.[28] One commentator doubted 'if any advocate of the
wheat board dwelling on its advantages in a purely one-sided manner would have
made the impression made by the first minister in his method of dealing with

the obviously bad as well as the obviously good sides of the proposal.'[29] Despite Bracken's effort the bill was defeated 24-21 with six government members voting against, including Craig, Cameron, and Black of the cabinet.[30]

Bracken was subjected to a great deal of criticism over the next few days. The *Regina Leader, Edmonton Journal*, and *Saskatoon Star* all accused him of breaking faith with the farmers of Alberta and Saskatchewan while closer to home his action was interpreted as an abandonment of responsible government.[31] Bracken saw it differently. He knew it was a vital issue and that passage of the bill would be a disadvantage to many Manitoba farmers. He believed, therefore, that it should not be resolved by party in-fighting. To have forced it through by using the whip would have been unfair. To him it was more in keeping with responsible government to make the vote an open one, thus allowing MLAs to reflect more faithfully the interests of their constituents. Bracken, of course, was also well aware that the bill was likely to be defeated even if the whip was exercised. It would have been political suicide to attempt it. Thus, his actions over the Wheat Board revealed an ingenuity for marrying his principles and his personal goals. It was a tactic that over the years many in Manitoba were to find both frustrating and infuriating.

Another important issue that had to be dealt with during Bracken's first year in office was the liquor question. Bracken's handling of it and his personal stance throughout the discussions were further proof of his deep-rooted commitment to non-partisan politics. The UFM had in their election platform of 1922 pledged themselves to hold a referendum on prohibition if they obtained office. Bracken had clearly committed himself to a referendum during his campaigning in The Pas. Both the UFM and Bracken made these commitments, although the one as an organization and the other as an individual were opposed to any modification of prohibition. Bracken rarely took a drink throughout his life. He had been raised in a prohibitionist 'ban the bar' atmosphere and he still adhered to this practice on the assumption of political office. However, he realized there was considerable opinion in favour of legalizing the sale of liquor provided it was under government control. Therefore, he agreed to put the matter to a referendum and promised to abide by the result even if it meant the introduction of legislation to legalize the government sale of liquor.

The Moderation League had prepared a petition, including a full-scale bill, asking for government control and sale of liquor. By the time the petition was submitted on 21 January 1923 it contained 76,000 signatures, the largest ever to be presented to a Manitoba government.[32] There was also pressure on the government from the Beer and Wine League to allow the sale of beer and wine with meals in hotels. The legislature finally decided to hold separate referenda on the two issues. The date for the referendum on the Moderation League bill was set for 22 June and that on the proposed beer and wine legislation for 11 July.[33]

It was a lively campaign in which Bracken took an active part. He made it clear from the beginning that it was not a party issue and that everyone should vote according to conscience. Bracken himself spoke repeatedly, 'on economic as well as moral grounds,' in favour of the temperance cause and against any extension of the liquor business. A week before the initial referendum he chaired an over-flow meeting at the Walker Theatre organized by the Winnipeg Prohibition Committee and argued vigorously for the maintenance of the existing Manitoba Temperance Act.[34]

Bracken was fighting on behalf of a losing cause. The Moderation League bill was approved by an over-whelming vote: 107,609 for and 68,879 against. However, when the votes were counted in the referendum on the Beer and Wine bill, the total against was 65,072 with only 27,016 in favour. The people of Manitoba thus revealed that they wanted government control of the liquor business but they did not want a return to public drinking. As Bracken wryly put it, he had come a long way from being Worthy Patriarch of the Sons of Temperance in Seeley's Bay at sixteen to chief bartender of the province of Manitoba at forty.[35]

The Manitoba Government Control and Sale of Liquor Act of 1923 required every prospective purchaser of liquor to be twenty-one and have a permit costing one dollar. The permit holder then purchased liquor from the Government Commission, paid for it in advance, and the commission delivered it to his residence. A record was kept of all purchases made by each permit holder to prevent the purchase of large quantities by individuals. Transient visitors to the province could purchase a temporary one-month permit for one dollar.[36]

Unfortunately, the act proved hard to enforce over the next few years and by early 1927 was being branded a failure. In addition to widespread concern at violations of the law, strong agitation had developed for liberalization of the act to enable the sale of beer by the glass in public establishments. Bracken decided to submit the issue to a further referendum which was held on the same day as the 1927 election. The vote heavily favoured the sale of beer by the glass and the Bracken government introduced new legislation. The Government Liquor Control Act of 1928 authorized licensed hotels to open beer parlours for the sale of beer by the glass while government liquor stores were now permitted to sell on a cash-and-carry basis as well as for home delivery. The 1928 legislation, with minor amendments, determined Manitoba drinking habits for the next thirty years.[37]

By the autumn of 1923, after a year in office, the Bracken government was feeling more self-confident and assured. Three of the most sensitive and complicated issues had been handled satisfactorily and the premier and his colleagues had demonstrated to the electorate and the legislature that they were dedicated to non-partisan and businesslike government. The farm MLAs were settling into their surroundings and beginning to realize that they were unlikely to be removed from office.

The growing strength of the government was underlined at the end of the year. In early December Bracken decided to enlarge his cabinet. Neil Cameron stepped down as minister of agriculture because of illness but remained in the cabinet as minister without portfolio. Charles Cannon (Mountain) took over as minister of education from Bracken and Albert Prefontaine (Carillon) became provincial secretary and took charge of the Department of Land and Railways. D.L. McLeod retained only the office of municipal commissioner while Bracken assumed the agriculture portfolio. Before joining the farm movement in the early twenties, Cannon had been closely identified with the Liberals and Prefontaine with the Conservatives. The by-elections in Mountain and Carillon were set for 24 December 1923.[38] Cannon was opposed by G.R. Fraser of the Conservatives while Prefontaine had to contend with Maurice Duprey, an Independent.

The by-elections provided the first opportunity in over a year for the electorate to see Bracken on the hustings and to take his measure. From the start he challenged the Conservatives to prove their sincerity in seeking economy by withdrawing from the fight and permitting Cannon an acclamation. He asked all government workers to fight the election 'on educative lines and to avoid a wrangle of personalities.' In his speeches Bracken usually surveyed the deficit situation in the province and reminded his audience that wheat production had not increased in the past fifteen years. So expenditure had outrun revenue. There was no need, he said, to blame anyone; all were responsible. The important thing was to get together and solve the difficulty. Some might ask, 'Why cut expenditures?' 'Why balance the budget?' This, said Bracken, was necessary in order to protect the credit of the province: 'How could people demand lower taxation until such time as the government could pay its way.' As for income tax, he agreed that all taxation was very disagreeable, 'but surely it was agreed that it was only fair for those who had money to pay more than those who had not?'[39]

On the whole, Bracken succeeded throughout the campaign in avoiding political wrangling and confined his remarks to those of an educational nature, but occasionally he was led astray by the attacks of two Conservatives, John Haig and R.G. Willis, a former leader of the party. Willis, in particular, with his old 'country schoolhouse' style of political speaking, flayed away, hammer and tongs, defending the Roblin régime and accusing Bracken of extravagence. Bracken and Cannon could not resist mention of the Parliament Building scandal which aroused many approving chuckles in the pro-government crowds. It was usually an uncomfortable evening for Willis and company but an enjoyable one for the audience who preferred their political meetings to be lively and personality-ridden rather than debating societies where strictest accuracy was observed and no advantage was taken of an opponent. These country people knew who they were going to vote for but why take all the joy out of the combat because of it? Bracken quickly sensed this mood and was not loath to cater to it. For example, when he was accused at Baldur of paying overly high salaries to the liquor commissioners, Bracken shot back: 'The graft on the parliament building would have paid those salaries for 40 years.'[40]

The by-elections were a useful experience for Bracken. They familiarized him with other sections of the province and exposed him to some hard-hitting campaigning. Overall he and his colleagues had been content to place their record and their analysis of the province's problems before the public. The vote on 24 December was a vindication of their policy. Both Cannon and Prefontaine won overwhelming victories. Duprey lost his deposit and Fraser saved his by fewer than forty votes.[41]

The solid victories in the by-elections and the government's increasing dominance in the House were proof by 1924 that the farm group was gradually establishing its control over provincial affairs. This was a satisfying development for Bracken but the personal cost had been considerable. Pictures of him in the mid-twenties still show a trim, handsome, purposeful man with no signs of wear-and-tear. Certainly, his performance in a challenge soccer match at the Brandon Winter Fair in 1924 seemed like the Bracken of old: 'Bracken was easily the best player in a field which included athletes of all sizes, weights, and shapes. The slim, black haired youth ... was the spearpoint of every attack for his side. His footwork was good enough to satisfy his severest critic, and if his opponents hadn't concentrated on him he might have scored again and again.'[42] But the photographs and his soccer exploits were deceiving. Bracken had always worked hard, but since August 1922 he had been putting in a very long day, often into the early hours of the morning.[43] His personal schedule of cabinet meetings, departmental routine, talks with delegations, and speech-making in Winnipeg and throughout the province had begun to take its toll. The strain was such that by mid-1925 he was being advised to rest by his doctors. But it was too late. He had permanently damaged his health and for the rest of his political days he was subject to bouts of exhaustion and discomfort. Increasingly, he gave the impression of being under stress and of finding it difficult to unwind. Now he relaxed only at home – where he never discussed politics except in the most general way – or in farm houses and small communities across the West.

Throughout the twenties Bracken spoke surprisingly little in the legislature, preferring to let others such as Craig carry the burden of debate. When in the chamber he usually wore neat grey serge business suits and ties of serviceable yet sombre hue which gave the impression of a businesslike manner and quiet authority. His clothes were an accurate reflection of his attitude and performance.

After an initial boisterous and, at times, anarchic session in 1923 Bracken gradually established his control of the House. He did not do this with deeply moving and eloquent speeches, or a flamboyant and dramatic style. He was incapable of the first and the second would have been quite out of character. His manner was always considered and authoritative and his style more like that of a university professor than one normally associated with a politician. He was not a good platform or even legislative speaker. His speeches were dry and fact-laden and one had to be attentive. They were nearly always logical and carefully structured but they did not move or stir – no one would feel the need to rise and applaud spontaneously or rush to the barricades. Bracken usually wanted to examine a problem, open it out in all its dimensions, and explain to his audience the motives and conclusions of the government based on an examination of existing evidence. He did this throughout his political career. His very first speech in the Manitoba legislature on 22 January 1923 and his last in the federal parliament in April 1949 were cast in the same mold. Those who heard him in the twenties and thirties remark on the control which he had in the House, the way he treated it as if it were a schoolroom and he the schoolmaster. It was a quietly arrogant, patronizing stance but not offensively so because Bracken had no obvious personal arrogance – in fact he was quite a modest man. He did not flaunt his self-confidence. If he had done so, he would not have lasted long in a province as conservative as Manitoba.

Bracken was, of course, a detail man. And nowhere is this more apparent than in the work he would do on his speeches. The surviving manuscripts of his speeches in the Manitoba Archives are almost incomprehensible, so laden are they with addendums, insertions, overlays, second-thoughts, and marginalia, all written in a tight, crabbed hand of incredible minuteness. This was a trait throughout his university and political life. His natural drive toward excellence and his nervousness about the public platform made him compulsive. He worked hard on his speeches and found it difficult to employ ghost-writers. His constant revision led Ewen McPherson, the provincial treasurer in the thirties, to exclaim in exasperation on one occasion: 'Good Lord, that man would edit the Lord's Prayer if he could.'[44]

His professorial attitude and his careful marshalling of evidence were the natural outgrowths of his careers as an agronomist and university lecturer. His analytic, scientific, and logical way of presenting himself were to his advantage in the provincial field, particularly in those days when many legislators and most of the electorate wanted to be free of party politics. As Douglas Campbell has pointed out, Bracken was a pragmatist. He would not abandon principle or bend from what he thought was right, but he was sensible enough to realize what was obtainable and what was not. He was not intuitive but arrived at decisions by a slow, analytic process. This again was reflected in his whole manner and presence in the legislature.

Although Bracken steadily improved his political skills, eventually becoming rather a shrewd tactician, he remained aloof from the back-stairs machinations that have always been a part of traditional politics. In fact, he had very few advisers in the twenties and those he had were more close friends than political confidants. Inside the government he relied heavily in the early years on Craig and then on 'Billy' Clubb, a warm, friendly man blessed with an enormous fund of plain common-sense. Outside the legislature he would often chat with Bob Gourlay, the president of Beaver Lumber and a first-class curler, who became one of his closest friends, and occasionally with Frank Fowler, the general manager of the Winnipeg Grain Exchange. Although Fowler was an active federal Liberal, there is no evidence to suggest that Bracken was identified with the federal Liberal party during those years. He unquestionably preferred the Liberals led by Mackenzie King to the Conservatives led by Arthur Meighen, but he strongly believed that federal and provincial politics should be separate. In any case, he disliked partisan politics and took no part in the federal elections of the twenties. Within the Progressive camp he obviously preferred Thomas Crerar's 'broadening-out' tactics to the 'group government' philosophy of Henry Wise Wood of Alberta, and he repeatedly stated his government's desire to embrace people from all economic interests and of all political persuasions. Government by 'class' or 'economic interest group' was antithetical to his personal philosophy of consensus government.

Bracken was most at home with agricultural problems and with rural audiences, which was only fitting in a province like Manitoba. During the twenties he travelled extensively making dozens of speeches in the rural areas. It was during those talks to the assembled farm families that Bracken's deep-seated love and respect for the farmer and the rural life was most apparent. One easterner who by chance heard a Bracken speech in Deloraine in late 1926 captured the essence of the man's style and character. When he had first seen him on the train he had taken the serious, solemn-faced man for a Baptist preacher. That evening at the town hall meeting he was surprised to discover that his preacher was the premier of Manitoba: 'At first sight he is disappointing, apparently a quiet, mild-mannered individual, fitted more for school-teaching than influencing votes. His voice was fair, carrying well enough in the hall where we were, but not particularly strong nor pleasing ... ' As the meeting progressed Bracken's manner grew upon the visitor. The premier stepped down from the platform and mingled with his audience and in a quiet conversational tone outlined his government's economic policies. It was obvious that Bracken had everyone's close attention and was deeply respected. 'It was the queerest political meeting I have ever attended,' wrote the easterner: 'No hurrahing, no band, no flamboyant platitudes, but just a man of the people standing up before some of his supporters, giving an account of his public stewardship.'[45]

5

Wood, minerals, and Liberals

By the mid-twenties Bracken's 'pay as you go' policies, combined with the gradual return of prosperity to the West, were stabilizing the Manitoba economy. His cautious, pragmatic approach to government was meeting with general public approval and his party's command of the legislature was no longer seriously threatened. Increasingly, his attention was drawn away from the day-to-day concerns of finance, liquor, and education to the problems associated with the development of Manitoba's natural resources of wood, water, and minerals.

Bracken had been committed to diversifying Manitoba's economy and opening up the undeveloped regions east of Lake Winnipeg and north of The Pas from the time he had accepted the leadership of the farm group. He had argued long and hard within the cabinet about the need to diversify the economy. To him an overdependence on wheat was not sensible. By the mid-twenties he was making it clear on a number of public platforms that important as agriculture was, as serious as its problems were, and necessary as their solution was, the province could not continue to depend on agriculture alone. Forestry, mining, fishing, and water power would all have to be developed, as would secondary industry.[1]

As the western economy improved during 1924, Bracken actively promoted the formation of an Industrial Development Board. It was formally established in July 1925 and combined the interests and concern of the province, the City of Winnipeg, and the Board of Trade. It was financed chiefly by the city and the province, assisted by the Board of Trade, the Winnipeg Electric Company, and the Manitoba Power Company. The board's operations were quickly delegated to three main committees and by the end of 1925 a major survey of the industrial potential of the province had been launched.[2]

Bracken was anxious to promote the greatest possible development 'on sound lines' of every class of industry represented in the province. He realized that the completion of the Panama Canal had curtailed the distributing area of Winnipeg and an initiative needed to be taken in order to rebuild confidence in the province's business community.[3] He welcomed outside capital to Manitoba and was prepared to throw his government's backing behind projects if they were in the larger interests of the province and no outright monopolies were established.

One difficulty in developing the province was that the federal not the provincial government controlled Manitoba's natural resources. This had been the situation since 1870 when Manitoba entered confederation. It was joined in that colonial status by Alberta and Saskatchewan in 1905, although the financial arrangement with those two provinces was more attractive. Manitoba received no subsidy until 1882 when the federal government granted $45,000 per annum. In 1885 this was raised to $100,000 a year. In 1912 when Manitoba's boundaries were extended to their final position, the annual subsidy was again adjusted. The population-subsidy scale in use in Alberta and Saskatchewan since 1905 was applied to Manitoba and made retroactive to 1 July 1905.[4]

This arrangement far from satisfied Manitoba. In 1913 it joined with Alberta and Saskatchewan in sending a letter to Prime Minister Borden calling for the return of all unalienated land and for continued compensation for the land already alienated. The war prevented any sustained consideration of this complicating proposal, but when it was discussed at a federal-provincial conference in 1918 it ran into opposition from eastern provinces who interpreted the claims for compensation by the three western provinces as an 'infringement upon the purely fiscal arrangements between the provinces and the Dominion.'[5] Furthermore, there was no recognition given to the fact that Manitoba had not been compensated at all for the years 1870-82 and only partially for the years 1882-1905. It was becoming obvious that if Manitoba wanted to have its grievances redressed it would have to act apart from Alberta and Saskatchewan and it would have to separate clearly the issues of an annual federal subsidy, compensation for alienated land, and the return of the province's natural resources.[6]

By April 1922 the Mackenzie King government had agreed that the natural resources question should be adjusted so that the prairie provinces would be in 'a position of equality with the other Provinces of Confederation.' To this end the federal government was prepared to open negotiations and willing to submit contentious points to arbitration.[7] The concession of 'equality' was an important one and from that date the federal Department of the Interior had to consult with Manitoba before there could be any further alienation of resources.

Bracken first discussed the natural resources question with the King government in November 1922 and pressed for a solution of the problem. He wanted the return of the remaining resources and compensation upon a fiduciary basis for those already alienated.[8] Despite King's willingness to negotiate he was not prepared to accept Manitoba's conditions as a prelude to discussion. As problems over pulpwood concessions, mineral development, and water power mounted and intensified in Manitoba in the twenties, Bracken continually found himself and his government placed in an increasingly awkward, if not invidious, position by Manitoba's continued colonial status. He constantly pressured the King government for either a conference on the question or referral to independent arbitration, but by 1928 nothing of substance had been accomplished.[9]

One of the earliest issues to underline Bracken's difficulties was a dispute over pulpwood concessions in the region of Lake Winnipeg. In 1921 J.D. McArthur of Winnipeg had acquired pulpwood berth No 1 on the eastern shore of Lake Winnipeg. In looking for financial backing, McArthur had interested George Seaman of Chicago, a large distributor of newsprint, and Hugh Chisholm of the Oxford Paper Company of New York, one of the largest newsprint manufacturers in the United States. In May 1924 McArthur and Seaman announced their intention to build a 200-ton mill in St Boniface. At that time Bracken wrote to McArthur saying such a plant would be of 'inestimable benefit' to the province, to St Boniface, and to the City of Winnipeg, and if there was anything within its jurisdiction that his government could do, consistent with its responsibilities to the people of Manitoba, it would be glad to do it.[10]

For the scheme to be profitable, McArthur and Seaman claimed they needed an additional pulpwood concession capable of yielding 3,000,000 cords. They went to Ottawa that summer to negotiate the grant with Charles Stewart, the minister of the Department of the Interior. The size of the proposal alarmed not only other lumber operators in Manitoba but it also staggered Bracken, who was instinctively opposed to such a monopoly. Under the terms of the 1922 agreement on natural resources, Stewart did not want to make an outright grant unless Bracken agreed. The Manitoba premier refused to do so. Stewart therefore decided to offer the concession for open sale.[11]

In late October 1924 the federal government offered a huge 40,000 square mile tract of land in northern Manitoba for sale as a pulpwood berth No 2. The auction date was set for 16 December. The purchaser would be able to select tracts over a five-year period containing up to 3,000,000 cords of spruce pulpwood.[12]

The announcement caused an outcry in Winnipeg. Most critics, including the ILP, the UFM, and John Dafoe, the editor of the *Manitoba Free Press*, were appalled that a virtual empire in timberland would fall into the hands of one company. Such a lock-up of timber berths would prevent development and drive a number of smaller companies out of business. Dafoe, for one, wanted a mill – the *Free Press* would benefit from having a mill at its back door – but he did not think the proposed concession in the public interest. Everyone pointed out the dangers to Manitoba that resulted from the federal administration of the province's natural resources.[13]

Bracken shared these fears, and he quickly informed Stewart that he and his cabinet wanted the terms of the concession revised.[14] Bracken was in a difficult position. If his government refused to co-operate it would bear the responsibility of the loss of the pulp mill to the province. On the other hand, unless it tried to modify the arrangements it would be subject to the accusation of having 'sold out' to monopoly interests. Bracken had to have the mill but on more acceptable conditions. On 24 November Bracken went on record as whole-heartedly in favour of establishing a pulp mill and the sale of sufficient pulpwood to make it an economically sound proposition provided all existing activities, whether related to mining, lumbering, or the cutting of cordwood and trees by settlers, were not disturbed.[15]

During the next few weeks Bracken met frequently with representatives of McArthur, a special committee of the Board of Trade, and his cabinet, and was in constant touch with Ottawa. By 7 December negotiations had been completed and the final arrangements for the sale of pulpwood berth No 2 were announced. Bracken had won a number of concessions. Under the new terms the reservation would end as soon as 3,000,000 cords of spruce pulpwood had been selected. All unselected regions would automatically become open after certain dates. Settlers, existing sawmills, and homestead applications were protected.[16]

These changes did not sit well with George Seaman and the Oxford Paper Company and they immediately pulled out of their deal with McArthur. This placed McArthur in a difficult position and for a time he was prepared to listen to offers of a new partnership from E.W. Backus of Minneapolis, who owned the Minnesota and Ontario Paper Company, and William Hurlburt of the Spanish River Pulp and Paper Company. But when it became clear to McArthur that both Backus and Hurlburt were really opposed to the establishment of a mill in Manitoba – Backus referred to Manitoba 'as his backyard' – the talks collapsed. McArthur then told Bracken what had happened and, at McArthur's urging, the premier wired Ottawa that in his opinion the sale should be postponed. But the telegram was sent too late and the sale went ahead.

McArthur decided to bid without the support of outside capital. When the auction opened on 16 December both Hurlburt and G.R. Gray of the Spanish River Company showed up. Gray pushed the bidding to a very high level and then dropped out. As a result McArthur's Manitoba Pulp and Paper Company acquired berth No 2 at a bonus of $2.00 per cord above the required initial bid of eighty cents. McArthur soon admitted that the price he had been forced to pay would make the project impossible to finance successfully. Even Ottawa officials had been surprised at the price for which the berth sold. The ordinary price for pulpwood limits was about one or two cents over the upset price of eighty cents. It was seldom that more than a dollar a cord was paid for pulpwood.[17]

McArthur was still determined to bring a pulp and paper industry to Manitoba and he now approached Bracken and asked for government backing. McArthur argued that there would never be a pulp and paper industry in the province if one had to rely on American capital. He claimed the rulers of the American paper industry were trying to hold down production in order to create and maintain an artificial scarcity in newsprint: 'If we want our pulpwood resources developed we will have to do it ourselves.'[18] This plea proved unavailing. Bracken was sympathetic to much of McArthur's argument, but as the *Tribune* pointed out, pulpwood concessions at $2.80 a cord were not worth the paper they were printed on. A newsprint industry in Manitoba would have to compete with companies that had paid between eighty or ninety cents a cord for their pulpwood.[19] Bracken was not interested in investing public money in such an inauspicious enterprise.

By early 1925 it was obvious that McArthur would be unable to find additional capital and was faced with the probability of being unable to fulfil the conditions fixed by the tender. It was at that moment he was approached by the Spanish River people who were prepared to take over the enterprise from him and build the mill themselves provided he got a better deal from the dominion government.

In late April Bracken was asked by the federal government to consent to an arrangement worked out with McArthur and the Spanish River Company. The proposal was to merge berth No 2 and berth No 1, obtained by McArthur in 1921. The rate over both concessions would then be reduced to ninety-two cents – the upset price plus twelve cents. In effect Bracken was being asked to approve a new arrangement on the basis of a fixed charge without competition. He refused point blank to agree to the proposal. He wanted the federal government to put the limits up to auction a second time with a forfeit so large as to preclude bogus bids.[20]

While making this point in Ottawa Bracken found himself subjected to considerable pressure to give his approval to the federal government's scheme. He telegraphed Craig on 6 May 1925: 'Strong propaganda under way to get Winnipeg support to price reduction on pulpwood. Reported here Southam Press likely to come out in strong support. Am told statement has gone from Spanish River Counsel to Canadian Press. Also many wires to Winnipeg from same source requesting Winnipeg pressure on Stewart and self. Am advised this is beginning of organised effort to gain support for proposition and that if failure results Bracken administration is to be credited with the blame.'[21]

Bracken's objections and the difficulties Stewart would face in ignoring both the price bid in December and the principle of public sale resulted by mid-May in a modification of the proposal. The new arrangement did not call for a resale of pulpwood berth No 2 but was based on an exchange of timber berths held by

McArthur. He held berths Nos 1 and 1A; the first, centred on Pine Falls, contained 50,000 cords of pulpwood; the second embraced 1080 square miles of territory located northeast of berth No 1. Berth 1A was not a good proposition. The timber was scattered, and many gullies and ravines would make logging costly. The proposal was that McArthur exchange berth 1A for a territory, equal in extent, to be selected in co-operation with the federal government from elsewhere in the province. The original price bid – $1.65 for No 1 and basic for No 1A – would remain the same for both berths. If the exchange were to go through, the Spanish River Company would take over both berths and build a 100-ton mill at a cost of $3,000,000. Stewart was willing to recommend the exchange if Bracken approved. On 15 May the federal cabinet put through an order-in-council cancelling the sale of pulpwood berth No 2.[22]

Dafoe advised Bracken that he, for one, had no objection to the arrangement provided the public interest was protected. The *Free Press* would give 'guarded and moderate' support, saying that 'under the circumstances' the action was justified.[23] On 28 May Bracken announced that the Manitoba government had decided to approve the arrangement with the modification that the selection of the new stands of pulpwood was confined to the east of Lake Winnipeg and limited to an amount adequate to maintain a 100-ton mill. While protesting that his government should not be called upon to undertake any responsibility in the disposal of these resources while they were under the jurisdiction of the federal government, Bracken hoped there would be no delay in arranging for the immediate establishment of the industry.[24] Dafoe endorsed this arrangement in an editorial on 29 May. It was much more in the public interest than, first, the grandiose scheme of the previous November by which an empire of pulpwood was to be blanketed and locked up in the interests of American pulpwood speculators, and second, the more recent suggestion that the bonus on berth No 2 be reduced by private arrangement with the minister of the interior. A contract was finally signed on 12 June 1925 between the federal government and J.D. McArthur whose Manitoba Pulp and Paper Company was to operate the mill for its new parent the Spanish River Company.

The *Tribune* did not share Dafoe's opinion of the scheme. It claimed that an unnecessary delay of one year had occurred and that the final arrangements were in many ways as generous as those originally outlined in October 1924 and to which there had been so much objection. All that had resulted was delay and the loss to the city of a 200-ton mill. McArthur was to be permitted to exchange one of his berths, known to be lean in pulpwood, for one of equal size to be hand-picked and furnishing a far richer supply of pulpwood. For this his company would pay only eighty cents a cord. There would be no premium, no auction sale, and no sealed tenders. The *Tribune* accused both the *Free Press* and Bracken of hypocrisy: 'They have given their blessing to a principle they had recently denounced. They have shelved their convictions about auction sales, and sealed tenders and offered free right-of-way to a proposition that embodies all the objections registered against the Seaman project for the establishment of a pulp and paper-making industry in the city of St. Boniface ... Premier Bracken, in a truly amazing exhibition of weakness, lent himself to aims and objects, for which he could have had very little sympathy, but which for diplomatic reasons he felt he had to respect. For that weakness he pays the usual price ... He has had to publicly abandon principles that he had previously asserted ... '[25]

Why did Bracken change his mind? As recently as mid-May 1925 he had favoured another sale, yet two weeks later he had endorsed a private arrangement. The reasons are fairly straightforward. He knew Manitoba wanted a mill. It was unlikely to get one if the concession area was put up to auction because the bidding would undoubtedly be run up again to an unreasonable figure by other interests. Manitoba would be back at square one. The only way to get a mill was to make a private deal. He was not responsible for making it but he had to approve it in principle; therefore he was a party to it. Bracken had been boxed in by the big business interests and he had little alternative. They knew that Bracken was under pressure to bring a mill to Manitoba and that he did not have final control of the province's resources. The businessmen were therefore able to extract a very extensive concession at a ridiculously low price from the federal government.[26] If Bracken had not gone along he would have had to face considerable hostility in the legislature and in the province generally.

The Bracken government's pragmatic policies were also underlined by the negotiations surrounding mineral development in the Flin Flon region north of The Pas. Bracken had been fascinated by the north since his initial trip to The Pas in 1922. Its vastness and solitude appealed to the romantic in him. He was stimulated by the challenges its very existence seemed to present. From the start he was anxious to explore it as much as possible. He rode over the working portion of the Hudson Bay Railway and delighted in canoeing into isolated settlements and camping out along the way. He visited the bay itself in 1924 and after a quick change plunged into its chilly waters, emerging for an exhilarating run along the sandy beach. The sense of release that he experienced on these occasions was all too seldom indulged. Constantly under pressure, he kept his feelings and physical tensions under disciplined control, but the north gave him an opportunity to relax three or four times a year. And once aircraft began to be used with increasing frequency in the twenties, Bracken – an instant devotée – took every opportunity to fly over the sprawling expanse of Manitoba: the Manitoba-Ontario border area, the interlake, but particularly north of $53°$. Thus Bracken brought to the issues of northern development a deeper commitment than most of his colleagues. He had seen the north, he had talked with the trappers, the missionaries, the miners, and the storekeepers, and had shared their dreams and hopes. He was determined to ensure that the north was opened up and its riches developed.

The problems facing a developer in the north were enormous. The mineral bearing regions east of Lake Winnipeg and north of The Pas were isolated from main transportation links and from urban centres. Vast amounts of capital would be required to survey, test, and ultimately extract the ore, link the deposit with the outside world, and construct new towns at the site. For there to be any success there would have to be a marriage of private enterprise and government support. Bracken and his colleagues had to decide how far they were prepared to commit the government to the developmental process. There was never any doubt that Bracken was prepared, if necessary and within reason, to pay a fairly stiff price to ensure northern development. He was convinced that the future of the province rested to a considerable extent on the profitable development of the mining areas.

It had been clear since 1915-16 that there existed an extensive copper-sulphide-zinc deposit some ninety miles north of The Pas at the Flin Flon site. The presence of zinc created difficulties for the Flin Flon mine, since zinc could be refined only in British Columbia or Belgium and the lack of railway facilities made its profitable mining impossible. Moreover, its presence made the extraction of other minerals more difficult. Thus from the start the Flin Flon mine had problems owing to the complexity of the ore, 'its marginal value,' and its isolation. Capital, labour, and equipment, and probably government backing of some sort would be required before the mine could be profitably developed.[27] In 1920 the Mining Corporation of Canada acquired the Flin Flon mine but the mixed ore and the low price of copper made development impossible and the site lay untouched after 1921.

In 1925 the price of copper rose on the market and on 11 November 1925 the Mining Corporation of Canada granted an option on the Flin Flon property to Roscoe H. Channing, Jr, who represented Harry Payne Whitney, the New York financier and mine developer.[28] The rise in price would not have been enough to interest Whitney but in the early twenties a process for commercially extracting zinc at a profit had been discovered. This, plus the rise in price of copper, had added about $6.00 per ton to the potential value of the ore and since 1924 had resulted in experiments with samples of Flin Flon ore by Whitney and his associates. By late 1925 they were sufficiently satisfied of the mine's potential to take out the option.[29]

News of the option caused considerable excitement in The Pas but within a few days excitement turned to anxiety and anger when it was rumoured that the

CPR planned to build a line into the mining area from Nipawin, Saskatchewan, thereby bypassing the town. Bracken was soon deluged with letters and telegrams by the concerned and irate citizens and business interests of his constituency who saw their long held hopes of growth and prosperity dashed at the crucial moment. He immediately telegraphed George Graham, the minister of railways, and D.C. Coleman, vice-president of the CPR, seeking information. Graham told Bracken that he knew nothing of CPR plans while Coleman attempted to reassure him. The CPR had certainly surveyed such a line but nothing was planned. In fact the CPR did not have an option to build. Unless it got one nothing could be done.[30]

By mid-December Bracken and his colleagues were exploring the possibility of building an extension line into Flin Flon from Mile 7 on the CNR's Hudson Bay Railway. A survey of such a link had been made by the Norris government in 1921. The cost of construction had then been estimated at $2,500,000. By late 1925 these surveys had been pulled from the files and were being closely examined by Bracken and the cabinet. Bracken was by then prepared to have the government build the road provided the government were 'properly protected.' It was clear that no large-scale development at the Flin Flon site was possible without railway communication. It was unlikely that Whitney and his associates would be prepared to invest millions in a mine, a smelter, and a new town without having first made definite arrangements for a railway link. Bracken knew that.[31]

By early 1926 the CNR had also investigated the feasibility of a line from Mile 7 to Flin Flon. In March Bracken and Sir Henry Thornton, the president of the CNR, met to discuss its construction but Thornton was cautious. There was no guarantee that the new metallurgical process would be commercially profitable. Since the necessity for railway communication depended upon the development of such a process he thought it wiser to await the results of the investigations currently being conducted in Denver by the Whitney group.[32]

With the CNR reluctant to move and the CPR resurveying the Nipawin route, Bracken was more anxious than ever to establish the Manitoba government's control of the Flin Flon area. He asked Ed Brown, the former Liberal MLA for The Pas, to assess the various options. In a detailed memorandum Brown recommended that the province take the initiative and guarantee the bonds of a 'Flin Flon Railway Company' for construction of a line from Mile 7 to Flin Flon. In order to safeguard the interests of the province Brown suggested that the company should be obliged to arrange a long-term lease with the CNR for the operation and maintenance of the line on the basis of a rental sufficient to meet the annual interest charges on the bonds and to provide a sinking fund to redeem the bonds on their maturity. Thus, argued Brown, it would only be a question of the province lending its credit for the purpose of securing the construction of a railway and the successful development of the Flin Flon site.[33]

Bracken was impressed by Brown's arguments and he strongly supported them in cabinet discussions.[34] He and his colleagues had already agreed to support applications by the Winnipeg Railway Company and the Central Manitoba Railway in order to keep the potentially rich mining areas east of Lake Winnipeg tributary to Manitoba rather than Ontario, so similar arguments concerning the northwestern part of the province were equally persuasive. The cabinet agreed to throw its support behind an application for a railway into the Flin Flon mine. On 18 March the Mining Corporation of Canada, still the owners of the site, formally applied for a bill to be passed by the Manitoba legislature incorporating a company to be called 'The Manitoba Northern Railway Company' with power to construct a line from Mile 7 on the Hudson Bay Railway to the Flin Flon mine. The company asked for a government bond guarantee of $3,500,000 redeemable in four years at 4½ per cent per annum to cover the cost of construction. Bracken was informed that the Mining Corporation of Canada had been negotiating with the CNR 'and it is practically assured that that railway will take a lease of the proposed Manitoba Northern Railway over a long period at a rental sufficient to meet the annual interest charge on the lands, and to provide a sinking fund sufficient to retire the bonds at their maturity.'[35]

Bracken introduced the appropriate legislation in early April and the act received royal assent on 23 April 1926. Under its charter the Manitoba Northern Railway agreed to start construction in sixteen months and to complete the line in three years. The bill met with little opposition in the legislature. Both Liberals and Conservatives were anxious that development proceed apace and, after being assured that all necessary steps had been taken to protect the province's interests, they supported the legislation. Thus at the end of April 1926 the Bracken government had agreed to guarantee bonds up to $3,500,000 to facilitate the opening of the mining area of the northwest and to provide $25,000 per mile for a line opening the mining area to the east of Lake Winnipeg.[36]

Under the terms of his option Whitney was obliged after 1 September 1926 to carry on experimental work at the Flin Flon site. To do so he erected a fifty-ton pilot mill which began operation in March 1927.[37] The option expired on 1 December 1927 so there was a need to reach a quick decision about the site. By late October there was enough evidence to convince Whitney and his associates that they should develop the property. However, there was one hitch – the sixteen-month time period stipulated in the Manitoba Northern Railway Charter had lapsed and the Manitoba government's bond guarantees were now in abeyance. No provision for a railway any longer existed. Whitney would not develop the site without a railway. This caused an immediate flurry in provincial, dominion, and CNR circles.

While in Ottawa in November 1927 for the federal-provincial conference, Bracken lunched with H.J. Symington, the CNR lawyer, Charles Dunning, the minister of railways, and G.A. Bell, vice-president of the CNR. At this meeting Bell stated emphatically that the CNR would not proceed with the construction of a line unless the Manitoba government or someone else bonused it to the extent of $6000 a mile. Dunning said the dominion government would be prepared to take over the charter on that basis.[38]

Bracken did not favour a subsidy such as that proposed by Dunning and the CNR. Instead he suggested that the Manitoba government provide monies in case of a deficit. Dunning opposed this arrangement and initially refused to accept it.[39] Bracken would not budge and outlined his position to Symington and R.E. Phelan, the chief engineer of the Flin Flon site, at a meeting at the Chateau Laurier in Ottawa on 9 November. Three days later, with Dunning still unfavourable, Bracken wired Phelan, now in New York, asking if the site would be developed if a railway was not constructed. Phelan wired back immediately in emphatic terms: 'You have asked me whether the Flin Flon venture will be undertaken by us if a railroad is not put through to the mine and I unhesitatingly say it will not be.'[40] Later that day he wired again, putting additional pressure on the Manitoba premier: 'Immediate decision on railway necessary otherwise whole Flin Flon project will be jeopardized.'[41]

In face of Bracken's refusal to provide a subsidy and Whitney's refusal to develop the Flin Flon site without a railway, Dunning finally capitulated. He would accept Bracken's suggestion if offered. At a cabinet meeting in Winnipeg on 17 November it was agreed that the Manitoba government would contribute up to $100,000 per year toward meeting any operating deficits that occurred during the first five years of operation of the Manitoba Northern Railway. Bracken wired Dunning of this decision later that day.[42] In turn, the Whitney interests agreed to contribute $250,000 immediately toward the cost of the railway. They also agreed to build and operate a smelter at the Flin Flon site capable of treating 3000 tons of ore per day and to develop a hydro-electric plant capable of ultimately producing 270,000 horsepower. The initial Whitney investment would be $18 million. The charter of the Manitoba Northern Railway was to be turned over to the CNR and the line operated as a subsidiary.[43]

The transfer of ownership to the Whitney interests was completed in late November,[44] and on 27 December 1927 the Hudson Bay Mining and Smelting Company was incorporated and an operating company, Flin Flon Mines Ltd, formed. Construction began at the site in early 1928.

Bracken was well satisfied with the negotiations. He felt he had helped ensure the development of the northern region while protecting the interests of the province. Neither he, nor the Manitoba opposition, nor the federal government had given any thought to controlling the profits that might be made. In the 1920s all levels of government in Canada were only too happy to welcome outside capital in order to facilitate development. For Bracken it meant provision of work for a large local labour force and expansion into a hitherto inaccessible region. The only problem that now had to be resolved was the location of the hydro-electric power site. The Whitney interests favoured Island Falls on the Churchill River in Saskatchewan while Bracken wanted the White Mud Falls on the Nelson River to be developed.

While much of Bracken's attention in the mid-twenties was taken up with the development of the province's resources he was never completely free from political manoeuvring. It was during those years that the first discussions about a fusion or coalition of Liberals and Brackenites – increasingly referred to as Progressives – took place in Manitoba. They throw a revealing light not only on Bracken but on the state of Manitoba politics and the relationship of the federal and provincial Liberals.

Although Bracken had apparently given some thought to a coalition of his group and the Liberals in late 1923, he had not pursued it after the overwhelming by-election victories of that December. Norris was not interested and his own attention had been distracted by the resource issues.[45] Quiet soundings on either side in early 1926 had again revealed that Norris was a stumbling block. He would not contemplate joining a coalition except as premier, which was obviously impossible. Of more significance, he was unpalatable to Bracken's French-Canadian supporters because of his education policy of ten years earlier. There began to be talk in Liberal circles of bumping him upstairs to a seat on the Railway Commission.[46]

Serious discussions with Bracken were initiated in March 1926 by members of the Manitoba Federation of Young Liberal Clubs and owed much to the work of the president, Ralph Maybank, a resourceful Winnipeg lawyer. Maybank and another Young Liberal, Alf Rosevear, saw Bracken for the first time on a Saturday morning. Bracken was very busy and the interview was supposed to last only fifteen minutes, but the premier prolonged it:[47] 'He spoke quite frankly of the matter of coming together. It would seem to me that he figures he is going to lose his Tory supporters anyway and that the best thing for his Government is to form an alliance with somebody else. Liberals are best. I do not know whether he really has any political ambitions for the future and whether he is safeguarding them or whether as a matter of fact he is carrying on through a sense of duty, being ready to surrender the reins to someone else as soon as that someone else can be found, the main purpose being to keep the Tories out.' By this time Bracken knew that his most trusted confidant, R.W. Craig, wanted to retire from politics. To replace him in the cabinet he considered asking Judge H.A. Robson, a prominent Liberal, to join the government, thus cementing a Liberal-Progressive relationship. Maybank and Rosevear were encouraged by this development and, after Norris announced his resignation at a Liberal convention in late March, the two men again met with Bracken on 29 March and 8 April,[48] but nothing definite materialized.

For much of the summer and autumn of 1926 attention in Manitoba was focused on the September federal election. Maybank and Rosevear were both deeply involved in the campaign and it was not until mid-October, with the return to office of Mackenzie King and the Liberals, that they came back to provincial politics. For his part, Bracken simply bided his time. His group was in no danger in the legislature. Any initiatives would have to come from the Liberals.

By the autumn of 1926 the possibility of fusion, the leadership of the party, and the 1927 provincial election were being widely discussed in Liberal circles. A small group of 'die-hards' were opposed to coalition while the party at large seemed divided in its views. At the Liberal convention on 23 November there was a mixed reaction from the delegates to the idea of co-operation. The majority seemed to favour it, some because they thought Bracken was going to win anyway and an arrangement was therefore wise, but others because they believed that the Liberals could, in time, absorb the Progressives. Some, of course, were determined to maintain the separate Liberal identity and felt that if there was to be any accommodation the first move should come from Bracken. Toby Norris, the retiring leader, was quite frank. He found fusion a distasteful word. He was not prepared to go on his knees to the government. If it took a high and mighty position, then the Liberals would have to forget it. But he admitted he would sooner see a Progressive government than a Conservative one. Horace Chevrier of St Rose spoke for many of the delegates when he said: 'The question is not what we have against Bracken, but what possibilities there are of constructive proposals.'[49]

Despite the efforts of the Young Liberals to prepare the ground for fusion it was clear that there was considerable division of opinion in the party and by the morning of the leadership convention, 20 March, a readily acceptable candidate had not emerged. It was at that moment that Hugh Robson was suggested as a possibility. Robson, a man of fifty-six, had considerable standing in Winnipeg and the West. Appointed a judge of the court of king's bench in 1910, he had resigned in 1912 to become Manitoba's first public utilities commissioner. More recently he had served as chief counsel for the Union Bank of Canada. For some years he had been active in Liberal politics behind the scenes but had not previously stood for public office. Fifteen minutes before nominations closed he agreed to let his name stand. The Young Liberals, thinking Robson favoured a co-operative approach, boosted his name on the floor of the convention, and in the voting he swept to an overwhelming victory.[50]

It was only later that Maybank realized that Robson was 'more opposed to the

Government than I expected he would be. He counts on running a very spirited campaign against them ... He laid down his plan of campaign as being a candidate for every seat.'[51] It appeared that Robson's last-minute entry into the leadership had been planned well in advance in order to avoid revealing his thoughts too soon. Robson had been subjected to a great deal of pressure from Jimmy Gardiner, the Liberal premier of Saskatchewan, who fervently believed that the Progressives must be fought wherever they raised their heads. What Gardiner did not seem to appreciate was that the majority of the Progressives in Manitoba had originally been Liberals, rather than Conservatives as in Saskatchewan. Gardiner later admitted to King that he had done 'whatever I found it possible to do to encourage the choice of Judge Robson for the leadership.'[52]

The choice of Robson as leader had certain implications for the role of the Manitoba Liberal party. Initially, the reaction to him was favourable even among committed Liberal-Progressives like Crerar who thought him 'probably the best choice ... He has tact, ability, and common sense, which I rate as one of the virtues in public men, and I think he will lend his energies toward working out a rather difficult situation as well as possible.'[53] But by the middle of May Robson's attitudes toward co-operation had become clear. It now looked as if there would be three-cornered fights in every constituency. Crerar feared the development of bitterness between Liberals and Progressives: 'Robson is a good deal of a bitter ender, and frankly, I don't like the situation that has developed. It might easily have important reactions at Ottawa. Personally, I think that Gardiner is giving evil counsel to Robson and his friends.'[54]

On 18 April Robson issued a statement to the papers placing the Liberal party before the electorate 'entirely free from alliances,' and declaring that both class government and group government were unacceptable in Manitoba.[55] In private, he informed Mackenzie King that 'We have to open and continue this fight in an effort to place the Liberal Party in power. Understandings or entanglements will do infinite harm and we will not be led into them.'[56]

The 1927 election in Manitoba was held on 28 June. Bracken campaigned arduously defending his 'pay as you go' policies and the overall record of his administration. He was aided considerably on the hustings by two recent recruits to his cabinet – Billy Major, a Winnipeg lawyer, and Bob Hoey, the former MP for Springfield. It was soon apparent that they were shrewd choices. Major, who had replaced Craig as attorney-general in April, proved a tough campaigner who thrived on the cut-and-thrust, while Hoey, the new minister of education, was both an outstanding platform orator who could hold an audience spellbound and also a vigorous, resourceful debater. Unquestionably, Bracken had considerably strengthened his front bench.

Overall it was a quiet campaign centring around the government's performance over the previous five years. The Gardiner forces played an active role in the election,[57] one much resented by many Liberals, as well as Brackenites, but a role supported by Robson. Whatever bitterness of tone crept into the campaign was attributable to the presence of the Saskatchewan workers. Generally, the opposition groups focused their criticism on Bracken's economic policies. The Labour group was angry that its concerns had been shunted aside in the interests of economy while the Conservatives and the Liberals claimed that the government had not been frugal enough. Despite these varied criticisms, it was assumed by most observers and by the majority of his opponents that Bracken would win. The question was by how much. As one delegate had pointed out at the Liberal Convention the previous November: '... Bracken is going to be re-elected. They have given reasonably decent Government. You can't say much against them.'[58]

The prediction proved correct but Bracken did not get the large margin he had sought. The government was returned with twenty-nine, a gain of one. The best showing was made by the Conservatives who won fifteen seats, up from six in 1922. The Liberals stayed the same at seven. Labour won three, a drop of three, continuing their decline from 1920, and only one Independent was re-elected.

Bracken's government took twenty-seven of the forty-five rural seats, the same as in 1922, and won two of the ten Winnipeg seats. It had continued to attract a considerable portion of the Anglo-Saxon farm vote and, as usual, had the support of the bulk of the rural ethnic and the French-Canadian vote. The obvious reason for its failure to make any significant improvement in its overall position was the resurgence of the Conservatives who had finally thrown off the odium of the 1915 scandal and, under new, young leadership, had built a powerful, province-wide organization. In 1927 Bracken did not have a political machine to match the Conservative's. The increasing apathy and apolitical stance of the UFM had meant the virtual collapse of the organization that had been instrumental in the farmers' victory of 1922. Also, the emergence in southern Manitoba of a rival farm organization, the District Builders, had 'sapped the strength' of the UFM. It was no accident that the Conservatives took five seats and the Liberals four in that area. These developments had been accelerated by the electorate's drift back to the traditional parties after the return of prosperity in the mid-twenties. This had hurt Bracken's chances of making substantial gains and had obviously benefitted the Conservatives more than the Liberals.

The Brackenites had also been hurt by the continuing anger of some of the farmers at the government's refusal to support a wheat board in 1923. Others had felt betrayed over the abandonment of prohibition and their resentment had grown with the seemingly lax enforcement of the new liquor laws. Of equal importance was the fact that the Bracken government had taken office in the midst of a depression and had been obliged to institute harsh economic measures. A backlash from some voters was not unexpected.[59]

Overall, however, Bracken was satisfied with the results. Although not the landslide victory he had wanted, he felt justified in interpreting the win as a vote of confidence in his government's policies. He had held his own in the rural areas where he was obviously still closely identified with agrarian interests and he had gained encouraging support in Winnipeg. He now had a secure majority in the legislature, a strengthened cabinet with the election of Major and Hoey, and a solid mandate to continue his businesslike administration of provincial affairs.

6

The Seven Sisters site

'Good business but poor politics – can't be both.'[1]

In the months following the election the Liberals re-examined their position. Some of the younger members now thought it had been a mistake 'to join with the old crowd' in the campaign against Bracken,[2] and wished they had stayed with the policy of gradual penetration and control. Although Robson began to realize that the sensible attitude to adopt was one of 'benevolent neutrality,' he, Norris, and Edith Rogers really wanted to lambaste Bracken whom they disliked and considered 'a Tory.'[3] As for Bracken he was still prepared to co-operate with the Liberals and he made that clear to both Crerar and J.A. Robb, the federal minister of finance. Crerar was convinced that 'if Norris and Robson were out of the way there would be no difficulty ... There is no doubt whatever that at the moment sentiment in Manitoba is strongly Progressive. The Liberals at Ottawa should get it into their heads that the course of wisdom so far as Manitoba is concerned is to co-operate with Bracken.'[4]

King and Senator Andrew Haydon, the Liberal national organizer, were sufficiently distressed by the Manitoba situation to send party trouble-shooter Thomas Taylor to Winnipeg in late November. His primary task was to reunite the two wings of the Manitoba Liberal party and to lay the groundwork for a relationship with Bracken. During his stay Taylor continually argued the need for local Liberal co-operation with the Progressives. He also discovered that Norris who, as usual, had won his seat in Lansdowne was still an anathema to the French population of the province. Taylor feared that if he were to remain active in the party for much longer the French would turn away from the Progressives, not toward the Liberals but to the Conservatives, thus strengthening the Tory forces. He told his superior in Ottawa that any future co-operation or fusion in Manitoba to be wholly successful would have to entail the removal or elevation of Norris.[5]

Interestingly, by December Robson was of the same conviction. He wrote twice to King to press for Norris' appointment to the bench or to the Tariff or Railway Board. He pointed out that 'Provision for Mr. Norris, by you, would go a long way to encourage local Liberals to amity with the Progressives which is I am sure becoming increasingly necessary.' Also the French would be happier and dissension among his own supporters would be eased.[6] He elaborated later: 'Although it is a change of attitude on my part I am concerned about keeping the Progressives friendly. The appointment of Norris to a position would mean that the Bracken Government, which in a sense is Progressive, would get his seat in the Legislature. That would be an act of great significance in binding our Federal interests. Please do not overlook that.'[7] King was delighted to hear of Robson's change of heart, for only by welding Liberals and Progressives 'into one fighting force' would they be assured of defeating the 'common political foe.'[8]

Gardiner was one man who disagreed with this proposed co-operation. He believed dealing with Bracken was fatal not only to Liberal interests in Manitoba but in the West generally. On hearing that Bracken was prepared to take Donald McKenzie, a former secretary-treasurer of the UFM, off the Tariff Board into his cabinet in order to make room for Norris on the board and that this had the backing of Dunning, Gardiner was furious. As far as he was concerned the strengthening of the Bracken government would mean the weakening if not the defeat of the Saskatchewan Liberals.[9] King, of course, disagreed. He reminded Gardiner that most Progressives from Alberta and Saskatchewan were either uncertain quantities or opposed to the Liberal party. It was 'on the Manitoba Progressives alone that we are able to rely for the support which is necessary to carry on government with any degree of security.' It was not in the interests of the federal Liberal party to antagonize them. Co-operation with Bracken was therefore critical. King agreed that the Manitoba situation was 'about the most involved of any I have ever had to face,' but it now appeared that Robson was prepared to co-operate. That was exactly what King and his Ottawa colleagues wanted.[10]

Robson's change of attitude had been prompted to a considerable degree by the dilatory approach of the King government to the natural resources question. The continued unwillingness of the federal Liberals to reopen negotiations was damaging the provincial Liberals and giving the strengthened Conservative party just cause to make life difficult in the chamber for both the Brackenites and Robson.

Bracken had endeavoured to re-open the question early in the year. On 10 January 1928 he wrote directly to King reviewing the correspondence of previous years on the transfer of the natural resources. He drew attention to the recommendations of the Duncan Commission on the problems of the Maritime provinces, their generous implementation by the dominion government, and the favourable attitude at the recent federal-provincial conference of the premiers of Quebec, Ontario, and the Maritime provinces toward the natural resources issue.

'With the other provinces so favourably disposed,' argued Bracken, 'and the whole Dominion responsive to the spirit of the 60th Anniversary of Confederation, the time is singularly opportune for the settlement of this question by arbitration ... We cannot conceive any valid objection that can be taken to so fair and just a proposal at this time.' He requested an early decision.[11] When King did not reply immediately Robson wrote to Charles Stewart, minister of the interior, pointing out that a quick solution of the question was important for the Manitoba Liberals.[12] Two weeks later the Liberal leader wrote in a similar manner to King: 'Our relations with the Bracken Government are satisfactory and Liberals and Progressives should present a united front when occasion demands. But there must be progress in the resources matter or this amalgamation will fail to prevent heavy Tory inroads.'[13]

On receiving this letter, King took up the resources question in cabinet and succeeded in having a letter approved and mailed. After apologizing to Bracken for the delays, King asked that one final attempt be made to reach agreement by conference. Failing that, the two governments could decide about the terms of reference for arbitration and the composition of the tribunal to which the issue would be referred.[14] Despite efforts on both sides to find a mutually acceptable meeting date nothing had been determined by mid-March.[15]

By then Bracken was deeply immersed in the final stages of his government's negotiations with the Winnipeg Electric Company over the development of hydroelectric power at the Seven Sisters reach on the Winnipeg River – an issue that had concerned him since 1925.[16]

It had been established that the Winnipeg River with its tributary the English River was capable of producing over 1,000,000 commercial horsepower; over 700,000 in Manitoba and the balance in Ontario. The 700,000 in Manitoba would be concentrated in seven places. Of these seven, three – Pinawa, Great Falls, and Pointe du Bois – had already been developed, the first two by the WEC and its subsidiary the Manitoba Power Company and the third by the City of Winnipeg. One, Pine Falls, was under lease to the Manitoba Pulp and Paper Company. And three – McArthur Falls, Seven Sisters, and Slave Falls – had yet to be developed.[17]

There were three agencies by which this power was made to serve the public – the WEC, Winnipeg Hydro, and the Provincial Hydro (technically known as the Manitoba Power Commission). The WEC distributed power in the city of Winnipeg and in certain areas of eastern and east-central Manitoba; Winnipeg Hydro distributed power almost entirely in Winnipeg; the Provincial Hydro distributed power in southwestern Manitoba. The latter was only a distributing concern and had no guarantee either of an adequate supply of power for its own use or of low rates for such power. It was dependent on either the WEC or Winnipeg Hydro, and its contract with Winnipeg Hydro was due to run out in 1930. Estimates indicated that if Manitoba were to experience the same average growth in consumption of power as certain districts in Ontario where similar conditions existed, an additional power supply would be required by 1930. To many, the best source was the reach at Seven Sisters.

Looking at the Seven Sisters reach on a map, one sees that the Winnipeg River divides above the site into two channels, the Pinawa channel and the Seven Sisters channel. On the Pinawa channel was located the powerhouse of the WEC, capable of producing about 58,000 horsepower. Under its lease the WEC was entitled to divert to this channel – in perpetuity – nearly half the water in the river for its own use. For many years the Waterpowers Branch of the Department of the Interior had wished to have the Pinawa channel closed and all the water diverted into the Seven Sisters channel. Development on a massive scale of a higher head at Seven Sisters would mean the power production of the Winnipeg River would be permanently increased by 50,000 horsepower.[18]

This was the general situation in the summer of 1925 when the WEC became alarmed by rumours that the Seaman-Backus pulpwood interests were after the Seven Sisters location. On 21 August 1925 the WEC applied to the federal government for a lease to develop the site. Bracken wrote immediately to Charles Stewart requesting that Seven Sisters be reserved for the province. Stewart refused both applications, pointing out that maximum development of the reach was essential. When Bracken renewed his government's application in early 1927, Stewart indicated that no disposition would be made until an arrangement was entered into by which the WEC plant on the Pinawa channel was abandoned and the Seven Sisters site developed. Stewart suggested it might be an opportune time for the province and the WEC to come to a mutually satisfactory understanding covering the development of the combined Pinawa-Seven Sisters reaches. Bracken agreed that discussions between the province, the WEC, and the federal government were essential but in March 1927 he still insisted that the province should have Seven Sisters reserved for its use.[19]

During the 1927 election and for much of the year the dispute over Seven Sisters received little notice but on 13 December S.J. Farmer, the Labour MLA, drew attention in the legislature to rumours that the WEC was buying land adjacent to Seven Sisters Falls.[20] Bracken wrote immediately to Andrew McLimont, the president of the WEC, warning him that the provincial government had asked to have the site reserved for its use and would oppose any effort of the WEC to put itself in a preferred position with the dominion government.[21]

This firm response resulted in an exchange of letters with McLimont and a private talk with Edward Anderson, the WEC lawyer, which effectively opened negotiations between the company and the Bracken government. Over the next three months Bracken was to see a lot of Anderson. As WEC counsel he had been charged with Seven Sisters since August 1925 and was thoroughly familiar with the policy of the Waterpowers Branch in Ottawa. During the critical discussions over Seven Sisters in early 1928 Anderson drafted most of the WEC correspondence and handled nearly all the personal negotiations. However, he later made it clear that he always worked within guidelines established by McLimont. As president, McLimont was the dominant factor on the WEC side: 'What he wanted pretty much was done.'[22]

By the end of January 1928 it was clear that both the WEC and the Bracken government agreed that the main flow of the Winnipeg River should be diverted from the Pinawa channel into the main channel, thus allowing maximum development at Seven Sisters. But that was all they agreed on. McLimont wanted the government to withdraw its application so that the WEC could develop the site. Bracken refused to consider such an action. He wanted to be assured that when Seven Sisters was developed the province would receive cheap power sufficient to its needs for a long time to come. He was not convinced that development of the location by a private company would guarantee that. Perhaps the best solution would be for the government to develop the site itself. Bracken assured McLimont that the government's firm stand was necessitated by the desire to resolve the issue 'in the best interests of the Province as a whole.'[23]

Bracken decided to seek outside advice before making a final decision. This was not a deliberate delaying tactic. He was as anxious as McLimont to resolve the issue but he did not wish to act hastily. He wanted to be sure that, whatever his decision, it would be defensible as the best possible solution. He knew the issue would plunge his government into the midst of a major battle over the question of public versus private ownership of hydro-electric power. He needed expert advice if he were to make the correct decision.

Bracken was determined to proceed carefully even though he was desperately tired and in need of a holiday. Always operating on his nerve ends anyway, he was weakened by flu for much of the spring of 1928. His doctors, aware that he was in danger of stretching himself beyond his physical limits, advised a lengthy rest away from the city. For much of February and March, during the vital Seven Sisters negotiations, he was therefore anxious to get away. It is against this background of conflicting pressures that one has to examine those crucial weeks.

At the end of January Bracken asked Dr T.H. Hogg, the chief hydraulic engineer of the Ontario Hydro-Electric Power Commission, to advise his government for 'a short time.' He also arranged for J.T. Johnston of the Waterpowers Branch to come to Winnipeg for a conference on the disposition of Pinawa and the effective overall use of Seven Sisters. Hogg and Johnston arrived in Winnipeg on 6 February.[24]

Bracken's choice of Hogg as an adviser raised many eyebrows in Manitoba for it was assumed that since he worked for a public corporation he would naturally favour public ownership. Although Bracken later admitted that the same thought had occurred to him he stressed that Hogg had not been chosen because it was expected he would provide a certain answer. He had been selected because he was considered to be 'the most outstanding hydraulic engineer in Canada.'[25] During the trip to Winnipeg Johnston provided Hogg with a detailed background of both the Seven Sisters and Winnipeg River questions and the policy of the Waterpowers Branch. By the time they reached Winnipeg Hogg was fully aware that the federal government wanted maximum use of the Seven Sisters site, and that this would involve abandoning the Pinawa channel. However, he had no clear idea what he would be asked to report on.[26]

On their arrival in the city Hogg and Johnston met with Bracken in the premier's office. Also in attendance were Clubb, the minister formally in charge of the provincial hydro since 1922. The conference lasted two hours during which the problem facing the Manitoba government at the Pinawa-Seven Sisters reaches was 'exhaustively reviewed.' It was made clear to Hogg that the Manitoba government wanted a complete analysis of the power resources of the two reaches. It wanted to know the best way to obtain the maximum utilization of the river's flow. Bracken asked for cost estimates of all possible alternatives so that his government could decide whether it should proceed with public development or whether the WEC should be allowed to develop the site alone. In order that he and his colleagues would have all the relevant information before them, Bracken asked Johnston to provide detailed memoranda on power development on the Winnipeg River and a specific statement of federal government policy toward the use of the Seven Sisters site.[27]

All the talking for the Manitoba government at these early February meetings and, in fact, until mid-March was done by Bracken, although he was very ill and had been strongly advised by his doctors to get away. But Bracken was reluctant to delegate responsibility in such a crucial matter and insisted on handling the negotiations himself. Neither Clubb nor Major, the new attorney-general and already a trusted colleague, made any significant contributions to the discussions. Bracken got out of his sick-bed to meet Hogg and Johnston at the Legislative Building on 6 February but later that day and again shortly before Hogg left the city Seven Sisters was discussed at the premier's bedside at 604 Stradbrooke. It was obvious to Hogg that Bracken was 'a very sick man.' Bracken was not unaware of the dangers to his health – that is why he had urged Hogg to get the report in as quickly as possible – but he was determined to see the issue through to the end.[28]

Shortly after meeting with Hogg and Johnston, Bracken asked John Allen, Manitoba's deputy attorney-general, whether or not it would be difficult for the

Manitoba government to expropriate the Pinawa plant of the WEC.[29] In Allen's opinion it would, because the land at Pinawa still legally belonged to the federal government. Bracken asked A.B. Hudson, a prominent Winnipeg lawyer and Liberal stalwart, for a second opinion but by 21 February it was clear that Hudson agreed with Allen.[30] So, by late February 1928, a major obstacle to public development of the Seven Sisters site had emerged. This was of particular concern because at the beginning of the month the Bracken government had supported S.J. Farmer's resolution in the legislature urging continued public development of hydro resources and a few days later the Manitoba federal MPs had written to Charles Stewart requesting that the Seven Sisters site be retained for the use of the Manitoba government.[31] It was becoming increasingly obvious that Bracken would not be able to avoid a major controversy over the issue of public versus private development of hydro resources.

This was confirmed on 5 March when Hogg delivered his draft report. On turning it over to Bracken, Hogg made it clear that he had concluded 'it would be economically unsound for the Government to develop the Seven Sisters site and that it would be better for the Government to try to get out of the development its maximum needs for a rural hydro at a low rate ... ' Bracken discussed every aspect of this conclusion with Hogg and then asked him if he would object to his report being shown to the cabinet. Hogg had no objection as long as it was understood to be incomplete. Bracken then discussed the report and its conclusions with his cabinet on 5 and 6 March. However, he never showed the report to any of his colleagues. He simply read extracts from it to the assembled group. Thus no one but Bracken saw Hogg's draft report in early March. The cabinet reached no formal decisions at that time, although it was agreed to contact McLimont about possible prices for a block of power. Nevertheless, it was clear to both Bracken and his cabinet that Hogg's conclusion was already a firm one, and certainly there was no difference between the draft and the final version on that point. All that was to change over the next two weeks were certain cost and price estimates which did not alter the substance of the case that Hogg had already made.[32]

The Bracken government had no idea what the possible cost of power would be before Hogg arrived. Now that the decision against public ownership seemed the most likely it was decided to raise the matter with McLimont of the WEC. Hogg helped prepare a letter which was mailed to McLimont on 5 March. Bracken asked McLimont for information on two matters so that Hogg could complete his report. First, what value would the WEC place on its Pinawa plant and its transmission line if the government decided to purchase them; and, second, if the government withdrew its application for the Seven Sisters site, what would be the best price the WEC would give the government for a block of 30,000 HP to be taken as and when the provincial hydro required it?[33] McLimont replied two days later pointing out that although the WEC had no intention of selling the Pinawa plant its estimated value would exceed ten million dollars. As for price, if the WEC were given a lease for the development of Seven Sisters it would be prepared to supply 20,000 HP at $17.50 per HP, the same price at which the company had agreed to sell power to Winnipeg Hydro.[34]

Not long after this exchange of letters Bracken received a visit at his legislative office from Anderson who wanted to know what Hogg was likely to report. Bracken told Anderson that the report was unfinished and gave the lawyer 'as little satisfaction' as he could. He revealed nothing of the contents of the draft report but simply said 'the Company would have no chance whatever unless it was prepared to make us the best contract in Canada ... ' Bracken made that statement having already received the $17.50 offer. Not many days later Anderson phoned Bracken and asked if he could bring McLimont in to see the premier. Bracken agreed and Anderson and McLimont saw Bracken for a few minutes in his bedroom on their way to the office. During the brief conversation McLimont intimated that the WEC could probably do better than the earlier $17.50 offer. No further details were discussed at that time, and as it happened that was the only interview Bracken was to have with McLimont over the next two months.[35]

One other matter discussed at the cabinet meetings in early March was the possibility of making a preliminary report on Hogg's findings to the legislature which, though still in session, was rapidly drawing to a close. It was finally decided not to do so because it would be unfair to both Hogg and the legislature to discuss an incomplete report. Moreover, if the nature of the probable decision and the details of the report became known, it would hamper the government in its negotiations with the WEC.[36] Bracken was later to argue that the provincial government was under no obligation to take a report to the legislature because water powers were under federal jurisdiction. One may or may not accept this argument. Certainly Bracken did not use it at the time. What does carry weight, however, is the shrewd point that if the Hogg report – whether draft or final – had gone to the legislature it would have seriously weakened the government's bargaining position. Bracken had to decide whether to table it and weaken his position or make the agreement and then table. The situation never arose because the report did not arrive until after the session ended. Many critics were to say this was highly convenient but the truth, of course, was that Bracken had been constantly urging Hogg to get the report in, so that he could leave Winnipeg.

Although the cabinet had discussed the issue constantly since Bracken's conversation with Anderson and McLimont, no final government decision had been reached when Hogg mailed his finished report from Toronto on 15 March. It was delivered to Bracken on Saturday morning, 17 March, between 10:00 and 11:00

AM, while the cabinet was in the process of tieing up the loose ends left by the closing of the session the previous day. On receiving the report, the cabinet immediately put all else aside in order to consider it.

Hogg concluded that public ownership would be economically unsound. If the province could obtain from the WEC an adequate supply of power, say 30,000 HP, for a long term at a reasonable price, Hogg recommended that it would be 'advantageous and desirable' to do so. He argued that the province could ensure the maximum possible power output from the potential power capacity 'equally as well by adequate supervision and control, as by the actual development itself with public moneys.' Also, the WEC could be contractually bound both to furnish power in Winnipeg for a stated lease period and to turn over the Seven Sisters site under a recapture clause at the end of the first period of the lease or at time of renewal. Hogg reasoned that since the control of the natural resources would likely be handed over to the province within a few years, the federal government would probably be prepared to insert in any lease granted to the WEC such clauses as the province desired.[37]

Hogg's conclusions were not unexpected. In fact, they did not differ from those of his draft report earlier in the month. Now that the conclusions were final, Bracken and his colleagues were guided entirely by them. As a result there were no technical advisers present during the cabinet discussions that morning nor at any subsequent meeting. Almost immediately the cabinet decided that it would be unwise for the government to develop the site; so if the WEC would agree to terms the government would be prepared to withdraw its application leaving the way open for the company to negotiate with the federal government for a lease of Seven Sisters. Clubb, Major, and Bracken were authorized to negotiate with the WEC. By 5:00 PM the draft of a letter to McLimont had been prepared.

During the afternoon Anderson phoned and learned that the Hogg report had arrived. Since he knew that both McLimont and Bracken were due to leave Winnipeg within the next three days – McLimont on the 18th and Bracken on the 20th – he was anxious to begin negotiations immediately in the hope that the matter could be resolved before both had gone. Anderson was, of course, the man responsible for the negotiations for the WEC, but he would need McLimont's formal approval of a contract before anything could be finally settled with the provincial government. Under these circumstances, Bracken read the substance of the draft letter over the phone. Anderson then asked for a meeting that Saturday evening. Bracken agreed and after dinner Anderson, Major, and Clubb, the latter having been extricated from a curling game at the nearby Granite Club, assembled at Bracken's house for the first of the key negotiations. Although Anderson was not shown the letter at that time – in fact, he did not see it until Monday, 19 March – its central points were discussed, so it would be best to outline it here.[38]

It was a shrewdly written letter. Bracken deliberately left the impression that the government was still seriously considering public development. When it was drafted the government had already decided to make a deal with the WEC. But if that were revealed too early in the negotiations the government would relinquish its advantage and probably end up paying far more than it would like for the power. So it had to be made to seem that all options were still open and that the government would still recommend public development if a reasonable contract could not be arranged with the WEC.

If the WEC wanted the government to withdraw its application the Pinawa channel would have to be closed and the full possibilities of Seven Sisters developed; the WEC would have to undertake to turn over the plant at Seven Sisters to the provincial government after thirty years if the government wanted it; and the company would have to agree to supply the Provincial Hydro with up to 30,000 HP for thirty years. But the key issue was price. Bracken made it quite clear that if the WEC adhered to its $17.50 offer of 7 March then the government would proceed on its own. He argued that the price of power would have to be no lower than $10.00 and no higher than $13.50 per horsepower per annum. This last condition was a deliberately tough bargaining point. Hogg had suggested in his report that the price of $14.70 per horsepower just negotiated by Ontario Hydro was the most favourable obtained in Canada in recent years. He had suggested that Manitoba would be doing well if it could arrange something similar. Bracken set his price deliberately low, no doubt hoping that when he had to go up, as he must have expected he would, he could still remain under the $14.70 figure. He was also aware that by coupling a low price with a veiled threat of public development he might be able to obtain a much lower price than $14.70. In concluding his letter, Bracken revealed that he would be leaving town in three days.[39]

With these conditions in mind Bracken, Clubb, and Major conferred with Anderson that Saturday evening at the first of a number of meetings that were to stretch over the next three days. During those sessions all aspects of the proposal were thrashed out. Most were quickly agreed to. The stumbling block was the cost of power. At the initial gathering no change in price was made. The next morning they met again at Bracken's house and Anderson, having consulted at length with McLimont,[40] now lowered the price to $15.00. This was already a considerable gain for the government, but Bracken and his colleagues rejected it. This angered McLimont who thought the government was driving too hard a bargain.[41] Nevertheless, before he left Winnipeg that evening he and Anderson prepared a draft reply to Bracken's letter – not yet received. McLimont assured Bracken that although the government's price of $13.50 was 'away below any figure that power can be produced for by the government under existing or anticipated conditions,' he was prepared to reduce his $17.50 figure. He wanted negotiations to continue.[42] At a meeting on Monday afternoon, 19 March, Anderson went down to $14.00 but still the government held firm. The next morning, at what proved to be the final meeting, Anderson dropped his price to $13.90. Major suggested they should split the difference, but Anderson refused. They finally agreed on a price of $13.80 and a minimum price of $11.00 rather than the suggested $10.00.[43] Bracken immediately wrote to McLimont summarizing the conclusions reached over the previous three days. On receiving the letter later that day, Anderson replied on McLimont's behalf approving the terms. They became the basis of a formal contract signed on 25 April.[44]

The agreement was very favourable to the government. It was to receive 30,000 HP for thirty years at a very low price plus the right to recapture the Seven Sisters site at the end of that period. The WEC had also agreed to abandon the Pinawa channel, thus permitting maximum development of the Winnipeg River. As Major later put it, 'the Government practically dictated the terms of the lease.'[45] Both the federal government and the WEC recognized the terms as 'exceptionally favourable' to the province.[46] Anderson had found negotiations between 17–20 March very hard, with price and compensation issues fought out 'quite stubbornly. I thought they were not giving us a fair deal. I was pretty much annoyed several times during the negotiations.' Anderson also said that if he had known the contents of the Hogg Report, especially Hogg's suggested price, he would not have made as favourable a bargain; certainly he would have obtained a better price. As it was, the Manitoba government had succeeded in obtaining the lowest rate for power on the North American continent.[47]

Now, if the agreement was so generous for the province, why had the WEC accepted it? The reason is obvious. Despite the deal they had been obliged to make with the government, the WEC still obtained a large supply of power for thirty years. In fact, their control at Seven Sisters and Great Falls now amounted to about 50 per cent of the power of the Winnipeg River. Undoubtedly, given normal increase in demand and continued expansion and development in the province, a good profit would have been realized. Neither the WEC Board of Directors nor its two negotiators could have foreseen the depression of the thirties and the resultant undermining of a large profit margin.

A matter which caused considerable comment later was the speed of the negotiations – the whole matter having being resolved, or so it seemed, between Saturday, 17 March, and Tuesday, 20 March. This was, of course, a deceptive time period. Both parties to the negotiations had already accepted the federal government guideline for the maximum development of the power on the river; thus they had both accepted the abandonment of the Pinawa channel. The major item left for debate was the price. And, admittedly, it is a puzzle as to why Anderson, as the WEC man most involved, did not realize after his weekend meetings that the Manitoba government was not as committed to possible public development as it had appeared. Surely he would have sensed this, and, in turn, dug in his heels. McLimont later testified that Anderson had authority to go as low as $13.80,[48] but that seems an *ex post facto* argument. What appears incontrovertible is that the WEC was quite prepared to accept fairly hard terms in order to gain control of over 50 per cent of the power on the river for thirty years. This raises the question as to whether or not it was a bargain in the public interest. On balance the answer still appears to be yes, given that the province would have been unable to take over except at enormous cost which would have meant extra taxes – an anathema to all parties – and because control of the site could return to the province in thirty years.

Bracken finally left the city on the evening of 20 March for a holiday in California. He was to be away about a month. Before leaving he dictated a letter to Stewart, informing the minister of the successful conclusion of negotiations with the WEC. As soon as a contract was drafted the government would be ready to withdraw its application for the lease of Seven Sisters, leaving the way open for negotiations between the WEC and the federal government.[49]

The decision to have Seven Sisters developed by a private company caused a major controversy in the province. This had considerable political repercussions and led to a delay in the issuance of a lease to the WEC by the dominion government. Not only were Bracken and his government attacked for abandoning public development but the manner in which it was revealed to the public was much criticized. The legislative session had ended on Friday, 16 March, and the agreement had been announced and the Hogg Report released on 21 March. It seemed as if Bracken had deliberately avoided a debate on the issue in the legislature.[50] This, of course, was not the case. However, it was unfortunate timing and the *Winnipeg Tribune*, the Labour group, and the Conservatives under Taylor soon began to flail Bracken, the former two for the preference of private to public interests, and the latter for not consulting the legislature.[51]

By the time Bracken returned from California on 14 April the controversy had become intense and remained so for much of the summer. The opponents of the contract – all the Labour interests and many of the federal MPs – urged the city to intervene and apply for the site. On three separate occasions in April and May, first in the Public Utilities Committee and subsequently at special sessions of City Council, this proposal was voted upon and defeated. Undaunted, the Labour MLAs and city councillors and the two Labour MPs, James Woodsworth and A.A. Heaps, continued their criticism of the government and attempted to persuade Mackenzie King not to sanction the contract. It soon became difficult to keep abreast of the various resolutions and petitions flowing to Ottawa from either side of the ideological divide.[52] By June Fawcett Taylor was publicly calling for a special session of the legislature to consider the issue.[53]

Bracken was not much impressed by the opposition to the contract. As he pointed out to Stewart, the agreement complied completely with federal government policy and was obviously the most efficient and economic way to proceed with the development of the Seven Sisters site. Bracken made a special journey to Ottawa in early May to put his case to the Manitoba Liberal-Progressive MPs and, although he did not succeed in winning them all to his side, he made a considerable impression.[54] But he had little success with Stewart, who was obviously disturbed by the outcry in Winnipeg. Thus, when the power question was being discussed in the House of Commons on 6 June it was really no surprise that Stewart indicated he was not prepared to dispose of the Seven Sisters site while grave differences of opinion existed.[55]

Both Robson and Bracken were annoyed by this decision. For some time Robson had felt that the federal government's delay over both Seven Sisters and the transfer of natural resources was 'a very great impediment to Liberalism' in Manitoba. He also knew that Bracken was anxious to resolve the natural resources issue. In a private conversation in late April the premier had told Robson that 'if the resources question were fixed up the blending of the two parties would be easy.' Robson urged King to take action: ' ... we are beginning to feel almost helpless as a Provincial Party. This will help the Conservatives federally if it continues ... the Resources question is an overhanging pall. And I have to support Mr. Bracken in such matters so as to keep him from attacking us at Ottawa. If he comes in for more abuse regarding Seven Sisters he may have to resort to the Resources question by way of defence.'[56] Robson realized that the Seven Sisters issue was no longer a departmental matter. It was now a political question that demanded attention at the federal level.

Bracken agreed. It is clear from a hastily scribbled note to himself of late May or early June that he believed there was a concerted effort underway to make Seven Sisters a political issue. As far as he was concerned, his government would 'continue to regard it as what it is – an economic question to be settled on business principles. Good business but poor politics – can't be both ... If Leg. doesn't like our decision can tell us so. Will have an election and see whether people want Dev. by business Govt. or Stag. by pol. Govt.'[57]

Bracken was fed up with the delay in granting the lease and in calling a natural resources conference. He reasoned, much as Robson had earlier suggested he would, that a decision on natural resources by which Manitoba got effective control of water power would stifle opposition criticism, or, at least, give him control. But he had to make King realize that a solution to the problem was to his advantage also. He attempted to do so in an extraordinary letter of 15 June. It is one of the very few surviving letters written by Bracken and in it we have a clear indication that the Manitoba premier was not above playing the political game he so publicly despised. After briefly outlining the history of the Seven Sisters issue, Bracken got to the heart of the matter:

Due to delay in issuing the license, the matter has become one of political controversy through the efforts of the Independent Labor Party and the Winnipeg Tribune. International labor, the business interests, the Provincial Liberal Party, the City Conservative Members and the Manitoba Free Press strongly support the Government's agreement. The country Conservatives are now watching the situation with a view to obtaining political advantage if they can. Delay only adds to the prestige of the Independent Labor Party and the Tribune, it contributes to the disintegration of the Liberals, creates discontent among the Progressives, encourages friction between Liberals and Progressives, and tends indirectly to the advantage of the Conservatives. It is creating a disagreeable situation for us and you, insofar as cooperation and better understanding are concerned. Mr. Robson has acted splendidly, and everything has been moving in the direction you desire and that I have been working toward but unless immediate issue of the license is made the agitation will continue. If it were granted, it would be followed by a collapse of the agitation and by the continuance of harmony between the Liberals and Progressives.

I am afraid that the Natural Resources question and other constitutional questions may also become embarrassing to both of us if the agitation is fed by further delay.

From the point of view of development of harmony between Liberals and Progressives, as well as from the point of view of the well-being of the Liberal Party itself in Manitoba, it may easily prove disastrous if there is undue delay.

I am therefore taking the liberty of writing you personally to ask your consideration of the whole matter and to request your direction that the license issue at once to the Company in order that the agreement between the Company and the Province may be consumated and the best interests of all be served.[58]

There seems to have been no reply to this letter and it is difficult to know how King reacted to a missive that bordered on political blackmail. Perhaps it was a salutary shock. In any event, it was obvious that concrete solutions were essential to both the Seven Sisters and the natural resources issues. Final arrangements were made for a conference in early July on the return of the resources to Manitoba, and on 28 June the Canadian cabinet decided to return control of water power to the western provinces. King admitted to his diary that the issue of private or public ownership of Seven Sisters was a difficult one, but he convinced himself that to turn the water powers over to the provinces and thus probably Seven Sisters to a private company was 'certainly the right one, as in accord with our policy of the Nat'l Resources.'[59]

The conference between Manitoba and the federal government over the transfer of natural resources opened in Ottawa on 3 July. Discussion began with King reading the correspondence which had been exchanged since 1922.[60] This caused him to wince inwardly: 'I confess I felt ashamed of our side of the record, the continuous procrastination. Bracken was very nice in speaking of it disclosing great tolerance on each side.'[61] King then pointed out that the federal government was prepared to recommend the immediate return of the natural resources without further question but that Manitoba was not prepared to accept the return of the remaining resources as full settlement. He therefore proposed that the question of additional compensation, whether a lump sum or an annual payment, be referred to arbitration. Bracken and his colleagues agreed. That evening, after dinner at Laurier House, it was decided to have a three-man arbitration commission and a start was made on a draft agreement.[62]

By the time Bracken returned to Manitoba the following night most of the details had been worked out and both he and Mackenzie King were pleased with the outcome. The prime minister confided to his diary that his 'whole guiding principle in this matter has been to get free of technicalities and right what seems to me a wrong situation existing at present.'[63]

To a degree King was undoubtedly sincere but one has to take his rationalizing with a grain of salt. He knew that federal retention of natural resources was a source of concern to Manitoba Liberals as well as to Bracken. If he wished to effect a fusion in Manitoba, the resources would have to be transferred as soon as possible. He also knew that if anything went wrong in future with mineral or power development the responsibility would not rest with the federal government.[64] As King saw it, 'we will create a real issue, which will be forced by others if we delay longer. We can bring Libs. and Progs. in Manitoba together on this. We can use every argument the Tories have used and leave them not a leg to stand upon. If we go the right way about it, we may win all three Western provinces to our side on this return of their resources ... '[65]

Over the next few days, from their separate bases in Ottawa and Winnipeg, King and Bracken spent a good deal of time ensuring that the agreement was properly drafted and met the concerns of their colleagues.[66] All ended amicably. Mr Justice Turgeon of Saskatchewan, C.M. Bowman of the Mutual Life Assurance Company of Canada, and Thomas Crerar were accepted as commissioners by the Manitoba government, and the agreement was released to the press and published on 12 July 1928.[67] Under its terms Manitoba was to be placed in 'a position of equality' with the other provinces with respect 'to the administration and control of its natural resources' from the date of its entry into confederation. A commission was to determine what financial adjustments would be required to fulfil that aim. Once the financial terms had been agreed upon both governments would introduce appropriate legislation to effect the transfer of resources. Of particular interest to all those concerned about the disposition of the Seven Sisters site was clause six of the agreement, which stated that until the transfer was completed the federal government's administration of Manitoba's natural resources would be 'in accord with the wishes of the government of the province.'

In the days following the press release there was considerable public concern over clause six and its application to the Seven Sisters issue. Knowing that he would be asked about this on 16 July when he spoke to the Young Men's Section of the Winnipeg Board of Trade, Bracken telegraphed King on 13 July seeking clarification. As he understood it, there would be no exceptions and the wishes of the provincial government 'would be accepted in this as in other natural resources question.'[68] King agreed but tried to get Stewart to confirm it. When nothing had been heard from his minister by early on the 16th, King replied to Bracken himself: 'my understanding corresponds with your own.'[69]

This was the statement that Bracken was able to make at the Board of Trade dinner that night and again to the press on the 17th. The speech itself was a vigorous defence of the Seven Sisters contract. His government, he said, believed in public ownership 'perhaps more than any other group in the Legislature excepting only the Labor group,' but it also believed that the best way to kill public ownership was 'to go into unsound business propositions or to take a "dog in the manger" attitude and stand in the way of development, or refuse to settle a complicated problem in a common sense way because it departs temporarily from the letter of the principle of public ownership.' Anyway, the question was not so much one of public versus private ownership: it was a 'question of development versus stagnation, a question of being assured of cheap power for rural hydro users versus going on at present with no assurance either of power or of low rates.' His government, said Bracken, had acted in the best interests of the province. No other scheme had more advantages or fewer objections than the arrangement with the WEC.[70]

Robson and Dafoe both agreed with Bracken. Dafoe could not 'see any two sides to this question. It seems to me all the considerations of reason and business and common sense are on one side.'[71] The day after Bracken's speech Robson urged King to hasten the grant of the lease: 'There is a growing demand here that public ownership cranks and opposing schemers be ignored and that the lease be granted and the work go ahead immediately ... If the Provincial request is not heeded there will be a stormy time. The settlement has taken well and you are occupying a fine position and these good impressions should not be jeopardised ...'[72]

The decision having been made to transfer the resources, there was nothing much that could hold up the granting of the Seven Sisters lease. But Stewart continued to be dilatory and, as it turned out, somewhat confused. Bracken and Stewart discussed the lease for the first time on 20 August in Winnipeg. The reason for the discussion had been a letter to Bracken from Stewart, dated 18 August, stating that the federal government had decided 'to offer the Manitoba Government the right to develop' Seven Sisters. Bracken must have been astounded when he read the letter. After all that time and all the controversy it was apparent that Stewart had not grasped the essentials of the issue. After discussing the matter with Stewart, Bracken wrote a polite but pointed reply carefully traversing the all-so-familiar ground, indicating that Stewart's offer was not in conformity with the agreement of 12 July, and respectfully urging him to hurry the process up.[73] Thereafter, matters moved more smoothly and an interim licence was granted on 18 September to North Western Power Limited, a WEC subsidiary set up for the purpose.[74]

7

Scandal

'The Tories made so many assertions about Bracken that he appointed a Royal
Commission and they are digging up rather more than any of the political
parties cares about. My sympathy is with Bracken. That Taylor is such a
mean-tongued thing I would like to see him get what he needs and that would
be kicked out of office.'[1]

By the time the Seven Sisters lease was granted in mid-September and the Turgeon
Commission met for the first time in mid-October, Bracken was engrossed in the
complexities of the Manitoba political scene. Shortly after his return from California in April he had asked Donald McKenzie to contest the Lansdowne seat,
soon to be vacated by Norris, with a view to joining the cabinet as minister of natural resources. When the controversy developed over the contract with the WEC
Bracken asked Norris to delay his resignation and the seat was not vacated until
September. The by-election was then scheduled for 10 November.

McKenzie was formally adopted by both the Progressive and Liberal parties as
their candidate in Lansdowne on 20 October and two days later was sworn in as
minister of natural resources, as provincial secretary, and as the minister responsible for the provincial hydro. His nomination was strongly endorsed by Bracken
and Robson. The Liberal leader also publicly supported the government's stand
on Seven Sisters and approved its general policies on hydro development.[2] This
outright endorsement of McKenzie and of Seven Sisters by the Liberal leader left
many Liberals throughout the province unhappy. In the ensuing campaign J.W.
Wilton, a Liberal 'die-hard' from Winnipeg, openly challenged Robson's stand,
and urged all Liberals to vote for Dr Harvey Hicks of Oak Lake, the Conservative
candidate, and thus against association with Bracken.[3]

The campaign was a heated one. The main issue was the Seven Sisters lease.
From the outset – Hick's nominating meeting on 4 October – Fawcett Taylor,

the Conservative leader, denounced the government's action. He termed the lease 'the most glaring breach of faith between a government and a people which had ever been recorded in Manitoba politics. The premier had violated every thread of the principles upon which he and his party had been elected ... '[4] He criticized the lack of opportunity given the legislature to debate the issue; he claimed that Bracken had flouted the decision of the house to uphold public ownership; and he accused the government of abandoning its own commitment to public owner-ship and of selling out to private interests.

The most important, and certainly the most sensational charge, was levelled against Bracken's apparent collusion with the Winnipeg Electric Company. Taylor charged that the Bracken government, in return for campaign funds, had entered into an agreement with the company as early as 1927. He was convinced that as much as $50,000 had changed hands, although he suggested that $1,250,000 was unaccounted for in the WEC books. He also pointed out how many officials and directors connected with the WEC had served on the Bracken campaign committee in 1927.[5] Furthermore, he drew attention to the fact that as soon as the 1927 election was over the stock of the WEC had started to climb. It had risen from 74 in July 1927 to 128¾ in May 1928. During the time the legislature had been sitting it had gone as high as 127. Taylor claimed that company earnings did not warrant such a rise. The only explanation was the expected acquisition of Seven Sisters Falls.

Although these were highly serious charges, Taylor admitted that he could not prove them. He believed he would be able to, but if he were proved wrong he was prepared to resign the Conservative leadership. This added a truly bizarre touch to the whole campaign, and nothing is more revealing of the unsophisticated na-ture of Manitoba politics in those days. Needless to say the whole campaign was fought over Taylor's statements and the issue of the Seven Sisters lease. By the end Taylor was calling for an investigation by a Royal Commission.[6]

Bracken, McKenzie, and Major bore the brunt of the campaign for the govern-ment. It had a severe effect on the premier's health. Bracken was ill throughout the campaign, having picked up yet another bad cold, and by the end he was un-der a doctor's care. He was physically and mentally drained. He had never fully recovered from his illness of the previous winter, and the tension and anxiety in-duced by Taylor's charges, coupled with the cold and problems of diet, brought him as close as he was ever to come to a full breakdown. Nevertheless, in his stub-born fashion he campaigned arduously. Bracken asserted throughout that Tay-lor's charges were baseless, and he accused the Conservative leader of deliberately misleading the electorate. On 30 October at Oak Lake, from the same platform used by Taylor the previous evening, Bracken declared Taylor's accusations 'ab-solutely and positively false. That is the most cowardly insinuation that I have ever read coming from the lips of a public man. Colonel Taylor knows full well there is no truth in it.'[7]

Over the next ten days Bracken, Major, and McKenzie were at pains to explain the advantages of the Seven Sisters deal. All three declared that it was a sound business arrangement that would ensure a solid financial foundation for the development of hydro-electric power. They emphasized that the government had not abandoned the principle of public ownership. Not only could the site revert to the province in thirty years but during that period the company's discretionary power would be limited by the terms of the contract and the continuous assessment of the Public Utilities Commission. The advantages of the arrangement were outlined at every meeting to the exclusion of virtually every other issue.

Toward the latter stages of the campaign, as Bracken's strength ebbed, Major assumed more of the burden. He also took it upon himself to be the hatchet-man for the Progressives. He openly called Taylor a coward and held his own in the verbal in-fighting. Tough language and inflammatory phrases sounded better coming from him than from either McKenzie or Bracken. The former could not afford the luxury and Bracken personally disliked engaging in such crude party-politicking.[8] He preferred to adopt a rational approach. As he pointed out to a Griswold audience on 7 November with respect to Conservative accusations of extravagent government: 'Every Conservative member approved of the budget. They only urged that more money be spent. Strangely, however, they have been opposed to all forms of taxation.' And to the same audience he summed up his attitude to the whole campaign: 'We want to know in this bye-election whether or not you want your government run on a business basis, not on a basis of theory.'[9] Toward the end of the campaign both groups had a number of outside speakers at work, but by then the main issues had been repeated in wearisome detail from platforms in every town and hamlet of the constituency.

The constituency was a traditional Liberal seat. It had been held for years by Norris who had won the last two elections by over 1000 votes. The Conservatives, therefore, had the odds against them. The result of the by-election on 10 November was a victory for McKenzie over Hicks by a margin of 268 out of a total vote of nearly 2800. This was considered by Bracken and his supporters to be a public vindication of his policy, but was viewed by the Conservatives, probably with more justification, as a slap in the face to the Seven Sisters arrangement. Whatever conclusions could be drawn, one was obvious. Bracken would now be under considerable pressure, personal and public, to have Taylor's charges investigated.

Bracken took no immediate action on Taylor's charges. In fact he left the province on 29 November, the day after the Liberal convention, for Battle Creek, Michigan, where he spent almost two months in a sanatorium recovering his health and seeking advice on diet and exercise. He did not return to Winnipeg until 21 January 1929.

This visit to Battle Creek was the culmination of a lengthy period of illness for Bracken. For most of his life he was susceptible to colds and viral infections which sapped his strength and obliged him to spend many days each winter in bed. In addition, Bracken had been suffering since the mid-1920s from severe stomach pains, constipation, and a general weariness and fatigue. He had been ill in bed for much of late 1927, again in the spring of 1928, and the condition had been aggravated in late 1928 by the tensions of the by-election. Bracken's problems were probably the result of anemia and extreme nervous tension. He was always a very tense man who kept his emotions under a strong rein and did not often give vent to his feelings or share his thoughts with others. His long working hours and his constant tension played havoc with his stomach and his bowels. He was often in considerable pain and much distressed.

In his anxiety for a solution to his medical problems, or at least for a key to understand them, he was an avid reader of medical works. Two that he consulted constantly during those years were *The Fast Way to Health* by Dr Frank McCoy, the fifth edition of which was given to Bracken in September 1927, and *The Health Question Base or A Thousand and One Health Questions Answered* written by Dr John Harvey Kellogg of Battle Creek, Michigan. It had first been published in 1917 but Bracken had the 1925 edition. Sections of both books dealing with stomach ulcers, hyper-acidity, constipation, diet, influenza, laxatives, enemas, pernicious anemia, 'Prolapsus, or Sagging of Organ,' and 'Rectal Troubles' were all heavily underlined.

Bracken was obviously much impressed by Kellogg's book and by what he had heard of the Battle Creek Sanatorium. As soon as the Lansdowne by-election was over he made arrangements to go south. He spent the better part of eight weeks there with a four-day trip to New York in early January. It cost him close to $1000 for accommodation at the sanatorium plus fares and incidental expenses. While there he lived on a vegetable diet, shunning the fleshy foods that were supposed to exacerbate sensitive stomachs, took sun baths, had regular gym classes, morning and evening, and had an infected tooth-root removed. All in all it was a much needed rest far from the political battlefield and the clamourings of Fawcett Taylor. However, he was not completely out of touch with the Manitoba acene, being kept informed by letters and newspapers and in late December by a visit from Major and Clubb. When he returned to Winnipeg on 21 January he was refreshed for the battle over power policy that was bound to erupt both inside and outside the legislature.[10]

During his absence the critics of the Bracken power policy had continued to flail the government. In late December 1928 Taylor made it clear that he intended to force an inquiry into the whole circumstances of the transaction, when and with whom it originated, how the negotiations were conducted, and generally the relations of the government with the WEC, beginning with 1927. His stand was unanimously endorsed by the executive of the Conservative Association of Greater Winnipeg.[11] In early January Taylor travelled the province on a 'power eduction tour,' repeating his assertions and criticizing private as opposed to public ownership.[12]

Immediately upon returning to Winnipeg Bracken reviewed what had been happening on the Seven Sisters question during his absence. After a number of meetings with his cabinet colleagues he decided to appoint a Royal Commission to investigate the charges made by Taylor. The announcement was made on 29 January and the order-in-council was dated 2 February. The three commissioners were Daniel A. McDonald, chief justice of the Court of King's Bench, and Andrew K. Dysart and James F. Kilgour, both judges of the Court of King's Bench. The commission was asked to find out whether or not Bracken or his government, or anyone acting on their behalf, had entered into a 'corrupt' bargain with the WEC over Seven Sisters or had agreed to let the WEC have the Seven Sisters site in return for a campaign contribution. It was also asked to investigate whether or not the WEC had directly or indirectly contributed $50,000, or any other amount, to the Bracken campaign funds for the 1927 provincial elections in return for an agreement over Seven Sisters or had contributed to any party's or individual's campaign fund for the 1927 election. The commission was granted full powers to summon witnesses and documentary evidence and to investigate the circumstances leading up to the making of the agreement provided it did not pass upon the merit or expediency of the contract. The government would assume full responsibility for such matters.[13]

Taylor did not find this last proviso satisfactory. He had wanted the commission to make 'a full and complete enquiry into all the circumstances' connected with the negotiation and completion of the agreement. He thought Bracken's proviso would prevent that.[14] Certainly it presented the commission with a major problem of interpretation, for 'it proved very difficult to consider the question of honesty apart from the question of expediency of the contract ... a palpably unreasonable contract would be strong, albeit circumstantial evidence of corruption.'[15]

The commission began sitting on 4 February. One week later on 11 February the Manitoba legislature began its session. For the next two-and-one-half months power policy and commission revelations dominated the Manitoba scene. Both the commission hearings and the legislative sittings were given extensive coverage in the newspapers and hardly a day passed without a new or dramatic twist being added to the stories. The Manitoba public sat enthralled, although somewhat bemused, with the goings-on in Winnipeg. Nothing as exciting or as full of fury, pomposity, rhetoric, and high comedy had happened in Manitoba politics since the days of the Roblin government.

Before the commission finished it had heard more than thirty witnesses, amassed over 5000 pages of transcript, and made a special trip to Los Angeles to interview Andrew McLimont, the former president of the WEC. Much of its time was spent listening to protracted haggling on the admissibility of evidence. For some weeks a relatively relaxed posture was adopted and questioning tended to be more wide-ranging than Bracken had wished. During this period both Major and Clubb were subjected to close questioning by Taylor's lawyers on such matters as comparative pricing, the urgency of the need for development, and the feasibility of public or private ownership. Eventually the commission grew tired of this and tightened the procedures.

There was also considerable debate over an audit of the WEC's books. An audit was demanded by Taylor's lawyers in order to clarify the question of the $50,000. But the commission adopted the position that it was beyond its powers to authorize an audit and the WEC representatives refused to permit it. From the testimony that did emerge from Anderson, McLimont, and Blodgett, the comptroller of the WEC, it was unlikely that any evidence would have been found either to confirm or deny the charges. The company did not keep a record of political donations. McLimont had simply had the authority to make discretionary withdrawals for such purposes and to spread them among the various operating accounts without indicating the use to which they were put. McLimont claimed he had not kept a personal record of such transactions. The commissioners did not press very hard to establish the honesty of this testimony. They seemed content with the word of those involved.[16] Suspicious though the testimony was it was true that a donation of the size suggested by Taylor would have required the approval of the WEC Board of Directors. This, as James Coyne, a WEC director, testified, had never been sought.[17]

While these problems were being sorted out by the commissioners, debate had opened in the legislature on 12 February with Taylor launching a predictable criticism of the government's actions over Seven Sisters. Some of the charges were familiar ones – failure to adhere to the agreed principle of public ownership and failure to consult the legislature before concluding the agreement – but to them Taylor added criticism of the Royal Commission. He considered it a means of preventing a full-scale examination in the legislature of the Seven Sisters lease. Astonishingly, in light of his charges and fulminations of previous weeks, Taylor asserted that 'the royal commission was appointed to investigate some subsidiary charges made in the Lansdowne bye-election ... '[18] Now that his bluff had been called and he had to assume the responsibility, and the expense, of proving his charges, Taylor was attempting to treat them as off-hand remarks, not to be treated seriously. His problem was that Bracken had every intention of treating them as such. Robson was also critical of Bracken's decision to appoint a commission. He claimed that he had never taken seriously any of the remarks during the Lansdowne election: 'I don't think these matters should be followed up. You make a man popular if you abuse him.'[19] These comments revealed a complete lack of understanding of the premier. Bracken was highly sensitive to any slight or to any suggestion of personal dishonesty. It was not in his nature to allow public criticism about his integrity to pass unexamined or unchallenged.

The intensity of his feeling was dramatically revealed on Friday afternoon, 15 February, when he rose to speak in the legislature. Bracken indicated that he intended to treat a motion introduced the previous day by John Queen calling for a special committee to investigate the Seven Sisters deal as one of non-confidence. Until the government knew that it had the support of the House no major legislation would be introduced. This in itself was a shock but the real drama unfolded towards the end of his speech when he referred directly to Taylor's charges. The scene is best described by George Ferguson, the young legislative reporter for the *Manitoba Free Press:*

For more than 40 minutes the premier sketched the legislation which would flow from the throne. Dry, accurate sentences followed one another in military precision from his lips ... Suddenly, as the hands of the clock reached the hour of four, he turned fiercely upon Colonel Taylor. The whole tone of the speech changed. With his opening sentence he made a savage reference to the famous Oak Lake speech of the Conservative leader ... His dispassionate voice rang on a suddenly querulous note. Deep-seated anger was held back only by an obvious effort ... Statements made at Oak Lake said Bracken, in the midst of a silence that hung like a black mantle over the house, had branded the premier of Manitoba as a thief ... 'No public man could take those charges lying down,' said the premier, and the silence around him grew deeper and heavier. 'I hope I am not thin-skinned. Perhaps I was wrong in taking notice of the charges. Perhaps that is the price we have to pay.' Pale and drawn, Mr. Bracken fumbled through the papers on his desk, and read the statement he had received of a speech made by Mr. Newton, of Roblin, who was reported as saying 'I knew Bracken received a large sum of money for putting through the Seven Sisters deal.' Asked how he knew, Mr. Newton was reported as saying, 'I saw the cheque' ...

PREMIER BRACKEN: 'I will not be called a thief.' His voice was hoarse and almost broke, and he stood in his place, staring across the floor at the Conservative leader who rose slowly from his seat.

COLONEL TAYLOR: 'I never made a single charge of personal dishonesty against him, and he cannot produce any evidence that I did. Any charges I made were against his government.'

PREMIER BRACKEN: 'I am glad to hear that, because of Colonel Taylor's reported statement that Mr. Bracken, for a consideration which some time might be known, agreed to let the Winnipeg Electric Company have the power site.'

COLONEL TAYLOR: 'There was no such imputation in my address. I made no personal charge whatever.'

THE PREMIER: 'Well, I accept that' ...

The scene ended as quickly as it had begun. Controlled and restrained once more, the premier finished his speech. On the motion to adjourn, the Conservative leader rose once more to make three ... statements: he had never suggested any questions for the consideration of a commission; he had never made any charge of personal dishonesty or impropriety.[20]

This was, of course, ludicrous question-begging. Anyone who had followed Taylor's speeches the previous November and many of his subsequent assertions had been in no doubt as to the intent of his comments.

What had added to Bracken's tension that Friday afternoon and caused him to be uncharacteristically revealing of his private feelings was the knowledge that while he was defending the validity of the Seven Sisters lease and his personal honesty in the legislative chamber, Bill Clubb was across the street in the Law Courts building admitting to the Royal Commission that he had purchased WEC shares in March 1928 while discussions with the company were in progress. In itself, this would have been bad enough, but Bracken knew that Clubb had not been alone in his actions. Two days earlier, shortly after the start of the session, both Clubb and Major had come to Bracken to tell him that they had both purchased WEC stock the previous March.[21] Neither had indulged heavily and Major had sold his after a few days. Nevertheless, this was a grievous indiscretion by two leading cabinet ministers and confronted Bracken with a serious political problem. Although both men offered their resignations, Bracken initially refused to accept them. The premier considered their actions injudicious and indiscreet but did not believe their judgment on the contract had been affected. He preferred to delay a decision on the future of the two men until the Royal Commission had finished its task.

When Bracken revealed his ministers' indiscretions and his decision to retain them in the cabinet to the legislature on Monday, 18 February, it was as if a bombshell had exploded in the chamber. Taylor called for the ministers' immediate resignations and Robson concluded that the revelation of 'fraud' in connection with Seven Sisters rendered both the agreement and the lease null and void. The criticism and furour mounted throughout the week and Bracken was under constant pressure from within his party to accept the resignations in order to save the government any further embarrassment. During those feverish and pressure-packed days it was rumoured that the government would either resign or that Bracken would be replaced by McKenzie and a new administration formed. Bracken had no intention of complying with either course, but on Friday, 22 February, ten days after he had first heard of the indiscretions, he finally agreed to accept the resignations. That he did not see them as permanent was revealed a few days later when Hoey and McKenzie were sworn in respectively as *acting* attorney-general and *acting* minister of public works.[22] Immediately after making his announcement, Bracken moved the adjournment of the House until 20 March. After much rhetoric and jockeying for position by the various groups in the legislature, the motion finally passed 27-17 on 1 March, but only after closure had been introduced.[23]

The whole incident revealed very clearly the contemporary attitudes towards such issues as a politicians's use of inside information, government-business relations, and personal inter-party relationships. For not only Clubb and Major had taken a flier. It was later revealed that John Haig, Taylor's principal lieutenant, John Queen, the ILP member, and P.A. Talbot, the speaker of the House, had also bought shares. None of them seemed to consider their actions unusual or themselves wanting in judgment. Clubb and Haig were quite frank on this point to the commission. Despite being on opposite sides of the political fence, Haig had been Clubb's close friend and solicitor for years. Thus Clubb had not been at all surprised when Haig had walked across the floor of the House in the closing days of the session the previous March and had asked him if the government had any report from Dr Hogg. Clubb admitted they had. 'Well,' asked Haig, 'is the Province going to develop?' 'I don't think so,' replied Clubb. 'Well,' said Haig, 'I think it would be a good time to buy Winnipeg Electric Stock ... I am buying some and I think that you should too.' Clubb agreed, 'All right. You can buy me 100.' Over the next few days, Haig, using his own name, bought Clubb 350 shares of WEC stock. Clubb admitted under questioning that he had purchased the shares because he knew that when it was eventually revealed that the government did not plan to develop Seven Sisters the WEC stock would go up. Although he had never invested as heavily in stock before, he was emphatic that it had 'in no way influenced' his decision in securing the best deal possible for the province. Thus he did not think his action improper. The air at that time had been full of talk about WEC stock which had been rising steadily for some months and many people both in and out of the legislature were speculating.

Although Clubb assured the commission that he had not spoken to anyone else, it was obvious that he did not think it particularly wrong to have revealed a cabinet secret to Haig nor to have used inside information in the hopes of turning a tidy profit. He claimed continuously that his conscience was clear. Apparently, he did not consider it unusual for cabinet ministers to use inside information to their own advantage.[24] Haig agreed. He told the commission that he did not think Clubb had done anything wrong in buying the stock. Nor did Haig seem to think it odd that he had been the one to offer John Queen advice on stock purchases, nor that Queen, a supposed ideological foe of capitalism, had purchased $75.00 worth.[25] Major had also made use of his inside information when he had agreed to buy fifty shares on 15 March 1928. His partner, Rod Finlayson, had been planning to invest, so Major had simply said 'all right get me some as well.' Unlike Clubb, Major soon had second thoughts and had sold his stock on 23 March because, or so he told the Royal Commission, he thought it unwise to hold shares in a company one was dealing with.[26]

These close friendships across party and ideological lines and the casual use of inside information were not uncommon in Manitoba politics in those days. Even Bracken, a man of strict integrity, did not consider the actions of Clubb and Major so heinous that the two men should be permanently expelled from political life. Always the pragmatist, Bracken knew that they had not shaped the agreement to their own advantage, so why get rid of them for trying to make a little money on the side? In the event, none of the purchasers made any money. The hard bargain that Clubb and Major had helped drive coupled with the depression of the thirties severely limited the company's development, and Clubb lost $5000, Talbot $3000, and Queen his $75.00. As Haig sardonically replied when asked by A.E. Johnston, the government lawyer, if he was a business man: 'Not very good. I bought Winnipeg Electric and I don't think anybody who bought it would be a good business man.'[27]

Although Bracken had been engrossed in party and legislative problems since his return from Battle Creek, the question of fusion with the Liberals had never been far from his mind. During the three-week legislative recess he gave serious consideration to coalition as a solution to his government's difficulties. When it had become obvious that Clubb and Major would have to resign, Bracken had opened negotiations behind-the-scenes to see if Robson would come into the cabinet as attorney-general in place of Major. If he agreed, Bracken hoped the other five Liberal MLAs would follow him to the government benches and allow the administration to ride out the Seven Sisters storm.[28]

King and the Ottawa Liberals watched these developments closely. As always, they were kept well-informed by Dafoe who was quick to recommend that advantage be taken of the situation to bring about fusion. He wanted the local Liberals who were currently 'in a hopeless minority,' without any chance of forming a government for years to come, to join the Brackenites and work for Liberalism from within. It was 'nonsense' to argue, as Gardiner was inclined to do, that the Liberals should go it alone. That would only result in a Tory victory at the next election. Dafoe recommended that King take advantage of the adjournment of the Manitoba legislature to 'judiciously take a hand ... in impressing upon both factions here the necessity of cooperating upon some permanent basis if disaster, in which they will all share, is to be averted.'[29]

Dafoe was, of course, preaching to the converted. King was firmly committed to an alliance, or a coalition, between the Liberals and Progressives of Manitoba.[30] On 4 March he outlined his ideas to Robson. By then the Manitoba Liberals had decided to hold a convention on 19 March to discuss the issue of co-operation with the Bracken administration. Although there had been considerable discussion within the party and much public debate, no official offer had been received from Bracken when King wrote to Robson.[31]

In his letter King pointed out that he had refrained from commenting on the Manitoba political situation but since 'provincial and federal politics are inextricably interwoven' in the province, he felt it his duty to express his opinion. He saw two alternatives open to Robson: first, a repudiation of Bracken's government by the Liberals; and, second, 'a joining together,' to be decided on in conference between Liberals and Progressives, in order that the government could carry on so that an election and a possible Conservative victory could be avoided. King thought it should be recognized that the Conservative party was the common enemy of both the Liberals and the Progressives. He reminded Robson that 'The Progressives in Manitoba *need* your help today, and as a consequence you should be able to make your own terms with them. You should make them in the name of Liberalism, as opposed to Toryism. To keep the Conservative Party out of control in Manitoba is an all-sufficient ground for you, as a Liberal, finding means of honourable cooperation with those members of the legislature who are opposed to the Conservative Party.' The alternative to co-operation with the Progressives was a Conservative administration which would be disastrous.

Switching to the federal scene, King pointed out that the federal Liberals had the wholehearted support of the Liberal-Progressives of Manitoba. The Liberals of Manitoba could, by acting properly on the provincial scene, guarantee the Liberal-Progressive combination against the Conservatives in Ottawa. An opposite course by Manitoba Liberals might, in a moment of crisis at the federal level, prove disastrous. 'Moreover, the strengthening of Conservative forces in Manitoba, combined with hostility between Liberals and Progressives in that Province, might not only injure us materially in Manitoba but would, I believe, have as well unfortunate consequences in Saskatchewan.' It was, he said, an opportunity for statesmanlike action.

King's letter was delivered personally to Robson on 7 March by Thomas Taylor, who had again been sent to Manitoba by the prime minister. King wanted Taylor to explain the position to Robson and to persuade the provincial leader to comply with federal needs. Taylor was to report directly to Senator Haydon, the national organizer, and was to use the code name 'Longbury.'[32]

On 6 March, the day before Taylor arrived in Winnipeg, Bracken finally, 'after the usual hesitation,'[33] broke silence and officially opened the possibility of cooperation. The following is the complete text of his letter to Robson dated 6 March 1929:[34]

With regard to the present political situation in the Province, it seems to me opportune and desirable, from the point of view of the public interest, that the situation ought now to be considered carefully with the object of determining whether a greater measure of cooperation between our two groups cannot be worked out, upon terms honourable to both Parties and in the Public interest.

I have canvassed the situation very carefully and have satisfied myself that the Government can carry on, even under the most adverse conditions likely to develop, yet I think a larger majority in the House would be in the public interest. Under these circumstances, I am willing to meet you personally to consider the whole matter; or, as an alternative, we might institute a joint committee of carefully chosen representatives of both Parties, to consider the possibilities of effecting an arrangement by which the Government of the Province might rest upon a basis of greater numerical strength in the House.

I am very definitely of the opinion that the public interest can best be served in this way, and I would respectfully solicit your sympathetic consideration of this proposal.

Taylor met with Robson for the first time on Thursday evening, 7 March.[35] Over the next few days the elderly judge and the young Liberal intriguer were to see a lot of one another. Neither formed a particularly favourable view of the other. Taylor, anxious to carry out his mission successfully, tried to persuade Robson that it was his duty to go into the Bracken cabinet. In order to make the decision more palatable, Taylor even managed to get Bracken to agree to the admission of two Liberals if that were the price of securing a fusion of Liberal and Progressive forces. But Robson continued to hesitate and to Taylor seemed unduly influenced by Gardiner. In an effort to resolve this dilemma Taylor made a flying visit to Regina and asked Gardiner to view fusion more favourably. Though the Saskatchewan premier wavered more than usual, he was still deeply suspicious and was only prepared to help if Bracken would agree to retire in a year and turn the leadership over to Robson.[36] Taylor knew that if fusion were to depend on such an arrangement it was doomed to failure. Bitterly disappointed, he wrote pessimistically to King. 'I am awfully sorry,' he said, but 'the whole situation is very unsatisfactory.'[37] By 14 March it appeared to him that the whole project had collapsed.

Robson, of course, had never been anxious to join the Bracken administration. His reasons were well founded and not purely personal.[38] He knew that many in his party disliked Bracken and that a large number of Manitoba Liberals were still influenced in their attitudes by their experiences during the formation of Borden's Union government. These 'die-hards' were refusing to have anything to do with fusion. Robson realized that the unity of his party was at stake. He concluded that he could best serve Liberalism at both the provincial and federal levels by preventing an open split in his ranks. Within a week of Taylor's arrival, Robson had decided that the best he could do was to comply with Bracken's offer and have the convention agree to the appointment of a committee to confer with one from the government side about a merger. While the negotiations were under way the Liberals would give the government general support in the legislature.[39] Having made up his mind Robson fled to Minneapolis on 14 March to escape the various pressures upon him, particularly the importuning of Taylor. He did not return to Winnipeg until the morning of 19 March, the day of the Liberal convention.

During the few days left to him Taylor, on the advice of King, attempted to pack the convention with delegates favourable to fusion.[40] Meanwhile, King put pressure on many of the prominent 'die-hards,'[41] and also wrote to both Robson and Gardiner stressing how important fusion was for the federal Liberals.[42] He pointed out to Gardiner that the entire cabinet, as well as all the Liberal and Progressive members from Manitoba, had agreed that co-operation was the right course to pursue. King explained that the support from the *Manitoba Free Press*, 'which we can have guaranteed for both Provincial and Federal fields from now on, if coalition is arranged, is another factor of utmost importance to us Federally and should also be helpful to your province as well as Manitoba.' Even if Gardiner could not support fusion, King asked him not to oppose a move toward that end by others. King hoped Gardiner would impress the importance of the situation on Robson. In the event, Gardiner agreed to help bring about fusion – or at best co-operation – between Manitoba's Liberals and Progressives, and he sent his provincial librarian, W.F. Kerr, to Minneapolis in an attempt to persuade Robson to listen sympathetically to Ottawa's arguments.[43]

The result of the convention on 19 March was very close to the wishes of King and Bracken, although not quite the ultimate solution they had wanted.[44] As expected Robson opposed any precipitate action and declared a sound understanding on policy would have to be reached before he would support united action. Most of his colleagues tended to agree, so they unanimously approved the appointment of a negotiating committee. In the meantime, the Liberals would support the government in the legislature.[45]

King's initial reaction was one of delight. He confided to his diary on 19 March: 'From word received tonight the Liberal Convention at Winnipeg has fulfilled our highest hopes in bringing together Liberals and Progressives in that province. In other words a fusion of the two parties. It has taken a lot of manoeuvring, but Gardiner has played his part well and the pressure put on from Ottawa has worked like a charm. If only the same result could be effected in Ontario and Alberta we would be back to the two old parties with gain to the Liberal cause. I am greatly pleased at this result.'[46] King was jumping the gun a little, but the two groups in Manitoba were soon meeting to discuss coalition.[47]

Bracken and Robson met on the 21st and the Liberal leader wrote of it to King. It was not the positive statement that the prime minister had expected: 'Mr. Bracken and I had another conversation yesterday. We understand each other all right and will keep the Progressive and Liberal Parties friendly. For the good of Liberal prestige here, and the retention of Progressives who are former Tories, we may continue on the group basis. Do not think that delay in, or even absence of fusion will have any undesirable meaning. Mr. Bracken is feeling stronger, has regained his poise. We help him in consultation now and then. But I hear so often that the Liberals must retain their identity – and there is a lot in it.'[48]

Bracken must have watched the scrambling and infighting among the Liberals with some amusement. He was, of course, interested in fusion and prepared to take in Liberal members, but it would be on his terms. He knew that the Liberals would be obliged to support his government on the power question because the thought of a Conservative government, or another election, was anathema to them. Therefore, he did not press too hard at this point. He did not feel it necessary to make great sacrifices in pursuit of coalition. To a degree Bracken was also held back by the attitude of the Tory members of his cabinet who resented the thought of working with the Liberals. Hoey managed to pacify them, but it was obvious that Bracken had to play his hand cautiously.[49]

On 20 March the three-week recess ended. Feeling well rested and certainly more confident about his political position, Bracken plunged back into the public arena. Soon after the House reassembled he made it clear that he wished to proceed with his programme as rapidly as possible. Earlier, he had assumed that by the time the adjournment ended the Royal Commission would have been near the end of its work and its decision soon known. It was now obvious that the hearings would drag on for some weeks, so further delay was unwise. Nevertheless, before either the budget or any major legislation was introduced, he wanted the debate on the address to be completed and Queen's motion for a special committee to investigate the Seven Sisters power deal disposed of.[50] In this he had his way and on 3 April, the same day that he appeared to give his initial testimony to the commission, Queen's motion was defeated 31-19 with the Liberals siding with the government. On 4 April Bracken made his budget speech, and on the 5th, 8th, and 16th he completed his testimony.

Although Bracken must have felt a certain strain as he settled into the witness box at the Law Courts Building on 3 April, the hearings did not prove arduous for him. The government counsel, Isaac Pitblado, took him through his evidence in a straight-forward, matter-of-fact manner and the premier never had to deal with a difficult or awkward question. On 3 April, shortly after he had completed his initial testimony, the WEC made it clear that it would permit no audit of its books. With that Hugh Philipps, Taylor's counsel, withdrew from the hearings and took no further part in commission proceedings. As a consequence, Bracken was never properly cross-examined nor his attitude and assumptions queried. He was recalled to the stand briefly on 16 April in order that Marcus Hyman, representing the Labour party, could ask questions, but Hyman's examination soon spilled over into the area of merit and had to be abandoned. In those few minutes in mid-April when he faced a sceptical opponent, Bracken was rather stiff-necked. He was quick to stand on his integrity, resenting the slightest implication of impropriety, and his answers were often abrupt and snappish. If Philipps had stayed the course and cross-examined the premier, the Manitoba public would undoubtedly have been treated to another dramatic spectacle. But that was not to be.

There were no real surprises in Bracken's testimony. The premier's position on the development of hydro-electric power in Manitoba and his specific approach to the Seven Sisters question were well known. What the commissioners now heard were the details of the negotiations from 1925 to 1928. Bracken also made it clear that he had had no knowledge of any monies coming to the government from the WEC before or during the 1927 election nor had he been aware, before 12 February 1929, of the stock speculations of Major and Clubb. Bracken claimed he had 'honestly relied' on the Hogg report and had made the contract with the company believing it to be in the very best interests of the province. All this was backed up with an impressive mass of documentary evidence.[51]

With the completion of Bracken's testimony the commission had virtually ended its inquiry. Its report was tabled on 30 April. Its conclusions were no surprise to those who had followed the proceedings of the past two-and-one-half months. Although Justice Dysart was critical of the commission's failure to press some of the witnesses hard enough, particularly the representatives of the WEC, he agreed with his two colleagues that there was not 'a tittle of evidence' to justify Taylor's charges.[52] Bracken and his cabinet were completely exonerated of any corruption or dishonesty in connection with the Seven Sisters power agreement, and all the assertions that Taylor had made proved unfounded.

It was clear that Taylor's case had been built on hearsay evidence. During his testimony Taylor said he had heard about the $50,000 changing hands from Ray Elliott, who had been told about it by his brother-in-law, James Coyne, the WEC director.[53] When the charges were made public, Elliott denied having told Taylor or being told by Coyne.[54] Coyne denied saying anything of the kind to Elliott.[55]

In his investigations for the government lawyers, Ralph Maybank, the coalition activist, had established that Ray Elliott, a staunch Conservative, had been a drug addict, and was now a probable alcoholic. His family had urged him to enter a sanitarium. Coyne had had virtually no relations with him, and their meeting had been accidental and nothing of substance had been mentioned. As Elliott's father said, his son 'would be the last person in the world to whom Coyne would give any confidence.'[56]

When Elliott testified on 15 April he was out of hospital for the day.[57] He admitted that he might have mentioned a $50,000 figure to Taylor in their casual conversation of July 1928, but he was emphatic that he had not received any information from Coyne about campaign funds. Elliott was unclear how he had arrived at the $50,000 figure but suggested he may have assumed it would cost about $1000 to contest each constituency. Elliott asserted that Taylor had drawn the wrong inference in July, and certainly it was obvious from Taylor's testimony that the Conservative leader had been grossly lax in his handling of whatever he thought he had heard.[58] He had not written Elliott's remarks down; he had never asked Elliott for a written statement; and he had never made any effort to see if Coyne would substantiate the rumour. Elliott, on the conclusion of his testimony, admitted that he had had no grounds for mentioning $50,000, or for connecting it with Coyne, the WEC, or Bracken. Taylor did not have the grace to admit any such error in judgment. In fact, he asserted in his silly, headstrong fashion that in political life he had no hesitancy making charges on flimsy evidence.

As the commission hearings had revealed, the only donations that had been made were as follows: $3000 to Bracken's party; $3500 to the Conservatives; and $500 to the Liberals. McLimont's testimony on this matter was corroborated by the testimony of Coyne, Haig, and Anderson.[59]

Thus ended the Seven Sisters affair with Bracken completely cleared. All the other pending issues soon fell similarly into place. The government's decision to issue a priority permit to the British Dominions Power Syndicate of London,

England, for the development of White Mud Falls on the Nelson River was approved by the legislature on 3 May with support coming from Sanford Evans, the leading Conservative.[60] Two weeks later, on 16 May, after last-minute efforts by the Conservatives to delay its passage, the legislature finally ratified the agreement and lease of Seven Sisters Falls to the Northwestern Power Company. The legislature prorogued on 17 May and the next day Major and Clubb were sworn back into office. With the signing of the White Mud lease by the federal government on 21 May, all the major power issues that had preoccupied Bracken's time and energies for the past eighteen months had been successfully concluded.

By June 1929 Bracken was anxious to put the cares of the province behind him for a few weeks and take a well-earned rest, but there was one key matter to attend to before he could relax completely. On Sunday, 23 June, the premier left for Ottawa to take part in the final discussions of the *Turgeon Commission Report on the Transfer of the Natural Resources to Manitoba.* To this point, Bracken had not been involved in the hearings, having left Manitoba's case in the hands of Craig and A.B. Hudson, the Winnipeg lawyer. The Manitobans had based their arguments on precedent – that in the past the self-governing colonies had been given control of their public lands. They argued that the first clause of the July agreement was the crux because it recognized the equality of Manitoba with the other provinces of Canada with respect to natural resources and stated that the principle should be applied from the date of Manitoba's entry into confederation in 1870. The Manitobans wanted the dominion government to continue the existing subsidy and to pay a lump sum compensation of approximately $6,000,000.[61]

The Turgeon Commission accepted most of Manitoba's arguments. In outlining its decision to King, Turgeon emphasized how complicated the resources question had become as a result of delay, the numerous proposals and counter-proposals, and the make-shift arrangements that had been tried. This had made the whole issue 'nearly impossible of clear, unanswerable solution. I mean that enough ammunition can be found in past records to attack any proposed solution from both sides.' The commission recommended the payment of a lump sum totalling $4,584,212.49 and the continuation of an annual subsidy.[62]

At the Ottawa conference King indicated immediately that he was prepared to accept the recommendations of the commission.[63] Bracken was equally agreeable, and it was decided that the formal drafting should be undertaken by the Department of Justice and the Department of the Interior in consultation with Craig and Hudson for Manitoba. The province's sixtieth anniversary, 15 July 1930, was agreed upon as the date of formal transfer.

On Saturday, 14 December 1929, the agreements on natural resources between Ottawa and Manitoba and Ottawa and Alberta were signed at the Parliament

Buildings. In keeping with the importance of the occasion the ceremony took place in the Privy Council chamber of the East Block where the proclamation of Confederation had been read on 1 July 1867. For King it was a symbolic occasion: 'This completes the real autonomy of those two Western provinces and gives them a fresh start, with additional assured financial assistance ... It is interesting that these agreements should have been made with Progressive governments. It should help to bring closer together Liberal and Progressive forces.'[64] Finally, on 15 July 1930 the natural resources of Manitoba were officially transferred by the Dominion of Canada in a ceremony at the Legislative Building. King gave Bracken a cheque for $4,700,000. Bracken, on receiving the resources, said it was the 'culmination of a long and tedious controversy which arose out of an unfortunate misunderstanding of Confederation days.'[65]

With the settlement of the resource question Bracken could finally relax. He badly needed a rest for he was still mentally and physically exhausted. The man who had loved to play practical jokes, who drove recklessly and much too fast, and who exulted in the chance to test his strength and athletic skills against younger men on the soccer and rugby fields was gradually being ground down by the restraints of public office and the remorseless toil it demanded of him. Middle-age was also taking its toll. In the twenties the opportunity to fly and travel the north had given him some respite and he had undoubtedly thrived on the exhilarating sense of freedom that flight in a small craft provides. But there had rarely been a prolonged absence from the legislature, the statistics, the board rooms, and the offices of Winnipeg.

During the last five months of 1929 Bracken had more opportunity to relax than he had had for years. The province was in sound financial shape, there was no important legislation pending, and all the major issues of the previous seven years had been resolved. Now was the time to get away. He took full advantage of it. Immediately after the successful Ottawa meeting of June 1929 he continued on to New York where he spent a short time with relatives. In July he spent a week at Battle Creek, having a check-up and receiving further advice on diet. Finally, on 13 September he left for Europe. He was away for two months.

The trip was essentially a well-deserved rest. Shortly before leaving he had indicated in an interview that he had a three-fold purpose in making the journey: to study the British contributory system of old-age pensions; to investigate the causes of Danish agricultural efficiency; and to look into European markets for Canadian barley.[66] In the event, he did spend some time talking with British civil servants about old-age pension schemes but he does not appear to have given any attention to agricultural conditions in Denmark or to European barley markets. Instead he played golf, visited the sights in Scotland, England, Holland, and France, and went to the theatre in London and Paris.[67]

He returned home on Sunday, 24 November, tanned, rested, and fully recovered from the vigours of the past two years. He was going to be in need of his good health. A month earlier the New York stock market had collapsed. North America and the world generally were on the brink of a devastating depression. Canada, and particularly her western provinces, were to feel its full impact.

8

'Work, Economy, Patience'

Bracken walked briskly up the steps of the Legislative Building on Monday morning, 25 November, refreshed from his two months overseas and eager to tackle the accumulated backlog of correspondence and administrative detail. Minutes after entering his office his euphoria dissipated and he was abruptly reminded of the stresses and difficulties that he had managed, for a time, to shut from his mind. On his desk he found a note from Robson, dated 23 November, curtly breaking off relations between the Liberals and the Progressives.[1]

Robson had never liked Bracken, and had only agreed to co-operate with him in order to prevent the Tories from forcing an election and to comply with King's federal interests. He had begun to question the wisdom of that decision during the summer. As his views became known there had been widespread talk about the need to get rid of both Bracken and Robson if fusion was ever to be achieved. Some doubted that the two parties could ever be merged under Bracken's leadership,[2] while others thought that both might have to go, perhaps Robson to the bench and Bracken into a major research post.[3]

There is some indication that before going overseas Bracken had been considering withdrawal from politics. Ed Brown, his predecessor as MLA for The Pas, had spoken to him about retirement and had concluded that a place on the National Research Council in Ottawa would appeal to him if he could take over as chairman after H.M. Tory retired. It is possible that in his weary condition Bracken did think of retirement but one cannot place too much faith in Brown's remarks, for he was convinced that Bracken should step down and was liable to interpret the premier's musings to his own advantage.[4] It is unlikely that Bracken seriously considered withdrawing from politics. Why should he? Despite all the difficulties of the past year he and his party were still in the driver's seat.

Contact between the two parties was at a minimum while Bracken was in Europe. King does not seem to have made any firm decisions about the Manitoba situation, although it is likely he was prepared to sound both men about retirement. If anything he recognized that Robson, more than Bracken, was the impediment to fusion and he was undoubtedly giving more thought to Robson's future than to Bracken's. It was suggested to him by Dr J.P. Howden, the Liberal MP from St Boniface, that Robson would adequately fill the vacancy on the Manitoba Court of Appeal. Howden even suggested that if such a move were made and if Ewen McPherson, the federal Liberal MP for Portage la Prairie, were to take Robson's place in the legislature, Bracken could include McPherson in the cabinet and groom him to take over as premier 'in a comparatively near future.' Howden thought such an arrangement would solve all the problems in Manitoba.[5]

Robson's letter of 23 November re-emphasized the gulf that divided the two men and caused considerable anxiety in both Manitoba and Ottawa. It had apparently been occasioned by Robson's belief that Bracken would not allow the Liberals a clear field in the forthcoming Mountain by-election unless the premier had absolute assurance that the Liberal elected would support the government at all times. Furthermore, Robson believed Bracken was not prepared to hold the by-election before the coming session. If that were so, the Liberal party was through with co-operation.

McKenzie, Hoey, Clubb, and Major had initially associated these actions with a recent visit to Winnipeg by King, but once the real reasons were established the four cabinet members were anxious to set matters right. They were prepared to call the by-election immediately and to support the Liberal candidate. They asked Dr Bissett, the MP for Springfield, who acted as intermediary with King throughout this episode: 'to impress as strongly as possible on Ottawa the fact that until Mr. Robson is put on the Bench, or otherwise disposed of politically, trouble, and serious trouble will constantly arise. Further, Mr. Robson's letter should be withdrawn ... It was suggested that I [Bissett] see Mr. Bracken, but knowing he would be in Ottawa shortly I decided not to. But rather lay the facts before you, knowing that you will see him personally. He is about as difficult to deal with sometimes as Mr. Robson ... All matters referred to in this letter I have fully discussed with Mr. Crerar, who is going to see Mr. Bracken regarding the Mountain by-election, and I feel certain that he can have the matter fixed up to the satisfaction of all concerned.'[6]

Meanwhile, in Ottawa, King was working hard to resolve a number of problems associated with the Manitoba situation which, he admitted to Howden, he found 'somewhat baffling.'[7] He finally had an opportunity to talk over the Manitoba political scene with Bracken on Friday evening, 13 December, the day before the two men signed the natural resources agreement. He later confided to his diary: 'I had Bracken to dinner with me tonight and we talked over Manitoba politics. He thinks Robson is weak, wd be better out for union of Libs and Progs., wd favour his going to bench – he himself wd be glad to take position in Int'l Research later on, not till after election, if he could get out honourably.'[8] A few weeks after this conversation Robson was appointed to the Manitoba Court of Appeal. He resigned as leader of the Manitoba Liberals on 3 January 1930 and from the Manitoba legislature a week later. The Mountain by-election was then called and Ivan Schultz was adopted as the Liberal nominee. Neither the Bracken party nor the Conservatives fielded candidates, and Schultz was declared elected by acclamation on 29 January in time to sit during the session. The Liberals decided not to select a successor to Robson immediately and the impetus for fusion languished. It was raised sporadically over the next eighteen months, but not until Bracken formally reopened the question with invitations to all parties in September 1931 did coalition once again become a major factor in Manitoba politics.[9]

By the time the difficulties with the Liberals had been sorted out it had become clear that much larger problems faced Manitoba than the personality conflict of two of its political leaders. Within a few weeks of the stock market crash in October it was obvious that Canada, the prairies, and Manitoba were enmeshed in a world-wide depression. Bracken began grappling with its ramifications long before the fusion issues were clarified. For the next ten years he was to think of little else. Its impact on Bracken and on the Manitoba political, economic, and social scene was considerable.

The depression that held Canada in its grip during the thirties was exacerbated on the prairies by one of the most prolonged dry spells in the continent's history. It began in 1929 and continued almost unabated for ten years. Drought, dust storms, grasshoppers, weeds, and rust would have been enough to cripple the prairie economy but these nightmare conditions coincided with a glut of wheat in other exporting countries and the erection of tariff walls around the traditional European markets. The price of wheat began to fall and by 1932 No 1 Northern at Fort William had plunged to thirty-four cents a bushel, the lowest price in 300 years. Although Manitoba was not as heavily dependent on the external wheat market as were Alberta and Saskatchewan, it still reeled under the impact of the general collapse. The prices for oats, barley, and other grains also plunged dramatically, so that the Manitoba farmer who had heeded Bracken's advice to diversify soon found himself trying to sell in a falling market. Low prices, prolonged drought in the southwestern section of the province, and increased unemployment in the scattered cities, towns, and villages caused severe strains on municipal revenues and forced Bracken and his colleagues to grapple with the basic economic and constitutional questions involved.

Bracken's initial concern was for the farmer. In dozens of speeches throughout the province Bracken outlined the causes of the current crisis, and advised his audiences to work, to economize, and to have patience. It was not a time for pessimism. What was needed was a 'frank facing of facts; a sympathetic approach to farmers' problems; and the cooperation of all in meeting the situation.' The West had survived birthpangs before and would do so again. It was not a question of whether or not the West would survive, but rather what the cost of survival would be in 'abandoned farms; thwarted hopes; bankruptcy; and pyramided debt.' It was a time for 'clear thinking; sane programs, economy in public and private undertakings; and efficiency in private life, municipal life, and government activities.'[10]

'What Canada needs is markets.' Bracken hammered at that refrain continuously during the early thirties. He was particularly disturbed by the deliberate high tariff policy of R.B. Bennett's Conservative government. To Bracken that more than anything demonstrated that the western farmer beset by falling prices, collapsing markets, and devastating drought still had to contend with policies designed to appease eastern manufacturing interests. He asked if the farmer had to carry the whole shock of the depression alone? Bracken realized that the farmer could not escape, but he needed help with the tariff from the federal government. For over forty years the Canadian tariff had led either to an increase in the cost of commodities or had prevented the lowering of costs; it had restricted trade and interfered with markets. It was not equitable. If there was to be a policy of restricted markets, then the farmer should be compensated at the national expense as the manufacturers were protected at the farmers' expense.[11]

In late November 1930 Bracken spoke at the Royal Winter Fair in Toronto. It was a frank statement of farm opinion and indicated that he had strong ideas about national policies. He was emerging in his careful, sincere fashion not only as the recognized spokesman for western farm interests but also as someone who realized the need to rise above sectional concerns in the establishment of federal policy: 'The West does not ask for sympathy only for understanding and a frank and thorough examination of the facts. It asks only for an equally frank and equally thorough and truly National policy – one aimed to cope with the Western situation in the best interests, not of Western Canada alone, nor of Eastern Canada alone, but in the best interests of Canada as a whole ... The question is whether or not the price shall be equitably borne by the Nation which framed and carried into effect the policies of over-development or whether it will be borne alone by that section of Canada which is now suffering but which is not the cause of its suffering.'[12] Bracken's response to the mounting difficulties of the depression did not change during the thirties. He continually called for economy, personal restraint, and a sharing of the burden. He argued that the most serious crisis in the economic history of the world could only be solved by intelligent planning and a general acceptance that sacrifices were necessary.

One of the earliest and most dramatic developments that confronted the western premiers during the depression was the sudden financial inability of the wheat pools to meet their obligations. In 1929 the pools had advanced their members $1.00 per bushel for No 1 Northern, basis Fort William. In financing these advances the pools had guaranteed the banks that the value of their wheat-holdings would always be 15 per cent greater than the total of their borrowings. Plunging world prices had now made that guarantee virtually impossible to uphold. In order to prevent the banks from forcing the pools to sell their grain on weak markets the governments of Manitoba, Saskatchewan, and Alberta agreed to guarantee the necessary 15 per cent margin.[13] This major commitment of February 1930 was an ominous sign of the perilous state of western agriculture. It was also an action accomplished with startling ease and a minimum of dissent. The three premiers met and decided to act, the details were then drawn up and agreed to, and the necessary legislation quickly passed.[14] In Manitoba even Fawcett Taylor and John Haig knew better than to be critical, although by 1931 they were to forget momentarily that they had in fact supported the Bracken government's action.

Throughout these negotiations Bracken did not play a leading part in the formulation of policy but he tended to act as spokesman for the three western premiers. He believed deeply in providing support for western agriculture and the necessity of protecting the western farmer. When speaking in support of the Pool Guarantee bill in the legislature on 27 February he explained that the action of the prairie governments would prevent a serious slump in wheat prices owing to possible forced selling on weak markets. He was convinced it would stabilize the market.[15] It is clear that no one, certainly not Bracken, expected prices to continue falling. They never imagined, for example, that they would ever have to make good their support of the pools because they never believed that the price of No 1 Northern at Fort William would fall below $1.00.[16] By the end of 1931 this illusion had been shattered and hard bargaining ensued with the federal government in an effort to have the dominion authorities bail out both the provinces and the pools. By late 1932 the pools were dead and the western provinces had to meet their obligations. For Manitoba the cost was $3,374,939.78.[17]

Besides showing a willingness to throw the backing of the state behind private enterprise in the interests of the western farmer, Bracken was also among the first to argue that in such calamitous times creditors would have to work out a reasonable and equitable arrangement with debtors rather than attempt to extract their pound of flesh. In September and October 1930 the Bracken government called two creditors' conferences to discuss the matter of debts.[18]

Bracken spoke at length on the rural position at the opening of the first meeting on 22 September and some of his remarks were quite revealing. He explained to the assembled representatives of the loan and credit institutions that the prices of agricultural products were lower than at any time since the war while the cost of living was much higher than before 1914. After paying the out-of-pocket expenses of producing the crop many farmers had little left to meet the necessities of life, let alone other obligations. The net value to the farmer of the wheat, oats, and barley that he produced was about one-third what it had been in 1928. Under these conditions 'undue pressure being exerted by the creditors will result in an even greater drift from the country to the city, and in some cases in abandonment of farms.'

Bracken made it clear that the Manitoba government recognized the rights of the creditors and had never interfered with those rights either by way of a moratorium or compulsory debt adjustment. 'We realise,' said Bracken, 'that if capital is invited here and its rights are arbitrarily interfered with that other capital will hesitate about coming in.' 'Nevertheless,' he went on, 'it is the Government's duty to interest itself in the welfare of the community as a whole. When we find an emergency situation develop then it becomes our duty to analyze it and to see whether greater justice to all cannot be done without serious injury to the community or to a section of the community.' Now, the government did not contemplate any revolutionary solutions such as a moratorium and it had no faith in overnight panaceas, but it was capable of recognizing brute reality: 'the operation of competitive collection agencies at this time might do great harm, unless tempered with reason and some kind of cooperation.' To Bracken it was obviously impossible to adopt laissez-faire attitudes in such an emergency situation. He asked the creditors to consider the establishment of either a debt adjustment bureau with legislative powers or a voluntary agency, possibly a government board, to referee in cases brought before it.[19]

While this first meeting was profitable it was decided a second was needed with both farm and creditor representatives in attendance. It was held on 17 October. Again Bracken spoke, this time even more ominously, about the worsening economic situation. He emphasized the need for co-operation between farmer and creditor in order to avoid mass abandonment of farms. It was not a question of asking the creditor to take losses, though that might be necessary in many cases, nor was it a question of writing off a portion of the farmers' debts, though in some cases that might be wise. The problem was how to help keep men on the land; how to lessen unemployment in the cities; and how to save the agricultural industry intact until the depression passed. The international market was outside Canada's control, but what was within their control was the efficiency of the production and marketing machinery: 'Personally,' said Bracken, 'I am convinced that whether Mr. Bennett plans to help us or make our burden heavier it will be in our own interest to *Roll up our sleeves. Tighten our belts. Loosen our coats.*

Make ourselves more efficient ... outside the question of markets we shall have to *save ourselves*.'[20] The result of these two meetings was the establishment of a voluntary debt adjustment bureau with A.E. Darby, secretary of the Canadian Council of Agriculture, as director.

Bracken's actions revealed that while he was prepared to use the government's authority to persuade the creditors to react sensibly to a sensitive and difficult problem he was not yet willing to intervene arbitrarily. It would have been uncharacteristic of Bracken to tamper so critically with business interests. Not only was he anxious to preserve the province's credit in order that it could continue to raise loans to meet its obligations, but temperamentally he shrank from tinkering with the basic mechanism of capitalism. As he put it in 1931 after a further conference: 'It was the feeling of the meeting that if there were no interference with the operation of ordinary economic laws the situation would right itself more quickly and more fairly than it would if temporary and more or less unsound measures were resorted to. It was considered that arbitrary or radical measures at this time would not only work out inequitably but do more harm than good.'[21]

In addition to the problems facing the western farmer a major concern for Bracken in the early thirties was unemployment. From late 1929 the premier grappled with a steady increase in the numbers of unemployed dependent upon municipal and provincial resources. Unemployment had not been much of a problem during the twenties and the Bracken administration had only occasionally had to face a responsibility in that area.[22] Nevertheless, Bracken had firmly believed for some years that the federal government should share in the costs of unemployment relief since federal tariff and immigration policies were at the root of many of the West's unemployment difficulties. The breakdown of the social structure in the early thirties and the worsening of the unemployment picture only hardened his views. He became a major critic of federal policies, particularly those of the Bennett government. He also, in his pragmatic fashion, began to alter his opinions about the role of the state. He continued to believe in hard work and, if anything, grew more resentful of slackers, but it was obvious that no matter how anxious men were to work, work was not to be had, either on the farm or in the city. People could not be left to starve. The state would have to assume more of the burden.

It would be wrong, however, to leave the impression that Bracken became a saviour of the people or that he was breaking with his own past or society's norms. In general, his response was predictably restrained and conservative. The rising costs of unemployment relief were met by increasing taxes, cutting civil service salaries, and eliminating capital expenditures. During his last three years as provincial treasurer, 1930-2, Bracken exercised tight budget control. His primary aim was to balance the budget. By 1932 he was close to achieving this, but only by paying for rising direct relief costs with the money received from the federal government at the time of the natural resources transfer. Also, he strongly favoured a programme of public works as a means of providing employment and he and his ministers constantly provided the Bennett government with lengthy lists of public works projects. Since the capital had to come from the federal government, not many were undertaken, but the Salter Street Bridge, the Norwood Bridge, the Auditorium, and the science building at the University of Manitoba were a few of the large-scale projects initiated at that time. Bracken's support for public works projects was in line with later Keynesian thinking but it is doubtful that Bracken approached the problem from that perspective. He was more concerned that people earn the money the state provided rather than simply receive it for nothing.

Bracken was first confronted with the unemployment problem in a personal way on 20 December 1929 when three hundred unemployed men walked from Market Square to the Legislative Building to appeal for assistance. He met them in the rotunda at the foot of the grand stairway and promised that the government would do everything possible to help.[23] In January he wrote to King in Ottawa pointing out that the unemployment situation was becoming 'acute' and was causing 'considerable agitation.' He claimed that the unemployment problem was largely a federal one and required federal government participation before a cure could be effected. King disagreed: 'We feel very strongly that this is a municipal and a provincial matter and, in no sense, one of federal obligation.' If it turned out that the provinces and the municipalities could not cope with their unemployment problems, then the federal government would consider what to do. Until that time no action would be justified by Ottawa. This remained Liberal policy until the July election when they were defeated by the Conservatives under Bennett.[24]

Throughout the winter of 1929-30 the Bracken government assisted municipalities in providing work by paying one-third of the excess cost of winter work over summer work and by assuming one-half the cost of administration and transportation and one-quarter that of direct relief such as the supply of food and shelter. During the summer various construction programmes were speeded up in order to provide employment. It was clear by then, however, that Manitoba could not long continue to bear the burden alone. The federal government would have to become involved.[25] In a meeting with municipal representatives in September Bracken asserted that the responsibility was 'very largely if not wholly federal.' In his opinion the municipalities should not bear the brunt nor even a major portion of the cost of relief.[26]

In a special session of parliament in September the Bennett government passed the Unemployment Relief Act appropriating $20,000,000 to be spent throughout the dominion. While welcoming Bennett's initiative and hoping to obtain as much as $2,000,000 for Manitoba, Bracken had one serious criticism. It was apparent that the federal government would pay out monies for public works only on the understanding that the municipalities would borrow and spend double the amount spent by either the province or the dominion. Similarly, the provinces would be expected to go into debt for an amount equal to that spent by the dominion. The ratio would be 50:25:25.[27]

Bracken pointed out that if that policy were rigidly adhered to the majority of municipalities in Manitoba would be unable to participate in the federal appropriations. Every million dollars the provincial government or the municipalities borrowed would take $50,000 a year for fifty years to pay off. This would mean a vast increase in taxes at both the municipal and provincial levels. The Manitoba government, said Bracken, would go to Ottawa 'prepared to pay dollar for dollar with the Dominion on the understanding that the Municipalities shall not be asked to go further into debt in order to participate in the Dominion cooperation.'[28]

As a result of a conference in Ottawa on 30 September Manitoba was allocated $900,000 for public works in Winnipeg and rural municipalities. The money was to be spent primarily on bridges over the Red and Assiniboine Rivers in Winnipeg, a drainage scheme in Winnipeg and adjacent municipalities, and roads and general public works projects throughout the province. The federal government did agree to reduce the rural municipalities' commitment to 20 per cent while assuming 50 per cent itself for the designated projects, but for all the other schemes the major financial costs had to be assumed by the municipalities and the province. In most instances the provincial government was obliged to match the dominion dollar for dollar. The dominion also agreed to pay one-third of the expenditures of municipalities for direct relief, where suitable work could not be provided for the unemployed, and one-half of direct relief in unorganized districts. Again the province was to match dominion expenditures dollar for dollar.

Bracken was under no illusions about these arrangements. He and his colleagues had recognized before going to Ottawa 'that spending public money was no cure for unemployment ... what the West needed was a market for its agricultural products.' Although willing to co-operate in Bennett's relief schemes, Bracken emphasized that there was little new in them. In requiring the provinces to pay dollar for dollar and insisting on significant municipal involvement, the federal government was 'forcing the major part of the burden onto provinces and municipalities.'[29]

As it turned out the work provided in the province by the Unemployment Relief Act barely touched the fringe of the unemployment problem. Bracken wrote to Bennett in January 1931 emphasizing that employment was at a very low ebb in Manitoba. The new year had begun with forty-two cities, towns, or municipalities resorting to direct relief measures and with 15,513 individuals receiving relief in the province. Bracken requested that the federal government assume 80 per cent of the cost of direct relief in both financially straitened unorganized districts and in organized municipalities. He also called Bennett's attention to the extreme conditions in the urban centres, particularly Winnipeg which was having to provide relief for many non-residents who had drifted into the city from various parts of the West. There were over 4000 single men being given meal and bed tickets daily in Winnipeg alone and in addition nearly 2000 families on relief. Bracken urged greater federal assistance.[30]

By late April there had been no reply from Bennett, so Bracken wrote again indicating that the situation was growing worse. A demonstration of some 6000 at the Legislative Building on 16 April underlined that there were 19,000 unemployed in the Winnipeg area affecting a total of 56,000 people. And this did not include those unemployed in other parts of the province. The work in sight would only take care of 1000 men. Bracken did not wish to be overly pessimistic but the unemployment problem was likely to be much worse in the coming autumn and winter. The municipalities had virtually exhausted their efforts to deal with local difficulties while the province's finances were such that it could not enter upon any large new undertakings.[31]

By June Bracken was pointing out that the unemployment situation was 'becoming more and more a national one.' He argued that 'the burden of the economic depression is falling upon Western agriculture to a greater degree than upon other industries, and in my opinion municipalities of Manitoba and the Province itself are paying a greater share of the cost of this National problem than they should be called upon to pay, and indeed cannot continue to do so without financial embarassment.'[32] Bracken's views were endorsed by a meeting of municipal representatives on 17 June and conveyed to Senator G.D. Robertson at a special meeting in Winnipeg later in the month.[33]

The Bennett government's Unemployment and Farm Relief Act finally passed the House in August and a conference was arranged for the 25th in Ottawa to discuss Manitoba's provincial and municipal undertakings and the degree of federal involvement. Clubb, the minister of public works, went east to meet with Robertson, and Bracken discussed matters with Bennett, Robert Weir, the minister of agriculture, and Thomas Murphy, the minister of the interior, in Winnipeg on 29 and 30 August. Manitoba wanted a twenty-million dollar programme of which sixteen million would be joint undertakings and four million straight federal grants. The government also urged the necessity of agricultural relief as well as unemployment relief, and requested that the drought area in southwestern Manitoba be treated in exactly the same manner as southern Saskatchewan. Manitoba also wanted co-operation from the dominion government in providing additional assistance to keep rural schools open ten months a year. The inability of the prairie provinces to finance 25 per cent of old-age pensions because of crop failure was also pointed out and the dominion was asked to assume the full cost.[34]

Travers Sweatman, a Conservative and a long-time critic of Bracken, interpreted these demands to mean that Bracken was getting ready to fight an election by blaming the federal government for Manitoba's difficulties. He advised Bennett to beware of him.[35] It is unlikely that Bracken had been thinking about an election at that time, but after Clubb's talks with Robertson in Ottawa, and his own with Bennett, Weir, and Murphy in Winnipeg he did begin to give serious thought to a political solution to his government's problems. It was clear from the talks that Bennett was opposed to a federal invasion of the provincial field. If it did have to intervene, said Bennett, the province would have to revert to territorial status and an administrative committee would have to be appointed. Bennett insisted that there was no obligation on the federal government to assume larger responsibilities.[36]

The assistance offered by the federal government was much less than expected. They agreed to pay 50 per cent of the cost of relief works outside Winnipeg and a minimum of 35 per cent inside the city while paying 50 per cent of direct relief. While an improvement on the previous arrangement, Bracken considered it insufficient. Municipal and provincial financial resources were limited and could not be stretched very far. Work on relief projects during the coming winter would have to be drastically curtailed. Similarly, the federal government had not heeded Bracken's pleas on behalf of southwestern Manitoba. Although it was evident by August that there would be a severe crop failure in the area, the Bennett government refused to consider these municipalities on a par with Saskatchewan. Instead, it recommended road work in the area as the best means of alleviating distress. The Bennett government also refused to assume the costs of old-age pensions and was only prepared to loan money to aid weak school districts.[37]

In a letter to all the western premiers on 4 September, Bennett reiterated that 'any effort on the part of the Dominion to undertake the direction of purely provincial or municipal undertakings would be in derogation of the constitutional rights of the provinces.' Nevertheless, he slightly changed the percentage of dominion contributions. In addition to its own undertakings and its assistance to provincial activities, the federal government would contribute 50 per cent of the cost of approved relief undertakings in cities and towns and loan to the provinces the additional 50 per cent, leaving the responsibility to the provinces of making satisfactory arrangements with the cities and towns about their contributions. All this assumed the cities and towns would deliver their bonds to the province as security and that treasury bills of the province would be delivered to the federal government for 50 per cent of the amount loaned.[38]

As far as Bracken was concerned these actions did not resolve the basic problem. The burden on the municipalities and on the province was still intolerable. Over the next few weeks he stepped up his criticisms of the Bennett government and endeavoured to ease or redistribute the burdens in the province. He wiped out the land tax and cut down provincial hydro rates in thirty towns. These actions, coupled with his cut of rural telephone rates earlier in the year, helped relieve individual difficulties in the rural areas.

A year earlier he had called for departmental economies, now on 1 September he resorted to the first of a series of civil service salary cuts. In making the announcement to the press Bracken said the government believed those with jobs should 'bear their proper share of the burden of the depression.'[39] As a further means of reducing costs and balancing the budget, he decided that the government would make no further capital expenditures except for carrying out existing unemployment relief schemes; that no new services of any kind would be authorized; that no new grants would be made for any purpose; that there would be no further appointments to the civil service; and that there would be no further salary increases to anyone until it was possible to give equal consideration to all.[40] These came into effect on 30 October 1931. On that date Bracken wrote to each of his ministers about the necessity for large reductions in expenditures both in the current year and the year commencing 1 May 1932. He asked for every possible reduction to be made 'forthwith.'[41]

The cuts continued over the winter. In December a five- instead of a six-day week was substituted for cleaning staff, and on 2 January Bracken called on his ministers to effect economies in travelling expenses, the use of telegraphs and telephones, and the use of government automobiles. Later in the month a further 6 per cent cut was made in cabinet and civil service salaries.

Bracken considered this increasingly stringent economic programme essential if he were to have any hope of balancing the budget or of stabilizing the province's plunging credit rating. But he also knew that it would be preferable to have a united political front in order to deal with both Bennett and the bankers. Consequently, in late September 1931 he invited the Liberals, the Conservatives, and the Labour leaders to form a union government to cope with the critical situation in the province arising from unemployment, agricultural depression, and straitened municipal and provincial finances.

Despite the bitterness and misunderstanding surrounding the collapse of coalition negotiations in late 1929, Bracken had never abandoned the hope that one day the Progressives and Liberals in Manitoba would fuse. He and his colleagues had kept in touch with the Liberal leaders, particularly after Bennett's victory. The triumph of a high-tariff group had seemed to underline the necessity of not splitting the low-tariff forces. In June 1931 the Liberals had chosen Dr Murdoch Mackay (Springfield) as their new leader and had left the door open for co-operation with the government. Crerar, as always, was in the thick of things, and he informed King that 'Bracken understands the situation and is apparently very anxious to cooperate ... while the provincial Tories are finding the growing unpopularity of Bennett a load, growing steadily heavier to carry.'[42]

Bracken's reasons for reopening formal negotiations with the other parties in September were two-fold. Firstly, he recognized that Manitoba's financial circumstances had become severe by late 1931 and that the province's relationship with the Bennett administration was strained. If all Manitoba political parties could approach these problems on a united non-party basis Bennett would have a more difficult time rebuffing their ideas and overtures. Secondly, as Crerar pointed out to King, Bracken probably wanted to put the provincial Conservatives in an awkward position. If they rejected his offer, as he expected them to do, then he would be able to say later that they had put party ahead of the interest of the province. In turn, he hoped a Conservative refusal would lead to an organic union between the Liberals and his party.[43]

In placing his suggestion before the leaders of the other parties for the abolition of party government, Bracken reasoned that in a time of economic crisis a radical change in administration was required, and that efficiency and economy in government would be furthered by abolishing partisanship. The details of the proposal were as follows: the union government would be made up of two representatives of the Conservative party, one from the Liberal party, one from the Independent Labour party, and four members of the existing government. All adherents would be committed to the elimination of party government in the province for five years. An amendment to the Legislative Assembly Act would be required to make such a government possible and would postpone a provincial election until such time as the legislature decided.[44]

Bracken acknowledged that he and his colleagues risked misrepresentation as a result of the offer but 'that price public men have always had to face, and no doubt always will. My associates in the cabinet and I chose to risk misrepresentation. We chose the way our best judgement dictated. It was not an easy choice to make. It was not a selfish one. It was made in the hope that energies now directed to partisan advantage and government defence might at this time be directed to more constructive purposes. It was made because we felt it would enable the legislature to try a united effort and not a divided one to the solution of our problems.'[45]

The response of the Conservatives and of Labour was predictable. Taylor immediately refused to have anything to do with the scheme and suggested that if Bracken felt so uncertain about his government's capacity to handle the affairs of the province he should call an election. John Queen said his group would have nothing to do with participating in a government formed for the purpose of reducing expenses by reducing wages and by curtailing the amounts paid to widows for child welfare and unemployment relief.[46]

Interestingly, the *Tribune*, not a staunch Bracken supporter, admitted the plan had merit in the abnormal times facing the province. There was good reason why party lines should be abolished and the best men and energies of all the parties united to provide Manitoba with sound government. Reminding its readership of the recent British example, the *Tribune* stated there were times when patriotic considerations must override the supposed merit of the party system. The *Tribune* shrewdly pointed out that even if the Conservatives did win in the next election, which they obviously thought they would do, theirs would not be an easy row to hoe. Any government in Manitoba over the next two years, regardless of its complexion, would be forced to do many unpopular things. Expenditures would have to be cut unsparingly and taxation would have to be increased to take care of extraordinary expenses. The editorial concluded:

The best brains we have should be in position of responsibility, and we have no time for party warfare. Men and women of vision and understanding in Manitoba regardless of party affiliations will support the union government proposal because it is in the public interest.

The party leaders will do well to give this situation most careful consideration.[47]

The plan was widely discussed throughout the province over the next few weeks. Although it was clear that many in both the Conservative and Labour rank-and-file sympathized with Bracken's viewpoint, neither party changed its stance. Only the Liberals continued to show interest. Taylor made a number of speeches critical of Bracken, and the premier took Taylor and the Conservatives to task for pursuing narrow political ends while the province was in difficulty. Crerar's predictions were proving true.[48]

On 17 October in a major speech to government supporters and business and financial leaders Bracken announced that there would be no election until 1932. This disposed of all the rumours about an early election that had been circulating throughout the province. He also took the opportunity to lambaste Taylor and the Conservatives pointing out that many thousands of dollars could have been saved the province by the adoption of non-partisan politics. Bracken was not as critical of Labour, sympathizing as he did with their humanitarian position. But he argued that all services in the province would have to share in the burden during difficult times. He was scathing of Taylor's promises to balance the budget when no budget in the world was being balanced. He accused Taylor of making political capital out of the depression. He said neither the Conservatives nor Labour had a lien on administrative efficiency or humanitarian instinct. No budget would be balanced at the expense of widows, orphans, aged people, the sick, or the unemployed nor by placing the whole additional burden on the tax-paying public. Both Conservatives and Labour knew that reductions would be made where they would cause no undue social maladjustment and additional revenues would have to come from where they could most easily be borne. He accused both leaders of being afraid of sharing the responsibility of making cuts and raising revenues. It was a scathing attack and one to which there was no adequate response, although Taylor continued to splutter in pretended indignation for some weeks.[49]

By November it was clear that the Liberals under Mackay were favourably inclined toward coalition, but before serious negotiations could begin Bracken had to deal with the rapidly disintegrating financial situation in the province. It had been evident since October that Manitoba was in severe straits. It was experiencing difficulty floating loans either with the Canadian banks or on the New York money market. The abandonment of the gold standard by the British and the decision of the Ottawa government to maintain the value of the Canadian dollar made it virtually impossible for Manitoba, without refinancing help, to meet its maturing obligations, and by late October Bracken was enquiring whether the federal government was prepared to assist the province refinance maturing issues.[50] It also became necessary for Bracken to press the federal government to forward monies to Winnipeg, as loans, to cover provincial and municipal relief expenditures.[51] Bracken found this continual recourse to Ottawa and to Bennett frustrating but he was careful to be polite in public statements.[52]

By December Manitoba's financial situation was grave. Unless Ottawa advanced both the dominion and provincial share of direct relief it would be impossible for the Manitoba government to finance it. Although all capital expenditures for purposes other than unemployment relief projects had been discontinued, the government still required $683,000 to meet commitments. The government had also estimated that the province would require overdraft privileges of $3,500,000. The province's bankers had agreed to an overdraft of $2,500,000, leaving the province to obtain $1,000,000 in some other manner. Manitoba also had the following maturing obligations to meet: on 15 January 1932 at the Royal Bank of Canada in New York a treasury bill of the province for $2,000,000; on 15 February 1932 at the Bank of Montreal in Winnipeg a treasury bill for $320,000; on 1 May 1932 at the Royal Bank in Winnipeg treasury bills totalling $1,627,000; and between December 1931 and May 1932 Manitoba Farm Loan Association bonds for $300,000. It was also becoming clear that the Provincial Savings Office was in a weakened position, having lost $1,500,000 to the National Service Loan and with an overdraft of about $1,300,000.[53]

Bracken and R. McN. Pearson, the deputy provincial treasurer, went east in early December to try and arrange additional financing for the province.[54] Bracken met initially in Montreal with Morris Wilson, the general manager of the Royal Bank, on 7 December, then with Edgar Rhodes, the minister of finance, in Ottawa on the 8th. On Wilson's suggestion Bracken asked the dominion for assistance on both the capital requirement of $683,000 and the current account requirements of one million, but Rhodes was not sympathetic. After returning to Winnipeg Bracken wrote at length to Rhodes pointing out how difficult it was for Manitoba to raise further loans. The American money markets would not take a public offering either by the dominion or any of the provinces, and the Canadian market was not prepared to absorb a public offering by any of the western provinces for a considerable time in the future. Bracken asked the federal government to loan Manitoba an amount sufficient to enable it to refinance its maturing obligations; the amount necessary to cover the provincial and municipal share of direct relief; the $683,000 for capital purposes; and to request 'one or other of the banks doing Provincial business to arrange additional overdraft privileges to the extent of $1,000,000,' so that the province could continue to make prompt payment of its obligations on ordinary account until such time as it was possible 'to bring about a complete budgetary balance.'[55]

On 18 December Bracken asked to see Bennett personally with respect to unemployment and financial problems which, he asserted, had reached 'the stage of possible embarrassment if not dealt with immediately.' Bracken, Bennett, and Rhodes met in Ottawa on 22 December and went over Manitoba's difficulties.[56] Bennett still refused to make any promises and had not done so by the time he left on New Year's day for the West despite another telegram from Bracken indicating that the province would cease all expenditures for direct relief unless Ottawa agreed to help.[57]

That the situation in Manitoba was strained was underlined by Ralph Webb, the mayor of Winnipeg and a strong supporter of Bennett, in a telegram to the prime minister: 'Situation here most intense. Apparently Government can do nothing and bankers will not. Urge you to stop off here for day or night to see what can be done to clear air on Government's financial position which effects ours.'[58] Despite this plea Bennett refused to interfere in 'local government's business.'[59]

Bracken believed there was an element of bluff in Bennett's attitude. The premier knew that some of the local Tories were advising Bennett to remain obdurate, even to the point of forcing default, so that they could seize power in the ensuing crisis. Bracken was determined to prevent this and during late December and the early days of January he worked feverishly with the help of Crerar and Joe Thorson, the former MP for Winnipeg South Centre, to finalize a fusion of Liberals and Progressives.

He had the sympathy of Dafoe and Harry Sifton, Clifford's son, who was a lawyer with the Armadale Corporation in Toronto. The latter thought Bracken had a good case and should take it straight to the people. The public should be made aware that though the wealth of the nation came from the farms and the forests, Canada's fiscal policy was designed to put the producers of wealth at a disadvantage compared with the manufacturing industries and their allied forces. Industry, feeling the pinch, dumped its workers onto the generosity of the state. The businessman then complained that the provincial governments were not balancing their budgets. 'Bracken's cue,' said Sifton, 'should be to *fight* openly, frankly and generously.'[60]

Bracken, Crerar, and Thorson were in almost continuous session at the turn of the year preparing a letter to be sent to Mackay. Although Bracken often found Crerar rather too inclined to give advice, he recognized his importance in the federal party and was happy to rely on his judgment on this occasion. As for Thorson, he was a powerful figure in Manitoba Liberal circles and his opinions were valuable.[61] Separate drafts of the letter were prepared by both Thorson and Crerar on 2 January, and after these had been threshed out Thorson prepared two more, one on 5 January and another on the 6th. Bracken went over them all very carefully and his final draft was based on the best phrasing and thoughts of Thorson and Crerar plus his own ideas.[62]

In his letter Bracken thanked Mackay for his offer of co-operation and invited the Liberal party to unite its forces with the government's 'in order to further the best interests of the Province.' Bracken cited the worsening economic conditions as the main reason for the creation of a coalition. He admitted he would have preferred that the Conservative and Labour parties had been agreeable and he made it clear he would welcome them if they changed their minds. In the meantime, the Liberals would be given larger representation in the cabinet than originally suggested. Bracken emphasized the need to maintain a balanced budget, to re-establish agriculture on a more profitable basis, and 'to find a way to bring about greater security of employment for our citizens.' He suggested that cabinet re-organization wait until after the session.

Mackay and the Liberals were agreeable and negotiations were opened almost immediately between the two groups. It was generally known by early January that Bracken was prepared to take two or three Liberals into the cabinet.[63] It was also clear that the proposal would meet with strong opposition from the 'diehard' group within the Liberal party which was now much better organized than in previous years. By the time Bracken's letter had been released to the press on

8 January the 'die-hards' had swung into action. A central committee of sixty had been organized in Winnipeg to which had been added at least twenty rural representatives. The 'die-hard' faction intended to go to the annual meeting of the Manitoba Liberal Association on Tuesday, 12 January, and attempt to put over a three-part programme: official rejection of any proposals for union with the present government; election of its own slate of officers for the Manitoba Liberal Association; and the replacement of Mackay as provincial leader. Failing this the 'die-hards' would organize a new Manitoba Liberal party. Thus the stage was set for a major confrontation on 12 January at the Fort Garry Hotel. It was especially piquant because Mackenzie King, privately favourable to fusion, was to arrive in the city at 9:00 AM on the 12th and address both a luncheon meeting and the banquet in the evening.

While the Liberals were preparing for their crucial meeting, Bennett disembarked from his CPR train at Brandon where he was met by a number of Manitoba Tories. In the drive to Winnipeg they attempted to persuade him not to loan Bracken any more money for direct relief. Bennett was admittedly angered by the Manitoba premier's frequent criticisms of his policies but he was not prepared to be persuaded so easily. After lengthy conversations with Mayor Webb and Bracken – who had arisen from a sick-bed – on Saturday, 9 January, he decided that Manitoba had to be helped. He ignored the advice of the local Tories and agreed to loan the province sufficient funds to cover the costs of direct relief for the last four months of 1931 and to meet maturing obligations in New York on 15 January.[64] Temporarily relieved, Bracken returned to bed to nurse his cold and to await the results of the Liberal convention.

Heavy snowfall had blanketed Manitoba for some days and many of the country delegates had difficulty getting to the Fort Garry on Tuesday. Nevertheless, the meeting opened as scheduled at 9:00 AM. Mackay recommended to the convention that the Manitoba Liberal Association accept Bracken's offer of a union government. In the three-hour debate that followed Thorson and Crerar spoke vigorously and at length in favour of fusion while Fred Hamilton, E.J. McMurray, and others of the 'die-hard' camp were critical of Bracken's record and his handling of current problems and warned of the dangers for Liberalism if the Manitoba Liberal party was absorbed by the Brackenites. Two amendments, one urging that the coalition proposal be laid over for six months, and the other questioning the right of the convention to deal with the matter, were overwhelmingly defeated. By a majority of approximately three to one the convention endorsed the recommendation that the Bracken and Liberal parties unite in coalition after the forthcoming provincial election.[65]

Although Mackenzie King made no public statement about coalition while in Winnipeg, he did talk with Bracken and a number of Manitoba Liberals, among them Crerar, Dafoe, Hudson, Frank Fowler, J.S. McDiarmid, and Thorson.[66] He considered the decision to merge the Liberal and Progressive forces in the province 'a good move. Some of the die-hards don't like it, but it will help both provincially and federally.' On Thursday, 14 January, King saw Bracken in his bedroom at 604 Stradbrooke, and later jotted his impressions into his diary: '... had a talk with Bracken who was laid up in bed. He will try to make the Coalition a success, says Bennett has been harder on Manitoba than on other provinces ... He thinks they will get over the financial difficulties but feels they are considerable. Believes Bennett favors National Govt. – tried to get his following in Manitoba to go in with Bracken on that basis but they wd. not ... The whole Winnipeg visit had been a great success ... I believe the impression made will mark a real advance forward, especially accompanied as the week was by the acceptance by the Liberals of Bracken's offer of three to go into his government. Bracken himself appears to be the real difficulty. If Crerar could get that post as Premier and get Ewen McPherson and Thorson to go in with him it wd. be the best possible step at present.'[67] Bracken was naturally pleased by the Liberal decision and interpreted it as evidence of the desire of most Manitobans to solve economic problems rather than to strengthen partisan positions.[68]

During the next few weeks the Brackenites and the Liberals attempted to work out the details of their new relationship, the five Liberal MLAs sided with the government in the session, and the 'die-hards' organized a Continuing Liberal Association. It was at that time that Bracken made his appeal for a union government of the three prairie provinces arguing that expenditures and unnecessary triplication should be reduced in the interests of economy. It is hard to know how seriously Bracken considered his suggestion. Perhaps it was meant to demonstrate to Bennett how parlous matters were in the West. It met with a mixed reaction and soon died a natural death.[69]

Bracken did not have long to dwell on the successful fusion of Liberals and Progressives. Barely had he emerged from his sick-bed when his government was faced with the possible collapse of the Provincial Savings Office. Bracken had known since December that the bank had a heavy over-draft and no adequate backing. He had hoped it would be able to ride out its temporary shortage. But the news that two treasury officials had stolen considerable sums from provincial funds and the general knowledge that Manitoba was in difficult financial straits had led to the circulation of rumours in early January that the bank was on the verge of collapse.[70] This started a run on the bank. Despite a personal attempt by Bracken to reassure the long lines of people waiting to withdraw their money, the run continued.

In late January Bracken and E.K. Williams, a legal adviser to the government and a close friend of Bracken, went east to confer with Montreal banking interests and with Bennett in an effort to restore the office's stability and prevent its collapse. The bankers told Bracken they were prepared to loan the dominion government any amount necessary to cover deposits, provided the dominion would reloan it to the province and guarantee the total.[71] Bennett refused to consider such a guarantee on the grounds that Bracken and Williams had indicated to him on 27 January that they preferred the office to close. Bracken vehemently denied Bennett's interpretation of that meeting. Far from wanting to see the office close, Bracken had wanted it to stay open. The province could not provide the monies itself. It was in a difficult position over the wheat pool guarantees and it was unable, despite rigid economies, to meet provincial and municipal expenditures for unemployment relief. It had therefore turned to the banks and the federal government for help.[72]

The immediate result of Bennett's refusal to help was Bracken's decision to inform patrons of the office that henceforth they would be obliged to give thirty days notice of withdrawal. He did this reluctantly, fully realizing that it probably meant the end of the office. Before he could act, however, Bennett intervened. Under pressure from the banks, the prime minister agreed to guarantee the banks if they covered deposits transferred from the Savings Office to their accounts. This action infuriated Bracken and many others in Manitoba who interpreted it as federal support for the private sector during a time of stress for both the provincial government and the public sector. No action better exemplified the degree to which the private banks dictated to governments during the depression. To many in Manitoba and the West it was yet another example of the close relationship between the Bennett government and the financial interests of central Canada.

Despite his annoyance Bracken had no alternative but to comply. The Provincial Savings Office closed on 19 February 1932 and a bill enabling the funds to be transferred passed the legislature in March.[73] A Special Legislative Committee was appointed to investigate the operation of the office and the origins of the rumours. The report exonerated Bracken and the government of all mishandling charges and placed the blame for the rumours on a number of indiscreet or malicious-minded individuals of whom two were the prominent Conservatives Errick Willis and John Haig.[74] The whole experience left Bracken exasperated and embittered and more willing than ever to be critical of Bennett and his administration.

In the following weeks Bracken continued to grapple with the province's general financial problems. Despite the commitment by Bennett to assist Manitoba, reaffirmed in further meetings in late January, it took continual reminders and pressure from Bracken until May to ensure that the money was forwarded for the purposes of covering direct relief commitments and maturing obligations.

Bracken must have wondered more than once if Bennett would have given a Conservative provincial government the same treatment.

The 1932 legislative session was Bracken's last as treasurer. His budget reflected the worsening conditions in the province. He had resorted to vigorous measures. He cut expenditures a further one million dollars. He repealed the child welfare tax on land ($325,000) and the soldiers tax relief levy against land ($90,000). He provided for new levies on the sales of liquor, cigarettes, cigars, and tobacco, and he slightly increased business taxes. But the bite really came in the personal income tax area. The exemptions for married couples and householders was reduced to $1500; for single persons to $750; and for dependents to $300. The 20 per cent discount on all personal income was removed and there was an across-the-board raise in personal income tax of one-half per cent. Gasoline taxes were raised from five to six cents a gallon, and rebates reduced from five to three cents a gallon.

Bracken said he found no pleasure in proposing either the reductions or the tax increases, but the aim of the government was to maintain essential services. It had tried to be reasonable. 'We,' he said, 'have endeavoured to place the burden as uniformly as possible having regard both to the ability to pay and the responsibilities of citizenship ... The conditions demand rational treatment, the courage to make unpopular decisions, a sacrifice on the part of many, and tolerance on the part of all.' 'Any modern state,' said Bracken, 'has the option of paying its way or of having deficits. We have chosen to pay our way. No responsible administration would decide otherwise.'[75]

Bracken had often spoken of the need to share the burdens of the depression, but as the *Free Press* pointed out many low-income people would now be paying tax who had never paid before. It seemed to be hitting those least able to absorb the blow. Moreover, it was patently an urban tax, for the lowered exemptions, the abolition of the flat 20 per cent reduction, and the ½ per cent increase would hurt the low-income bracket urban dweller more than either the farmer or the high-income bracket.[76] These taxes coupled with the lowering of mothers' allowance in February[77] revealed the essential business orientation of the Bracken government. It believed that the free market system should not be too over-burdened if it was going to be able to respond to the depression.

While Bracken had been wrestling with the province's finances, discussions between the Liberals and the Progressives had continued and by February a joint committee of five Liberals and five Progressives had been formed to discuss strategy for the approaching election. It was given full powers. Meetings were held on the weekend of 13 and 14 February and according to Thorson the two groups worked 'harmoniously together, making considerable progress in the matter of organisation for the coming campaign.' It was decided to open an office and meet on a regular basis.[78] Over the next few weeks Thorson, Crerar, Hoey, and Bracken worked out the details of the coalition. It was during those meetings that J.S. McDiarmid, Ewen McPherson, and Murdoch Mackay were agreed upon as the Liberal members of the cabinet.[79]

The three men joined the government on 27 May 1932, and the election was finally held on 16 June with two deferred elections – The Pas and Rupertsland – on 14 July. Bracken had initially intended to run solely on his record but he was quickly persuaded by his new Liberal colleagues that an anti-Bennett and anti-Conservative campaign would reap the best rewards. As a result most of his speeches and those of his supporters were heavily larded with criticisms of the Bennett government's high tariff and unemployment relief policies.

Bracken also defended his administration's record, berated the Conservative and Labour parties for not participating in the coalition, and outlined the measures that his government proposed for further reducing expenditures and spreading the burden of the depression. He pledged the Liberal-Progressives to a non-party business administration, to necessary financial adjustments with the least loss of services, to the creation of jobs in productive industry, to security of tenure for farmers and homeowners, and to an adjustment of the burden of indebtedness.[80]

His most enduring theme was his government's intention not to play 'petty party politics' but to do what was best for Manitoba. In a speech at Holland at the end of May Bracken declared: 'I have no sense of party politics. The only political platform I have is whatever is best for Manitoba, not just for farmers, not just for city people, but for all the people without respect of class or creed.'[81] Later, in June, he told an audience at Roblin that it was not his purpose to make a political speech: 'I don't know how to make a political speech. My only desire is to give you a business government pledged to do what is good for everybody ... '[82] He even went so far as to apologize for the election, saying: 'I am sure I am expressing the sentiments of every reasonable-thinking person when I say that this is no time when the welfare of a political party should be allowed to interfere with the administration of public affairs.'[83]

In their turn, the Conservative and Labour parties flailed away at the government, accusing it of gross mismanagement of the province's economic affairs. The Conservatives with Taylor in the vanguard made outlandish promises of reduced taxes and a restoration of Manitoba's credit if they were returned to power. The ILP under the leadership of John Queen were equally critical of Bracken's remorseless and, to them, inhumane budgetary policies but they saw little difference in the basic assumptions about society held by the government and the Conservative party.

All in all it was a vigorous but predictable campaign and Bracken bore the brunt of it for the coalition. He travelled extensively throughout the province right up to the eve of the election, but though he pushed himself hard he withstood the brutal hours much better than in earlier years. By election day he was tired and a little hoarse but was suffering no ill-effects.[84] He and his colleagues were helped immeasurably throughout the campaign by an excellent network of constituency organizations put together by volunteers from both the Liberal and Progressive camps.[85] Not since 1922 had the Manitoba electorate been so well-canvassed by the government side.

The results of the election were not unexpected. The Liberal-Progressives won an overwhelming victory with thirty-eight seats. The Conservatives won ten; Independent Labour five; and Independents two. Once again most of the government support came from the rural areas while the Conservatives and Labour had picked up seats primarily in the cities of Winnipeg, Brandon, and Portage la Prairie. Their aggressive organization enabled the coalition to take four of the five seats in southern Manitoba won by the Conservatives in 1927. The key reasons for the sweeping government victory were the failure of the provincial Conservatives to enter the coalition and the high tariff policies of the Bennett government.[86] Bracken was more than satisfied with his mandate.

9

Hanging on

Unemployment relief expenditures and maturing obligations in the United States and eastern Canada continued to be the main concern of the Bracken government during the middle thirties. The province continued to be hit by a series of crop failures and by 1936 had suffered from six consecutive years in which its net value of production was little more than half that of the late twenties. The strain on municipal and provincial finances was considerable. Although most of the rural municipalities were able to maintain their solvency this had only been achieved by repealing the major portion of the land taxes and by a drastic retrenchment of educational and general expenditures. But even those actions had not helped the municipalities in the sub-marginal interlake or those in the drought-stricken southwest corner which were in chronic distress, nor had they helped Winnipeg and its suburbs where virtually all of the Manitoba relief problem was concentrated.

The province was particularly affected by the problems of Winnipeg and the suburban municipalities. Winnipeg had entered the depression in a strong financial position but it suddenly found itself bearing the heaviest relief burden. Since most of the provincial revenues were derived from the city, there was little margin for increasing municipal revenues. As a result Winnipeg had to rely on the province for assistance. By 1936 the city had borrowed $3½ million from the province. In turn the province had had to loan municipalities one-third of their total expenditures on relief. These loans were roughly one-third of the province's borrowings from the federal government. To make matters worse the province had guaranteed the principal of suburban municipal debentures issued at a more ambitious and optimistic time. Now the municipalities were defaulting and the province had to make good its guarantees when it was least prepared to meet them.[1]

Obviously the province could not afford any further indiscretions. Thus it was a blow to both public and government morale when it was revealed only days after the 1932 election that J.A. Machray, the bursar of the University of Manitoba and also the chairman of its Board of Governors, had embezzled $901,175 from the university and $800,000 from the Church of England. A Royal Commission of Enquiry later established that Machray's activities had begun as early as 1902, and it rapped the university and the Norris and Bracken governments over the knuckles for administrative laxity.[2] These revelations did nothing to improve Manitoba's stock with either the Bennett government or the bankers, which was unfortunate because Bracken had to turn to them constantly over the next two years.

Soon after the election Bracken warned his ministers to exercise rigid economy for the remainder of the fiscal year, and, as of 1 September, he slashed cabinet and civil service salaries a further 7 per cent. He also decided that there would be no further guarantees of municipal debentures or overdrafts. Bracken pointed out that with continued reductions in revenues, the necessity for continuing expenditure on unemployment relief, and the substantial amount of money which the province had to pay to meet principal and interest obligations, 'the government had no alternative but to put into effect very drastic economies.'[3]

While continuing to cut back on expenditures as far as he could, Bracken also kept the pressure on Ottawa to provide more assistance to the province for unemployment relief. The federal government had ceased lending money to the western provinces to cover provincial and municipal direct relief costs on 31 March 1932. During the summer and autumn of 1932 and throughout the grim winter months, Bracken, his new provincial treasurer Ewen McPherson, and the premiers of Alberta and Saskatchewan repeatedly asked Bennett and Rhodes for the continuation of assistance. In letter after letter they pointed out that there was a danger of provincial bankruptcy if the federal government did not help. Bracken and McPherson constantly told Rhodes that the suburban municipalities, the large towns, and the cities of Brandon and Winnipeg had little or no borrowing power. As for the province, it *could* borrow for a time but that was becoming increasingly more difficult. In any event, it would have to pay a higher rate of interest for money than the federal government. Why, asked Bracken and McPherson, should Manitoba pay that higher rate if the dominion government could borrow money for less and reloan it to the province? They contended that 'the unemployment problem is a national one, incapable of local control or solution, and therefore its relief is likewise largely a national problem.'[4]

For the most part the pleas of Bracken and McPherson fell on deaf ears. Rhodes and Bennett were obdurate. They insisted that the federal government had no obligation, and no intention of assisting the province, beyond 31 March. They reminded the Manitobans that the province had already received considerable help from dominion authorities. In the future, Manitoba would have to make its own financial arrangements.[5]

Bracken was both frustrated and alarmed by the federal stance. In addition to the problems of financing relief, the Manitoba government had maturities worth more than $12,000,000 falling due between 1 October 1932 and 1 May 1933, including one for over six million on the New York exchange on 15 December.[6] In an effort to repair the province's financial position Bracken, McPherson, and Pearson consulted with the Royal Bank and various bond houses in Montreal and Toronto in late August. While they were promised overdraft privileges and given some hope that provincial bonds could be floated on either the British or American markets, the experience was a depressing one. Both the Royal Bank and the bond houses 'emphasized several times the need for the utmost retrenchment, and the need to balance the Budget as quickly as possible.' The official bank memorandum of the meeting stated that 'It was pointedly brought to the attention of the premier that, of course, the most vital thing in the Province's picture is that they should balance their Budget.' In reply Bracken could only say that he was aware of the need to do so but that it would be impossible to bring about a balanced budget within two years 'without precipitating an impossible situation.'

The meetings ended with the bank promising to intercede with Bennett on Manitoba's behalf to see if the federal government would agree to a three-year extension on monies falling due to it on 22 February, while Bracken promised to try and arrange relief financing with the dominion. As it turned out, neither the bank nor Bracken were successful in their overtures. Bennett simply said that Manitoba would have to meet its obligations.[7] The prime minister did relent a little in December when he agreed to help Manitoba pay the maturing loan in New York and thus avoid a major default, but he remained intransigent on matters of relief.[8]

Manitoba's relationship with the Bennett administration reached its nadir during February and March 1933. Rather than listening sympathetically to the argument that the western provinces were entirely at the mercy of the banking institutions, Bennett launched a major attack upon them and demanded that they pull up their financial socks.[9] His letter to Bracken was sternly worded. The financial condition of Manitoba had 'recently been the subject of earnest consideration' by the federal cabinet. It appeared that

no convincing evidence has been adduced to show that every possible effort is being made by the Legislature and Government of your Province to adjust your affairs and work into a position of self-reliance. ... it certainly appears that your course has been pursued without due regard to the ever-increasing difficulties involved, not only for the Province but for this Government ...

It becomes my absolute duty to say to you in the plainest terms, and I do so with all respect, that in case you anticipate in making further requests for financial aid, either by loan or by guarantee or in any other form, favourable consideration cannot be given to such request unless your Government is prepared to pledge itself to present a balanced budget by further reductions in proposed expenditures or by increased taxation, or by both, or if convincing evidence is adduced that under existing conditions such balanced budget is impossible, then your Government must adopt a definite prescribed plan whereby the maximum estimated deficit under your proposed budget shall be well under One Million Dollars.

Should your Government be unable or unwilling to comply with the above requirements, any alternative which can be accepted must be one which meets with the imperative necessities of this time ... the only alternative I can propose, meeting such necessities, is that the finances of your Province be supervised ... by a financial controller who may be nominated by your Government but who must be satisfactory to the Government of Canada ...

Bennett apologized for writing in such terms but some limit had to be placed upon borrowings from the dominion treasury.[10]

When this letter arrived at the Legislative Building it created a mild furour. Bracken quickly took the Conservatives into his confidence and rumours of a fusion began to circulate.[11] For some weeks before the arrival of the letter Bracken and his cabinet had been discussing what kind of budget to bring down. Early in the year McPherson and Bracken had decided that additional taxes would have to be levied in order to meet the federal government's and the banks' demand for a balanced budget. By February they were unsure if such a policy would work. The lack of earning power of the citizens of Manitoba might make an increase in taxation impossible. They had then considered other courses of action such as the absolute discontinuance of relief, of old-age pensions, and mothers' allowances. The first would have meant starvation while the last two would mean an increase on direct relief rolls and could not be considered. They also contemplated shutting down the schools, withdrawing police protection, and closing the courts. The first would have meant sending boys and girls onto the street without employment and the latter was quickly discarded because 'In our opinion at no time in [Manitoba] history has protection of the peace been more necessary.' The cabinet had eventually decided that all the suggestions were unacceptable because the abolition of such services 'would destroy the whole social system and cause hardship and suffering, the effect of which could never be wiped out.'[12]

The very fact Bracken and his colleagues had contemplated such actions reflected the depths to which Manitoba had sunk by early 1933 as a result of the depression, the grip of the banks, and the stoic attitude of the federal government. Nevertheless, it was clear that the government had no alternative but to conform to Bennett's stipulation if they wished to preserve any degree of financial stability and credibility and to have continued access to federal finances. Thus on 18 March Bracken agreed to cut general expenditures even further and introduce additional taxes in an effort to bring the provincial deficit under one million dollars.[13]

The Manitoba budget was brought down in the last week of March and it reflected the government's response to Ottawa's pressure. A 2 per cent tax on all salaries and earnings was included while expenditures were reduced by $650,000. The changes would hopefully lower the deficit from an estimated $2,650,000 to approximately $500,000. The reaction was predictable – an uproar from the Labour ranks, cries of woe from the business community, and exhortations from the Conservatives to cut both expenditures and revenue. The storm raged furiously for some weeks. The Board of Trade went so far as to demand that the government balance its budget and then accept a Board of Trade appointed committee as its economic adviser.

The 2 per cent 'wage tax,' the highest such tax in North America, was the most severely criticized aspect of the budget. In a major speech in the legislature Bracken met this criticism head on. He condemned the criticisms of the Labour and Conservative members. Labour wanted the province to default on interest payments while the Conservatives did not want the government to borrow, or impose new taxes, thus allowing nothing for relief and sixty-four other essential services. 'We must be consistent,' said Bracken. 'If we are going to pay for our needs, we have got to get the revenue.' The premier went remorselessly through item after item challenging the opposition to say that each one should be further reduced or cut out altogether. They could not do it. The budget could have been balanced only by smashing essential services. The government had no desire to do that. It had hoped to be able to borrow enough to carry on but that had proven impossible. Increased taxes were not popular but they were the only way. 'New taxes are bad and the government knows it,' said Bracken, 'but default of our obligations or repudiation would be worse.'[14]

Whatever might be said about these drastic measures they did gradually have an impact on revenues. By 1935 the province finally balanced its budget – except for a small portion of its sinking fund appropriation – on all accounts except relief. After 1935 revenues were maintained at roughly $14 million while expenditures, excluding relief, but including $400,000 to $500,000 annually for sinking funds, were slightly less. British Columbia was the only other province to report current surpluses in the late thirties.[15]

The effort by Manitoba to balance its budget was sufficiently impressive that Rhodes and Bennett were more willing over the next two years to help the province meet certain of its maturing obligations to the banks. It did not, however, change their attitude toward unemployment relief financing. They still maintained that Manitoba and the other western provinces would have to make their own arrangements to finance the provincial and municipal share of relief. Bracken pointed out repeatedly that Manitoba could only meet its relief obligations by borrowing at high rates of interest. Bennett and his advisers were unmoved by these arguments. They claimed that the existence of high rates of interest was no excuse for not selling bonds. Bracken was thoroughly frustrated by this attitude. It was all very well to balance the budget but stripping expenditures to the bone and bleeding the tax payer was a pointless exercise if the province could not slow the inexorably mounting debt that was threatening to engulf both it and the municipalities. Increasingly, Bracken had the support of J.A. McKerchar, the chairman of the City of Winnipeg Finance Committee, Sanford Evans of the Conservatives, the *Free Press*, and even the *Tribune* in his pleas to the federal government. More and more the Bennett administration seemed unsympathetic, even unknowing, about the West's problems.[16]

During the winter of 1933–4 the western provinces continued to argue for a refunding of their debts at lower rates of interest. The federal government, on the other hand, wanted to get away from the tripartite system of relief. It proposed to devote to public works the money it would ordinarily spend on provincial and municipal relief operations. Bracken favoured work projects over the dole but pointed out that the programme would be ineffective if it meant that the money spent on relief by local governments would be decreased to the extent that works expenditures were increased.[17]

The termination of the unemployment relief scheme on 31 March 1934 finally brought matters to a head. At a meeting with the western premiers in July Bennett informed them of his decision to cut back on federal expenditures. As far as Manitoba was concerned the dominion agreed to continue the current provision for single unemployed men in camps, its contributions to provincial expenditures for the construction of the Trans-Canada Highway and provincial highways, and its policy of settling people in need of relief upon the land. With that understood the dominion agreed to pay the province $135,000 on the last day of each month, until 31 March 1935, as a grant-in-aid to assist the province with direct relief.[18]

The agreement meant, in effect, virtually a 20 per cent cut in the dominion contribution to direct relief. Bracken soon made it clear that his government could not assume the portion that Ottawa had jettisoned. The municipalities would have to assume the extra burden. The province would continue to pay its one-third share of direct relief costs but would only pay 20 per cent as the dominion share, meaning that the municipal share of relief would be over 40 per cent. This placed a heavy burden on urban municipalities where the relief load was acute.[19]

Despite repeated pleas by Bracken the dominion grant-in-aid was not changed until after the defeat of the Conservatives in the 1935 election. Within weeks of being returned to power the Liberals increased Manitoba's grant to $236,230.00 for December 1935 and the first three months of 1936. This allowed Bracken to reduce the municipal burden for direct relief to 30 per cent.[20] The dominion grant was lowered to $200,812.50 for the early summer months and in July 1936 Manitoba received $3,000,000 of the $30,000,000 allotted by Ottawa to dominion-provincial relief agreements.[21] These slightly more generous arrangements still did not resolve the intolerable burden being placed on the municipalities and the provinces. Like Bennett, King complied strictly with the BNA Act. But matters could not long continue in this fashion and by late 1936 and early 1937 the parlous state of western finances was causing major concern in Ottawa.

Apart from the problems of mounting debt, shrinking revenues, and an intransigent federal government, Bracken also had to contend during the mid-thirties with threats to the established order. His response was in keeping with his long held beliefs about society and general human conduct.

One characteristic that stayed with Bracken throughout his life was his belief in the capitalist system and in the virtues of hard work and individual achievement. Although as an agricultural scientist and a practising farmer he had a deep-rooted faith in co-operatives, he did not see that form of organization as a step toward the overthrow of the existing laissez-faire system. To him the co-operative principle was a means of introducing more business efficiency into marketing. It was a reformist technique not a revolutionary one. He never questioned the basic system, only its inefficient and disruptive methods. If they could be reformed the system was satisfactory to Bracken. He, like most of his contemporaries, had little sympathy for socialism and none at all for communism. His attitude toward trade unions was ambivalent. He recognized the right of collective bargaining and the need to protect it, but he also wanted the game played within the rules. Any hint that the rules were being transgressed and Bracken could be hard in his response. He was not prepared to recognize that the rules of appropriate conduct had been drawn up to the advantage of those in power with the primary concern the protection of the *status quo* and the stability of the existing political and economic system.

Yet, under the pressure of the depression, Bracken, like many of his contemporaries, was driven to ask certain basic questions about the society around him and the way if operated. He realized that the mechanisms of that society were at fault. In his search for alternatives, Bracken, on occasion, appeared to recognize the inhumanity of the profit motive and the self-centred national policies that it engendered. But these thoughts really never lasted very long nor do they appear to have been deeply held. Bracken was a man who was fundamentally an adherent of hard work, order, and loyalty. His record, on occasions when he had to face a challenge from those of different ideological persuasion, was not a happy one. He too quickly assumed that all criticism and questioning were the work of agitators or communists. It rarely seems to have occurred to him that there might be merit in much that was said or done by those not in the main stream of contemporary virtues. Bracken was a conservative, as were most Manitobans, particularly those in the small towns and villages and on the farms. He spoke for them, or seemed to, and that was the source of his political strength. In his search for a solution of the problems of the depression, he never questioned the fundamental principles underlying the Canadian economic and social system. If he did he hid it well. Neither his public pronouncements nor his actions and policies could have been readily interpreted as anything but those of a staid, unimaginative man cloaked in the puritan ethic.

There was considerable distress in Manitoba from the early months of 1930 as the depression quickly took its toll. Farm workers were laid off and moved into Winnipeg where they joined the rapidly mushrooming legions of urban unemployed. Trade unions, workers councils, and various other organizations of the unemployed and of labour made repeated appeals to the government for assistance and understanding or a change in legislation.[22] Often meetings in Market Square resulted in marches on the Legislative Building where thousands of unemployed would demand to see their premier, usually without success. Sometimes in the early thirties delegations of workers would wait upon Bracken in his office and more rarely Bracken would come out on the steps to listen to complaints or to address the crowd. Bracken did not particularly enjoy these occasions. He disliked confrontation and preferred more amicable and rational settings. He instinctively distrusted mass demonstrations which by their very nature questioned the existing political, economic, and social order.

Occasionally, frustration spilled over into violence and damage was done to property. These were never well co-ordinated actions but the result of pent-up hostilities and anxieties, and were usually aimed at government offices and property, the symbols of a seemingly unfeeling and uncaring authority. Two of the most dramatic developments took place in late 1932 when the depression was at its most intense.

In early October over 500 farmers marched into the city from the north and northeast of Winnipeg. Organized by the Farmers' Unity League, a communist affiliate, the farmers had come to Winnipeg to dramatize their plight. Although

Bracken had seen the leaders of their delegation he had turned down their suggestions. He had also refused to provide free transportation to the farmers so that they could return to their homes. He had, in fact, seemed rather curt and unsympathetic.[23] He had pointed out in clear terms that 'Law and order will be preserved.' Such demonstrations were unacceptable. He accused the farmers of allowing themselves 'to be used by Communists for propaganda purposes.' It was unnecessary, said Bracken, 'to go to all this trouble and inconvenience to see government.' He never refused 'to see a delegation that was sincere in its proposals.' From his vantage point the farmers had used the appointment for propaganda purposes rather than as an opportunity to discuss problems in a rational manner.[24]

These attitudes were typical of Bracken during the thirties. His files contain correspondence from various labor organizations in Winnipeg and Manitoba, bringing to Bracken's attention conditions throughout the province. He usually replied perfunctorily or through his secretary. He saw a number of delegations but invariably argued that his hands were tied. He was so often out of the city that he was unable to see many delegations, and he always advised Winnipeg organizations to go and see the Greater Winnipeg Unemployment Advisory Board.[25]

In late November 1932 another incident occurred, this time in Arborg. Five hundred disgruntled farmers marched into the town, 'stormed the municipal offices, manhandled the clerk and forced him to resign office. Many files of municipal records, including assessment records, were scattered to the winds.' Composed for the most part of Ukrainian men and women, with a sprinkling of Poles, the demonstration had been organized by the Farmers' Unity League. The reason for the parade was a proposed tax sale which the municipality had intended to conduct on the day of the march. The crowd had gathered from Gimli, Poplarfield, Chatfield, and from the unorganized area north of Bifrost municipality. As a result of the demonstration the tax sale was cancelled for that day. Bracken's reaction to this is unclear, but Major and both Winnipeg papers attributed the demonstration to organized agitators.[26]

Bracken's major brush with organized labour and a strike situation during his political career occurred in June and July 1934 in Flin Flon. On Saturday, 9 June, 1300 employees of the Hudson Bay Mining and Smelting Company went on strike demanding recognition of their newly formed union, the Mine Workers Union of Canada, reinstatement of certain employees alleged to have been discharged without sufficient cause, return of wage scales to the 1929 level, pay every fifteen days, and certain changes in the method of paying overtime. W.A. Green, the general superintendent of the company, refused to recognize not only the committee of twenty that presented these demands but also the Mine Workers Union which had been organized by the Workers' Unity League, another Communist affiliate.

At 3:00 PM that afternoon picketing began. The company quickly issued a statement establishing its position and adhered to it throughout the month-long strike. It would not recognize the MWUC nor the committee as properly representative of the miners even though the committee represented the approximately 700 members of the local unit of the union. The company was willing to pay twice a month, but it argued that the pay scale was as high as anywhere for similar services and, 'contrary to conditions in almost every other copper mine in North America,' full-time work had been given to all employees throughout the years of depression. It considered the present scale of pay, averaging $4.26 per eight-hour shift, more than fair in the prevailing depression conditions. What appeared to offend the company most, and what eventually offended the town council, the mayor, the local business community, the local newspaper – the *Flin Flon Miner*, and Bracken and his cabinet, was that 'These demands are not from a majority of the Company employees but are the result of a communistic organization outside who have come to the camp to cause trouble for their own purposes.'[27]

On Monday, 11 June, an extra detachment of seventeen RCMP officers headed by an inspector was sent to Flin Flon. The RCMP had been acting as the Manitoba provincial police since 1932 and Bracken had had to sanction the use of extra officers, but he made it clear in an initial statement on 11 June that the government itself had not yet been asked to intercede. As always, he underlined that it was the responsibility of the authorities to see that property was protected and law and order maintained. The sending of the RCMP to Flin Flon was solely for that purpose and 'there would be no interference with legal rights of strikers.' As long as the strikers kept within the law the police would be no threat to them. Bracken did point out, however, that if the crisis continued it would be serious for the community as a whole. He knew better than anyone that the province was in grave financial difficulty. The relief rolls were already overburdened. The possibility of an extra 1300 men to provide for was not attractive, especially when, with a little common-sense, they could be working. Similarly, the government's commitment to Flin Flon and the mine was considerable. Bracken was not prepared to see that jeopardized.[28]

Over the next three weeks the situation in Flin Flon remained stalemated although the initial sympathy of the press for the strikers waned, an anti-communist league was formed, and the issue of the communist affiliation of the MWUC and the Workers' Unity League became increasingly major issues. Throughout, Bracken kept a close watch on developments. On 23 June he declared: 'So far as the strike at Flin Flon is concerned, if there are any real differences between the employees and the company I feel sure that they can be settled amicably without the assistance of any outside agitators belonging to organizations representing the Communist Party whose interest would seem to be not so much in the wellbeing of

the workers as it is to stir up unrest and trouble regardless of the disastrous effects it might have.'[29]

The tensions in Flin Flon finally boiled over on Saturday, 30 June. The town
council had made arrangements for a vote to be taken and one hundred special
constables were sworn in for the occasion. The strikers and their wives formed a
cordon around the Community Hall and attempted to prevent prospective voters
getting in. This led to a wild free-for-all, resulting in two constables being sent to
hospital and the arrest of two men. The RCMP had intervened with billyclubs but
were outnumbered and beaten back. The vote was called off at 2:00 PM. If anything, the incident had demonstrated that many of the miners were determined to
remain out and that they were not involuntary supporters of the strike.

The riot so alarmed Mayor Foster and his council that they immediately telegraphed Bracken asking for fifty additional police officers. Foster claimed the
utilities were in danger, that intimidation prevailed, that lives were threatened,
and that martial law might be necessary. He asked either Bracken or Major to come
north immediately.[30] RCMP reinforcements were rushed to the town and by 4 July
there were ninety officers patrolling the streets.[31] As far as Roscoe Channing, the
president of HBMS, was concerned the events of 30 June could have only one interpretation: 'The fight is now a plain issue between law and order and Communism. The Company stated its position at the beginning, reiterated it ... on June
23rd, and from this point it will not yield one inch.'[32]

It was in this atmosphere of tension and recrimination, highly conscious of
the province's financial difficulties, and under pressure from the mayor, the company, and the Anti-Communist League, that Bracken decided to make a personal
visit to Flin Flon to assess the situation and interview the various groups involved.

By the time he arrived in the town on Saturday, 7 July, his own position and
assumptions were quite evident. Five days earlier he had been briefed by C.C.
Sparling, chairman of the Anti-Communist League, Councillor McSheffrey, Inspector Brown of the RCMP, and R.E. Phelan, the general manager of HBMS, who
had all travelled down to Winnipeg for the purpose. Needless to say the information and opinions obtained were one-sided. The strikers were referred to as cowardly in their tactics, putting women and children in the front lines, and fighting
from behind them. McSheffrey did not think the issue was any longer, if it ever
had been, over wages but whether or not there was to be communism or law and
order.[33]

Bracken's rough notes drawn up on his way to Flin Flon reflected how his assumptions warred with his desire to seem impartial. On the one hand he wanted,
he said, to get at the facts of the situation; on the other he wanted 'to help Flin
Flon end this suicidal policy.'[34] Despite this seeming ambivalence it is clear that
by the time he went north Bracken was sure in his own mind that the strike was

communist inspired, that it was therefore unrepresentative, and that it had to be ended. He had maintained throughout a concern for the preservation of the legalities and principles of collective bargaining and strike action, but the breakdown, as he saw it, of law and order in late June had obviated any further need to maintain a distance from the Flin Flon scene. Bracken now believed he could openly intervene and do so with complete justification. At no time did Bracken move significantly away from the legal and constitutional plane to concern himself with the wage and living conditions in Flin Flon. He was deferential to the company and accepted its information at face value. This was not surprising. He wanted an important mine to get back into production.

During his first day-and-a-half in Flin Flon Bracken met with the town council, the Elks, representatives of the men wishing to return to work, the Odd Fellows, Father Dublois, businessmen, the Anti-Communist League, the Knights of Columbus, and the German-Canadian League. The information he received from all these sources was the same: the strike committee was not representative of the majority of the men; many of the men who had supported the strike had been 'misled by Revolutionary agitators'; and the majority of men now wished to return to work. Foster did admit that conditions in the mine were not all they should be but his was not a prevailing view. Most considered the strike the work of outside communist agitators who had not conducted vote proceedings properly. Most of the men, it was agreed, had been either duped or misled into joining the union, and a real strike vote had never been taken. The Anti-Communist League said 90 per cent of the men had not known the MWUC was communist affiliated. It claimed the union took the unemployed, bootleggers, and pimps.[35]

By Sunday afternoon Bracken had still not spoken to any representatives of the Strike Committee. Thinking they were not going to be heard they wrote to Bracken requesting a meeting. Bracken said he had been busy but he would be happy to meet a representative group of the committee. However, he refused to meet 'anyone representing the Workers' Unity League or the Canadian Labour Defence League or the Mine Workers Union or paid strike leaders from outside.' On that basis he would meet representatives at 5 PM that afternoon. Five of the committee met Bracken and claimed they represented 824 employees. They asked Bracken to enforce the law giving them the right to collective bargaining and the right to join the union of their choice.[36]

Despite this assurance, Bracken was convinced by Sunday night that more than half the employees had not belonged to the union and that a proper strike vote had not been taken. He concluded that an organized minority was preventing the majority from returning to work by intimidation. Such a situation would not be permitted. He therefore told Channing that if the company were prepared to reopen the mine, and the men wanted to go back to work, the government would see that they were protected and that law and order were maintained.[37] When Channing agreed, Bracken prepared a statement to be circulated to the miners.

In his first sentence Bracken flatly stated that 'the plant of the Hudson Bay Mining and Smelting Co. was closed down, largely, in my opinion, due to the activities of Communist organizers operating through the Mine Workers Union.' He referred to the great investment made by the province, the company, and the business community in the town. Bracken declared that he was in Flin Flon in the interests of a company that had supplied jobs for 'every willing worker'; of the taxpayers of Manitoba whose government had pledged $100,000 a year for five years to help start the industry; and of the workers many of whom had been misled by the activities of the few. He made it clear that he had no sympathy for 'revolutionary activities' or for 'paid agitators.' The provincial government would use its every resource to preserve law and order 'to protect any and all men who desire to go to work.' Employees would not be compelled to return, but if a majority so desired then 'no radical or revolutionary group' would be allowed to stand in the way.[38]

Bracken's statement was prepared and circulated to the mine employees after 9 PM on Sunday evening, 8 July. He urged them to return to work Monday morning. At 9:30 PM Channing announced the mine would open the following morning. And so it did. At 7:30 AM 700 men, divided into three columns with a constable at the head of each and two policemen at the rear, marched between lines of RCMP constables to the main entrance to the plant. They were greeted by jeers and cries of 'scab' from several hundred stand-pat strikers and their supporters, but no violence resulted. Bracken watched the march past from the verandah of the company's staff house. Later that morning he left Flin Flon for Winnipeg well satisfied with his weekend's activities.[39]

Over the next few days the men gradually returned to work. At a closed meeting on 13 July the remaining strikers voted 201 to 18 in favour of ending the walkout. As a result of the strike the company restored 50 per cent of the wage cut retroactive to 9 July, initiated a twice-monthly pay day, and cut electricity charges by two cents to seven cents per kilowatt hour. A company union was also organized, and when HBMS refused to hire anyone of communist leaning or affiliation, especially anyone who had any association with the Canadian Labour Defence League, the WUL, or the MWUC, the new union happily agreed. When Bracken was informed of these developments in September he entered no complaint. He and the company were at one in their fight against communism.

The whole incident stemmed as much from a dislike of unionism as from a fear of communism. Nevertheless, it was a fearful and repressive decade. The Bennett government was cracking down on communist activity and making frequent use of section 98 of the Criminal Code. All levels of government across

Canada were instinctively protective of business interests and wary of trade unions. Bracken was no exception. Although claiming to be concerned with union rights he was quick to accept the company's, the town council's, and the business community's views. He heard what he wanted to hear, and what he heard reinforced his own predilections.[40]

In August Bracken was congratulated by Thomas Deacon, a former mayor of Winnipeg, for his courage, firmness, and sagacity in handling the strike. His actions, said Deacon, had protected the industry and Manitoba's reputation as a stable area for investment. Bracken thanked Deacon: 'We did what obviously was the right thing to do, and we are pleased that our action in this respect is appreciated. Personally, I would have gone up sooner, but other advice counselled delay. In any event, the final outcome was very satisfactory.'[41]

The Flin Flon strike was Bracken's major brush during the 1930s with communism and with the social tensions generated by the depression. Although he became concerned in July 1935 about the possibility of trouble developing from the On-To-Ottawa Trek, no real difficulties materialized and Bracken did not have to take any untoward action. He did insist that the government would provide relief to the trekkers for only two days, after which they would either have to return to their homes or to their camps or accept work available to them.[42] The strike committee soon bowed to governmental pressure and men began to leave Winnipeg and the province. The Manitoba government provided the money for transportation and a free meal provided the men took the first train available.[43]

Bracken's perceptions of society and of the individual's responsibility within it were only confirmed by his experiences during the thirties. While he now recognized that the state had to intervene on behalf of the citizen in times of stress, he still believed that the individual had a responsibility to himself and the state to work and to attempt to resolve his own problems. There was nothing necessarily inhuman in this position. In fact, it was sound nineteenth-century liberalism and it was shared by the majority of his contemporaries. The problem was that Bracken could sound unwittingly harsh and uncaring in the face of real suffering and this angered many of those caught by the vicissitudes of the depression. Shortly before the 1936 election he was burned in effigy in Market Square after a torchlight procession of single urban unemployed.[44]

The legislative chamber in the mid-thirties never offered anything to match the drama and the controversy of the Flin Flon strike. The drastic cuts in capital and current expenditures severely limited the programme of the government, and even more than usual the legislature became a glorified municipal council concerned with good housekeeping and administrative measures. Bracken's main opponent, Fawcett Taylor, retired from the Conservative leadership in 1933 to the bench and, until his own withdrawal from political life in 1936, Sanford Evans was the Tory leader. Though a powerful financial critic, Evans was far less flamboyant and aggressive than Taylor. Party politics disappeared almost entirely from the chamber and it was a dull and dreary place, lacking in ideas, humour, vigour, and incisiveness.[45]

If politics were at a low ebb in Manitoba they were not in the rest of the country. It was one of the most interesting political decades in Canadian history with new parties emerging at both the federal and provincial levels. Of most significance to Westerners was the joining of agrarian and labour interests in the Cooperative Commonwealth Federation in 1932 and the startling and sweeping victory of William Aberhart's Social Credit party in Alberta in 1935. In Manitoba the CCF absorbed the ILP and a Social Credit organization was soon established, but no one was sure how much support the new parties commanded.

They were soon to find out for on 12 June 1936 Bracken announced that a provincial election would be held on 27 July with deferred elections in The Pas and Rupertsland on 21 August. It was an odd time for an election to be held in Manitoba, and since the government still had a year left in its term the announcement caught the opposition groups and most government supporters by surprise. Harvesting would be in full swing in the rural areas and many city dwellers would be enjoying their annual vacations. The need to fill vacancies in the legislature did not seem a sufficiently plausible explanation since there would not be another session until 1937. Whatever Bracken's reasoning his snap call was much resented even within his own party.

Bracken drafted the government manifesto himself and it was issued on 3 July at the Marlborough Hotel to an audience of 400.[46] It reflected his dilemma of having to defend the record of his administration while also trying to meet the demand of frustrated and depressed Manitobans for a 'new deal.' At the same time that he called for endorsation of his government's 'sound, economical and business-like administration' he also promised to undertake 'a new deal for agriculture,' to work for lower interest rates on private and governmental loans, and to exert pressure for the assumption by the federal government of a larger share of relief and social service costs. As usual, he placed emphasis on providing 'a square deal and sound business administration to every section of the province, urban and rural, industrial and agricultural.'[47]

Despite Bracken's efforts to publicize his 'new deal' he spent much of his time throughout the campaign rigorously defending his government's retrenchment policies. Essentially, he ran on his record and asked for a mandate to continue the same pragmatic approach. There were no lavish promises. It was an administrative platform. It reflected, as the *Tribune* put it, Bracken's proven technique 'of plodding common sense.' It was also a platform in which many avenues led to

Ottawa. As the *Tribune* again pointed out, 'all the noisiest babies are laid neatly on Mr. King's doorstep; only the more manageable infants are recognised as provincial responsibilities.' Although this seemed like buck-passing it was simply a reflection of an increasingly insoluble problem in federal-provincial relations.[48]

The election was hard-fought and, at times, vituperative. Earlier in the year the rural Conservatives had succeeded in forcing the retirement of Winnipeg businessman Sanford Evans and had chosen as leader in his place Errick Willis of Boissevain. The son of a former party leader, Willis was a farmer and small-town lawyer who had sat as a Bennett Conservative in Ottawa in the years 1930-5. With his folksy, down-to-earth style Willis had a considerable appeal in the rural south and southwest where he concentrated his campaigning. The main object of his attack was the government's financial record. The Conservatives promised to reduce the costs of government by $1,000,000; to 'honourably' reduce rates on provincial borrowings; to wipe out the 2 per cent wage tax; to set licence fees for all passenger automobiles at a flat rate of $5.00; and to treat as uncollectible all overdue advances to farmers for seed and feed in drought areas.[49]

These were highly ambitious promises, and were vulnerable to criticism from the government forces and the newspapers. Bracken and Major were particularly critical. They pointed out that rarely in the previous six years had the Conservatives made constructive proposals for the reduction of expenditures or the increase of revenues. If it had been possible to pare $1,000,000 the government would assuredly have been quick to do so.[50] The *Free Press* rightly pointed out that these promises would be hard to keep and the public would have to take the Conservative party on faith. Even the *Tribune*, still a Conservative supporter although not as vehement or as vitriolic as in the twenties, thought Willis had overreached himself in his promises.[51]

The CCF party deplored the Conservative platform because it would involve the sacrifice of services but found the government no more imaginative in its efforts. Accusing them both of being middle-of-the-road parties concerned more with ledger accounts than with people, it offered itself as 'the humanitarian party' and appealed to the public on a platform of social ownership of natural resources, the appointment of an economic council, and improvement in financial and social services.[52] J.S. Woodsworth, the national leader of the party, M.J. Coldwell, and Angus McInnis all took part in the campaign.[53]

The newest addition to the Manitoba political scene was the Social Credit League. Benefitting from Aberhart's sweeping win in Alberta the previous August, Social Credit made a strong emotional impact during the election. While making the usual promises to reorganize the province's economy, the new party's greatest vote-getter was the pledge of a $25.00 dividend for all to assist in the costs of food, clothing, and shelter.

Bracken pushed himself hard during the election, travelling hundreds of miles over dirty, unsurfaced roads in the intense prairie heat. It was probably his toughest campaign. The rural voters were downcast and frustrated after six years of depression while the electorate in the towns and cities were full of scepticism about the government's capacity to resolve its problems. Bracken faced many hostile audiences but his worst moment probably came on Friday, 24 July, during a speech in St James. As he presented the government's case he was constantly booed, jeered, and questioned from 9:15 to 10:30 PM. His reaction displayed his deep-seated attitudes to criticism as well as his fatigue. The *Tribune* reported the incident the following day:

As the noise rose to a steady din, Mr. Bracken retorted more and more bitterly to the unemployed in the crowd.
' ... this rabble kicking up a row. 'Forty million dollars the Manitoba government had paid to you folks, who don't appreciate it.
'Twenty cents a day is all you're worth.'
'Boo'
'Forty million dollars ... '
'Boooo'
'Forty million dollars ... '
'Boooo'
'Forty million dollars ' – seven times Mr. Bracken repeated.
' – taken out of other people's pockets and given to people like this howling mob, and that's how much it is appreciated.
' – this noisy bunch in front of me who wouldn't work if they had a chance.'
....
Mention of agricultural problems brought repeated shouts: 'How about Winnipeg?'
'Who are these disturbers?' Mr. Bracken asked near the end of the meeting.
'Communists?'
'No. Pure British subjects,' came the reply in a rich English voice.[54]

Despite such occurrences Bracken was convinced that he would receive a majority, perhaps a reduced one but nevertheless sufficiently large to govern without support from other groups. It was therefore somewhat of a shock to watch the returns as they came in at the end of July. The vote reflected the confusion and anxiety of the Manitoba electorate. The government was reduced to 22 members, the Conservatives increased to 16, the CCF-ILP won 7, the Social Credit took a surprising 5; Jim Litterick became the first Communist elected to public office in North America, and the colourful and aggressive Lewis St George Stubbs swept in at the top of the Winnipeg poll.[55] The vote in The Pas and Rupertsland on 21 August now assumed critical importance.

The government had lost heavily in the rural areas. In the Anglo-Saxon south and southwest seven seats had fallen to the revitalized Conservatives under Willis while the Social Credit League had taken its five seats in the usually faithful rural ethnic areas of west-central Manitoba and the Interlake. A closer look at the popular vote revealed that roughly one-third had gone against the traditional parties. Although the Conservatives had gained six seats, their share of the popular vote had slipped by 8 per cent while the CCF-ILP with two more seats had slipped 4 per cent. By comparison the government had not done as badly as its drop in seats would indicate. Its popular vote had fallen only 3 per cent, better than any of the other traditional parties.[56]

This must have been little consolation to Bracken. In the immediate aftermath of the election it was rumoured that he would hand over the leadership to another member of the cabinet, but the premier quickly quashed that rumour as he left for The Pas to plan his own election campaign. 'I am no quitter,' he declared, 'I never give up in the middle of a good fight.'[57] It was a proud and defiant remark, but Bracken's tense and worn look more adequately reflected his circumstances. Hoey, one of the strongest men in the cabinet, had been defeated; Nick Hryhorczuk, with him since 1922, had also been beaten; and both Donald Mc-Kenzie and Ewen McPherson, his treasurer and main support in his battles with Ottawa, had held to their retirement plans. Some means would have to be found in order that he and his government could continue. If he could win in The Pas his own position would be strengthened and his party's right to carry on re-affirmed.

Bracken's main concern was stable government. The province's financial circumstances were too perilous to permit a weak minority government to try and run its affairs. Bracken, therefore, began to consider ways in which a stable non-partisan administration could be assured. On 4 August, shortly after his return from The Pas, he wrote to Errick Willis stressing that what Manitoba needed more than anything else was stable government. He believed the present government with the co-operation of another group could give it. Failing such co-operation, it would be necessary to call another election: 'You will agree, I am sure, [wrote Bracken] that the maintenance of stability of government during these troublous times is of paramount importance. Personally, I am convinced that provincial affairs, particularly under these conditions, can be administered free from all party politics ... ' Bracken invited the Conservatives to join with the Liberal-Progressives for the next four years, thereby creating a government representative of the great majority of the people. He suggested that three or four Conservatives including Willis, be appointed to cabinet positions, even the treasury, and the Liberal-

Progressives to a similar number. He further suggested that the leadership of the united group be shared. He would carry on for two years and Willis would take over for the last two.[58] Willis replied the same day. Although he had been prepared to consider the idea, the majority in his caucus had not. He therefore turned the proposal down and reassured Bracken that the Conservatives also desired stable and businesslike government and would continue to work for it.[59]

This was not the first time Bracken had suggested coalition as a solution to the province's problems, but there was an element of political gamesmanship at work in this instance. Bracken knew that if Willis accepted, he, Bracken, would always receive credit for the suggestion. He also knew that the Conservatives would not be able to dominate his own group in the caucus. Similarly, if Willis refused, Bracken would always be able to say that the Conservatives were more interested in partisan politics than in the interests of the province. He had underminded Taylor that way in 1931-2, and now he was attempting the same thing with Willis. Willis and his supporters fell into the trap. After criticizing Bracken throughout the campaign, it was now difficult for them to associate with him.

Having made his offer, Bracken returned to The Pas and his own electoral future. His opponent was George Mainwaring, the mayor of Flin Flon. The issues were primarily local although provincial financial questions and the 2 per cent tax crept in constantly. Willis was in the riding for the whole time. Crerar came for a week to aid Bracken in what had been since 1935 Crerar's federal seat, and a number of other Liberal-Progressives appeared in a well-organized assault on the riding. It was seen by all observers as a key to the government's future, and speculation was rife over the result.

Then on 13 August, only eight days before the vote, Dr S.W. Fox, newly elected leader of the five Social Credit MLAs, personally pledged the support of his group in carrying on the government.[60] Despite the division that this announcement accentuated in an already divided Social Credit party, the action was endorsed by Aberhart. The Social Credit group insisted that in return for their support Bracken would have to initiate an economic survey of the province. He was only too happy to agree. The arrangement worked out with Social Credit was neither a coalition nor a fusion, such as Bracken had suggested to Willis; it was simply a promise of general support. No promises of a cabinet position were made, and, so far as is known, none were asked.

Bracken was, of course, delighted by this development. It virtually ensured him of victory in The Pas. And such was the case. On 21 August he won by almost 1000 votes, a larger majority than on any previous occasion. This left the coalition with a total of twenty-three seats, Rupertsland having fallen to an Independent. By early September he had conferred with all five Social Credit MLAs and was reassured of support.[61] He then proceeded to form his cabinet. Bracken added four new ministers – Stuart Garson (Fairford) as provincial treasurer; Ivan Schultz (Mountain) as minister of education; Doug Campbell (Lakeside) as minister of agriculture; and Sauveur Marcoux (La Verendrye) as minister without portfolio. By the end of September Willis declared that the Conservatives would not force an election.[62] The Bracken government appeared safe for the present.

10

Manitoba's case

During the winter of 1936-7 there was considerable speculation in the province about the future of the Bracken government. Much was heard about the possibility of a new coalition administration under a different leader. Despite the rumours these manoeuvrings never came to anything, and it is doubtful if Bracken was ever seriously challenged as leader. There was, however, more legitimate doubt about his administration's capacity to survive a meeting of the legislature, especially if it made no effort to cancel the 2 per cent income tax. Bracken's problem was that cancellation of the tax, and the resultant loss of revenue, was impossible to contemplate if other revenue sources were not available.

Bracken hinged many of his hopes for greater stability on a refinancing of the provincial debt and an assumption by the federal government of additional responsibilities. He argued that the problem of relief had been treated from the outset as if it were a passing emergency, but it could no longer be considered that. The financial situation in his own province was proof, if any more were required, of the necessity of a more settled policy. The budget was only just being balanced, without including relief expenditures. The several millions for that were being borrowed, and there was a steady increase in the annual debt charges. If the special 2 per cent tax were to be dropped, alternative means of raising revenue would have to be found because further taxation was impossible. The province's acute difficulty could be eased by the dominion assuming the whole cost of old-age pensions, and considerable relief would result from a lowering of the interest charges on the provincial debt.

This difficult financial situation was coupled with a touchy political one. The Bracken government was dependent on support from other groups in the legislature all of whom were committed to an easing of the financial situation by a cutting of interest charges. In order to retain power the Manitoba government needed the co-operation of both the dominion government and the bondholders.

Bracken had no intention of arbitrarily renouncing the province's debts but he did intend to sit down with its creditors and point out to them the unfairness of the existing situation and the urgent need for voluntary adjustment.[1]

The manner of resolving the problem of provincial debt had been a cause of concern to the King government since its return to office. A loans council scheme had had too many political complications and had been abandoned. A resolution looking to the amendment of the BNA Act to enable the dominion to guarantee the bonds of the provinces had been rejected by the Senate. Finally, Charles Dunning, the minister of finance, had suggested the establishment, on a purely voluntary basis, of a National Finance Committee for the continuing and properly organized discussion of taxation and federal-provincial financing.[2] This had been accepted, and one of the first opportunities to put Manitoba's case came at the initial meeting of the committee in Ottawa on 9 December 1936.

The session was attended by the federal finance minister and all the provincial premiers and treasurers. It proved to be a disappointment for Bracken and for all those who had expected some positive developments in federal-provincial financing. After outlining Manitoba's difficulties Bracken proposed that the dominion and the provinces should unite in an effort to secure adjustment of interest rates on provincial and municipal bonds. The only support came from Saskatchewan. Bracken also suggested a review of 'the economic basis of Confederation' in order 'to see whether, in the interests of the people of the Dominion of Canada, the provinces should not be relieved of some of the many responsibilities that were given to them at Confederation.' If a 'Royal Inquiry' into the broad federal issues was not advisable, he proposed a commission on the problems of the prairies similar to the Duncan Commission on the Maritimes.[3]

Unknown to Bracken both the Bank of Canada and Dunning were anxious to bring about some measure of dominion co-operation in debt refunding for the West, but Dunning was unwilling to risk a rebuff from the federal cabinet. King and Dunning had discussed the possibility of a royal commission on federal-provincial relations on 16 November but King had not been much committed and the two men had decided to leave it until 1937, 'if at all.'[4]

When it became clear that most of the other provinces were not prepared to support Manitoba and that the federal government would not contemplate any major additional contribution either by taking over some of the provincial social services or by giving the provinces larger financial relief, Bracken told Dunning that Manitoba had no choice but to approach its creditors and ask for an adjustment regardless of the impact on the principal value of the bonds. The premier assured Dunning that Manitoba would not oppose a loan council nor someone from outside Manitoba having something to say about Manitoba's future financing if either would result in a balanced budget. But if a balanced budget would not result Bracken saw little alternative to compromising with creditors if 'the rising tide of communism' were to be lessened.[5]

The failure of the National Finance Committee to do anything about the critical financial difficulties of the prairie provinces necessitated further intensive cabinet discussions in Manitoba and a conference between representatives of the Saskatchewan and Manitoba governments.[6] The urgent need was underlined in Manitoba by the difficulties confronting the city of Winnipeg. Faced with half a million dollar deficit, the city was seeking some kind of financial assistance from the government. In December it suggested that the province give it either a share of taxes on liquor, gasoline, and motor vehicles, additional powers of taxation, or relieve it of the entire cost of unemployment relief and a portion of the cost of educational, police, and fire protection services.[7]

It was impossible for Bracken to meet the city request, but he knew that it was imperative to preserve services throughout the province. To do that some form of financial relief was essential. Despite his worries Bracken had never mentioned the possibility of debt repudiation. In fact, he had made it a point to say that was definitely not his intention. Nevertheless, his words at the conference on 9 December were open to that interpretation and on 18 December Mackenzie King and his cabinet discussed the probability of default by Manitoba and Saskatchewan. Basically, the cabinet was unsympathetic and thought the two provinces should work out their own salvation: ' ... if it is known they must do so, the banks and insurance cos., etc. will help to save their going to default. So long as the Federal Government can be looked to for financial grants or loans they are likely to lean on the Federal Treasury.'[8]

The atmosphere was made much more tense with the announcement on 30 December that the federal government would not increase federal aid for relief that winter. This policy just added to the burden of Winnipeg and Manitoba. It simply meant they would have to borrow larger sums.[9] Also, the Saskatchewan government was attempting to persuade Bracken to do nothing that would rebound to the disadvantage of western credit. It wished Manitoba and Saskatchewan to unite in an effort to obtain larger subsidies from the federal government. Saskatchewan argued that after the Duncan Commission report the Maritime provinces received, 'temporarily,' larger subsidies which they were still receiving. Bracken argued that subsidies in themselves would not solve the basic problems. He claimed Manitoba had done everything possible to meet her obligations; that the province had reached the breaking point in taxation; that unless some adjustment was made either to enlarge means of revenue, to shift more of the social burdens such as relief and old-age pensions to the federal government, or to give federal help in financing provincial bonds, there was no other way out except a reduction in present Manitoba bond interest.[10]

Let's Be Calm

Bracken and his cabinet were in virtually continuous session during early January as they grappled with preparations for the new provincial budget that would have to be announced once the session opened. Their dilemma was obvious. If Bracken repealed the 'wage tax,' revenue would be reduced. That would further impair Manitoba's credit and her capacity to borrow. Ottawa would be less likely to lend the money for relief if the government repealed the 'wage tax.' That would be a backward step in balancing the budget. But, since more than half the legislature was committed to abolition of the 2 per cent tax, the government faced almost certain defeat if it did not repeal the tax. In his talks with Ottawa Bracken made it clear that the situation he faced was as much political as financial and that for political reasons financial aid was essential.[11] It was during this confused and tense period that rumours of the replacement of Bracken and the formation of a coalition government were rife in Winnipeg.[12]

Throughout those early January days Bracken hoped that Ottawa would relent in its attitude and agree to come to the aid of Manitoba and Saskatchewan. His spirits must have soared when Dunning invited representatives of both provinces to meet him in Ottawa on 17-18 January to discuss possible solutions. The invitation had resulted from a federal cabinet meeting on 8 January during which there had been 'a trying and difficult discussion on the position of the Western Provinces.' According to King, the cabinet had been fairly evenly divided on the matter of allowing Saskatchewan and Manitoba to go into default. Ilsley, Rogers, Elliott, and Cardin had been prepared to risk that step. King, Crerar, and Lapointe had not. King 'felt it would be much too great a risk to take at this time when we have vast refunding operations on the war debt account, and when the world is in the disturbed condition it is, and when unrest in Canada might assume alarming proportions at any time.' Also, he thought 'it would be unfortunate to have repudiation become general throughout the West and there is no saying where it might end.' It was finally decided to allow Dunning to try to make an arrangement with Manitoba and Saskatchewan which would enable them to issue securities at a lower rate, to be guaranteed by the dominion. Ottawa, however, would take the subsidies and some of the revenues of the provinces as security for any amount which might have to be paid out on the dominion's guarantee. The establishment of a royal commission to investigate the financial relations of the provinces and the dominion was also discussed. King and Dunning strongly supported the idea but Lapointe was opposed. No final decision was taken at that time.[13]

Bracken, Premier Patterson of Saskatchewan, and their colleagues met Dunning and his federal officials in Ottawa on 17-18 January 1937. Bracken's position was clear. Both he and Patterson wanted to maintain an orthodox system of financing but considered that attempts to impose further taxation would result in political upheavals. Bracken believed that the federal government's policy of distributing relief on a population basis without regard to special conditions was bad. Conditions in a city such as Winnipeg, for example, called for special treatment. He held that the whole question of the federal government assuming only a portion of relief payments on the prairies was wrong in principle and required investigation. The two premiers also said that the system of the federal government 'loaning' the provincial 'share' of relief payment was not only wrong but also impossible, for it was piling up a steadily increasing debt on which interest was charged which could not be paid.[14]

The two premiers suggested that their governments pass legislation calling in all outstanding provincial bonds carrying an average of 4½ per cent interest and issue new refunding securities at from 2½ to 3 per cent interest guaranteed by the dominion government. The old bonds would be paid off at par. This plan was rejected by the federal government. It also refused to assume any more of the relief or social services burden or to increase provincial subsidies. The majority of the federal cabinet were fearful of the implications for federal credit if the federal treasury were opened up any further to the provinces.[15]

This decision placed Bracken in an awkward position. He could not stall the opening of the legislature much further. By the time he arrived back in Winnipeg on 20 January he had more or less decided to have an interim suspension of debenture interest either by arrangements with creditors or by legislation. He was determined that no new taxes would be imposed and expenditures had already been cut to the bone. The only way to obtain any leeway in Manitoba's grim financial situation was to suspend interest and / or principal payments on its bonds.[16]

While Bracken and his cabinet huddled in Winnipeg, King discussed with Dunning and Graham Towers, the president of the Bank of Canada, the possibility of the bank making a report upon the financial relations between Manitoba and the federal government. Although Towers was initially reluctant to have the bank thrust into the limelight, he finally agreed, after a talk with W.C. Clark, the deputy minister of finance, that it would probably do no harm. King was happy with the decision: 'The more I think of it, the more I believe the quicker the whole situation is known and understood, the sooner we will be rid of it.'[17] The position of the western provinces continued to be a topic of major concern in the federal cabinet during the next few days. On 23 January King strongly urged that they not be allowed to default. He also suggested again the appointment of a royal commission, but no conclusions were reached.[18]

By late January Alex Skelton, chief of the Research Department of the Bank of Canada, was in Winnipeg undertaking a detailed study of Manitoba finances. A few days later Towers had a long conference with Bracken and Stuart Garson, the provincial treasurer, in the premier's office.[19] Bracken had already announced that the session would open on 18 February. He was anxious that a decision, one way or another, could be reached before then.

While Skelton and Towers conducted their investigation, Bracken was working hard to ensure that his government would have a majority in the legislature. On Monday, 3 February, he had half-an-hour's talk with Dr S.W. Fox, the Social Credit leader, and then joined the Social Credit caucus for an informal discussion. A basic understanding was worked out and Bracken left assured that his Liberal-Progressive group would have a bare majority in the session. He was already fairly certain of the support of Independent member Oddur Olafson. The understanding reached between Bracken and the Social Credit was not a coalition. The gulf in economic thinking between the two groups was too wide to bridge, but it seemed clear that the Bracken government's decision not to abolish the 2 per cent income tax met with Social Credit approval. What did concern the Social Credit group was the establishment of an economic survey of Manitoba. The willingness of the Social Credit to support the government the previous August had been based on the understanding that Bracken would launch such a scheme.[20]

A few days later, on 8 February, Bracken met with representatives of Manitoba's bondholders in an effort to bring about a voluntary agreement on measures for reducing the annual interest charges on the provincial debt. Bracken outlined the economic situation in the West, pointed out the budgetary position of Manitoba, and invited his audience to consider 'the proposal of voluntarily sharing with the rest of the community a reasonable portion of the burden of the depression.' The meeting was friendly and Bracken was sympathetically received. It was agreed that his proposals would be given further consideration after the Bank of Canada presented its report. The appointment of a royal commission to determine the division of taxing powers, the proper apportionment of money-spending responsibility, and general federal-provincial relations was thought to be essential by the majority present.[21]

The Towers report was completed by 11 February and was discussed by the federal cabinet on the 15th.[22] The analysis was broken down into three time periods, 1926-9, 1930-3, and 1934-7. The bank criticized the Manitoba government for lightening the tax load in the 1927-30 period. It believed greater advantage should have been taken of the good years to build up surpluses for bad times. It also thought that the province had made unduly large capital outlays during the 1929-32 fiscal years. But for most of the period under review, 'specifically during the last five years, the Government of the Province of Manitoba has made strong and commendable efforts to keep its budget balanced, and avoid unnecessary increases in debt, by imposing taxation on a scale at least as high as that of any other province in Canada, and of restricting expenditures as far as it was possible to go without curtailing services to an extent which would not have been in the public interest.'

The bank found that in spite of Manitoba's efforts, 'the percentage increase in its revenues during the period 1926-36 has been smaller than that of any other province except one.' This was due, first, to the fact that at the beginning of the period Manitoba taxation was somewhat higher than average and gave less scope for increasing the returns, and, second, that 'the incomes of Manitobans were more severely and continuously affected by the depression than were those of the people of most other provinces.' The bank agreed with the Manitoba government that additional funds were necessary for the maintenance of certain services such as roads, the educational system, and mental institutions. How much money was needed was questionable but it did not appear 'practical to increase revenues by further taxation.' Similarly, the substantial increase in debt for relief purposes over the past six years was causing serious concern, and there was a strong feeling that it was unwise to continue adding to the debt for that purpose.

The report pointed out that Manitoba had been affected by the low level of prices for agricultural products during the years 1930-5, by drought in some sections of the province, and by the indirect affects of drought and low prices further west. Towers thought Manitoba had been fortunate that the drought areas were predominantly outside the province. But 'Notwithstanding this advantage and the efforts of its Government, which, as we have indicated, have been very considerable, the province is either not in a position to carry on, or is able to do so with assurance for no more than a short period, unless some unexpected favourable factor should appear ... it seems to be the case that revenues are not adequate, or are not sufficiently elastic, to enable the province to bear the burdens which modern practices of government and the force of the depression have placed upon it.'

Towers did not believe that the various debt refunding proposals that had been made provided a solution to Manitoba's problems. In fact, they involved a severe blow to Manitoba's credit. He reminded the federal government that Manitoba did not stand alone in its difficulties as other sections of the country were facing problems which might differ in degree but were not much dissimilar. He therefore recommended the appointment of a royal commission to inquire into federal-provincial relations.

The federal cabinet met at noon on 15 February 1937. Within half an hour it had been decided to appoint a royal commission to investigate the whole system of taxation in the dominion, to study the division of financial powers and responsibilities between the dominion and the provinces, and to make recommendations as to what should be done to secure a more equitable and practical division of the burden to enable all governments to function more effectively and independently within the spheres of their respective jurisdictions.[23] Pending the report of the commission the government would give temporary aid to Manitoba and Saskatchewan. This was later set at $750,000 for Manitoba.

Bracken was naturally delighted with both the Towers report and the federal decision to appoint a royal commission. He believed the report vindicated Manitoba's stance of the past few years and that a royal commission was long overdue. Feeling considerably more at ease than at any time since December, he approached the opening of the Manitoba legislature with greater confidence. He broke from tradition almost immediately in order to stress the seriousness of the situation facing the province. Rather than assign the duty of introducing the motion for an Address-in-Reply to the Speech from the Throne to one of the younger government members, Bracken did it himself. He explained the procedures that would be followed during the session: the government was willing to accept majority decisions on all ordinary matters of policy and administration; thus an adverse vote on ordinary matters would not be considered as a want-of-confidence vote. Adverse votes construed as want-of-confidence would be on the Address-in-Reply, plans for the readjustment of dominion-provincial relations, and any question on which the government stated beforehand that it would take a firm stand.

The government was endangered only once in the session. Lewis St George Stubbs introduced a motion calling for the repeal of the 2 per cent 'wage tax.' Bracken moved an amendment that the tax should be repealed as soon as a majority of the House approved of sufficient reductions in expenditure to offset it. N.V. Bachynsky, a government supporter, then moved an amendment to the amendment that the tax should be repealed as soon as the House approved of an alternative tax. Both amendments carried, and the original motion was voted down by a small majority. To have abolished the 'wage tax' would have meant a loss of $1,500,000 easily collected revenue. Bracken did compromise by raising the income assessment, thus reducing the burden on people with moderate incomes. Although this concession relieved 35,000 people, it meant a loss of $500,000 in revenue. But it was probably worth it politically. A straight vote on the abolition of the tax could have resulted in the defeat of the government, thus precipitating a dissolution of the legislature and another election. Although most opposition groups did not wish another election, the 'wage tax' was such an emotional issue that they might have been left with little option but to defeat the government.

On 24 March 1937 Bracken submitted his plans for an Economic Survey Board to the legislature. He did not think the survey would be costly. The board would have an advisory committee to serve for a term of years. Government facilities and secretarial staff would be used and the government would call for the voluntary service of specially qualified people on the board. The survey would be wide-ranging and would include a soil survey and studies of primary and secondary industry, production, consumption, health problems, and labour conditions.

Bracken claimed that realities had to be faced. One-tenth of the province was unemployed, wealth production had been halved, young people were without employment opportunities, and agriculture had been bankrupted by economic and climatic forces. Most of these problems had reached their existing serious level because they had not been studied in the beginning. The time had come to lay the basis of a new deal. That basis would have to include whatever was necessary and valuable in socialism, social credit, and other policies.[24]

Only the Conservatives had any criticism to make and that was because they thought the survey was economically unnecessary and catered too much to Social Credit ideas. That may have been so, but it was also an idea that was in keeping with Bracken's thorough, cautious approach to the solution of problems. The board was approved, $15,000 was allotted for its initial expenses, and Clive Davidson was appointed director. Over the next two years the board supplied the government with a number of valuable reports on conditions in the province.

King did not make a formal announcement of the commission's terms of reference nor of its personnel until August, but the Manitobans began their preparations long before that. Representatives of Alberta, Saskatchewan, and Manitoba met in Regina on 3 May for a preliminary discussion. Garson was the Manitoba representative, and thus from the start assumed the duties he was to carry throughout the next year and a half.

Although new to cabinet responsibilities, Garson, at thirty-eight, was a ten-year veteran of the House. A lawyer by profession, he had been persuaded to enter politics in 1927 after Bracken had heard him speaking at a rural meeting. He had quickly shown his ability but fusion with the Liberals had meant that Bracken could not bring him into the cabinet until 1936 when he was given the crucial post of provincial treasurer. Garson was an extremely able man, hardworking, highly intelligent, and quick. Like Bracken he was a detail man and a compulsive explainer who, on any given subject, always knew more law than anyone else – even the minister concerned. In the House he was dry and serious and his manner gave no hint of his wry sense of humour.

After taking office Garson had soon become an expert on federal-provincial relations and on all financial matters. Bracken and Garson were completely agreed on the need to re-examine and revise the existing taxing powers and the need to shift responsibility for national matters such as unemployment relief and old-age pensions to the federal government. Garson played a prominent role in having Manitoba's case placed cogently and forcefully before the federal government and the general public. Bracken constantly sought his advice, and gave him more leeway than any of his other ministers. It was apparent by the end of the decade that Bracken considered Garson to be his most useful and powerful minister.

The actual relationship between the two men and the degree to which the policies of the late thirties originated with Garson rather than with Bracken will probably never be known. There is no doubt that Bracken was the master of his cabinet and that Garson had been chosen because he shared Bracken's attitudes. So, in that sense, Garson was reinforcing commitments and ideas that Bracken had long held. Also, Bracken had always been one to rely on outside expert advice in the preparation of a case or before making a major decision. He usually knew roughly what he wanted – sound economic practises; his concern was to maintain or obtain them in the most efficient and effective manner. Now, however, more than ever before, he left the organizing and the overall direction to someone else, and it is here that the degree and nature of Garson's influence is unclear. He was patently an important force in preparing and presenting Manitoba's case and he doubtless took Bracken further and faster than he might otherwise have gone. But until the Garson Papers are opened we will not know, and even then they may be unrevealing. The Bracken Papers contain almost nothing on the relations of the two men, and very little more on the methods of preparing Manitoba's case.

Bracken and Garson initially tried to persuade Jacob Viner, an economist at the University of Chicago, to take the job of director of research, but Viner was only prepared to act in a consultative capacity. Bracken must almost have dropped the phone when he learned that Viner charged $100 a day while away from Chicago. In the end Professor A.R. Upgren of the University of Minnesota was recruited as research economist and Viner and Professor Alvin Hansen, also of Minnesota, served as consultants in the preparation of the Manitoba brief.[25]

Bracken also turned for assistance to two local men, Hank Grant and Clive Davidson, and over the next three years their services were invaluable. Grant was a professor of Agricultural Economy at the University of Manitoba and had been a close friend and adviser to Bracken for many years. An expert on prairie agriculture, he was able to draw on considerable local knowledge in preparing his background papers for the outside economists. Davidson, although younger than Grant, had a wider range of experience. After completing his MA at the University of Saskatchewan he had gone on to do graduate work in economics and statistics at the University of Chicago, and from 1930 to 1935 he had been with the agricultural branch of the Dominion Bureau of Statistics. In 1935 he had joined the Wheat Board but by 1937 he was in Winnipeg engaged in private statistical work. Davidson's Ottawa and Wheat Board experience soon proved indispensable to Bracken and some of the most cogent and well-argued memoranda in the Bracken files were those supplied by the director of the Economic Survey Board.

By mid-May the Manitobans had worked out in general terms what their argument would be. They believed they would be able to show that Manitoba had suffered economic disabilities owing to national tariff and trade policies, national monetary policy, and national settlement policy. They also expected to be able to argue that 'the fields of taxation allotted to it under our federal system are inadequate to support the present-day conception of the provincial government's responsibilities; and that some realignment of these fields of taxation and functions of government, based upon the tax-paying capacity of the province, is essential.' Initially, it had been hoped that all the western provinces, but at least the three prairie provinces, could 'collaborate in the preparation of arguments common to all, at least to the extent of making certain that the argument of each should not be inconsistent with those of the other provinces.' If Viner had agreed to serve as director the Manitobans had planned to push that idea. Once he declined they dropped it, although they did continue to confer with Patterson's government in Saskatchewan.[26]

King finally announced the composition of the commission on 14 August. The commissioners were Newton W. Rowell, chief justice of Ontario, chairman; Thibaudeau Rinfret, justice of the Supreme Court of Canada; John Dafoe, president and editor-in-chief of the *Winnipeg Free Press*; R.A. MacKay, professor of political science at Dalhousie; and H.F. Angus, professor of economics at UBC. On 31 August Alex Skelton was appointed secretary of the commission and director of research. Unfortunately, before the first public session of the commission, the Honourable Mr Justice Rinfret had to resign owing to illness. His place was taken by Dr Joseph Sirois of Quebec City, a professor of constitutional law at Laval. When ill health also forced Rowell to resign in mid-1938, Sirois succeeded him as chairman. Hence the popular title – the Rowell-Sirois Commission.[27]

In recognition of Manitoba's initiative in having the commission appointed, public hearings opened in Winnipeg on 29 November 1937 and lasted nine days. Hearings concluded in Ottawa on 1 December 1938. Two provinces, Alberta and Quebec, did not make submissions and Ontario withdrew her co-operation in July 1938.

Bracken opened the presentation of Manitoba's case on 29 November with the declaration that:

In what we shall have to say we shall speak as Canadians, not as sectionalists. What we shall say we shall say as Canadian citizens who happen to live in this part of Canada. What we shall say will be said because it needs saying in the interests of Canada as well as of Manitoba ...

In presenting our case we shall feel that we are not less Canadian in spirit or in reality if we show that the economic picture which Canada, not intentionally but nevertheless actually has permitted to be drawn across this section of the Dominion is not just to those Canadians who happen to live here and is not in the interests of Canada as a whole.[28]

The case which the Manitoba delegation made to the Royal Commission during the first week in December was one familiar to those who had followed Bracken's comments since the early thirties. It outlined the difficulties under which Manitoba and the West had laboured as a result of federal monetary and tariff policies, stressed the impossibility of continuing a situation by which the prairies were responsible for expanded relief and social service costs on a narrow tax base, and pointed out that although Manitoba's debt was no more than average in a national context the ability of its citizenry to absorb that debt was far below the national average. The Manitobans called for a substantial shifting of responsibilities and of taxing powers between the federal and provincial levels of government.

After a lengthy and detailed analysis of Manitoba's treasury problem, Garson pointed out that the BNA Act did not provide the provinces with adequate financial capacity for the provision of social services, that the initial increase in Manitoba's debt charges had been primarily due to the province's borrowing for relief and social services, that the dominion subsidy, as a percentage of total current revenue, had dropped from 88.08 per cent in 1875 to 12.27 per cent in 1936, and that the provision of unemployment relief should not be financed as a capital expenditure by borrowed money but as a current expenditure out of current revenue. Garson argued that 'due in large part to the financial plan of Confederation as interpreted by the courts, Manitoba and other provinces and a number of municipalities in Canada are on the verge of default or have already defaulted.'

Garson did not think an enlargement of the provincial field of taxation was wise nor did he think that increased federal subsidies, federal retirement from the field of direct taxation, or a sliding allowance to the provinces from the federal treasury were sound or desirable solutions to Manitoba's long-run problems. He argued that the financing of relief would lead inevitably to the bankruptcy of many Canadian provinces. Garson claimed that the dominion government should assume the administration and financing of relief not only for reasons of efficiency and equality but because 'it would deal with a national problem by a national instrument upon a national scale, and could therefore be coordinated with national trade, monetary and tariff policies.'[29]

In concluding the Manitoba brief Bracken called for a reconstitution of the provincial debt and interest burden and a reallocation of responsibilities between the dominion and provincial governments. He wanted the dominion to assume full responsibility for the financing and administering of unemployment relief and old-age pensions and to assume on substantially a 50-50 basis the cost of such social services as mothers' allowances, hospitalization, the care of the mentally ill, public health services, highway construction and maintenance, and technical education. In return the province would give the dominion the sole power to collect succession duties. He urged upon the commission 'such a readjustment of Dominion-provincial relations as will make possible within Confederation, a workable plan under which the Dominion, provincial and municipal governments can provide for the people in every province of Canada, that common standard of public and social services to which as Canadian citizens they are justly entitled.'[30]

It was a strong submission with which to start the hearings. The commission was now aware of all the major problems facing the prairie provinces. In the event, Manitoba's brief turned out to be the most comprehensive and best argued of all those submitted. Bracken and his colleagues could feel satisfied with a job well done.

As if to underline the gravity of Manitoba's case, Bracken had to meet a special session of the legislature the day after the commission's departure from Winnipeg in order to grapple with the city's financial problems. In May the city had been told by the Bank of Montreal that it could borrow no more money for unemployment relief after 1 July. Although this deadline had been moved back to 20 July the bank had thereafter remained firm. The city had turned to the provincial government for assistance and it in turn had appealed to the federal government. The latter had been prepared to lend the additional sum to the province if the province would turn it over to the city while absorbing the interest and principal payments itself. Bracken had refused to add to the provincial debt in this fashion and had turned the proposal down. After considerable haggling between the three levels of government a conference was held in Ottawa on 19 July in an effort to resolve the impasse. After much persuasion, and very reluctantly, Bracken agreed to shoulder, only on a temporary basis, the 20 per cent of relief expenditures which the bank had refused to finance. Bracken deeply believed that of the three governments the province was the least able to bear the extra burden of the city's relief costs. He believed the city could use monies normally allocated to its sinking fund. Nevertheless, he called an early session so the city could be given new sources of revenue and thus relieve the province of the extra load.[31]

The city was given authority to raise $630,000 by extra taxation to meet its share of relief costs, but the provincial government was not happy with this arrangement and in June 1938 it appointed a Royal Commission to investigate the city's financial set-up. Its members were Carl Goldenberg of Montreal, chairman; A.L. Crossin of Winnipeg; and Joe Thorson of Selkirk. It reported in 1939. The commission found that the city's financial condition was basically sound and that it could afford to divert a proportion of its sinking fund payments into relief. As a result Bracken made no further changes in provincial policy and the city was left to handle its financial affairs as best it could.[32]

By early 1938 Bracken was becoming increasingly recognized as a strong federalist or centralist. During 1938 there were a number of opportunities for him to demonstrate that he was, in fact, both a strong federalist but also an equally strong champion of the rights and interests of the West. He argued that it was false to look at the country in regional terms. All parts of Canada were interconnected and dependent on each other. To dismiss the plight of the West or to try and hide behind existing constitutional imperatives was to work against national needs and realities. Similarly, he argued that low tariff policies were essential if the western farmer were to be able to buy automotive parts and farm equipment at reasonable prices. Bracken scorned economic nationalism as a narrow-minded and parochial approach to national and international problems. He attributed much of the world's difficulties over the previous ten years to that limited approach to trading problems. There were two issues in 1938 that revealed Bracken as a moderate but tenacious advocate of both the centralist and the western viewpoint: the concluding phase of the Rowell-Sirois Commission hearings and the problem of western agriculture.

In early May 1938, a few weeks after the session ended, Mitchell Hepburn read a thirty-page brief to a hearing of the Rowell-Sirois Commission in Toronto. Garson was in the audience as Hepburn made a dead set on Bracken and the Manitoba arguments of the previous year. The brief was a rebuttal and contained no positive proposals. Hepburn declared his government's emphatic opposition to any enlargement of the power of Canada's federal government. Any changes ought to be in the other direction: 'Canadians ought to strengthen the hands of government closest to the people.' He left no doubt that he stood for the complete maintenance of existing provincial rights. He thought the provinces should handle their own fiscal problems. There never would be equality between the provinces. He thought finances should be provided by broader provincial taxation and prior provincial right to the income tax field, the federal government stepping in only when provincial needs had been satisfied. He was especially critical of Manitoba's tariff brief, calling it 'a bit of political arithmetic awry with reality.' The West seemed to forget that the East bought the West's grain, meat, and dairy products behind a protective tariff wall.[33]

Bracken and Garson had little immediate comment on the substance of Hepburn's remarks although Bracken hoped that Hepburn was not speaking for any large section of central Canada; if he were Bracken was afraid that the prospect of a more united nation was much more remote than many had hoped. He still wanted the West's and Manitoba's case to be dealt with on its merits.[34]

That July during a trip to eastern Canada and in reply to a reporter's question, Bracken called himself a federalist as contrasted with a provincial rightsman. He was strongly of the opinion that Canada's future lay in the path of a strong federal union rather than in that of nine sovereign provinces.[35] His growing interest in national affairs had already been noted by many journalists. But in mid-October some began to speculate about the premier's future. One writer summed up the speculation best in the *Tribune* in an article entitled 'Whither Bracken:'[36]

On its face the record shows that Mr. Bracken is beginning to emerge from the cocoon of political provincialism into the larger statesmanship of the national field ...

Two provincial premiers, Messrs. Hepburn and Duplessis have forced themselves on the national scene in a rather startling way. Reversing an old grievance, they declare that they are sick and tired of being hewers of wood and drawers of water for Western Canada.

Obviously some sort of rejoinder on behalf of the West is called for – no more speechmaking, but some intelligent, responsible and consistent line of policy and action which will make sense and stay put.

Mr. Bracken is now the dean of Western premiers – indeed he heads the oldest provincial government in Canada. It is, therefore, quite natural that he should feel responsibility for raising a Western voice in national affairs. This responsibility he shares, of course, with others but he is in a special position to make his voice heard.

The need for strong representations from the West is nothing new in Canadian affairs, indeed it is exactly as old as the West itself. The fact that this is merely an old problem with new facets does not diminish the urgency of the Western case. A westerner may set out to confine himself to provincial politics, may base his political career upon provincial support, but in the very nature of things he is likely to be drawn into the wider arena of national affairs if not of federal politics.

A further opportunity for Bracken to speak for the West came at the end of 1938 at the final hearing of the Royal Commission. Bracken, Garson, and Viner all spoke before the commission and all were frank and forceful. When Bracken had finished his remarks there was little left of Hepburn's position and he was soon receiving congratulations from all over the West for his vigorous comments. Bracken was never a loud, boastful man. He was always even tempered and moderate in his conduct, but he could speak with conviction and vigour when motivated. Despite his poor speaking habits in the legislature, he could be animated and persuasive when he was speaking on a set occasion in a formal atmosphere on a topic about which he felt deeply and with a brief in front of him.

In his remarks Bracken defied anyone to prove that the wheat problem confronting Canada had its origin in the prairie provinces as Hepburn had alleged in May. The war had led to patriotic expansion of wheat acreage and post-war international developments had cut down markets. Bracken stressed the dire urgency of a more rational dominion-provincial relationship if inequities were to be reduced. He reaffirmed as clearly as he could but in a non-threatening manner that if no action resulted from the work of the commission, 'the province of Ontario and the Dominion of Canada may just as well make up their minds now as later that there will have to be a drastic adjustment of public debt burden in more than one province in Canada and in many additional municipalities.'

Bracken agreed with Hepburn that governments should live within their incomes. And western Canada could do that if, having sold its products in the competitive markets of the world, it could buy in the same markets. But that, unfortunately, was not the case. It sold in a low market and bought in a protected market to the advantage of Ontario. Bracken had nothing but disdain for Hepburn's reference to the 'capitalized wheat growing interests of the west.' Those capitalized interests were western tax-payers who had submitted to a heavier tax load than that in Ontario. They were the same people who had submitted for years to a tariff policy which had added to their costs and mainly benefitted other parts of Canada. 'They had paid high rates of interest, suffered drought, plagues and low prices as well as a monetary policy, whatever its virtues, not designed to relieve the desperate predicament of the wheat growers in the west.'[37]

The following day, 29 November, Bracken called for a tariff advisory council, representative of all regions, to deal continuously with the economic implications of the Canadian tariff, its effect on the national welfare, and on the basic economies of the various parts of Canada. The existing tariff structure was too much the result of the 'hurly-burly' of politics.[38] Most observers thought Bracken had won the verbal battle with Hepburn.[39]

By the end of 1938 Bracken was becoming widely recognized as a major spokesman for the West. Most of his comments so far had been directed at federal-provincial relations and the straitjacket of the BNA Act, but during the winter of 1938-9 he re-emerged as the leader of western farm interests.

Agriculture had never been far from his mind at any time in the thirties. He was actively involved in farming enterprises and he made a point of visiting farm communities on a regular basis. He had spoken out earlier in the decade, dissecting the causes of the depression and calling for more efficient farming and marketing methods. He and Hank Grant had attended a conference in Cincinnati in December 1932 on world wheat problems and this had led to Bracken becoming in the mid-thirties a strong advocate of acreage reduction. He had thrown his government's support behind a Wheat Problems Committee, representative of the prairie provinces, and had assisted Grant's activities on its behalf. He had also continued to speak out against 'the unregulated individualism and uncontrolled nationalism' which had resulted in a surplus of wheat in the world and a consequent plunge in prices.

Bracken defended the World Wheat Agreement of 1933 by which the main wheat exporting countries agreed to limit their exports over the next two years. He welcomed this arrangement as a reasonable first step to rational production policies but he emphasized that Canada's and the West's problems would not begin to diminish until there existed a national policy for agriculture covering all provinces and all products. The prairie provinces needed markets but they also needed a concerted attack upon the drought area 'by an intelligently conceived and scientifically worked out program of conservation.' Certain areas should be closed to settlement and the drought area reclaimed by conserving stream flows, extending the boundaries of forest reserves, creating new forest reserves and community pastures, and reforesting parts of the dry belt. When Bracken carried this programme into the Canadian Clubs of Montreal and Toronto in December 1934 and appealed to eastern businessmen to support a national programme, he was well received and his ideas widely publicized. He was described by the *Financial Times* as 'one of the most sincere men in Canadian public life and an outstanding expert in field husbandry.'[40]

Although Bracken's interests in western agricultural problems never slackened, his time and energies were increasingly preoccupied with financial crises and federal-provincial relations and it was not until the late summer of 1938 that he turned his attention back to agriculture in a major way. What drew him was the problem of wheat marketing. In 1935 Bennett had re-established the Wheat Board which had taken over the Central Selling Agency's wheat holdings, and the King government, somewhat reluctantly, had continued to operate it. Each year a price had been set for wheat but each year the board had not had to make any purchases from the farmers because the world price had remained slightly above the pegged price. By 1938 the Wheat Board had sold its accumulated backlog and King and Gardiner gave serious thought to abolishing the board. Both men favoured private enterprise over government involvement in the sale of wheat. In 1938, however, the world crop was very large and prices fell. The western farmer not only wanted the Wheat Board to continue but he wanted the board to guarantee him a reasonable return. After wrangles in the federal cabinet between eastern and western ministers, King succeeded by August in having the price pegged at eighty cents a bushel of No 1 Northern, basis Fort William.[41]

Bracken found eighty cents satisfactory. He thought western farmers should be happy with that price.[42] Satisfied he may have been, but, as Clive Davidson kept telling him, pegging the price of wheat was merely a compensating measure. It did not resolve the fundamental problems facing wheat marketing. In an effort to come to grips with these issues Bracken announced on 13 October that he was calling an international conference in December in Winnipeg to discuss the marketing of western agricultural products. The urgency had been occasioned by the plunge of the actual price of No 1 Northern, as opposed to the pegged price, to sixty cents a bushel, only seven cents more a bushel than the average for 1932–3, the worst year for western agriculture. Thus the future trend of prices and markets, and what to do about them, was of crucial importance. The eighty-cent price established by the Wheat Board had saved Western Canada in 1938, said Bracken, 'but what of next year and the years that are to follow? The situation is a challenge to western agriculture and a challenge to the nation as a whole. Adequate markets for our surplus agricultural products are absolutely essential to the economic well-being of Manitoba and other western provinces, and the Manitoba government feels that the time has arrived when the whole question should be considered in the light of our experience since 1930, and in the light of more recent developments.'[43]

By early November Bracken was speaking to a radio audience throughout western Canada of the need for national action to save the agricultural industry of western Canada. Either major tariff reductions in order to lower production costs or compensation through assured minimum prices were imperative, said Bracken, to ease the burden which the people of the West were now carrying. He warned his listeners that the price at which western wheat was sold was a matter not solely of western concern but of vital importance to all people in the dominion. He wanted the urgency of the situation understood not only by the western farmers but by the nation as a whole.[44]

The conference on wheat marketing problems met in Winnipeg from 12-16 December and was attended by over 200 representatives of organized agriculture, industry, business, and finance throughout Canada. Those present heard papers on the broad international trends and the specific domestic policies that had led to the current difficulties, and various alternatives for the future were discussed. At the end it was agreed, on Bracken's suggestion, to form a representative committee on markets and agricultural readjustment to carry on from the point where the conference left off. Bracken was given the responsibility of assembling the committee and organizing its work. Its primary function would be to carry on the campaign for wider markets and agricultural adjustment. Sub-committees would handle the examination of detailed questions.[45]

The conference was a natural sequel to Manitoba's briefs to the Rowell-Sirois Commission, and enabled the West to state to the nation the problems of agriculture. Bracken was widely acclaimed for his initiative and diplomatic tact in assembling the conference. *The Financial Post*, always supportive, went so far as to suggest that he could probably move on to the national stage anytime he wished. He was a shrewd politician, despite his denials: 'Sensing acute wheat difficulties ahead, Mr. Bracken called the recent conference. Through the medium of wheat he believed he could get varying western interests to speak with a united voice, possibly through a single leader ... Only a diplomat of the highest talent could produce such cooperation.' Many of those present were said to be 'much impressed with John Bracken's skill in getting unanimous cooperation from widely conflicting political and economic interests.' They were also impressed by the fact that he was still in his middle fifties and 'undisputed leader of a central and strategic Canadian province.' *The Post* suggested he could become the new Liberal leader within two years owing to the King-Hepburn split.[46]

Bracken's capacity to function on the wider stage was soon to be tested again.

The federal government was unhappy at having to pay upwards of $40,000,000 to prairie wheat growers for the 1938 crop and the cabinet was, by the end of the year, considering alternative methods of dealing with the question. The government longed to get out of the wheat business, but the real problem was how. Two proposals were apparently being reviewed by late 1938. One envisaged 'putting the wheat pools back on the job of cooperative marketing of wheat, plus a government guarantee of a minimum price at a reasonable average world market level.' The other was more complicated. It would be based on two factors: 'A sliding scale of government guaranteed payments increasing as the world price of wheat fell below a fixed level but paid on a percentage of normally cultivated acreage instead of seeded land.'[47]

It was with these problems that Bracken became involved in the first half of 1939. It was an issue that generated considerable emotion within the federal cabinet and led to public disagreement between Jimmy Gardiner, the minister of agriculture, and Bracken. As usual, Bracken relied heavily upon Hank Grant for advice in this area, and it was Grant who wrote many of Bracken's speeches. He also turned often to Clive Davidson who became the secretary of Bracken's Western Committee on Markets and Agricultural Adjustment.

During January Bracken stepped up his campaign to keep the public informed of the western plight. A lengthy article he wrote outlining the problems facing Manitoba and the West and analyzing current and proposed solutions was published in the *Ottawa Citizen* on 13 January 1939. Bracken spoke in Calgary on the 16th and again in Edmonton on the 17th, and hammered away at the same issues: 'We must strive to regain lost markets by more aggressive merchandising and advertising; by reciprocal trade treaties and by unilateral tariff reductions and by barter if necessary.' He argued that the state had to assist agriculture with the problems of wheat marketing and prices. Laissez-faire methods were no longer enough. They would lead to bankrupt farmers, abandoned farms, increased unemployment, general default in public debt, a lower standard of living, and 'perhaps peasantry in much of Canada.' It would be a national disaster to allow western agriculture to fail. He called for a united front in the West 'on a policy that is vital to Canada and is in the national interest.'[48]

By 20 January Bracken had assembled a committee of eighteen, six from each of the prairie provinces, representative of governments, agriculture, business, and industrial interests. It held its first meeting in Regina on 31 January.[49] It was a distinguished group strongly representative of both the grain trade and the wheat pools, as well as the universities. The ministers of agriculture of both Saskatchewan and Alberta were also included, though Douglas Campbell, the Manitoba agricultural minister, was not a member. Bracken obviously planned to look after Manitoba's interests himself.

The first meeting was primarily organizational. It did, however, recommend the appointment of a sub-committee to draft a federal wheat policy for 1939-40 that could be recommended by the Western Committee to the King government.[50] The Committee reassembled for a two-day conference in Saskatchewan in mid-February. There it was unanimously agreed to request that the Wheat Board should be continued for 1939-40, that a guaranteed price for wheat of at least eighty cents for No 1 Northern, basis Fort William, be set by the federal government, and, in order to assure all farmers of an improved maintenance income, that some form of subsidiary assistance by way of a crop insurance plan be introduced.[51]

Bracken was in complete sympathy with these requests. As he pointed out to the Saskatoon Canadian Club on 15 February: 'If we can afford to subsidize manufacturing to the extent of $47,000,000 a year, through tariff protection, then we can afford to subsidize western agriculture to the extent of $50,000,000 a year through the wheat bonus.' Bracken wired Ottawa and asked for an early appointment for the presentation of the wheat committee's views.[52]

The approach of Jimmy Gardiner was different from that of Bracken and the Western Committee. On 16 February Gardiner outlined a new wheat marketing policy in the House of Commons. The policy involved discontinuance of the existing system of a fixed minimum price and substitution of an acreage bonus to meet emergency situations arising from crop failure or lack of markets. He pointed out that the fixed price for the current year of eighty cents a bushel would cost the government $48,000,000 but its distribution involved giving more to those who had crops and nothing to those who had not. The bill, said Gardiner, 'will be drafted on the principle that assistance will be given in proportion to need, and calculated on an acreage basis and so adjusted as to encourage home building and maintenance rather than increased wheat production.' He thought the fixed-price system inequitable. It took no account of drought and grasshopper difficulties. It resulted in those having most receiving most and those having no crop receiving nothing.[53]

As Bracken knew, there was a need to make a clear distinction between relief and assistance in the marketing of the wheat crop. It was important to secure a fair price for the farmer with a crop as well as provide assistance for the farmer without a crop. Bracken's Western Committee had advised meeting these two demands by a fixed price and crop insurance, Gardiner by an acreage bonus system that had a form of crop insurance built in. Neither Gardiner's nor Bracken's plan was perfect. Gardiner's would encourage growth on marginal land and would not resolve the problem of low international prices. Bracken's was an emergency rather than a permanent solution. It would ensure the circulation in western Canada of a certain amount of money so that the economy could continue to function. Gardiner's plan was also a measure of the East's objection to the cries of the West and was thus a political compromise. The Bracken method of meeting the West's problems was full of defects; so was Gardiner's – but they both reflected the West's needs. It was now essential for the Bracken Committee, as the Western Committee was commonly called, to confer with the dominion government.[54]

The Bracken Committee met with the dominion cabinet for the first time on 1 March in Ottawa.[55] In introducing the committee to the cabinet, Bracken made it clear that neither he nor his colleagues were in Ottawa 'to hold a gun to head of Dom. Govt.' They were not present 'as fly by night organizations to demand continued handouts by Dom. Govt.' But they were there 'as a body of men sincerely concerned with the immediate economic future of Western Canada; a body of men sincerely desirous of tackling problems ahead of Western Canada along soundest possible lines; as a body of men determined to give the problem continued study in each of eight or nine directions.'[56] King was favourably impressed by the delegation: 'It was as fine a delegation as I have ever listened to. The material was admirably prepared and splendidly presented. I think every Minister was deeply impressed by the presentation which was most helpful. Was delighted to see the farmers getting themselves into the position where they could hold themselves against industrialists of large cities. I felt in the main they were right in their presentation ... It was an intellectual treat to listen to what was said, and one felt one was getting a really splendid picture of the whole situation in relation of Western Canada to the rest of Canada.'[57]

Over the next few weeks the debates in the House of Commons were followed with intense interest by Bracken and his colleagues. Gardiner was initially unsympathetic to any change but after the departure of the Bracken delegation he came under increasing pressure to alter his proposals.[58] Bracken, of course, continued to make speeches in Winnipeg and throughout Canada advocating the need of the nation to stand by the West during its economic and financial problems.[59] He repeated his usual and now well-known arguments about the causes of Western distress to the Winnipeg Canadian Club at the Royal Alexandra Hotel on 24 March, and made a major speech on 'Canadian agriculture from a Western Viewpoint' to the Eastern Canadian Conference on the Marketing of Farm Products in Montreal on 28 March.[60]

While Bracken was in Montreal William Euler introduced a bill amending the Canadian Wheat Board Act. It included the provision that as of 1 August wheat growers would receive a guaranteed initial price of sixty cents a bushel, basis No 1 Northern at Fort William, instead of the eighty-cent minimum paid in 1938-9.[61] Bracken found the new price unsatisfactory. He did not believe it was in the best interests of the West nor the nation as a whole. He reminded the government that it was essential to keep the special problem of relief resulting from crop failure, or partial crop failure, altogether separate from the main problem of assistance to the wheat industry as a whole in times of emergency. Sixty cents a bushel was an inadequate price 'to preserve the wheat industry and the economic structure of the prairie provinces with its many ramifications, in the national economy. Assistance rendered to farmers in the case of small yields, or crop failure, will not compensate for a less price to the industry as a whole, or inadequate protection to the farmer who harvests a crop in 1939.' He pointed out that if the government's support to the West was inadequate the western farmer would turn to the production of farm products for the domestic market with destructive results for all of Canadian agriculture. Thus the handling of the wheat problem was not a problem affecting the West alone, but a problem of far-reaching significance for the country as a whole.[62]

In Ottawa King had some doubts about the political implications of Gardiner's wheat policy but decided to rely upon his minister's judgment for the moment.[63] Toward the end of April, however, he was obliged to face the issue more fully. Bracken had assembled another meeting of the Western Committee in Calgary in mid-April where it had been decided to visit Ottawa again and press for an effective Wheat Board and a minimum price of not less than eighty cents per bushel.[64]

Bracken, now widely recognized 'as the undoubted champion of the western grain grower' and as the principal unifying force in the West, led the delegation to Ottawa on 24 April.[65] Most of the cabinet was present to hear the committee's arguments in favour of the continuation of the Wheat Board and an eighty-cent guaranteed minimum price.[66] On this occasion King was not quite as sympathetic, pointing out that his government had to consider the needs of the nation as a whole. The delegation represented only three provinces but to get anything through the House he had to consider what would be supported by his own following – and by the opposition – from each of the other provinces. He turned to his ministers and said he could not compel them to accept the view of Western Canada and ignore the views of the provinces they represented. He did not want to give evidence of a disunited country to Hitler. He was determined to avoid confusion and disruption. King said he and Gardiner wanted to meet the needs of the West without being driven into an impossible situation.[67]

The next day Bracken met King before the cabinet meeting. King was suspicious, as he usually was in tense moments. He confided to his diary: 'I felt, as he [Bracken] was talking, that while anxious to have it appear that he was most friendly to myself and the Government, in reality, what he said was so phrased so as to prepare the way for him, if need be, to go out on his own in agricultural policies which would appeal to Western Manitoba.' Bracken asked for a meeting with King and Gardiner. King doubted much good would come from the interview, 'knowing that Gardiner is strongly prejudiced against Bracken. I felt the interview would do more harm than good, so did not pursue it ... ' The cabinet meeting that followed was, in King's words, difficult. Gardiner was 'very definitely set in his own way, and Euler and Ilsley equally so in theirs.' Finally, King said there were only one or two courses. One was to drop some of the proposed legislation and simply let the Wheat Board Act stand, applying it next July, probably at the eighty-cent minimum; another alternative was to take the proposed legislation, make the minimum seventy cents, and agree upon some acreage spaces for the relief part, extend the legislation to cover Ontario and Quebec, and fix a penalty which would prevent persons receiving the guaranteed rate from making beyond a certain sum out of the public treasury. Gardiner said he would resign if the first course of action were adopted. Ilsley then said he would resign if the other alternative were chosen. He did not like compromising at the expense of the public treasury.

King assured Gardiner that he thought the cabinet would stand by him but that he would have to be reasonable himself. To Ilsley, King said he felt sure that once he saw the need to support western industry in the teeth of changed world conditions he would appreciate the reasonableness of meeting the situation in a way that would tide over the worst. It was left to C.D. Howe and the four members of the Wheat Committee of the cabinet, Euler, Ilsley, Gardiner, and Crerar, to see what changes could be made to satisfy and protect the West, the different cabinet members, and Liberal political fortunes.[68]

In the end, King's persuasive arguments prevailed. When the amended wheat legislation was introduced on 2 May the minimum guarantee was raised from sixty to seventy cents and adjustments downwards were made in the bonusing system.[69] This legislation subsequently passed through parliament. Although not satisfactory to many grain interests, it placated Bracken for the time being. He knew there was still a vital need for long-range policies and planning but a start had been made and the immediate problems of the western economy forestalled.

Bracken was widely recognized as being primarily responsible for ensuring that the federal government's agricultural policy had been subjected to such a searching examination. As never before, the Canadian public had become acutely aware of the interrelationship of the fortunes of the West with those of the nation. Newspapers across the country commented on Bracken's increased stature and heralded the emergence on the national scene of a man concerned more with Canada as a whole than with any one province or region.[70]

By mid-1939 Bracken had established himself as both the major spokesman for western interests and as a politician prepared to see regional concerns in national terms. Not all of the ideas nor the arguments were his. He relied, as always, on the advice and guidance of others, particularly Garson in the financial and constitutional areas and Grant and Davidson in the agricultural. But the issues of the late 1930s were ones that Bracken had been preoccupied with for more than a decade and about which he had strongly held opinions. This had enabled him to speak with assurance and common-sense at a time when the national spot-light had been concentrated upon him.

11

War

Manitoba political and administrative affairs were not overly demanding in the summer of 1939. Apart from the Royal Visit to Winnipeg in May and the accompanying formalities, life continued much as ever for Bracken. He usually spent every weekend on his farms at Great Falls and Marchand and often stayed a week or more at his place near Hudson Bay Junction. The only issues that continued to attract his time and attention were those related to agriculture.

But with the outbreak of war that autumn Bracken was soon urging a conference of provincial treasurers at Ottawa to determine how the provinces in their own interest and that of the nation could best work with the dominion in the prosecution of the war.[1] He pledged Manitoba's full co-operation with Ottawa's financial and economic plans and offered to modify the province's own financial policy in order to comply. Similarly, the Bracken Committee met in mid-September and agreed to support the federal government's agricultural policy and to act, if necessary, as the agency for mobilizing farm production resources of the prairie provinces.[2]

For the first year of the war Bracken's major preoccupations were the report of the Rowell-Sirois Commission and the difficulties confronting western Canadian agriculture. He was now the recognized and accepted spokesman for the West and he took advantage of every opportunity to hammer away at the Canadian conscience. He was much in demand as a speaker at Canadian Club meetings, Board of Trade gatherings, and various farm society sessions. At all of them he repeated his message: the problems of prairie agriculture were not regional problems but national problems. They could only be satisfactorily resolved by the state, and that meant by the federal government.

As the summer drew to an end and it became clear that storage facilities were inadequate for the grain harvest, Bracken was to the fore in urging that the federal government provide the western farmer with an advance on the guaranteed price per bushel in order that the western economy would not collapse. He maintained it was in the best interests of debtor and creditor alike that cash be available in farmers' pockets over the winter of 1940-1.[3]

Of even greater concern to Bracken at the beginning of 1940 was the pending report of the Rowell-Sirois Commission. Until it was released it was difficult for him to take any legislative action at the provincial level. In late January he telephoned King's secretary to find out when the report would be available. He had postponed the start of the session in the hope that he would be able to study it and make use of it in the legislature.[4] But King had no intention of releasing the report until after the federal election of 26 March and Bracken had to bide his time. The 1940 Manitoba session was therefore a hasty and tame affair.[5] When the report was tabled by King on 15 May it was greeted with satisfaction by Bracken. In essense it called for the assumption by the dominion of provincial debts and unemployment relief costs in return for the transfer by the provinces to the dominion of their personal income tax, corporation tax, and succession duties. The commission suggested a national adjustment grant as compensation to the provinces. Garson later estimated that for Manitoba it would amount to $2,100,000.[6]

Bracken believed the recommendations substantiated Manitoba's case, and he called for an early conference. But his hopes for a quick examination of the Rowell-Sirois Report were given a jolt in late May when King told him, 'much to his surprise that I did not think we could touch the Dominion-Provincial Commission's report till the war was over.' It was King's opinion that 'until we had discussed the peace, we could not touch this local situation.'[7] The fact was, of course, that King was afraid the report was too divisive. He feared that its recommendations were unpalatable to Ontario and Quebec and possibly to Alberta and British Columbia. To discuss the report immediately might generate the open hostility and disunity within Canada that King was always so anxious to avoid.

This delay annoyed Bracken. Coupled with his growing concern for a sound national agricultural policy, it suggested a lack of strength and leadership at Ottawa. It is probable that two developments can be dated from this moment. First, Bracken's decision to form, if possible, a non-partisan government in Manitoba in order to have a stronger political base from which to persuade the Liberals of the need to face national financial, agricultural, and constitutional issues. And, second, his growing disenchantment with the federal Liberals as a vehicle for change and action.

It is clear that by late June he was having private conversations with Willis, the Conservative leader, S.J. Farmer, the CCF leader, and Sydney Rogers, the Social Credit leader. These conversations continued through the summer and early autumn days, and after July were being openly discussed in the newspapers and behind the political scenes.[8] Bracken seems to have acted, initially at least, without consulting his own cabinet colleagues. But that was not in itself surprising. He had done exactly the same in 1936 and had often acted alone in the late twenties on other matters. Nor is it unusual that he appears to have discussed the matter with Dafoe who, while not giving his blessing to the scheme, did say that he had no strong objections.[9]

At that time, late June 1940, Bracken's idea had been to create a purely war government and to carry on for the duration. The details of the scheme were not yet clear but he had intended to drop some members of his cabinet and bring in representatives of the other parties. Even then, however, he had no intention of pursuing the idea far if any of the parties declined to co-operate. He did not wish a repetition of 1931 and 1936. If all was successful he would hold an election with all the sitting members standing for re-election and none being opposed by party candidates.[10]

During August and September Bracken and his fellow party leaders were pre-occupied with trying to persuade Ottawa of the critical situation facing the western farmer owing to the lack of storage facilities on the prairies. Unless the farmer could be paid an advance for grain stored on his land the whole prairie economy was endangered. Bracken called a conference for 15 August in Winnipeg of representatives of the three prairie governments and of western municipal, farm, and business organizations.[11] The meeting was a success and unanimously approved a scheme for a dominion guarantee of bank advances on the security of grain stored on the farms. No formal sum was recommended but most seemed to consider a figure in the thirty to forty cents a bushel range would be satisfactory as an interim payment.

Bracken wrote immediately to Gardiner and Crerar and later in the month to King, urging the federal authorities to consider the plan. In early September he led a delegation from the West to discuss the problem with the wheat committee of the federal cabinet, but it had little success. In fact, Bracken and the prairie provinces were accused of trying to place the full load on the doorstep of the dominion. Bracken bridled at that and said that was exactly where it belonged and nowhere else. But Manitoba and prairie pressure was to no avail and by mid-September Gardiner stated that no decision would be made on federal policy before 1 November and perhaps not then. He was reluctant to add to farm indebtedness by granting loans. Bracken thought that nonsensical. If the farmer did not receive any money he would still have to go further into debt and his creditors would also be placed in a grievous position. Not for the first time Bracken wondered if Gardiner really knew how the prairie economy worked.[12]

Bracken had also written to King in August and September about the necessity for a conference to discuss the Rowell-Sirois Report, but got nowhere. He wrote again on 18 October and this time King read the request to the federal cabinet on the 22nd. However, as King later put it in his diary: 'Council agreed that in view of Hepburn's opinion, it would be unwise to call a conference ... I said there would be no agreement on the report till Hepburn and in all probability his government along with him would be removed. To this, the Cabinet agreed.'[13]

This outcome was immediately conveyed to Bracken. On receiving it he decided to proceed with his scheme for a non-partisan government in Manitoba. It was now clear to him that the federal Liberal government was not prepared to listen to either a western regional or a provincial voice on either the constitutional or agricultural issues. He reasoned that a united political front in Manitoba might alter that stance. Despite his preoccupation in recent weeks with the agricultural crisis facing the West, Bracken had not ceased to talk with Willis, Farmer, and Rogers about a non-partisan government. On hearing of the failure of his latest overture to Ottawa he wrote at length to each man suggesting the formation of such an administration and outlining how it might best be done.

Bracken reminded them that he 'had never looked upon party politics in provincial affairs with any favour' and that at different times in the past he had tried to have it brought to an end. He now thought its elimination essential if Manitoba hoped to see the Rowell-Sirois Report implemented and 'a fair deal' for agriculture guaranteed. As a means of forming a non-partisan wartime administration two Conservatives and one CCF-Labour member would be included in the cabinet. In addition, two more part-time ministers – ministers without portfolios – would be appointed, one from the Conservative party and one from Social Credit. Also, a budget committee of the executive council would be created and Bracken suggested that it include one member from each of the three opposition parties.

In concluding his letters, Bracken was explicit upon one point:

In whatever we may do in this connection, if anything, there is involved no sacrifice or compromise of principles on your part or our own. But in our judgement the differences of opinion which divide us in peacetime become of secondary importance in time of war. From war new and greater issues emerge. We suggest no abandonment of the peacetime principles of the cooperating groups but only that each should be united in the support of these new and paramount issues upon which fortunately there is common ground for agreement. If we did not think that without the least abandonment of principle you could support the above-mentioned program with respect to war, the Sirois Report and our western economy under war and post-war conditions, we would not be addressing this suggestion to you. We do so with the confidence that you will accept it because, like us, we are sure, you do not in times like these believe in party first and the country last. We are not today only CCF-Labor or Liberal-Progressive or Conservative or Social

Credit, but rather Canadians and democrats and freemen. Our cause, even Manitoba's cause, is at this time greater than your party or our own.[14]

By the end of the month all three parties had agreed to join the non-partisan government on Bracken's terms. The decision had been given quick approval by the Conservative caucus but it had caused some distress at the national level of the CCF party. In the end the provincial convention went against the advice of its national executive and endorsed the idea. S.J. Farmer and Stanley Knowles, the party's provincial chairman, had been favourable from the start, but had felt it incumbent upon them to sound the other provincial and the national bodies.[15]

Why did the three parties join so readily? In part, they probably all shared the ideal of unity during wartime but Bracken's emphasis on this was quite specious, for a provincial government had virtually no involvement in running the war effort. He knew, however, that if any of the parties turned down an offer couched in those terms they would be committing political suicide in Manitoba. Even David Lewis, the CCF national secretary, had to admit that.[16]

More realistically, they all realized that Bracken's name was in the ascendancy and if he went to the country, as he suggested he would, the probability was that they would be severely damaged politically. None of them could afford that possibility, particularly the CCF and the Social Credit. The Conservatives reasoned that they might be able to direct the government from within and perhaps in time make it more to their fancy. They also knew that they were not sacrificing any true philosophic principles by entering a non-partisan administration. A coalition would have been a different matter. That, in time, it was to become virtually the same as a coalition was not to be guessed in late 1940.

There was also another reason. Even as late as 1940 there was in all Manitobans a degree of anti-partyism, and the concept of non-party government was not the anathema to many as might be supposed. Although Salome Haldorson refused to join her Social Credit colleagues in support of the new government, and the 'diehard' Liberal League frowned on the whole affair, they were not representative of Manitoba's mood. War conditions had also changed the atmosphere. While the country, the empire, and the Allies were fighting for their lives, it seemed parochial and narrow-minded even to Manitobans to continue the local bickering and jockeying for position. It was equally obvious that the West and the country had problems domestically that could only be resolved by firm federal leadership, and a united front might achieve the necessary unity.

Bracken knew all this. One need not question his genuine sincerity in wishing to see a co-operative effort behind the conduct of the war, but he also realized that he could secure office and his policies more readily through non-partisan government than by going it alone. Bracken may have been an idealist but he was also an astute political realist. He had boxed his political opponents.

By early November the new cabinet had been appointed. Erick Willis became minister of public works replacing Clubb; Farmer became minister of labour, taking over another of Clubb's responsibilities; and James McLenaghen, a Conservative, became minister of health and public welfare, replacing J.B. Griffiths. The two ministers without portfolio were Conservative Alex Welch and Social Credit MLA Norman Turnbull. Bracken resigned from three portfolios – provincial hydro, dominion-provincial relations, and railway commissioner. Hydro went to Garson; dominion-provincial relations to Major, and J.S. McDiarmid became railway commissioner. The new cabinet had twelve members, an increase of two. The government decided to face one more session of the legislature and then go to the country for a mandate.[17]

On 2 November, two days before the Manitoba cabinet was announced, Mackenzie King called a federal-provincial conference for 14–15 January 1941 to discuss the Rowell-Sirois Report. Many observers, including the ever-supportive *Financial Post*, thought that the formation of a non-partisan administration in Manitoba had a great deal to do with forcing consideration of the report. It is not clear that this was so. A sub-committee of the federal cabinet had been examining the report for some months and had recommended calling a conference.[18]

Bracken and the Manitoba delegation approached the January conference firmly committed to the recommendations of the Rowell-Sirois Commission. Bracken was convinced that no other reasonable solution existed to both the immediate and long-range problems facing the West and the nation. The Manitobans had been arguing for some years that federal-provincial financial arrangements had to be revised in light of changed socio-economic conditions. The experience of the West and particularly of Manitoba had confirmed that point. There was a need to shift taxing powers from the provinces to the federal government and for the federal government to assume the burdens of debt and unemployment relief that had been crushing the provinces with increasing harshness since the early 1930s. The Manitobans were hopeful that the conference would result in an acceptance of some of the key commission recommendations.

In the event they were to be sadly disappointed. The conference met on 14–15 January in the House of Commons chamber against a background of mutual suspicion and dislike between King and the flamboyant and arrogant premier of Ontario, Mitchell Hepburn. Almost from the start Hepburn had not supported the Rowell-Sirois Commission and he had been even less enamoured of its findings. He was convinced of two things: that if implemented the recommendations would undermine provincial autonomy and concentrate far too much power in Ottawa; and, second, that wartime, when national unity was essential, was no time to discuss a potentially divisive document. He came to the conference committed more to killing it than to any examination of crucial economic and constitutional problems. At the conference he found support from two western premiers, Aberhart of Alberta and T.D. Pattullo of British Columbia. The latter shared Hepburn's concern about provincial autonomy but, if possible, was even more securely anchored in his blinkered provincial stance. It was not clear what Aberhart feared but it was clear he did not fancy centralization in Ottawa. Of the three he was probably more prepared to talk than Hepburn or Pattullo, but not about the specifics of the report.

The attitudes of 'the three wreckers,' as they came to be called by some segments of the press, became clear during the plenary session on 14 January when all the premiers made opening statements. These attitudes were underlined the next, and as it proved last, day of the conference when they refused to go into committees to discuss details. [19]

Three of the remaining premiers, while not enthusiastic, were willing to discuss the report and considered it a document of major importance. They were Adelard Godbout of Quebec, Alexander MacMillan of Nova Scotia, and John McNair of New Brunswick. The other three were far more positive and were anxious to see many of the recommendations implemented. They were Thane Campbell of PEI, William Patterson of Saskatchewan, and Bracken of Manitoba. Of the three Bracken made the most searching and argumentative speech, one which was widely discussed by politicians and the press. Bracken emerged from the conference as the arch-champion of the report and with his reputation as a serious, reflective statesman considerably enhanced.

His speech was a long one and its essence was by now well known to western audiences. He argued that Canada's economic and political structure was interdependent and Canadians could not allow it, at any time, to disintegrate. Maximum political unity had to be maintained. That was a major reason why the federal government had to be given adequate powers to implement national policies consistent with the fact of a single national economy as distinguished from several provincial economies. Manitoba, therefore, wholeheartedly supported the commission argument that 'national unity must be based on provincial autonomy, and provincial autonomy cannot be assured unless a strong feeling of national unity exists throughout Canada.'

Fully aware that Hepburn was listening, Bracken argued that provincial autonomy would be enhanced rather than diminished by the report. As far as he was concerned, it was 'axiomatic that provincial autonomy in the practical and substantial sense means not only the constitutional power to discharge provincial government functions but also the financial capacity to discharge them.' The thirties had left the western provinces' legal autonomy unimpaired but that had done them little good without the finances to activate their legal powers. This sort of theoretical autonomy no longer appealed to Bracken: 'We prefer to have autonomy in the practical and substantial sense of having not only the legal power to do a thing, but also the financial means with which to do it.'

On turning to the issue of taxation, Bracken made the strong point that Canada's ill-balanced tax structure arose from the dominion's substantial reliance on indirect taxation. Income tax was progressive, that is, geared to the ability to pay. It hit the rich harder than the poor. But indirect taxation hit everybody for the same percentage of cost, and thus had a more severe effect upon the low income earner than the high income earner. The dependence of the dominion on indirect rather than direct taxation during the depression had slowed recovery. The inequities of indirect taxation had existed before 1929 but they were intensified by the depression, and they still existed. They could only be properly resolved by a transfer of direct taxing powers to the dominion in return for the assumption by the dominion of provincial debts.

Bracken also pointed out that if nothing were done to implement the report and the tax fields remained the same, it would not be long before the dominion government invaded the provincial fields for additional revenue to finance the war. But when it did it would not assume provincial debts. That would place the provinces in an even worse position and default might result. That, in turn, would have serious repercussions on both provincial and dominion credit. To Bracken it seemed clear that Canada could not effectively carry on during the war and after with 'the now obsolete governmental equipment of seventy years ago.'[20]

The next day the conference was obviously in difficulty when Hepburn, Pattullo, and Aberhart refused to attend committees. J.L. Ilsley, the minister of finance, filled an awkward gap by providing the conference with a rough statement of the demands of the war on the dominion economy. He made it clear that sheer need would necessitate the invasion of provincial tax fields if nothing were done to implement the report's recommendations. When he finished, T.B. McQuestion, the Ontario minister of highways, indicated that Ontario was withdrawing from the conference.

Bracken found Ilsley's remarks revealing. As far as he had been concerned it was for that kind of information from both the federal government and the other provinces that he and his colleagues had come to Ottawa. Unless people talked, how could they learn? Unless they learned, how could they make the right decisions? 'We came to a conference. We did not come here to fight with other provinces or to order anyone else around, but to get the facts from all quarters so that in the light of the situation as revealed to us we would be in a position to decide what should be done or not done ... What have we got here today? Fault being found with the only constructive plan put before us, and what alternative proposals made? Nothing but the status quo.'

Bracken's disgust was obvious. He reminded his fellow premiers that if the report were not implemented, if the tax fields were not changed, the federal government would have to invade the provincial field in order to finance the war effort. But if they did that they would give the province nothing back. Was that satisfactory? Was everyone satisfied to go home with that *ad hoc* arrangement facing them? Bracken was prepared to stay and discuss finances. His province had had to put on heavier taxation than any province in Canada and had accepted a lower standard of social and educational service than most of them in order that it might try to carry on and meet its obligation. 'We ask that that situation be looked at to determine whether it is wise, in the interest of the future of confederation, that certain provinces should have to put on a much higher percentage of taxation than others and be content with a lower average standard of services than others, or whether that could not be fixed up so that even in the poorer provinces of Canada we can feel ourselves Canadians, not better than anybody else, not the poor relations of Canada, but just Canadians getting an average standard of service.'[21] But Bracken's pleas were unavailing, and after huddling with his cabinet, King brought the conference to a close. In doing so he indicated that the federal government would be willing to take up discussion of the report again if the provinces wished.[22] While King managed to sound appropriately saddened in public at the failure of the conference, it is clear from his diary that he was not displeased at the result.[23]

Bracken returned to Winnipeg frustrated and annoyed at the failure of the conference. He told the newsmen that such a peremptory end solved nothing. The Canadian people could not afford to let a problem of such importance to Canadian unity and Canadian strength remain unsolved, particularly in wartime. 'Nor,' he said, 'can the nation afford to sit by and see a major policy scuttled because three governments out of ten refuse to sit down with the others to consider it.'[24]

On Monday, 27 January, Bracken spoke to the people of Manitoba in a radio broadcast. He called upon the dominion government to over-ride provincial opposition to the Rowell-Sirois Report and put the financial recommendations into effect. At the same time he vigorously attacked Hepburn, Pattullo, and Aberhart for their part in scuttling the conference, and called their actions 'a new low in democratic behaviour and in callous discourtesy and in useless waste of public money.'[25]

The speech was a measure of Bracken's annoyance for it was rare that he criticized so trenchantly in public, particularly other premiers. He was applauded for his remarks in the West but the *Globe and Mail* accused him of provincialism. This surely was absurd, as even the *Tribune* pointed out.[26] Bracken was the only one who continually argued on the basis of the interests of Canada as a whole. Despite the furour Bracken continued to hammer away at the need to implement the Rowell-Sirois Report.[27] But to no avail. The report was effectively dead for at least the duration of the war. In the months ahead Bracken and his colleagues therefore took the lead in working out with the federal government compensation for federal invasion of provincial tax fields.

Before they got far with that Bracken and his new government had to face the electorate, which they did on 22 April. It was a low-key affair, 'unmatched for brevity and serenity' in the province's political life.[28] By 1941 Bracken had held office as premier for almost nineteen years, a longer period than any politician in the Commonwealth, and he was at the height of his popularity. He went to the electorate as the head of a non-partisan administration that everyone conceded would win overwhelmingly. Only eighteen candidates opposed the government and sixteen others won by acclamation, including Bracken and five members of his cabinet. Bracken spoke a mere eight times and in only six constituencies and always in favour of the implementation of the Rowell-Sirois Report, the need for post-war planning, and a fair deal for agriculture. As predicted, the coalition swept to victory winning fifty seats. In future, opposition would come from two Conservatives, General H.D.B. Ketchen of Winnipeg and Reeve D.A. Best of Assiniboia, William Kardash of the Winnipeg Workers' Committee, and two Independents, A.R. Boivin of Iberville and the irrepressible Lewis St George Stubbs of Winnipeg. Nothing could have more heavily underlined the popular appeal of Bracken and the Manitoba public's disinterest in partisan politics.[29]

In the aftermath of the election debt adjustment, stabilization of grain prices, and negotiation of tax fields were the main immediate issues. Bracken and his colleagues went east in May and by the autumn had reached agreement with the federal authorities on the problem of federal invasion of provincial tax fields, but political developments elsewhere in Canada delayed a final announcement until January 1942. Under the agreement the provinces would vacate the personal income and corporation tax fields for one year beyond the end of the war. The federal government would pay the provinces compensation and in addition pay grants to the provinces sufficient to make up the amount by which gasoline tax receipts fell below the totals collected for 1940. Also, PEI, Nova Scotia, New Brunswick, Manitoba, and Saskatchewan would be paid 'fiscal need' subsidies to replace the subsidies granted in 1937 as an interim arrangement until the Rowell-Sirois Report had been completed and more permanent arrangements decided. Under these agreements Manitoba was to receive $5,034,740.92 as a grant in lieu of suspended taxes; $600,000 as a fiscal need subsidy; and her gasoline revenue was not to be allowed to fall below $2,678,148 per year.[30]

Bracken took pains to underline that this was only a temporary, stop-gap agreement that would have to be replaced eventually by more permanent arrangements. He still believed most of the provinces would have been better off if the dominion had carried out the recommendations of the Rowell-Sirois Report. The new arrangement remedied none of the long-standing grievances that the report had underlined. The financial relationship between the provinces and the dominion under the BNA Act remained unchanged. The new arrangement provided only minimum assistance to help the provinces get by during the war. 'The fundamental problem of getting an average standard of public service in the majority of Canadian provinces at no more than an average rate of taxation, still remains to be solved,' said Bracken. He advised King that the problems would have to be faced when the war was over, if not before.[31]

With the approval of the agreements one of the major issues in Manitoba's life came to a temporary end. For the past six years Bracken had been increasingly preoccupied with federal-provincial relations. It had taken him for the first time out of the provincial and western arena and onto the wider national stage. Bracken had found that he had enjoyed tackling the complex issues that had confronted him there and had also enjoyed being accepted as the recognized spokesman and leader of the West.

Leader of the Progressive Conservative party

By 1941 Bracken was a figure of national prominence. He had taken a leading role in the discussion over federal-provincial relations and had established himself as a politician with a deep commitment to Canadian unity. He was also recognized as the voice of western Canada, the one man who best represented the needs, interests, and ambitions of the prairie provinces. The formation of his non-partisan administration in November 1940 and the overwhelming electoral victory of April 1941 had seemingly confirmed his hold on the western public. He was a man who publicly opposed partisanship in politics, who favoured a national government, and who believed in the full utilization of all resources of the state, both material and human, in the successful prosecution of the war. Already he had been critical of the King government in its pursuit of that goal.

Despite his now considerable interest in federal affairs and his willingness to speak out on matters of national concern, Bracken harboured no federal political ambitions. He was considered a Liberal by most and in the past his name had been linked with openings in the King cabinet. But there had never been a firm offer and it is doubtful if he would have seriously considered one. Not only did he have a deep-seated and sincere dislike of 'politicking' but by the late thirties he had become disenchanted with King's protracted style. Bracken was quite happy in Manitoba and he planned to stay there.

Thus it was a considerable shock when Senator Arthur Meighen, the former leader of the Conservative party, suggested in early November 1941 that the Manitoba premier allow his name to be considered for the leadership of the Conservative party at the meeting of the general executive of the Dominion Conservative Association scheduled to be held in Ottawa on 7 November. Bracken had never shown the slightest interest in entering the federal political arena and he had spent much of his political life grappling with the Conservative party at both the provincial and federal level. To be asked to become the leader of that party by one of its most prominent figures was staggering, and, at first, Bracken was at a loss to know how to respond.

Meighen later admitted that he did not know Bracken very well. He had met him only once and they had corresponded briefly in 1940 over the passage through the Senate of the Creditors' Arrangement Act, but had had little else to do with each other. Meighen knew that Bracken had a good record in Manitoba, and although he was reputed to be a poor speaker Meighen 'could not but feel that any man with his experience must have developed powers of parliamentary presentation which would stand him in good stead in Ottawa.'[1]

This suggests how very little Meighen knew his man, and how much wishful thinking was at work. For, as he admitted, he thought it would be to the party's advantage to have a leader closely and prominently associated with agriculture. As he saw it, the success of the party at the next general election lay in capturing the rural vote, drawing disaffected Liberals away from King, and offering a firm alternative to the CCF who were likely to do well in urban centres. Perhaps of more immediate importance to Meighen was his desire to avoid having to accept the leadership himself. He knew that a move was afoot to have the conference call upon him, and he wanted to avoid that. At sixty-seven he dreaded the thought of leadership, particularly of a party that had been reduced to forty seats in the Commons in the 1940 election and which had little support outside Ontario. He therefore determined to find a competent and acceptable alternative. On his own responsibility he decided to go West and sound out Bracken.

Having written ahead to arrange a date, Meighen arrived in Winnipeg on Monday, 3 November,[2] and presented himself shortly afterwards at the Legislative Building. 'Needless to say, Mr. Bracken was greatly surprised at the object of my mission. He did not, however, give my proposal an immediate rebuff. At the same time he gave me no encouragement, or so little that it was far from inspiring. He emphasized what he felt was his incapacity for leadership in Dominion politics, principally because he was not a good public speaker and he felt on that account he would be a disappointment in the Federal arena.' After a couple of hours together the two men agreed to meet again on Tuesday. When they did Bracken called Garson in to take part in the conversation and the two Manitobans pressed Meighen about the progressive outlook of the Conservative party. Having assured them of his sincerity Meighen returned to Toronto to await developments.[3]

Bracken was left somewhat bemused and uncertain of his next action. He does not seem to have talked to others in his cabinet, aside from Garson, and it is likely that on thinking the matter over for two or three days he was very reluctant to let his name go forward. But he does not appear to have attempted to get in touch with Meighen even though he knew the conference opened in Ottawa on Friday, 7 November.[4]

As the conference progressed it was soon clear that there was a strong ground-swell in favour of Meighen. To have attempted to introduce an outsider's name, particularly that of an accepted Liberal, would have been ludicrous. Meighen realized this and on Saturday phoned Bracken to advise him: 'I felt that he received the news with a sense of relief, and told me on no account to permit his name to be proposed.'[5] By the following week Meighen, under considerable pressure and after much agonizing, accepted the leadership.[6]

The fact that Bracken had been asked to consider the Conservative leadership, and that he had not abruptly turned it down, created quite a stir in Manitoba. The *Free Press* and the *Tribune* gave considerable coverage to the issue and the Greater Winnipeg Young Men's Liberal Association felt sufficiently goaded to ask Bracken about his attitude towards Liberals and Liberalism in the province.[7] None of this disturbed Bracken. Quite relieved that he had not had to disrupt the familiarity and contentedness of his personal and political life, he plunged eagerly into the business of the session. He did not, however, cease commenting on national issues. His speeches were widely read and noted, and his name continued to be heard and his ideas talked about at the federal level.

The dramatic entry of Japan into the war in early December 1941 prompted the Manitoba legislature to call for the conscription of Canadian manpower for overseas service as well as home defence. Bracken did not speak in the debate but he endorsed the proposal. Like many others in western Canada, he was convinced that the time had come to make maximum use of Canada's manpower resources. He was not much impressed by King's vacillating homilies.[8]

During the next few weeks King considered ways in which he could, at one and the same time, free himself of his no conscription pledge and undermine the commitment of the Conservatives and Meighen to all-out conscription. King was only too well aware that the Conservatives were forcefully playing the conscription hand in the York South by-election in which Meighen was opposed by Joseph Noseworthy of the CCF. On 22 January in the Speech from the Throne that opened the 1942 federal session a plebiscite was announced. This effectively boxed the Conservatives in York South and despite the intervention of Mitch Hepburn on Meighen's behalf, or perhaps because of it, Meighen was defeated on 7 February by Noseworthy. On 27 April the plebiscite made clear that every province in the country save Quebec heartily favoured conscription. In June 1942 King introduced House of Commons Bill No 80 designed to remove the restrictions on the use of conscripts overseas. The Liberal policy was summed up by King as 'not necessarily conscription, but conscription if necessary.' The Conservatives had no alternative but to support the legislation.[9]

Meighen's defeat and King's action on conscription were heavy blows to the Conservative party. Although Meighen agreed in July to stay on as leader, both he and others were anxious that a replacement be found. Meanwhile differences in philosophy and over principles between Meighen and R.B. Hanson, the House leader, and the confused nature of Conservative thinking, made Hanson determined to try and reorganize the party and define its goals. Meighen's narrow commitment to conscription and national government no longer seemed realistic given King's policies and his majority in the House. By August it had been decided to hold a meeting of concerned Conservative at Port Hope, Ontario, to discuss Canada's war and post-war problems and to see if a more progressive platform could be fashioned that could, in turn, be recommended to a party convention.[10]

While Hanson and Jim Macdonnell, president of the National Trust Company and a prominent party organizer and 'ideas man,' made arrangements for the Port Hope meeting, Meighen turned his attention to his successor as leader. He already knew whom he wanted – John Bracken. On 19 August he wrote to the Manitoba premier and suggested he consider the question in the light of the 'very serious condition of our country and of the unequaled service you can render.' He invited Bracken to Toronto for further discussion.[11]

Bracken was taken quite off-guard by the letter. He did not reply until 1 September:

Your letter was received in due course. It has given me quite a headache. I am late in replying – for which I apologise – but frankly I have been in very great doubt as to what to say. Your obvious sincerity and very deep concern on a previous occasion is the only thing that keeps me from discouraging you in whatever phase of your plans relate to me.

Several times I have been on the point of calling you or writing you – and have hesitated, not seeing my own way in the matter too clearly and not wishing to be misunderstood.

I have never doubted that I should accept your invitation to go down to see you – no matter what the outcome. The consideration you have given the Canadian situation and the impression of sincerity that you have left with me, leave me no reasonable alternative.

I don't want to run away from any task that I can do, but frankly, I have no desire to go to Ottawa in any capacity for *any* party. One might have difficulty in declining to serve in a united effort if that were achievable and ones services required. A wise decision on such a matter could only be given in the light of the then existing circumstances. In any event no personal consideration will ever take me to Ottawa.

But I'll go down and see you. It will be out of consideration to you and the time and thought you have given to Canadian welfare. My going will carry no implication of a desire to leave my present work for any other. And fortunately or unfortunately I'll have to take along my prejudices against parties, and Ottawa, and attempting things I'm not equipped by training or inclination to do. But I'll go.[12]

Bracken finally met Meighen and George McCullagh, the outspoken publisher of the *Globe and Mail* and an ardent Conservative, at the Royal York Hotel in Toronto on Sunday, 20 September. Although no record remains of their talk, Bracken obviously made no commitment one way or the other at that stage and Meighen and McCullagh were not discouraged by what they had seen and heard.[13]

Before the three men met in Toronto the unofficial Conservative conference had been held at Port Hope and had resulted in a statement of aims and beliefs that was considerably more modern and progressive than any previously associated with the party. While calling for conscription and the maintenance of the capitalist system, the conference had also recommended a more enlightened agricultural policy, collective bargaining, low-cost housing, and improved unemployment insurance and old-age pension schemes, all of which Bracken supported.[14] Hanson was pleased with the results but suspected that the section on labour relations might cause some concern within the party.[15] Predictably, Meighen was upset by many of the Port Hope resolutions but he realized that some of them might prove attractive to Bracken and he continued to push his campaign. By the end of September it had been decided to hold a policy and leadership convention in Winnipeg on 9–11 December.[16]

Others beside Meighen had also begun to think of Bracken, particularly those in the party who were anxious for the adoption of the Port Hope proposals. Hanson, Ray Milner of Alberta, the convention chairman, Hugh Mackay, the party leader in New Brunswick, Percy Black of Nova Scotia, Jim Macdonnell, and Dick Bell, Hanson's secretary and the newly appointed convention secretary, all thought Bracken would make an excellent choice if he could be persuaded to contest the leadership.[17] Even R.B. Bennett, Bracken's former sparring partner, was persuaded that Bracken was the man, especially if he could successfully coalesce the anti-King Liberals, the rural and agricultural vote, and the anti-CCF urbanites.[18]

Finally, on 17 November Meighen wrote to Bracken. It was a long and powerful letter, drafted with all the considerable skill at Meighen's disposal.[19] Meighen told Bracken that the crisis in Canada's affairs was much closer than when they had spoken the previous year and that it was 'much plainer than it was then that the crisis points to you and to you only.' He then made a direct appeal to Bracken's sense of duty and to his ambition:

I cannot believe that you could ever justify to yourself in the future standing out against this national demand. It rarely comes to a man to be the object of such a demand. Never in this country has it fallen to anyone to serve a distracted and distressed nation as it now falls to you. There is no one else who can meet this crisis ... I do not know what is going to happen to our country if you fail us, and I cannot believe for a moment you will fail us ...

If you will only give the word, we will do the rest in loyal association with you, and when this world travail is over, you will always know that you heeded the call of duty in its sternest tones.

This was highly flattering and persuasive language and again Bracken did not know how to respond. He was not a party man, he disliked the Ottawa political scene, and he had little experience of most of the issues that a federal politician was obliged to handle. It was true that since the meeting with Meighen and Mc-Cullagh in Toronto in mid-September he had given considerable thought to his candidacy and to national issues. He had continued to criticize the government's manpower policy and only recently had outlined 'A People's Charter,' a fourteen point post-war programme that closely paralleled the Port Hope policies.[20] But all this did not mean that he had decided to enter the leadership contest. While his speeches were opportune and perhaps designed to nail his colour to the mast, they did not represent a departure from his long-held beliefs. If anything they could be interpreted as indicating to the party where he stood. If the party were interested in him it would have to adopt a platform approximating his beliefs before he would seriously consider the leadership.

On 16 November, the day before Meighen sat down to write at length to Bracken, the Manitoba premier had been outspoken in his criticism of the government's manpower policy. Speaking at the official opening of the new home of the General Sir Sam Steel branch of the Canadian Legion, Bracken declared that 'In the fourth year of the war, after all the talk there has been about national selective service, we find ourselves with a wholly inadequate and uneffective manpower policy. The trouble is that there has been no team play in working one out. The cabinet has not done it, and they have given no one else the power to do it. It is a poor way to run a war. I have no doubt we shall win in spite of such policies, but it will be at the cost of a longer war, more casualties and bigger war debts.'[21] Bracken's criticisms of manpower policies must have completely convinced Meighen that Bracken had to be obtained for the party. Equally, the more progressive forces in the party, Bell, Macdonnell, Milner, and Hanson, were undoubtedly pleased by the people's charter. Both wings of the party were determined to get Bracken. Over the next few days, under Meighen's influence, they united in their efforts.

On 22 November Gordon Graydon, the national chairman of the Conservative party, Meighen, and Hugh Mackay left quietly for Winnipeg where they were joined by Ray Milner. Their wish for secrecy was broken on arrival on 24 November when Meighen was recognized by a *Free Press* reporter. Considerable circumspection was then required. Grant Dexter, the *Free Press* reporter, later wrote that contact with Bracken was initially established through intermediaries and then by Graydon and Milner.[22]

Bracken was subjected to a great deal of pressure by his visitors. According to Dexter he was not unwilling to become a candidate for the leadership but thought his past pronouncements against partisan movements in wartime precluded his running. The name of the party appears also to have been discussed and the name 'Progressive Conservative' suggested as more congenial to Bracken but it is not clear that the premier, at that moment, thought of its acceptance as a pre-condition of his candidacy.[23]

The lack of hard evidence makes Bracken's position at this time difficult to determine. He was concerned with efficient government, optimum use of resources during wartime, changes in financial and constitutional matters, a more enlightened attitude to agriculture – and even to labour – and was highly critical of the King government's handling of the war. His speeches in November and early December underlined and highlighted the policies that he thought a national government should pursue. He was obviously aware that his proposals were national in scope and could only be brought into being through the agency of a party of national standing and recognition, and he realized that someone must assume responsibility and take the lead. But by the end of November, after much discussion with Stuart Garson and Doug Campbell – who did not want him to leave[24] – Bracken was still not sure that he should listen to the Conservative overtures. His initial reaction of the previous September still held – a realistic appraisal of his own limitations warred with a sense of duty, ambition, and his love of challenge.

On Monday and Tuesday, 7–8 December, the Resolutions and Policy Committee of the Conservative party met to prepare a draft platform. This task had been simplified by Port Hope and the preliminary work of the convention committee. The platform was presented to Bracken on Tuesday evening, 8 December, the day before the opening of the convention. The fifteen Conservative delegates sat huddled in Bracken's living-room until 2:00 AM while he quizzed them about various aspects of the platform. At the end he seemed happy with it, particularly with the agricultural portion. But he still did not think he could suddenly present himself to the convention as a convert to Conservatism. If the leadership had been unanimously offered to him he would have accepted that as an indication of the party's altered stance; but since there would be a fight for the leadership he felt he needed a gesture of faith from the party if he was to risk his standing in Canada and his own province. If the convention would agree to adopt the name Progressive Conservative before nominations had to be filed he would run. If it declined, then he would not enter the contest.[25]

Bracken reasoned that if the party agreed to change its name it would indicate, first, that he was the choice of a majority and not a small unrepresentative minority, and second, that the party had moved away from its previous reactionary policies. His own supporters could then rally to the cause of the new party. The delegation doubted that the party at large would agree to a change in name and the meeting broke up without completing a statement.[26]

The next morning, Wednesday, 9 December, Mackay and Milner returned and continued to argue the question with Bracken. The outcome was the drafting of a letter which was read that afternoon to the delegates at the convention.[27] It created a furour in the auditorium. The letter read as follows:

A number of delegates to the convention have visited me, urging me to allow my name to be placed before the convention for the leadership. They advised me that while the platform had not yet been completed it is following the progressive character of the Port Hope report, and they asked if I could not make a decision now before waiting for the final draft of the platform.

I said I would try to do so today.

The matter of the leadership has been presented to me as a challenge which I felt I would have to accept if the policies were satisfactory and my candidature could be effected in such a way that my political friends and associates of many years would feel that the principles for which we have unitedly stood were not being abandoned.

There is every indication that the principles and policies yet to be adopted by this convention will be progressive in character and will not differ substantially from my own convictions.

If that were the only thing to be considered, I would be prepared at once to offer my name as a candidate for the leadership. I cannot forget, however, that for 20 years I have been privileged to lead a Progressive group from whom and from many others I have had the most loyal and unswerving support. These people and their views I cannot desert.

If, however, the Conservative party is becoming in fact the progressive party that is indicated by the spirit of the Port Hope report there will be but little separating our respective views. That being the case I believe that my action in allowing my name to be considered for the leadership would not be misunderstood among my friends and those who think like them across Canada if the party became generally recognized as a national progressive movement and were not afraid to be recognized as such.

If therefore, the convention were prepared to give visible evidence of its progressive intent by association of these two names, Progressive and Conservative, I would be willing to become a candidate for the leadership.[28]

As Granatstein has pointed out, the letter faithfully reflected the previous evening's discussion and attempted to appeal to the progressive element at the convention. Nevertheless, Bracken's action and Meighen's approval of it seem, in retrospect, to smack either of stupendous arrogance or abysmal naïveté. Certainly Meighen should have been able to predict the mood of the delegates better than he did. Bracken's position is perhaps more understandable. He was an outsider, he was risking a good deal, he needed assurance. But sincere though he may have been, his letter was a politically insensitive act and suggested that he did not have the necessary antennæ of an aspirant federal politician.

After the letter had been read to the convention a motion was introduced to adopt the new name. Disorder immediately broke out on the floor and, in the face of such resentment, Ray Milner, the convention chairman, postponed debate until Thursday morning, 10 December. But the ill-feelings only intensified overnight. Not that the majority of the delegates disliked either Bracken or the name, but they resented being used. They were not about to be railroaded into a pre-arranged decision by a small élite within the party. If Bracken wished to contest the leadership, well and good, but he had no right to seek preconditions. None of the other candidates had so presumed. Jeers and boos greeted Milner's effort to have the motion debated that morning and again he was obliged to postpone discussion. When Earl Lawson of Toronto introduced the motion in the afternoon he could find no seconder and speaker after speaker denounced the attempt to 'fix' the convention. Finally, amid much disarray, Jim Macdonnell suggested that consideration of a change in name be postponed until after the new leader had been chosen. The delegates approved and the question of a new name for the party was shelved for the time being.[29]

The delegates' reaction to his ill-advised effort to predetermine his status left Bracken more confused than ever.[30] It was now clear, as it should have been from the start, that if he had serious interests in the federal arena he would have to enter the leadership race just like any other aspirant and put his fate in the hands of the delegates. Close to despair after the developments of the previous two days Meighen, with the help of Art Smith of Calgary, made a final effort to convince the Manitoba premier, but when they left him at 7:30 he had still not made up his mind.[31] There were only seconds to spare before the deadline when Bracken finally appeared at the convention and signed his nomination papers.

The atmosphere in the Winnipeg Auditorium was so tense that Bracken's last-minute entry brought the delegates to their feet as he walked to the platform. It was a dramatic moment, but it had not been planned that way. Bracken had not decided to run until about 7:45, and when he and his son, Doug, attempted to drive the short distance to the auditorium they ran into problems with traffic lights and an officious doorman. Mrs Bracken, who had not wanted John to enter the leadership race, wrote to her other sons about those last tense minutes:

> At four minutes to eight Mr. Smith of Calgary called and wanted to know where Jack was ... Mr. Smith asked frantically 'Mrs. Bracken, do you know what your husband is going to do. There are only four minutes to go and if he is not here soon, it will be too late' ... .
>
> For a moment I hesitated – here was an opportunity to 'scuttle' the whole thing by saying that I did not know where he was, which would have been correct, for by this time he most certainly should have been at the Auditorium, but that would not have been fair, and so I told him that Dad had gone to the Auditorium to speak and to be a candidate for leadership ...
>
> Douglas phoned me later on to say that everything had conspired to hold them up that night. Every traffic signal was against them, they got into a traffic jam, and arrived at one of the doors five minutes to eight, but it was not at the right entrance and had a reporter that knew Jack not been there it is doubtful if the committee would have gotten him in time to sign his nomination papers. As it was, he had just one minute to spare when the signatures were attached ... [32]

What prompted Bracken to contest the leadership? As in 1922 when he had decided to accept the premiership of the province, his reasons were probably mixed. Once again a sense of duty seems to have been an important ingredient. Bracken had always been a firm believer in public service and the responsibility of the citizen to the state. This strain in his thinking had been directly appealed to by Meighen and it was difficult for him to disregard those arguments. Similarly, his ambition and residual daring were obviously involved. Doug Campbell, one of the men he consulted, has pointed out how flattered Bracken had been by the attention and encouragement of Meighen. After listening to Meighen's arguments or reading his persuasive letters, Bracken must have felt enormously stimulated and quite capable of overcoming the traditionally difficult transition from the provincial to the federal arena. Moreover, Bracken's integrity had been queried by the delegates when he had submitted his letter to the convention. He had never liked his motives to be questioned and his back had stiffened in a manner familiar to his colleagues. Thus when the radio announcers suggested that evening that he might not contest the leadership without the advantage of the name change his stubborn pride had really been ruffled. This was probably the catalyst that prompted the final decision, but its firm base was rooted in his strong belief in the Port Hope programme and in his own capacity to achieve it at the national level. [33]

There were five candidates for the leadership: Bracken, H.H. Stevens who had broken with Bennett in 1934, Howard Green of Vancouver, John Diefenbaker, the MP for Lake Centre, Saskatchewan, and Murdoch MacPherson, a Regina lawyer who had contested the leadership in 1938. They drew lots for the order of speaking and Bracken went first. It was obvious that he had not prepared a speech and his performance was stilted and marred by tension. Meighen thought it a bad speech, but as Arthur Lower, an observer of the scene, later remarked: 'out of him [Bracken], as the disjointed, icy particles tear themselves from his lips, there stick two qualities that have redeemed many of his speeches in the past and have not deserted him now, character and sincerity. Without brilliance and without "presence" he dominates the platform.'[34]

Bracken spoke for the allotted twenty minutes. He referred to the letter he had sent to the convention and indicated that it was one of the main reasons he was present. It had been suggested that it gave him an unfair advantage. That thought had not been in his mind when he sent the letter. If someone else attained the leadership he would be happy. The leadership had appeared to him a challenge which he would not refuse to consider. He was honoured to be considered for the leadership of such a great party. He offered his services, he said, 'only because his twenty years of public life might be of some use to Canada. In Manitoba, races, creeds and economic groups differed – yet there was unity. He would rather live in Manitoba than anywhere else. Only duty would take him away. He could never speak with the fluency of the other candidates,' he continued, 'but perhaps he would speak in the language of the common people and express their thoughts and aspirations.' Bracken congratulated the convention on the war policies it had adopted. He also commended the resolutions on social security and the call for a square deal for agriculture. 'If you had not done that,' he said, 'I would not be here tonight.' He ended in his usual tense manner: 'If you take me, you take my views too. I don't seek this task, but if it is the wish of this convention I'll take it as a national duty, as so many of our boys on a more dangerous front have done.'[35]

The ballotting began at 2:15 the following afternoon. After the first ballot Bracken was only ten short of a majority with 420, MacPherson had 222, Diefenbaker 120, Green 88, and Stevens 20. Bracken won the second ballot handily by 283 votes. He had 538, MacPherson 255, and Diefenbaker 79.[36]

Bracken's acceptance speech was a more polished performance. Most observers found it thoughtful, vigorous, and sincere. He thanked the convention for the honour they had done him. He thanked the other candidates 'for this early evidence of team play. That is what is needed in any contest and I trust that we may have many similar evidences of it in the days that lie ahead.' Anything he had achieved in public service, he said, had been accomplished 'in cooperation with other men':

There is no one individual in our democratic system today who can fill the prophetic role of a Moses, no matter what his talents or the degree of industry he brings to the task. On the contrary I am confident that a group of men, working for a common aim, drawing upon the accumulated wisdom about us, can by co-operation achieve great things, certainly in a nation as young and progressive as ours. Therefore, rather than impose my personal views on any economic or social reforms, I would prefer to leave the thought with you that I, in cooperation with many of you, might sit down and refine to a working basis many of the admirable viewpoints which have been incorporated in the programme ... Speaking for myself, I want to help work out such a programme for the future as will give to the youth of this country, as well as to the middle aged and the old of every race and creed and economic group, ample justification for a militant faith in it.

I want team play in doing it, team play from the grand fellows who contested this nomination with me, team play from the officers of this organization and from the rank and file of the Canadian people, and team play from the best specialized brains of this country upon which we must draw, if, from out of the complicated structure of our economy, we are to arrive at wise national policies that will be best for the general good.

I want to help build a united Canada. I want to try to help get Canada back to the unity Macdonald and Cartier gave it in the beginning and that Laurier so well maintained. I want to try to arrest the trend towards separation so dangerous to Confederation.

Bracken then outlined his 'People's Charter,' thanked the people and his colleagues of Manitoba for the past twenty years, and promised to do his best for the Conservative party.[37] After he sat down the delegates unanimously endorsed 'Progressive Conservative' as the new name of the party.

That evening Bracken met the press in his home and the process of making John Bracken known to the nation was begun. The following day, Saturday, he met the caucus twice and left most of them with a favourable impression. The response of the political observers across the country was mixed. Most were sympathetic to Bracken, but wondered if he and the Conservative party would work easily in harness for very long. Those who knew Bracken doubted that he would be able to make the transition to the federal arena. He was not a good speaker or debater, he did not think quickly on his feet or arrive at decisions rapidly. He was not a man of original ideas but one dependent on the advice and expertise of others. Those who knew the Conservative party doubted that the leopard had really changed its spots. The more cynical thought the 'Old Guard,' the more reactionary wing of the party, may have momentarily submerged their deepest instincts in order to obtain a man they thought would make a broad appeal to the rural and western voter but at the first hint of weakness or hesitancy they would attempt to reassert their ideas and position within the party. Some doubted that Bracken had the capacity either physically or temperamentally to lead a federal opposition party. He was unfamiliar with federal problems, disliked the cut-and-thrust of politicking, and had never been in opposition where his vaunted notion of team play would do him little good. All recognized his courage, integrity, and sincerity, but many doubted that he was a political Moses.[38]

The most damaging comment came from a shrewd appraiser of political talent, Mackenzie King. After watching the goings-on in Winnipeg with mounting incredulity, King commented in his diary on 9 December: 'Were I wishing to see the Conservative party thrown into utter confusion and the worst possible choice made, and the one that would give me the least possible trouble, I would hope that Bracken might be chosen.'[39] Even so he was amazed when the Conservatives did choose Bracken. He was convinced that Bracken had made 'a terrible mistake' and that 'the Tory party, as a party, has made an even worse mistake.' Nevertheless it pleased him to think that Bracken was not 'the mean and nasty type' as were others King had faced.[40]

By late December Bracken had plunged into immediate problems. He had to decide whether or not to go into the House. He had to supervize the selection of a new House leader and make arrangements for staff in Ottawa. In addition, he had to begin to make himself and his party's new platform better known to the people of Canada. After some delay Bracken finally made his first radio address as leader of the Progressive Conservative party over the CBC on 21 December. In it he reiterated the need for a fair deal for all, careful use of resources during wartime, nationalization of the economy, and the necessity to work for a brighter future.[41] It was a dull and platitudinous performance and did not strike the expected sparks. Bracken would have to be more vigorous and inspiring if he hoped to have any success.[42]

It was also becoming clear that he might not get all the support that he required. Some 'old line Tories' were not very enthusiastic about developments in Winnipeg, and even Meighen, anxious to be out of the wars, told Bennett that while he intended 'to give Bracken such help as might properly come from a retired leader,' he hoped 'he will not expect me to do more.'[43] Bracken was on his own.

13

Out of the House

'I have heard it rumoured too that I am not a colourful figure. That isn't just
a rumour; that is the truth.'[1]

Bracken left Manitoba for Ottawa with mixed feelings. Never a man to look back
with nostalgia or to regret a decision already made, he nevertheless recognized
the security he was leaving and the enormity of the task facing him. He knew
little about the intricacies of national politics or international affairs and had
little sympathy for party infighting. He went to Ottawa hoping that he could reduce inter-party friction, bring rationality back into the discussion of problems,
and make use of the expert advice that was so rarely tapped by politicians. He
therefore arrived in Ottawa optimistic that he could be instrumental in reshaping
the Conservative party into a powerful progressive force in federal life. But he
also recognized the difficulties that he faced and in his darker moments his
stomach sank when contemplating the task.

In the 1935 federal election the Conservatives had suffered a devastating defeat, dropping from 137 to 39 members in the House of Commons. Bennett had
hung on to the leadership until 1938 when Dr Robert J. Manion, his former minister of railways and canals, had replaced him. Manion, a personable fifty-six-
year-old physician from Fort William, had soon run into difficulties with the reactionary, pro-imperialist, anti-French elements in the party – the 'Old Guard' –
who were centred in the Toronto area. Despite his efforts party organization and
finances were in a dismal state when King called a federal election for March 1940.

When it was over the Conservatives had won only 40 seats to the Liberals 184.
Once more twenty-five of those seats were in Ontario, eleven in and around Tory
Toronto, while the remainder were scattered across the country. There were five
in New Brunswick, four in British Columbia, two in Saskatchewan, and one in
each of Nova Scotia, Quebec, Manitoba, and the Yukon. Although the Conserva-

tives had one additional seat the party was in the weakest state in its history. Manion had lost his seat, so the party was leaderless in the House, and only three members of the new caucus had front-bench experience – R.B. Hanson of New Brunswick, Grote Stirling of British Columbia, and Earl Rowe of Ontario – and it was of the slightest. More than ever the party was dominated by the big business interests of Toronto who were devout conscriptionists, imperialists, and capitalists with little interest in a new socio-economic order or a more open stance toward French Canada.

Moreover, the defeat had left the party's federal organization near collapse and the situation was little better at the provincial level. No Conservative government held office in any of the nine provinces and there were party leaders in only five. The party had more or less disappeared in Alberta, Saskatchewan, and Quebec. Meighen had had no time to repair any of these deficiencies and the abysmal state of the party's organization was unchanged when Bracken assumed the leadership. Equally ominous for Bracken was the growing influence within the party of George Drew, the leader of the opposition in Ontario. Drew was a traditional Conservative wedded to the *status quo* who frowned on the adoption of the Port Hope programme. Over the previous four years he had spoken out regularly on federal issues and it was increasingly obvious that he and his Toronto colleagues wanted to control the federal organization.

Thus the party that Bracken inherited in December 1942 was weak and divided at both the parliamentary and constituency level, and it was predominantly an Ontario party, out of touch with concerns and pressures in the West and the Maritimes. He would have to guide the restructuring of the party and be the major spokesman for its new platform while holding the 'Old Guard' at arm's length. He would have to steel himself to work exhausting hours, travel thousands of miles without proper sleep or regular or balanced meals, and make hundreds of speeches. The strain would be enormous and Bracken knew it and dreaded it. He had never liked public speaking from the moment when he had first stood before an audience and his experience over the years had neither eased his tension nor improved his performance. Moreover, he was now half way through his sixtieth year and his health was still suspect. During the thirties he had not had a major recurrence of his difficulties of the late twenties but only because he had followed a strict diet, exercised regularly, and shifted many of the burdens of office to his ministers. His new responsibilities would make such a sensible regimen difficult, if not impossible. They would demand a constant all-out effort. Bracken had never been afraid of work nor had he ever shirked responsibility but, at times, he must have winced when he contemplated the gruelling life ahead.

The manner of Bracken's arrival in the capital was revealing of the man and of his approach. He had wanted his arrival kept secret, and it had been. There was no fanfare nor any public reception. He simply slipped into the city and began attending to his responsibilities. But he quickly discovered that he could not avoid the press nor public attention. His recent victory had been front-page news and people wanted to know all they could about him. Over the next few weeks the newspapers and magazines were full of profile articles. Descriptions highlighted his trim muscular figure, square jaw, eyes that looked straight at you, firm mouth, and punishing grip. His interest in curling was emphasized as it was to be throughout his years as leader. He was extensively photographed during those initial days in Ottawa and a favourite of many magazines was one of him taken on 27 January leaning forward in the Visitors Gallery of the House of Commons listening to his first debate, having just come from a party caucus where Gordon Graydon had been elected to succeed Hanson as House leader.[2]

There had been two issues demanding Bracken's immediate attention after the convention; the first was Hanson's successor and the second was whether or not he should go into the House. The mechanism for the first was set up at the caucus in Winnipeg and before the end of the year all MPs had been asked to write to Bracken stating their preference. The letters that came in over the next few weeks showed a slight edge for Graydon over Diefenbaker and when the vote was finally taken Graydon was chosen by one vote over the Saskatchewan MP. What had counted against Diefenbaker was his inexperience and his temperamental, oratorical style.[3]

The second matter caused Bracken considerable concern and was an excuse for a great deal of advice, both requested and unsought. Bracken was loath to go into the House right away and had made that clear soon after the convention. He knew he was not a good speaker or debater and that the House of Commons would be a trial for him. He was also acutely conscious of his lack of knowledge of various parts of Canada and his inexperience with many national issues. His inclination was to stay out of the House and to travel extensively across the country, not as a political partisan, but as someone anxious to meet the people and gain a better understanding of other regional concerns. This caution upset many in the party. It left Hanson 'rather cold.' Both he and Rodney Adamson, the member for York West (Ontario), thought Bracken should be in the House which was 'the sounding board of the country.'[4] Dick Bell and Jim Macdonnell were also anxious to see Bracken in the House. It seemed essential to them if the Port Hope platform was going to become a permanent feature of Progressive Conservatism and if Bracken was going to secure himself firmly as leader both within his party and in the eyes of the electorate. The House of Commons was, after all, the public cockpit of politics. Bracken should be in it.[5]

Despite considerable pressure from within the party, Bracken stuck to his initial decision not to contest a seat. In addition to his personal inhibitions about the House of Commons he argued that the party's fortunes had to be rebuilt from the grassroots. Others could handle the House; no one but the leader could resurrect the organization.[6] Although the question of Bracken's entry into the Commons was raised again later in the year, he did not change his mind.[7]

Bracken's decision not to enter the House was the most crucial one of his federal career. It eventually weakened his position within the party and in the country. More than anything else it suggested, at an early date, that Bracken's style was not suited for the federal arena. A more self-confident, aggressive, and politically alert man would not have hesitated to enter the House and grapple with King and the Liberals, thus restoring party morale and attracting public attention. But it was not in Bracken's nature to act that way. He was not by instinct a political partisan. If anything, he thought it the duty of the opposition during wartime to support the government and not to indulge in negative criticism. He preferred to travel the country, meet its citizens, and broaden his knowledge.[8]

The other matter demanding immediate attention during Bracken's initial weeks was party organization. Macdonnell, Ray Milner, and Bell were all anxious that decisions should be made about organization and research.[9] The most persistent and the one with ideas was Bell. Only twenty-nine, Dick Bell already possessed considerable political experience. He had been an assistant private secretary to the minister of national revenue in 1934-35, an assistant dominion organizer during the 1935 election, and private secretary to both Manion and Hanson. Bell feared that 'unless we get things moving right away ... we are going to fall back into the same state of desuetude that confronted us six months ago ... '[10] 'We must strike while the iron is sizzling hot,' urged Bell. 'Team play,' he told Milner and Bracken, 'is not easy to secure. During my experience in official capacities with the party, commencing first in 1934, it has never existed, and my great fear is that it will not exist now unless we at once set about to perfect organization.' Bell made detailed suggestions for revitalizing the party structure, its finances, and its publicity and research activities,[11] but much to his regret bureaucratic inertia prevented any rapid consideration of his ideas. Although Rod Finlayson, Bennett's former private secretary, was appointed speech-writer and research director for the party at the end of January, Bell was not appointed national director in charge of party organization until 19 April. By then much of the early impetus had been lost. Ross Brown did not become publicity director until the early summer and a party monthly newspaper, *Public Opinion*, only began appearing in the autumn. One positive development was the graceful removal from office of John R. MacNicol, long a bane to Bell, and the selection of Gordon Graydon as the new president of the party during the annual meeting in March.

The main reason why the 'Port Hopefuls' had urged a quick and sweeping reorganization was to ensure that the 'Old Guard' in Toronto did not continue in control of the party. Macdonnell wanted the 'Port Hope crowd' to be influential in establishing a 'new management' in the party as well as 'a new organization and a new breath of life.' He thought it crucial that it soon be clear that different men had taken over or there would be widespread disappointment in the party and a feeling that there had 'really been very little change except the advent of a new leader, and incidentally a feeling on the part of the leader that he is in a rather false position.' Macdonnell believed Bracken was going to need a good deal of advice on such matters. He thought it might be necessary to make a decision for him: 'I understand he is very slow in his decisions and we cannot afford to wait too long.'[12]

It is doubtful that Bracken was aware of the complexity of these issues or if he was that he was capable of handling them. When he had met the prime minister on 19 January King had commented that Bracken 'had a pretty difficult reactionary wing to deal with.' Bracken's reply reflected his integrity but also his naïveté and what was to prove his incapacity for dealing with the hard-nosed men in his party: 'He said he had never taken a party part in politics. That he was just interested in the public service. He would not be afraid of the extreme wing in his party as he had laid down his own conditions.'[13] This reply seemed to beg a number of questions. If he did not produce results he would be abandoned as would his policies.

During 1943 Bracken stuck closely to his conviction that it was his responsibility to meet people and learn about Canadian problems and not to indulge wilfully in partisan criticism of the government. He opened his cross-Canada tour in mid-February with a ten-day trip to New Brunswick. He carried his 'acquaintance calls' into Quebec in late March and early April before launching a six-week tour of western Ontario, British Columbia, and the Yukon during late April and May. On his return he left immediately for Nova Scotia and Prince Edward Island and then spent much of July and August in rural Ontario. He was in the West briefly in late July and early August and toured Saskatchewan and Alberta extensively in October and November.

It was an arduous undertaking for a man who was sixty in June. It meant hours of tedious travel in all forms of transport, often over dusty, jolting prairie and rural roads. It meant missed or hurried meals, many of them too starchy or greasy for his sensitive stomach. He was rarely in bed before midnight and usually up and on the move by 6:00 AM. Those who travelled with him said he averaged four hours sleep a night during those trips and they marvelled at his stamina, his physical and mental resilience, and his constantly equable manner. However, the cost was heavy. Photographs taken of Bracken in mid-May reveal a very worn and lined face with hollow eyes and pinched cheeks. He was obviously driving himself too hard. What sustained him initially was his basic fitness and strength, but even that began to ebb. Always a tense man, Bracken found the travelling, speechmaking, and the constant meeting of new people a strain. His stomach began to trouble him in a way reminiscent of the twenties. He felt bone-weary and had to summon all his will-power to drag himself out of bed in the morning into another round of meetings and polite conversation. He began to find it difficult to remember names, surely not unnatural under the circumstances, but for one who prided himself on that ability it was a sign of fatigue.

By the end of the year Bracken had met thousands of people, sat around scores of hearths, had listened to the ideas, attitudes, and anger of hundreds of Canadians from one coast to the other. He had been down the mines of Cape Breton, had revisited the scenes of his youth in Seeley's Bay, had walked the Pacific shore, and watched the construction of the Alaska Highway. Everywhere he carried his message of national unity and the need for post-war preparation.

During the year Bracken relied heavily on Finlayson and Macdonnell for drafts of speeches and background memoranda. Both men knew what Bracken's predilictions were and kept within his non-partisan framework. Finlayson appears to have accepted that role but there is evidence that Macdonnell grew impatient with his leader's caution and wanted him to make more emphatic statements. The background memoranda were compilations of history and contemporary analysis of the people, milieu, and institutions of a given area. Bracken was also supplied with copies of speeches by others and with pamphlets and booklets written on various subjects relevant to a particular region. Memoranda were prepared suggesting suitable topics for discussion in various areas. These were sound, forceful documents, sketching the psychological condition of a community as well as its socio-economic situation. Most of this material was closely read by Bracken and heavily underlined and marked up.[14]

Bracken usually addressed groups about twice a day but refused to be drawn into any discussion of a political nature, restricting his remarks to stressing the need for adequate post-war planning. Everywhere he went he called for Canadian unity, the quick resolution of regional and sectional grievances, and less 'hyphenated Canadianism.' He continually pledged himself to the Port Hope creed and programme. His philosophy was a simple one: 'Human beings desire and deserve a better world than they have ever had before.' He argued that every man should have, as a right, the opportunity to make his own living and to be rewarded fairly for his work. But, at the same time, man would have to accept responsibilities and carry his own weight in the community. Unemployment should never be allowed to exist on such a wholesale scale again, but unnecessary state paternalism would have to be avoided. Thus, legitimate enterprise which guaranteed employment should be assured fair treatment by the state and should be assisted in difficult times. Bracken believed that the greatest danger threatening the material prosperity of Canada was 'the danger of discouragement to free enterprise.' Nevertheless, the state also had to ensure that the 'exploitation of the many by the few' was prevented. Similarly, all groups and sections of the community should be treated fairly. He was particularly concerned about the plight of the farmer who wanted parity, 'a square deal – no more and no less – a fair share of the nation's income.'[15]

Bracken indulged in partisan comment only once during those arduous months. In late June he had returned to Toronto to prepare for a major speech at Massey Hall on 2 July. He found that many people in the party thought it time that he dealt with the issues of the day. As usual Macdonnell was one of them. He considered it vital for Progressive Conservative success in the Ontario election of 4 August and for the party's chances federally that Bracken 'speak firmly and bluntly' on manpower.[16] Bracken had always had strong opinions on the subject, so he was more prepared to be aggressive than he might otherwise have been. The result was his most pugnacious speech to date.

Entitled 'First Essentials,' it was a strongly-worded criticism of the government's manpower policy. Bracken called on King to adopt 'a rational system of compulsory selective service for the farms, factories and forces.' In uncharacteristic phraseology but in a firm and calculated manner he asserted that: 'The war policy of the government of Canada, having been, in too many of its aspects, prompted by political cowardice, couldn't help but result in the sometimes disgraceful and all too often chaotic and wasteful conditions which now prevail across this Dominion.' He challenged the government 'to forthwith abandon its negative, partisan policy with regard to manpower.' He asked why the Home Defence Army was not made available for the tasks of the farm, the factory, and the mine. It was ridiculous to think that it would be able to repel any invading force if two oceans and the allies could not. It drained $150 million per year from the Canadian taxpayer to no good effect. 'The men are out of agriculture, out of industry, out of war, and out of everything but the Public Treasury.' He urged the government to rectify its inefficient use of manpower.[17]

King was stung by this attack, so unlike anything that Bracken had previously launched. In an angry reply from the floor of the House he claimed that 'a charge of "political cowardice" comes with ill grace from a leader of a political party who, throughout the whole of a session of parliament following his appointment as leader, had avoided attempting its leadership on the floor of the House of Commons.' Writhing with righteous indignation, King stormed that if Bracken had been in the House he would have asked the Speaker to see that Bracken withdrew the charge.[18] But Bracken was not in the House and his lance had pierced King's armour. The Conservative press was delighted as were those in the party who had long wanted an attacking style of leadership.[19]

This speech plus one of Bracken's regular tours in rural Ontario in mid-July seems to have had a beneficial effect on the Ontario provincial election of 4 August. George Drew's Progressive Conservatives won 38 seats, the CCF 34, and the Liberals 15.[20] Despite the great boost Drew's victory gave to the Progressive Conservatives cause, it was the strong showing of the CCF that most observers noted. It was tangible proof of what many in the party had feared since the early forties – the electoral appeal of socialism.

Although his pungent attack of early July was obviously considered a success by traditional partisan politicians, Bracken quickly reverted to type as if slightly embarrassed by his outburst. His tour of Ontario and the West in the late summer was low key, in keeping with his earlier trips; fact-finding not partisanship was the order of the day.[21] He did not make any major policy statements until his swing into Alberta in October.

By then Mel Jack had joined his staff as his private secretary. An employee of Great Lakes Pulp and Paper, Jack had formerly been private secretary to former Ontario premier George Henry and to Earl Rowe. He was experienced and had considerable organizational ability and political flair. Arthur Meighen had 'persuaded' him, much against his will, to take the job with Bracken. He joined the Progressive Conservative leader as he was about to embark on his western tour. By the autumn it was clear that many in the party were getting restless at Bracken's cautious leadership. Meighen wanted Mel Jack at Bracken's elbow in the hope that the energetic and resourceful Jack could persuade Bracken to become more aggressive in style.

The business and financial interests in the party that Meighen represented were alarmed by the seeming strength of the CCF. A poll released on 30 September showed that for the first time the CCF had a slim 1 per cent edge over the Liberals and Conservatives.[22] This appeared to prove what many had suspected: that the Progressive Conservative party was not establishing itself successfully as a viable opposition. In mid-September John Bird, the editor of the *Winnipeg Tribune*, concluded that 'The impetus of the Port Hope Conference, the Winnipeg Convention and the election of John Bracken has not been maintained.'[23] Similar fears had earlier been voiced by Macdonnell. Rodney Adamson was even more scathing and more specific in his indictment. When Bracken had refused to contest one of the August 9th by-elections Adamson had angrily scrawled in his diary: 'This is the end of the Conservative Party. Bracken is frightened to run and is an absolutely useless leader ... The Conservative Party as a political force is ended, killed by the political appeasement of Bracken.'[24] In late September he complained to Graydon that the party had failed to give leadership, 'We are old and fossilized. And incapable apparently of learning. In other words Gordon – we stink. And you know it.'[25] Others, though they thought Bracken was doing a reasonably good job and making a fine impression in the country, believed it was now time for him to get into the House and provide vigorous leadership in Ottawa.[26]

To some degree Bracken silenced his critics when he made a tough, hard-hitting reply in late September to a statement by King that the opposition groups should curb their criticism or he would appeal to the country.[27] Bracken thought all King had done was set up a series of conditions that would give the Liberal prime minister an excuse for calling a general election suddenly and then placing the blame on the opposition groups.[28] Many people in the party were happy with the reply. Meighen would 'like to have seen it stronger, but the public certainly is well pleased with it.'[29] What is interesting about all this is the response that just one tough speech from Bracken could elicit. It underlined how little aggressive speaking he did and how so many were anxious for it.

Bracken spent much of October and November in Alberta and Saskatchewan. It was during that trip that he announced the first plank in the party platform. At Lethbridge on 26 October he outlined a thirty-point agricultural policy whose objective was 'Equality for Agriculture.' Nearly all his subsequent speeches during the tour were summations of that initial statement.[30] Bracken's concern was the future of agriculture after the war. He wanted 'to correct Canada's greatest social inequity – the inferior economic position into which agriculture has been allowed to fall, and for all too long ... to remain.' A post-war collapse of agriculture had to be avoided. Those engaged in agriculture had to be assured a position of economic equality. He called for a more efficient administration of the ministry of agriculture, an expansion of export markets, progressive lowering of trade barriers, the provision of a floor price to prevent wide fluctuations of farm prices, the passage of federal marketing legislation to facilitate orderly marketing, provision of credit facilities, debt adjustment legislation, improved agricultural research, consideration of a fully integrated system of transportation in Canada, conservation plans, and adequate education and medical facilities.

Although still rather general, it was an interesting programme and one Bracken's farm audience thronged to hear. He constantly had anywhere from three to six hundred people gathered in town halls throughout the two provinces to hear him on farm matters. Unfortunately, Bracken did not take proper advantage of these opportunities. Nothing is more revealing of his inadequacy as a speaker and as a party politician than this western trip. He was an atrocious reader of audience moods and bored even the most sympathetic. He was still marvellous in small groups and in private conversation where his essential friendliness, strength of character, and integrity were clear. He once said to Victor Mackie of Sifton Newspapers that if he could meet every Canadian and shake his hand the Conservatives would win. Mackie agreed that might be so but the party could not wait that long and Bracken would not live that long.[31]

Bracken's first mistake was to speak for too long – anywhere up to two hours. What was worse he spent most of the initial time, when people were fresh and alert, outlining his own personal political history and the delights of his tours across Canada. After about forty-five minutes or an hour of this he would rush hurriedly through a few points of his farm platform and that would be that. Alice and Mel Jack were in despair at his stubborn refusal or sheer incapacity to change his tactics. The two resorted to a warning system. When Jack, placed at the back of the hall, detected gathering restlessness in the audience he would wave a handkerchief. Alice would then tug her husband's coat-tail. If he ignored her, as he usually did, she would tug harder and repeatedly. It usually had no effect. All Bracken would do was smile ruefully at his wife afterwards and say, 'You almost tore my coat off my back.' But at the next stop he would do exactly the same thing. His advisers were frustrated and his audiences departed dissatisfied. Bell tried to warn Bracken that he had heard criticism that his speeches were too long, but this had no effect either.[32]

The reaction to his tours and speeches was mixed. Many both inside and outside the party thought he should be in the House rather than 'gallivanting' around the country. They doubted the effect on the electorate of such bland, hit-and-miss tactics. Others thought the trips and meetings had been useful and that Bracken was establishing a good rapport with Canadians across the country that would materialize in votes at the next election. A number were highly critical of his speeches. They seemed full of platitudes and generalities that attempted to appeal to all segments of Canadian life. Bracken was depicted by the cartoonists as travelling across Canada with statements on anything for everybody poking out of his baggage. Even those most enthusiastic after the Winnipeg Convention had to admit that the impetus of that gathering had dissipated a year later. Much of this was attributable to the showing of the CCF but Bracken's cautious, uncharismatic, and non-partisan style had not helped.[33]

By the end of the year the Progressive Conservative party was still in poor shape. Finances had been found from big business sources to pay everyday expenses – Bracken was receiving $1000 a month – but efforts to start a fund based on small donations had not yet been fully launched and in the event were to prove unsuccessful. Ross Brown had done a creditable job obtaining coverage of Bracken's trips and of securing profile articles in both daily and weekly newspapers as well as in weekly and monthly magazines, but the Progressive Conservative journal *Public Opinion* was too stodgy and introverted to have much appeal. Bell as national director had put enormous effort into attempting to build up a viable federal organization and give advice to provincial bodies but by late 1943 he had to admit that there was no real overall control. Too many people were in separate compartments working without proper understanding of other activities. The organizations at the provincial level were not strong, particularly in Quebec,[34] and some were having internal difficulties, such as in Manitoba. Bracken was often out of touch with Bell and party headquarters and little direction came from him. Even if close contact had been maintained it is doubtful he could have been of much help. He had never been a strong party organization man in Manitoba and he was completely inexperienced at the federal level.[35]

On his return to eastern Canada in mid-November it was soon clear to Bracken that he was going to have trouble with the 'Old Guard' in the party. Restless at Bracken's caution and alarmed by the strong showing of the CCF, they began to put pressure on him to change his ways and also made an attempt to shift the engine-room of the party from Ottawa to Toronto. Bracken learned from Bell that plans were afoot in Toronto to have a national organization committee established there, consisting of Henry Borden, a Toronto corporation lawyer and Robert Borden's nephew, as chairman; Harry Gundy, president of the investment house of Wood Gundy; E.W. Bickle, a stockbroker; James Duncan, the president of Massey-Harris; and Alexander Mackenzie. Bickle and Mackenzie both worked for Drew, Duncan was a close friend and admirer of the Ontario premier, while Gundy was an associate of George McCullagh, the publisher of the *Globe and Mail*. It was intended that the group would be the guiding and directing force in all organizational matters throughout the country. Liaison would be established with private enterprise groups across Canada to fight socialism and to direct activities to the party's advantage.

Bell was highly critical of the idea. It ignored existing party structures and would antagonize the rank-and-file, most of whom hated Toronto at the best of times. The real danger was that the committee's primary loyalty would be to Drew and not to Bracken, for their main concern, said Bell, was to fight the CCF and a 'bulldog determination to retain at any cost their favoured position in society.'[36] Supported by Bell, Bracken refused to permit the 'Old Guard' to proceed with their plans. Nevertheless, he was well aware that this did not resolve his problem. From now on he was to be constantly at odds with the 'Old Guard' centred at Queen's Park.

By 1944 it was apparent to most of the hierarchy within the party that they had made a mistake in choosing Bracken as leader.[37] It may have been that no one could have provided the kind of leadership required for the disorganized and confused Conservatives, but Bracken did not have the ability or the capacity to stimulate a resurgence. He gave no real lead in policy formation, he was ineffectual as a party broker, he was an atrocious public speaker, and he seemed politically naïve on the larger stage of national politics.[38] Nevertheless, the Conservatives could not afford to get rid of Bracken. It was suspected that King would call an

The Truant

election in 1944, but even if he waited until 1945, or until the end of the war, it would be too soon. To dump Bracken only a year after choosing him and so close to an election would destroy the party's already limited credibility. The party was stuck with Bracken until at least the next federal election. If Bracken were to lose that would be the end of him. If he won he would have to be given his chance in the House. Thus by the winter of 1943–4 the party hierarchy was resigned, frustratingly so, but resigned nevertheless, to Bracken's continued leadership.

Bracken was aware of his difficulties. He knew he led a divided party and that the Toronto element was particularly critical. He struggled to convince his colleagues and associates of the importance of a non-partisan approach during wartime and the need to emphasize broad, optimistic goals for the future. But he was incapable of the kind of leadership required of him. Not only had he dismissed many issues of national and international concern, but his temperament and training were also against him. A man fashioned by the rhythm of the seasons with the pragmatic, almost fatalistic, attitude of the farmer was not to be stampeded into hasty statements or ill-considered actions. He preferred to gather the evidence and a variety of opinions and mull them over. Despite his difficulties Bracken did not succumb easily to pressure. As many had learned in Manitoba, he could be a very stubborn man. Throughout 1944 he and the 'Old Guard' were often at odds.

During the early months of the year important additions were made to the party's staff. Charlotte Whitton had been appointed consultant on social services the previous May and W.M. Drummond, professor of agricultural economics at the Ontario Agricultural College, had been named eastern economic adviser in October. They were now joined in January by Dr E.C. Hope, professor of farm management at the University of Saskatchewan, as western economic adviser, and H.H. Stevens as legislative adviser for the 1944 parliamentary session. Bracken also persuaded Hank Grant to send memoranda on a variety of economic and agricultural subjects. In April C.P. McTague, former chairman of the National War Labour Board and a justice of the Ontario Supreme Court, became national chairman of the Progressive Conservative party while Henry Borden became party secretary. Borden was to be of considerable help to Bracken, but he was also a close friend of Drew and McCullagh and his appointment could be seen as a strengthening of the Drew-McCullagh influence. McTague was more of an enigma. He was known to be favourable to labour, but he was also an out-and-out conscriptionist. In the event, he was to have a considerable impact on Bracken.

One of the first issues that Bracken had to tackle in the new year was that old chestnut, empire relations. On 24 January he and George Drew sat on the platform at a Toronto Board of Trade dinner when Lord Halifax, the British ambassador in Washington, called for 'closer unity of thought and action' and, if possible, a common foreign policy for the British Commonwealth in order to ensure that it would have an assured position in the world with the three great powers – the United States, Russia, and China.[39] Although Halifax was probably not expressing official British opinion, his attitudes were anathema to Mackenzie King and King said as much in his speech to the House of Commons on 31 January. Bracken also recognized that opinions in Canada had changed and he had no intention of becoming associated with Halifax's remarks nor with making it a major political issue. He simply stated his hope that the discussion of Commonwealth problems would not become 'the subject of small political discussion.'[40]

Bracken's caution on this issue, an emotional one for many Tories, aroused considerable indignation within the party. It probably further alienated Drew, a convinced proponent of 'co-operation,' and it certainly antagonized Howard Green of Vancouver, Murdoch MacPherson of Saskatchewan, and Arthur Meighen.

MacPherson did not think the party could 'hesitate or straddle or be indifferent to the issue. It cannot evade it or avoid it ... A strong Commonwealth and Empire is essential for world peace.' He claimed many in the party stood for the 'Halifax idea.'[41] Green confirmed this in a speech in Vancouver.[42]

As for Meighen, he wrote at length to Bracken and concluded that 'No one with a clear mind can contest Lord Halifax's position unless he is quite ready to contemplate the impairment of this Empire's position in the world, or indeed its liquidation.'[43] Halifax had not called for the centralization of power, as Lionel Curtis and the Round Table people had done years ago, 'but merely for machinery for continuing consultation in the hope of acting together.'[44] Meighen and General Arthur Charles persuaded Macdonnell to try to convince Bracken that a more positive statement was essential for the good of the party. Macdonnell dutifully suggested to Bracken 'that it ought to be possible for you to say something which will give cheer to many of the rather old-fashioned members of the Conservative party without frightening off any of the people that you wish to bring in.'[45]

In mid-April Bracken issued a statement on Canada's position and function in the British Commonwealth. He spurned both isolationism and empire centralization and called for Canada's full co-operation in the partnership of the Commonwealth. By so doing Canada would not jeopardize her autonomy but would contribute to a more stable world.[46] The statement was appropriately bland and could have meant almost anything. That this was so is demonstrated by Meighen's reaction. He thought it a 'complete and definite' endorsation of Halifax's speech. It was hardly that and it is doubtful that many of the right wing were as easily satisfied.[47]

While debate raged over the party's stance on Commonwealth relations, Bracken continued to outline his economic and social policies. Most of his speeches were now being drafted by Rod Finlayson and H.H. Stevens and strongly reflected the ideas of W.D. Herridge whose writings Bracken read and heavily marked up. Herridge's 'New Democracy' arguments on 'reformed capitalism' reinforced many of the points Bracken had been making earlier about the responsibilities of the citizen, the role of the state, and the need for a rational approach to the uses of capital.[48] Many of his comments must have sounded very strange, even alien, to a great number in his audiences.

For example, in a speech to the annual party meeting in Ottawa on 3 March he argued that the job facing the party was to make good on the word 'progressive.' This could be done by retaining private initiative and free enterprise, and by ensuring that the state protected the welfare of its citizens. The Progressive Conservative party had to demonstrate that it had a programme, personnel, and plans adequate for government and that it intended to have no master but the

The Ark in Heavy Weather

ordinary man. He then said: 'I would like you to understand that the Party is not being built up just to win elections. It is being built up to serve Canada ... I look upon it, not as a Party in the ordinary sense, but as a movement of the Canadian people in all walks of life who are determined that Canada shall be freed from whatever shackles hold her back.' It was a party dedicated to equal opportunity and community of purpose. The state would have to ensure that no class or group was disadvantaged. It would have to control greed while preserving profit and ensuring the maximum of essential needs for its citizenry. The party would have to put 'security for the many before profits for the few.'[49]

Whatever the reaction of his audiences, it was clear by the time Bracken spoke that it would be virtually impossible for the Progressive Conservatives to become identified in the public mind with the ideas Bracken was outlining. The CCF successes of 1943 had resulted in a move to the left by the Liberals, and the Throne Speech of 27 January 1944 had reflected Mackenzie King's intention to undercut both the CCF and the Conservatives with a programme of social security measures.

Bracken and the party suffered a further setback on 15 June in the Saskatchewan election. The CCF under Tommy Douglas won 47 of 55 seats while all forty Conservative candidates ran third and lost their deposits. It was a major catastrophe for Bracken. It demonstrated that 'progressive' policies were not being identified with the Progressive Conservatives and it raised serious doubts about Bracken's ability to rally western votes to the Conservative cause. For all intents and purposes, it spelt the end of the Progressive Conservative party's identification with, or willingness to pursue seriously, the Port Hope proposals.[50]

The CCF victory in Saskatchewan and the Liberal endorsation of social welfare policies had severely shaken most of the Tories. An incident on 19 June in Guelph further complicated matters. A nomination meeting for C.P. McTague had been organized for that day. McTague, who had just seen a major CCF victory take place and whose own ideas about social security had been adopted by the Liberal government, apparently decided that another tack had to be taken. With Bracken on the platform with him he came out in favour of sending the home army overseas. Referring to the problem of manpower, he said:

Now as to where *this party stands on this matter*, let me state in simple unequivocal terms. To our army overseas and their relatives here we say you should have reinforcements now, and they are available now, from the trained troops not now and never required for home defence, so called ... National honour demands that without an hour's delay the necessary order in council should be passed making these reinforcements available ...

The government's persistence in leaving these trained soldiers of the Home Army in Canada, can only be construed as deference to the will of the minority in the Province of Quebec ... [51]

It is doubtful that Bracken knew the exact words McTague would use but he was certainly sympathetic to criticism of the misuse of civilian and military manpower. This was the one issue on which Bracken and the Tories in the party shared common ground. Although Bracken had made a number of visits to Quebec and was anxious to establish a sound party base there, he still did not know very much about French Canada. He appreciated that to mention conscription outright would be political suicide but he still did not fully understand or accept the French-Canadian attitude toward fighting overseas. As recently as February in a speech in Quebec Bracken had criticized French Canada for disrupting Canadian unity. He thought French Canadians should pull their weight both for their own good and that of the country.[52] Therefore, when he rose to speak after McTague it was not particularly surprising that he endorsed the party chairman's statement about reinforcements.[53]

The Guelph remarks received considerable press coverage for two reasons. It seemed to indicate that the reins of leadership were gradually being taken from Bracken's hands and policy statements were now being made by someone associated with the Toronto group. Second, it seemed to shift the party away from Quebec toward English-speaking Canada and thus toward conscription. Though conscription was not mentioned at Guelph, only Dr Herbert Bruce, the member for Parkdale (Toronto) and a strong conscriptionist, was really happy with the statement.[54]

It is hard to know exactly what Bracken's thinking or involvement was in the decision to have McTague speak out on manpower. He was constantly under pressure from the Toronto group and he was always being phoned and bullied by McCullagh who was the principal financial backer of the party at the time. Bracken did not know how to handle McCullagh. He told Bell that he would rather do a hard week's work on the farm than have a ten-minute telephone conversation with George McCullagh.[55] Whether Bracken had succumbed to McCullagh's pressure or had reached his decision independently, the Progressive Conservative party had by June 1944 publicly moved closer to an outright conscriptionist policy.[56]

The furour over the Conservative manpower policy was still raging within the party when Bracken had to address himself to the government's bill on family allowances. For almost two years he had spoken in favour of social security measures and the responsibility of the state to ensure the minimum needs of its citizenry. It might have been expected that for these reasons alone, apart from any political considerations, he would have favoured the idea. Admittedly, it would deprive the Progressive Conservatives of a major argument but not to support it would make John Bracken seem a hypocrite and the Progressive Conservative party foolish. But initially Bracken did oppose the bill, at least in the form proposed. He had never favoured the dole as such and had always disliked the politician's penchant for buying votes. On 24 June he said that the plan had 'all the earmarks of a political bribe' and he criticized the expenditure of an extra $200,000,000. The fact that the government did not intend to bring the plan in until after the election seemed to him to be 'legal bribery of the electorate.' If the plan was good, said Bracken, then bring it in now. Why wait for a year? Bracken suggested much the same end could be achieved by raising the ceiling on low wages and relieving low income workers of their tax payments.[57]

Both Dr Herbert Bruce and George Drew were critical of a plan that to them appeared to bonus 'families who have been unwilling to defend their country.'[58] Others in the party such as Howard Green and John Diefenbaker had different opinions and were much in favour of the measure. The position the party should take was debated in caucus during early July. At one stage Bracken even had

Meeting of the Bracken Club

And Still They Come

Charlotte Whitton come into the caucus and give her views, and Henry Borden came up to Ottawa from Toronto to give Bracken the opinion of the Toronto group. The Toronto attitude was to oppose it as a political dodge. Bracken agreed completely with this. Borden reported back to Drew and McCullagh that Bracken would stand his ground. In caucus Bracken spoke against the allowances as he had promised and was supported by at least nine others including Adamson. However, after listening to much impassioned rhetoric Bracken finally bowed to the pressure of Diefenbaker, Green, and the maritime and western members. When the vote on second reading was taken in the House on 28 July not one Progressive Conservative MP voted against it.

The Toronto group was furious at this development and saw it as a further example of Bracken's lack of forcefulness. To them he was not a decisive man in caucus. A more realistic interpretation was that Bracken finally appreciated that his party could not afford to oppose a popular social security measure. If it did so it would lose whatever hold it had, or hoped to have, on the progressive instincts of the electorate. Whatever his motivation, the whole incident did Bracken no good either inside caucus, with the Toronto group, or in the country at large. To many it seemed that the Progressive Conservatives were opposed to social welfare and that Bracken had lost his battle to convert the party. [59]

All these crises brought Bracken's leadership under closer scrutiny. In July newspaper reports suggested that the Toronto group, particularly Drew, Meighen, and McCullagh, were trying to make sure that Bracken did not get a safe seat for the next election in the hope that he would lose and they would be able to get rid of him quickly. The argument went that Bracken had proven too independent for them, and that he was not making a wide appeal in the country. [60] So strong were the rumours and so destructive were their implications that Bracken felt obliged to respond. During a major policy statement over the CBC on 26 July he said:

Speaking of leadership reminds me that a rumour is abroad concerning the leadership of this party. The rumour is to the effect that efforts are being made to dominate me by a certain business group or groups – perhaps to oust me for another leader. May I say emphatically there has been no domination; there has been no attempted domination; and domination, if attempted by any one section anywhere, will not be allowed.

As for ousting me, no one has tried that; and they wouldn't succeed if they did; and, in any event, there are no aspirants that I know of. When I accepted the leadership of the Progressive Conservative Party, I accepted it from a National Convention because the Party had indicated its intention to be progressive, in fact as well as in name, and I intend that it shall *remain* a Progressive Conservative Party ...

I have heard it rumoured too that I am not a colourful figure. That isn't just a rumour; that is the truth.

He went on to assert that the party he led was no longer the Conservative party. 'It is a new Party which will give business, big and little alike, a square deal but no more ... On its behalf I am preaching a revolutionary economic doctrine, the death of scarcity Capitalism and the birth of abundance Capitalism. And I proclaim a revolutionary Party plan. Reactionaries have no place in it. This Party we shall purge of everything that is reactionary. If there be in it any groups which put their own before the people's interests, if there are reactionary influences which aim to keep us on the backward path, let them be gone and join some other Party. They will have no place here. So let the reactionaries move out, if there are any left, and leave the forward looking ordinary people of this Party ... ' He called on Canadians, of whatever political persuasion, possessed of goodwill and high ideals, to rally to the 'reformed capitalism' of the Progressive Conservative party.[61]

This was an extraordinary speech not only for his remarks about his leadership but for his stubborn hitting back at the reactionaries in the party and his comments about 'reformed capitalism.' But what was one to make of it all? There were no specifics, no plans, just generalities. It sounded well but how was it to be achieved? Bracken had not said and he never did. He rarely indicated how his ideals could be realized. The voter was bemused, many of his colleagues and supporters were angered and frustrated, and his enemies within the party became ever more hostile. By late July 1944 Bracken was not in control of his party, and really he never had been and never would be.

By the time Bracken had delivered this speech he had also sent a toughly worded telegram to Bona Arsenault of Quebec City repudiating an attack on Senator T.D. Bouchard that had appeared a week earlier in *L'Opinion Publique*, the French-Canadian counterpart of *Public Opinion*. Bracken took exception to the use of the term 'quisling' and to the appearance of unauthorized statements. The party, he said, 'cannot and will not adopt one policy in Quebec and another for the rest of Canada.'[62] Arsenault was both editor of *L'Opinion Publique* and president of the Progressive Conservative Association in Quebec, and he had worked hard since January 1943 to establish the party in Quebec. *Public Opinion*, the English-language publication, had been sympathetic to an attack by Senator Bouchard on the Order of Jacques Cartier which Bouchard claimed was deliberately aiming at the destruction of French-Canadian unity. *L'Opinion Publique* had referred to Bouchard as the 'Quebec Quisling.' The discrepancies between the two responses had been seized upon by *Le Droit* in Ottawa and *Le Devoir* in Montreal as evidence that the Progressive Conservatives were speaking differently to the English- and French-speaking communities in the old-fashioned Conservative way. Bracken's intervention was an attempt to refute that.

Whatever the nature of his reasoning it was an unfortunate reaction. Arsenault resigned on 29 July as president of the Progressive Conservative Association in Quebec and *L'Opinion Publique* was discontinued.[63] The Progressive Conservatives now found themselves in grave difficulties. The resurrection of the manpower question by McTague had hurt them and the quarrel with Arsenault was disastrous, for most French Canadians had sympathized with the attack on Bouchard. Moreover, efforts to make contact with Duplessis and the Union Nationale had proven very difficult despite the newspaper theories of Grant Dexter.[64] Duplessis believed that association with Bracken and the Progressive Conservatives would hurt his chances provincially. On 8 August 1944 he won the Quebec provincial election. After his victory, with the Progressive Conservatives increasingly identified with conscription, Duplessis was not interested in co-operating. For all intents and purposes the Progressive Conservatives were dead federally in Quebec by mid-August 1944.[65]

Throughout these various crises Bracken had continued to work at a remorseless pace, taking long and uncomfortable trips and making dozens of speeches. By October he was desperately tired and undoubtedly depressed that his efforts did not seem to be having much effect on party fortunes. The Liberal press continued to write about divisions within the party and even loyal party members were concerned and disillusioned that most people within and outside the party seemed confused about the specifics of party policy.[66]

In early September the Liberals had won the New Brunswick election, a result that had not been unexpected. Nevertheless, Hugh Mackay, the Progressive Conservative provincial leader, had regretted not being able to give the federal party a boost. He was 'discouraged from the standpoint of the Party, as we seem to lack cohesion, and it is awfully hard to get our friends ... to work for us.'[67] In October H.H. Stevens told Bell that Bracken's trip to British Columbia was not receiving adequate or reliable coverage: 'He is seldom mentioned, is not known and there is little effort to make him known.' The Liberals and the CCF were arguing that the '*Tory*' party was 'anti-labour and for the Big Interests, and they are making it stick.'[68]

The only positive development was the adoption of Bracken as a candidate in Neepawa. It was a good western Conservative seat in his old province and was ideal for his needs, effectively rebutting the rumours that he was being denied a safe seat. But Bracken's nomination did not resolve the party's major difficulties. What they needed more than anything else was a good rallying-cry. By early November they thought they had found it – conscription.

Bracken had never ceased to hammer away at King's manpower policy. In mid-October he accused the government of 'criminal folly' in sending undertrained men into action while a huge army of trained men remained at home. Later in the month he suggested that Quebec had 'borne a lesser burden in the human sacrifices of the war' which had resulted in 'an alarming state of disunity' in Canada.[69] Bracken was obviously ready to take advantage of any government difficulties over manpower or reinforcements.

By the end of October the Liberal cabinet had been plunged into crisis over the question of reinforcements. For months the Liberals had sincerely believed that reinforcements were not required in Europe, but they had been misled by their army advisers. In his trip to the front and to Army Headquarters in Europe that autumn Colonel J.L. Ralston, the minister of national defence, was told that 15,000 additional trained infantrymen would have to be sent overseas by the end of 1944. Shaken, he returned to Ottawa on 18 October. Six days later he informed the cabinet that he could see 'no alternative but for me to recommend the extension of service of NRMA personnel to overseas.'[70]

King and his colleagues were dumbfounded and for the next few weeks the crisis preoccupied the cabinet and eventually the nation. The King government came close to falling as the cabinet split over the issue. King disagreed with Ralston's assessment that conscription was necessary and he tough-mindedly accepted a long-held letter of resignation. General A.G.L. McNaughton, who had earlier been approached by the Progressive Conservatives,[71] was sworn in as Ralston's replacement, promising to persuade a sufficient number of NRMA men to volunteer for overseas service, thus avoiding the conscription issue. It was soon clear that this policy had failed. Faced with a revolt in his cabinet, King finally decided to send 16,000 conscripts overseas. This would apparently be enough to meet the emergency and appeared to avoid the major issue of wholesale conscription. Only 'Chubby' Power, a Quebec MP, resigned from the cabinet and of the fifty-seven French-Canadian MPs voting on the question in the House twenty-three continued to support King. King's main concern throughout had been the maintenance of Canadian unity and for the most part he achieved it, although riots did erupt in Montreal and Quebec City.[72]

Once the crisis became public most Progressive Conservatives were quick to react. Bracken called for the despatch of reinforcements overseas while Earl Rowe and others now thought the party had 'an outstanding issue at last that may drive Coldwell and King into one camp.'[73] After King announced that 16,000 men would be despatched, both Graydon in the House and Bracken outside it called for the use of all NRMA men anywhere in the world.[74]

When it was revealed that McNaughton would contest a by-election early in the new year in Grey North (Ontario), serious consideration was given to having Bracken run against him. It caused many 'sleepless nights,' said Bell, but the decisive factor was that if Bracken ran the CCF would probably not field a candidate but align themselves with the Liberals to defeat Bracken. The stakes were considered 'too high' and Bracken was advised not to run.[75] That decision having been made, Bracken and Mel Jack left Canada for Great Britain and Europe on 26 December to assess the situation at first hand. They did not return until late January 1945.

Bracken's trip to Europe was his first since 1929, but unlike his previous experience this was not a relaxing holiday. He took every opportunity to learn more about the whole question of reinforcements. He was accompanied in his visits to the front and to bases in both Great Britain and Europe by Rod Finlayson, upon whom he heavily depended, Mel Jack, and Colonel Brooks. The pace that he maintained was exhausting. He visited Canadian bases and hospitals in Great Britain, Belgium, Holland, France, and Italy. He had a number of meetings with both high-ranking Canadian military personnel and British political and military leaders. He met Churchill in his bedroom at No 10 which quite impressed him, although he thought Churchill 'aging fast.' In addition he talked with Vincent Massey and his staff at Canada House and visited a number of schools and institutions. Everywhere Bracken and his colleagues went they made a point of asking questions about the reinforcement problem. Bracken learned that no proper understanding had existed of the number of front-line casualties that would result after invasion. Consequently, after D-day the Canadians had become seriously undermanned, and men trained for other duties had had to be quickly retrained for an infantry role and shoved into battle. The result had been continued high casualties and eventually an unavoidable reinforcement problem. Bracken often heard complaints that men were being sent back into the line although they had been wounded many times. In some instances, it was asserted, the wounds had not healed completely before they were moved back. It was also pointed out that although the government call-up was for 16,000, this would probably produce no more than 8000 owing to illness, accidents, and transfers.

Bracken ended his tour convinced that the King government had to accept responsibility for the year's delay in reinforcing infantry units after the experiences in Italy and the further delay of several months after the invasion of Europe. It also annoyed Bracken to think that many men theoretically physically unfit for active combat were being moved to the front while over 60,000 men sat in Canada, many of them of 'A' category.

Before leaving for Canada Bracken had dinner with Lord Bennett in London on 16 January and Bennett offered advice about the Grey North by-election. He advised Bracken to tell the constituents what he had seen and heard: 'Make the keynote of campaign British connection. At issue is the reputation of Ontario.'[76]

By the time Bracken arrived in Canada on 26 January the by-election had been underway about two weeks. Primarily a Protestant rural riding it was not one that General McNaughton with a Catholic wife and a stubborn attachment to a private railway car would have a natural advantage in. The Conservative candidate, Garfield Case, was the mayor of Owen Sound whose main appeal to the electors was his local origin: 'Do you want a man from Grey North for Ottawa or a man from Ottawa for Grey North?'[77] As Bell had predicted, once it was clear that Bracken was not going to run the CCF had finally nominated a candidate, Air Vice-Marshal Godfrey of Gananoque. When Bracken returned it was estimated that Case was running first, with Godfrey second, and McNaughton third.[78]

A number of Conservatives, including Gordon Graydon, John Diefenbaker, Earl Rowe, and Karl Homuth, had been staying in the riding, attending meetings, and conducting an extensive house-to-house campaign. Nevertheless, Drew, Mc-Cullagh, McTague, and Bell thought it essential that Bracken speak in the riding soon after his return. Since the primary issue was the reinforcement question they wanted Bracken to make a hard-hitting speech on that subject. Rod Finlayson agreed and he, Drew, McTague, and McCullagh all prepared drafts for Bracken's consideration.[79] The final draft was put together by Finlayson using primarily the ideas and words of Drew and McTague. Bracken, exhausted by his trip and urgently in need of a rest, played no part in the preparation of the substance of the speech.

The speech, a vigorous criticism of the King government's reinforcement policy, was delivered by Bracken at Owen Sound on 31 January. He told the electors that the eyes of the boys overseas were upon them: 'They want only to know what your answer will mean to them in terms of the reinforcements they so badly need ... They expect you to rebuke the leader of a government which left them, after five years of war, inadequately supported in the face of German guns.' He urged the electorate to lift the morale of the men overseas by sending 'a strong clear voice ... across the water.' If they defeated McNaughton they would let the government know that a united nation had to be built on 'one national standard of sacrifice and duty ... the acceptance of equal responsibility and equal sacrifice in time of war, as well as in time of peace.'[80]

McNaughton quickly replied and accused Bracken of lack of knowledge and of making statements about reinforcements 'brazenly devoid of truth.' He promised to tear Bracken's address to pieces.[81] This to George Drew was like waving a red flag at a bull and in his suggested draft response he included a passage based on information received from one Lyle Kraft about an incident concerning rifles and equipment on the troop-ship *New Amsterdam*.[82] Bracken was due to speak at Meaford the next night, 1 February, and in preparing the speech Finlayson included a passage closely parallelling Drew's. On reading it over Bracken made only minor changes. The result was a devastating accusation: 'Let General McNaughton tell you about those who were sent over. Let him tell you the whole sordid story.

Let him tell you what happened on troop ships carrying draftees overseas. Let him tell you why some of those men arrived in Britain without rifles which they are expected to have. Let him tell you about how they threw their rifles overboard. Let him tell you how they threw their ammunition overboard. Let him tell you the truth, which is a condemnation of the complacency, the lack of leadership, the inept mishandling of the entire manpower problem in this nation.'[83]

Bracken's charges caused a furour, and McNaughton angrily denied them the next day. Both the Liberals and the Conservatives expended considerable energy over the next few weeks investigating them. It was clear by April that Bracken's advisers had been misinformed. Only one man, in a moment of personal anguish, had thrown his rifle away. No one had followed suit. The Liberals were so indignant, particularly since Bracken repeated the charge on 2 March, that they seriously considered taking him to court. But cooler political heads prevailed and it was decided to roast Bracken's goose on the campaign trail.[84]

Most members of the Progressive Conservative party thought Bracken's action a grave mistake and feared for its ramifications. Earl Rowe later claimed it was 'a damn fool thing to say.'[85] Mel Jack is probably right when he suggests that Bracken would never have said anything of the sort if he had been rested and well. It was totally uncharacteristic. But exhausted and under severe strain he had accepted the advice of men supposedly more experienced than he in the sort of cut-and-thrust into which Grey North had developed.[86]

The particular remark did not appear to hinder matters too much. Both the Owen Sound and Meaford speeches and the two other brief statements that Bracken made had also dealt with the more general question of reinforcements in a vigorous style that had appealed to his audiences.[87] Probably the most emotional and influential moment in the campaign came at Owen Sound on 3 February when two young officers, Captain Howard Sale and Major George Hees, movingly testified to their personal familiarity with the lack of proper reinforcements.[88]

The result of the poll on 5 February was Case 7333 votes, McNaughton 6097, and Godfrey 3118. The Conservatives were jubilant and Bracken emerged from the campaign with his reputation enhanced. The hard-hitting aggressive leader that so many within the party had wanted for so long suddenly seemed to have blossomed. But it was not so. Tired and without much resilience Bracken had allowed himself to be persuaded by his advisers that the bare-knuckle form of battling was the best. It is possible that if the evidence they had used had been correct Bracken might have continued to try to be more aggressive and less reflective. It is doubtful, however, for it was essentially not in his nature. And it would have been a strain for him to try to sustain it. When it was clear that his evidence had not been reliable, he backed away completely and resumed his less assertive style.

As a result of the Grey North by-election the Progressive Conservatives were now strongly associated in the public mind with conscription. As long as the war lasted that might be a valid electoral ploy in English-speaking Canada but if the war were to end soon, as it seemed by February it might, then not only would that not be a sound platform for a federal campaign in Quebec but probably not in the rest of Canada either.

It was not long before this dilemma presented itself. On 16 April Mackenzie King announced that a federal election would be held on 11 June. He was gambling that the war in Europe would be over by then. By early May it was and the issue of conscription or of reinforcements ceased to be a major concern to the bulk of the Canadian people. Admittedly, the war in the Pacific had not yet ended but there was little enthusiasm for it in Canada.

Despite the heavy criticism that had been levelled at them throughout the war the Liberals were actually in a good position for an election. They had linked their party and their platform to the post-war reconstruction measures of social security and full employment. By mid-1944 it was evident that this ploy had seriously undercut the Progressive Conservatives' Port Hope programme and had left them clinging to Bracken's vague remarks about 'reformed capitalism' and national unity. The CCF party had also been hurt by the Liberals' ideological and programmatic shift and was increasingly isolated as too extremist for Canadian tastes.

The Progressive Conservatives had no difficulty with money throughout the campaign but it was a different story when it came to organization and policy. Their organization was almost non-existent in Quebec and there were serious weaknesses in all provinces except Ontario. Matters of policy were more or less decided by default. The party had commissioned an advertising firm to plan general themes and it had finally been decided to centre the campaign around Bracken, emphasizing his free enterprise interests. This was dubious strategy because not only did it leave the Conservatives open to the Liberal charge that Bracken was being sold to the Canadian people as if he were 'a new breakfast food, or a new brand of soap,'[89] but it took little account of Bracken's obvious leadership deficiencies.

Bracken and the party also wedded themselves to the support of conscription in the Pacific theatre. This tactic is hard to appreciate, particularly since the caucus had rejected conscription in March. Henry Borden, the party secretary, later claimed that neither he nor Drew favoured the idea and that Bracken did not initially push it as part of the platform.[90] It is likely that Bracken was again subjected to pressure by McCullagh and others who thought that party concern for the Pacific war would have electoral appeal in English Canada. These elements within the party had already written off Quebec. Undoubtedly Bracken was influenced by these arguments; it is also clear that he was deeply convinced that Canada had an obligation to meet its responsibilities in the Pacific and that all Canadians, French as well as English, should share that responsibility. His speeches throughout the campaign were little different from those he had made on manpower and Canadian unity in the past. The result was a party and a leader undermined by the social security programmes of their opponents and committed to an outdated and unattractive wartime policy in an election to determine postwar leadership.

As usual Bracken wore himself into the ground during the campaign and on election day he was tired and haggard. He visited all sections of the country but spent only a brief time in Quebec. As expected most of his speeches were dull, overly long, and vague. Yet again Bracken demonstrated that he was not a charismatic or stimulating campaigner, and that he had little of the traditional politician's arsenal of weapons. He never went along to the club car to have a beer or even a ginger-ale with the newspaper reporters, and he often had to be reminded to get out on the platform and wave when his campaign train arrived or departed. So concerned was the party by Bracken's lack-lustre performance that George McCullagh gave the final Progressive Conservative broadcast over the CBC.

An overwhelming victory by George Drew's Conservatives in the Ontario provincial election on 4 June gave the federal party an important psychological lift a week before polling, but in the event it proved to be false optimism. Although the Liberal majority was reduced, King still had a clear command of the House with 127 seats (down from 184). The Progressive Conservatives won 68 (up from 40), the CCF 29 (up from 8), and the Social Credit 13 (up from 10).

The Conservative party had improved its standing in the House, but the result was a disappointment to Bracken and those who had tried to broaden the appeal of the party. The explanations for the poor showing were not hard to find. By taking the Liberal party to the left in 1944 Mackenzie King had outmanoeuvred the Conservatives. As a result, the Port Hope programme no longer seemed as attractive or imaginative as it had in 1942-3. Similarly, the West and the Maritimes obviously did not believe that Bracken had succeeded in breaking the influence of the 'Old Guard.' As far as the electorate was concerned the Progressive Conservative party remained synonomous with Ontario, especially with Tory Toronto. The returns bore out those assumptions. The party had succeeded in picking up only five additional seats outside Ontario – including one by Bracken in Neepawa – but had increased its Ontario representation by an impressive twenty-three. Ironically, the party was more than ever an Ontario party. Bracken's difficulties were only increased, not lessened, by the election results.[91]

14

In the House

One of Bracken's and Dick Bell's first concerns after the election was party organization.[1] Bell had resigned as national director on 12 June, the day after the election, pleading a desire to get back to his law career, but Bracken prevailed upon him to stay. It was unthinkable that Bell, a strength within the party, should be lost at this crucial juncture. Bell had been understandably frustrated by the divided leadership that had bedevilled the party since 1943 and, having done his duty through the election of 1945, he wanted out. Bracken persuaded Bell to outline his concerns in a memorandum and make recommendations. This he did.

Bell pointed out that certain actions were required in order to build a firm foundation for the future. The centre of gravity of party organization would have to be shifted back to the members of parliament, the elected executives of the Progressive Conservative Association, the chairman of the finance committee, and the national director. Revealingly, he said: 'The suspicion, whether justified or not, that a shadow government of the party existed in the background has occasioned me more difficulty than any other single factor ... This Party will not tolerate even the appearance of junta direction; and success can only be achieved if there is no ground for suspicion of it. Provincial headquarters, constituency groups and others will work loyally and faithfully for the leader and the national organizer but will not work if they feel, as they have at least in some degree felt, that a dictatorship of special interests of privileged persons exists in the background.'[2]

As a first step in the reorganizing process Bell drafted and Bracken revised a letter that was sent to all Progressive Conservative MPs at the end of July. Bracken argued that Conservative success in the upcoming session would depend on careful and thoughtful planning. He believed the party would benefit most if all MPs took an active and vital part in debates, each directing his interest and energy to those areas he was most qualified to discuss. It was not desirable that too large a part of the burden should be left to the leader and a few members: 'My objective as Leader will be to make possible for every member the opportunity to take an active and important part in all the work he is or should be interested in. If we perform our duties as a team and demonstrate to the House and to the public that we have a good program, know where we are going, and know also the strength and weaknesses of the Government's policies and administration, our future success will be assured.' Bracken wanted each member to make himself familiar with two or three aspects of policy. Therefore, he proposed ten committees, suggested a chairman and secretary for each, and assigned members to the committees according to their probable interests and qualifications. He was anxious that the work begin immediately. He wanted each committee to outline criticisms of government policy and to provide an alternative constructive policy on each issue. Attached was a list of committees, chairmen, and proposed members.[3] The various committees began meeting during the second week of September and caucus was arranged for Wednesday mornings.

This was an encouraging start and much needed but a suggestion that Bracken's personal stance on policy might prove difficult was reflected in a letter by Earl Rowe to Mel Jack in late July. Bracken had recently commented on the British election and Labour's victory. He had seen it as an indication of a desire for a progressive-thinking approach to peacetime problems. Bracken thought that the need for a progressive approach was seen by all Canadian parties. Rowe, a traditional Conservative, commented:

It is to be hoped we do not add to public confusion between progressive thinking and socialistic planning. Some back benchers of our Party boast about standing on common political ground, but so long as they belong to one Party it can be a temporary comedy; but when the right and left get on common ground, it might well develop into more of a tragedy.

I hope this is only a shadow of Port Hope. I regret basically I cannot interpret it as a shadow of New Hope.[4]

Bracken decided not to take a prominent part in his initial session as a member of the House of Commons, a decision that struck many colleagues and opponents alike as incomprehensible. Much of the criticism directed against Bracken and the Conservatives since early 1943 had opposed Bracken's absence from the House. Now that he had finally arrived he was still going to study it all. What on earth had those long hours in the Visitors' or the Ladies' galleries been for? Had he not learned anything then? They expected Bracken to grasp the reins of leadership in the chamber immediately and with authority.

But Bracken knew his limitations and preferred to soak up the ambience of the House and become familiar with its nuances and sensitivities. He made his first speech on 10 September on the Address. It does not read well, although it may have sounded better. It wandered, had no punch, tried to cover too much ground, and was obviously heavily dependent on notes. In it Bracken touched on a number of themes that he was to return to again and again over the next three years. He indicated his distaste for partisan politics by stating that he saw the role of the opposition to be 'constructive cooperation and constructive criticism.'[5] He criticized the Liberals for government by order-in-council and their departure from responsible government. He called for an examination of federal-provincial relations, particularly tax-sharing, and for a relaxation of bureaucratic controls.[6]

His first major speech in the House was on wheat pricing policy on 27 September.[7] He called, as usual, for a square deal for the producer, and protested against setting the maximum price at $1.55 and the floor price as low as $1.00 per bushel No 1 Northern at Fort William. He was followed immediately by Gardiner and the difference was obvious. Gardiner was much more fluent, less detailed, harder-hitting, and less schoolmasterish than Bracken. It was clear that Bracken had a sound grasp of the details of agriculture but that he had difficulty rising above them when speaking.

Towards the end of the session he again lectured the Liberals on their fall from cabinet government and criticized their emergency powers bill.[8] Bracken recognized that there was merit in some measure of control, such as price and wage control, but the specific advantages of such measures did not justify giving blanket approval to the principle of controls. He thought the government's bureaucratic policies not only removed the control of government from the elected representatives of the people but made a hollow mockery of government itself. He thought that provincial jurisdictions were being unnecessarily invaded and that the governor-in-council was given too much power.[9]

Most members of the party were reasonably satisfied with Bracken's first session.[10] But Bracken was tired. Although he had not spoken a great deal, the tension of his new position and the need for constant alertness and the awareness of his own failings had left him drained and exhausted by the end of the session. While back in Winnipeg at Christmas he went to the Winnipeg Clinic for a complete physical and x-ray examination. The check-up revealed a recurrence of his problems of the twenties compounded by fatigue and nervous strain.[11] Over the next two years he was to become increasingly tired and twice had to be hospitalized in Montreal because of extreme fatigue and nervous exhaustion. This was eventually diagnosed in 1948 as pernicious anaemia requiring constant medication. Thus by 1946 John Bracken, in his early sixties, by nature non-partisan, and suffering from a debilitating condition, was not in the best of health for the leadership of a major party.

A further indication that not all was well was a visit by Dick Bell and Mel Jack to New York to examine the radio training facilities available. The result was a recommendation to Bracken that he spend one week taking instruction in speech and the use of the voice from a Charles T. Harrell of the American Broadcasting Company.[12]

Bracken had always been aware of his deficiencies as a speaker and his first session in the House of Commons had underlined them. Not only did he speak for too long and too diffusely but he still had the bad habit of mumbling into his waistcoat or of addressing the government front bench rather than the Speaker, either of which meant that he could not be heard properly in the Press Gallery. The result was a continuously poor coverage for his speeches and actions in the House.[13]

Bracken spent the second week of February in New York with Harrell receiving instruction in pitch, tone, pace, emphasis, and enunciation. It was a mark of John Bracken's character and his pragmatic approach to problems that he was prepared to accept such instruction. He found it rather a difficult experience but in his tough-minded manner he wrote himself a memorandum outlining his deficiencies: 'Big trouble lack of colour – change of pitch, change of pace, more spontaneity, more emphasis, too fast, not enough pauses. Practice a style. Put life and emphasis into it – now too much reading. Too monotonous – practice pitch. *Assume the importance* you have. Give assumption of *Confidence* in what I say. Pitch dead. Voice dead. Breathing exercise. Open mouth. More air in lungs. Speak loudly.'[14]

From late February through to the opening of Parliament in mid-March Bracken was preoccupied with preparations for the session. One idea that he and Mel Jack had talked over was the limitation of the number of speeches on the Address from the Progressive Conservative side to three or four, so that the Conservatives could then turn to the government and argue that they should bring in their budget earlier to allow for fuller debate. Jack suggested that Graydon speak on external affairs, Diefenbaker on justice and dominion-provincial relations, and Howard Green on demobilization and rehabilitation. If a fourth speaker were required, A.L. Smith could speak on labour.[15]

It is not clear if Bracken ever raised this in caucus. If he did, he did not push it because in the House a number of Conservatives spoke. Bracken's own speech was a monster and suggested that he was finding it difficult to apply the lessons of February. After making a point of scolding the government for its slow methods and admonishing it for its 'lack of cabinet teamplay,' he spoke for two-and-a-half hours. The good ideas that he had were buried in the detail and the verbosity. He was right in criticizing the archaic methods in the Commons and the unbusinesslike approach to the appraisal of expenditures, but the force of his argument was lost in the drone of his voice and the shuffle of his notes. The substance of the speech demonstrated yet again that Bracken believed government should be more administrative and less concerned with the partisan politicking that wasted both the country's and the participants' time and energies. To a degree he had a point but he was talking to the wrong audience and in the wrong setting.[16]

During the session Bracken also spoke briefly in the House on the budget, the atomic energy commission, international relations, farm implement prices, federal-provincial relations, the United Kingdom wheat agreement, and co-operatives.[17] Most of his remarks were again devoted to agricultural matters, particularly to the problems of food supply. Basically Bracken was critical of the government's price ceiling policy and the burden it imposed on the agricultural community. He pointed out that farm production had slowed down since 1944 because costs were outstripping income. Thus, there was a growing inequity in the economy to the disadvantage of the farm population. The CCF disagreed with Bracken, arguing that the removal or raising of the ceiling on farm prices would increase the cost of living for Canadians and further harm livestock producers. Bracken realized that might happen but he was more concerned with the disparity between the world price for wheat and the price the Canadian farmer was obliged to take. Again his speeches on agriculture contained a number of interesting ideas, but they were too detailed and he was often too concerned with making petty, academic points.[18] Gardiner, his main antagonist throughout this protracted debate, emerged as the more shrewd debater, at ease on his feet, quick in rebuttal, with a familiar mastery of facts. It was clear to most of his colleagues by the end of the session that Bracken had difficulty holding his own in the House in his chosen area of expertise.

During the session an effort was also made to put the Quebec organization back on its feet. Bell had recommended this action as early as the previous July and in March had strongly stressed the need to repair the general image that the party was anti-Quebec and anti-French.[19] Macdonnell made several visits to Montreal in early January and each time met with Ivan Sabourin, a party stalwart, and John Hackett, the MP for Stanstead. On the last occasion Bell had also been present. In addition, Macdonnell had a number of meetings with several groups of English-speaking workers. It had finally been decided that longtime Conservative Sam Gobeil should make 'a tour of the constituencies for the purpose of contact and reviving of interest' previous to a representative meeting in the spring.[20] The primary purpose of the reorganization was to make the Progressive Conservative party's point of view understood and appreciated in Quebec. As Bracken informed a French-speaking correspondent: 'The Progressive Conservative Party is a national, not a sectional Party, and it must, and will, make its appeal to all provinces and to all groups, on the basis of a forthright and vibrant

Canadianism ... I have always looked on Canadians, wherever they may reside, be it in Quebec or in British Columbia or Ontario, as simply Canadians, entitled to equal rights, equal opportunities, and invested with equal responsibilities.' The spring conference was designed to let the Progressive Conservatives in Quebec decide on the organization best suited for presenting the Conservative side of the story to the electors of the province. Bracken did not intend to intervene in discussion or influence decisions. He simply wanted to see a permanent and efficient organization established.[21]

In early April Sabourin was chosen president of the Progressive Conservative party in Quebec.[22] Although Bracken had hoped that Sabourin would be able to resuscitate the party organization, it was soon clear that the Progressive Conservatives had little chance of developing support in Quebec. As one observer, J.H. Bender, pointed out to Macdonnell in November: 'Let us be frank about the obstacles to our success in Quebec. Both Messrs. Bracken and Drew made statements to win the Ontario vote which will not be soon forgotten in Quebec. One referred to the empty tables in Ontario; to the filled seats in other provinces. The other said Ontario would not pay for the baby bonus of provinces which refused to do their bit in the last war.'[23] Bell and Macdonnell were also concerned about Nova Scotia and New Brunswick where the local organization was 'deteriorating rapidly.'[24]

While problems of organization continued to plague the party, Bracken spent a few weeks in October and November at the United Nations meeting in New York as a member of the official Canadian delegation. Though he read through all the material and attended sessions, he took no active part. It was a pleasant and relaxing interlude for him. He enjoyed the trip and he and Alice visited relatives, toured the sights, and went out to the Music Hall, to dinners, and to the theatre. It was a wrench to have to leave and return to Canadian political and party problems.[25]

The first half of 1947 was taken up with a session of the House and with preparations for the by-election in Halifax scheduled for 14 July. Bracken spoke sparingly in the House. He continued to call for 'a square deal' for the provinces and for agriculture, commented critically upon the government's old-age pension plan, and spoke of the advantages of democracy and the threat of totalitarian communism. As usual his speeches were too long, contained too many newspaper quotes, and lacked bite and verve.[26]

By early 1947 Conservative morale was low. Bracken was not taking charge of the caucus and was relying on others for advice.[27] It was to Bracken's credit and still is that he was primarily responsible, with the assistance of Dick Bell, Mel Jack, Rod Finlayson, and Jim Macdonnell, in bringing organization to the Progressive Conservative caucus. Committees were set up, chairmen appointed, and briefs and position papers were prepared in all the major fields of government concern. This was a major step forward. The chairmen of committees had the responsibility for speaking on issues within their field in the House. Thus Bracken helped initiate in Canada the idea of a shadow cabinet. This in itself was fine, but where it broke down was that Bracken failed to provide any overall framework of policy within which the others could operate. For the years that he was leader he was also the chairman of the caucus. But he was not a good one. He was very tolerant of all points of view and seemed to be happy that a good discussion had resulted rather than that a line of direction in policy had been established. Increasingly, members left caucus frustrated and embittered and many simply stopped attending.

Bracken was also being much criticized for his non-adventurous approach to opposition. The major concern was his lack of aggression in debate. He did not give a lead in the House. So often the advantage was taken away from the Progressive Conservatives by the better-organized, better-prepared, and quicker-witted CCF who under M.J. Coldwell's leadership were a far more effective opposition party than the Conservatives under Bracken. Attendance in the House had fallen so badly by 1947 that often there were as few as five or six Conservatives on the benches. It was also obvious that many in the party and in the population at large were not clear what Conservative policy was on a variety of issues. Despite Bracken's arguments for a constructive alternative he, ironically, was not helping to provide one.

Not everyone came to Bracken with their complaints but some, such as George Hees, who respected Bracken, felt they could write frankly to him. Hees and his colleague Davie Fulton thought it essential that the party answer the questions of young Canadians more specifically than it was doing. Platitudes and generalities promising a better life for all did not impress the young. Hees enclosed four memoranda on labour relations, housing, social security, and immigration.[28] Bracken met with Hees and Fulton and others on 19 April and went over their grievances and ideas with them, but there was little noticeable change in his subsequent actions.

Bracken was feeling driven and buffetted at this stage. He knew that criticism of his leadership existed within the party but he did not know how to deflect or remove it. He was working as hard as he had ever done in his life. He was conscientiously attending the House, and he was speaking out whenever he could on government policies. He was frustrated by government bureaucracy and the complacency of the Liberals and equally frustrated by the ineffectiveness of opposition in determining policy. More than that he found himself under pressure within the party from the right wing who wished him to lead an all out assault on the government programme. The problem was that Bracken agreed with much that the government was doing. He may have disapproved of details and of methods, but essentially he favoured much of the legislation. It was further proof, if any were needed, that Bracken was in the wrong party.

Despite the criticisms that were levelled at Bracken during those years almost no one had any personal dislike for him, although for some it was hard to disentangle professional frustration from personal response. Bracken was a friendly, self-effacing man, open to his colleagues at the personal if not the public and professional level, and everyone acknowledged his integrity and character. Alice Bracken was universally admired and respected as a gracious, wise, and beautiful lady – 'John Bracken's main asset.' So there was little personal animosity but a considerable recognition of his failings as a politician and a leader.[29]

The by-election in Halifax was held on 14 July. Bell went down to help and Bracken visited the constituency briefly. The party candidate was A.A. McDonald. The Progressive Conservatives had experienced difficulty with organization in the constituency but they probably did as well as could be expected in the time available. When the vote was counted John Dickey had retained the seat for the Liberals and McDonald had finished a poor third behind the CCF.[30]

After the defeat there was considerable heart searching within the party. Some argued that the party should start articulating a moderate socialism just to the right of the CCF, so that the party would be seen to offer something hopeful to the voters. They argued that the 'Tory die-hards' would have to realize that their overriding financial concerns were negating party effectiveness. Those who were anxious that the party eschew all remaining vestiges of Port Hope thought the reverse. The sooner the Conservatives nailed their banner back to the mast of free enterprise and protection and freedom of the individual the better.[31] What all seemed to agree on was Bracken's suspect performance as leader. In the weeks following the Halifax by-election it was more common to hear the refrain 'Bracken must go. We can never win with him.'

This time the criticism did not die away or splutter out as it had in the past. Small groups of MPs meeting for coffee, drinks, or dinner would inevitably talk about Bracken and the party's future. Diefenbaker, who had remained essentially aloof from Bracken, going his own way and doing his job, was heard to fume more than once that Bracken was useless and would have to go. Meighen was inclined to agree and George McCullagh began to be more critical in print during the winter of 1947–8 than he had been before. Even Jim Macdonnell, long a Bracken supporter, began to have doubts in late 1947 but he was not yet ready to face the brute reality of arranging Bracken's demise.

Others were not so hesitant to put their thoughts on paper. In response to Bracken's request for advice on party strategy both Earl Rowe and Davie Fulton wrote at some length in the autumn. Rowe, a friend of Drew and McCullagh, a man always suspicious of Port Hope but not unsympathetic to Bracken, argued that the pendulum of political power was 'obviously swinging, perhaps slowly but not less surely, toward the right.' He was convinced that the Progressive Conservative party 'must be on the right. The left is already crowded. We must be vigorously reidentified as the party of enterprise, of development, opportunity and hope. We must assure the public there is no compromise with the Liberal Doctrine and no conciliation with Socialistic trends.'[32]

Fulton was even franker than Rowe. He appreciated Bracken's argument that there were disadvantages attached to making a policy statement too early. Nevertheless, in his view, 'our main fault has been and still is the lack of a concise and definite statement of our policies.' Again and again in his travels across the country people both in and outside the party had asked what the party stood for? What were its policies? Fulton had usually found it difficult to be precise because 'it is dangerous, if not irresponsible, to say things which you know have not been endorsed or even discussed by the Party officially.' It was essential to be able to produce up-to-date and concrete statements of constructive and progressive policy when confronted with queries. Moreover, if the Conservatives hoped to win the next election they would have to have a definite and positive alternative policy that would differentiate them from both the Liberals and the CCF. The strength and appeal of the CCF was that it did have a definite policy. A further reason was the necessity of inspiring and enthusing the party organization. Fulton attributed the very bad local effort in the Halifax by-election to the fact 'that our own workers had not much to be enthusiastic about in the shape of policies. Unless you know what you are working for you cannot be very enthusiastic about the job ... ' He recommended the preparation of a number of short policy statements that could be distributed in pamphlet form.[33]

Before Bracken could act on these suggestions both he and the party received a further jolt when the Progressive Conservative candidate in the York-Sunbury (New Brunswick) by-election on 25 October came in a poor second behind the Liberals. The result was not unexpected for it was a traditional Liberal seat, but the Conservatives had hoped for a respectable showing. This loss, coupled with the earlier disaster in Halifax, resulted in the preparation by Bell of a confidential memorandum on the state of the party. It was a devastating indictment of the current shape of the party and by inference of Bracken's leadership.

Surveying the events and trends of the past few months, Bell asserted that popular support for the party was in decline and that a continuance would result in a full-scale assault upon the party leadership. As far as he was concerned there were two chief causes for the decline: first, a lack of discipline in the party, particularly in the party caucus. This was evident in the conflicting attitudes taken by members both in the Commons and outside, disgraceful absenteeism in the

House, 'shameful, and in some cases, deliberate indiscretions with the press,' refusal of certain members to carry their part of the burden, either in or out of the House, and 'an attitude of unrest and suspicion among the Members – with expressed jealousy against those who do well. Small cabals and incipient rebellions are constantly being noted amongst the House membership'; and, second, 'the lack of a clear restatement of Party principles and policies':

The Winnipeg Convention is five years behind us. The policies therein enunciated have either been adopted or are obsolete. Subsequent declarations of policy have not been well-coordinated, and Party members have been far from consistent in adherence to such policies. Important statements of policy, made by the Leader have been ignored, and the first principle of politics, namely, that it is repetition that sells, has been forgotten.

So-called friendly newspapers preach policies which are in opposition to declared policies of the party, and our opponents exploit these against us. The net result is that the public's impression is that we have no policy or, alternatively, that we have tried to be all things to all men.

What could be done to rectify the problems? First, restoration of party discipline would require the appointment of a new chief whip to replace A.C. Casselman; 'the imposition and enforcement by the Leader and the new Whip of a rigid rule that no member may leave the precincts of the House of Commons while the House is in session, without the prior permission of the Whip'; 'a forthright, decisive statement by the Leader, that leaks from caucus will be investigated and formally dealt with, even if it involves the reading of guilty persons out of the Party'; a full caucus to be summoned at least five days before the next session and kept sitting until the strategy of the session and the restatement of party aims and policies had been approved; more regular meetings of caucus; and a more effective liaison between the caucus and the national headquarters.

Second, before the next session began 'a complete restatement of Party principles and policies should be issued to the public. This document must represent a forthright, vigorous and dynamic approach to existing National problems, and must be explicit and specific in its content. The full adherence to this new document by all Party speakers must be secured by disciplinary action, if necessary.'

Another difficulty was 'the serious deterioration of our relationship with the Parliamentary Press Gallery. Gallery members complain that they are unable to see the Leader, and that other members will give them nothing but back-door gossip. Consideration should be given to the designation of someone, such as Gordon Graydon, as the official press liaison officer of Caucus.'[34]

This was a highly critical document and underlined grave difficulties within the party. Obviously, Bracken's leadership was seriously impugned although never directly attacked. Bracken's stomach must have knotted as he read through these memoranda, but there is no evidence that he initiated any of the suggestions made by Rowe, Fulton, and Bell.

Criticism of Bracken continued both within and outside the party during the last weeks of 1947. The press criticism was particularly devastating. The *Winnipeg Free Press* regretted the demise of a national party and its cartoonist lampooned Bracken's reversals in policy.[35] The *Montreal Gazette*, the *Financial Post, Saturday Night*, the *Ottawa Journal*, and the *Ottawa Citizen* all argued that the Conservatives needed to take stock of their ideas and their methods and come up with a hard-hitting integrated platform that would provide an alternative to the Liberals and the CCF. Harold Dingman, who had written a folksy friendly article on Bracken two years earlier, now was scathing in his criticism of the party and of Bracken's ineffectual leadership in a December 6th article in *New Liberty* entitled 'Can the Tory Party Survive?'

The Printed Word was more blunt. It simply asserted that the Progressive Conservatives had to get rid of Bracken. He was a failure who in five years had done nothing to capture the imagination or to fire the enthusiasm of Conservatives as a class or to win the support of independent voters. Bracken was neither an orator nor an organizer and he was certainly not a Lincoln - 'in the realm of statesmanship, Mr. Bracken is not even a Model T.' The Progressive Conservatives needed a new leader with definite policies and principles or they would disappear as a party.[36]

Despite this criticism Bracken, suffering badly from fatigue and strain, dug in his heels and fought back. In December he criticized the government for its manner of handling the wheat agreement with Great Britain,[37] and he began to make arrangements for caucus meetings to discuss policy.[38] He also took a slightly more active role in the session that lasted throughout the first six months of 1948. His comments were confined essentially to the same issues - price ceilings, high cost of living, problems facing the livestock producer, freight rates, and communism. He was as critical as always of government by order-in-council - by 'secret decree' as he put it. He disapproved of the centralization of authority. He favoured production increases and less credit to curb inflation. But his style remained much the same - dry, without humour, overly detailed, and lacking flair and spark.[39]

Morale was low throughout the session. Rod Finlayson, who worked as closely with Bracken as anyone, admitted to Ralph Maybank, the Liberal MP, that it was doubtful if it would be possible to get rid of Bracken before the next election. He was afraid the Conservatives 'were nursing a "sick canary." '[40] As far as Bell was concerned there was too much defeatist talk within the ranks, too much pessimism and gloom.[41] Many of the back-benchers in the party were by now very restless and the young members such as Fulton were ruthless in their condemnations of Bracken's ineffectuality. It is doubtful that a more forceful man, one more in tune with their principles, could have done a great deal better in the political circumstances, but Bracken's irritating caution and reserve served as a lightening rod for all the tensions and frustrations of being in opposition.

Cal Miller, the recently elected MP for Portage la Prairie, became so depressed at the state of affairs within the party that in early May 1948 he indicated to Bracken his desire to resign his seat.[42] Miller said quite bluntly, but in personal friendship, that he was 'not too happy about the situation in Ottawa.' There was considerable hue and cry and criticism of Bracken within the party. Some of this Miller shared and some he did not. Nevertheless, the overall situation was not good. He did not like the organization of the party in the House and did not feel the most was being got out of the party. He felt that the whip, A.C. Casselman, should be removed. Someone else should be appointed and organization given serious attention. He did not believe the party had taken sufficient advantage of its opportunities in the House to deal the Liberals a telling blow or even a knock-out punch. He believed the party was 'bowed down with traditions and seniorities.' Some of the senior men could play valuable roles but the younger, more vigorous men should be listened to also. They were good men but 'some of them are being allowed to rust and rot and lose complete interest in the House of Commons when they should be an integral part of a fighting Opposition.' After receiving this letter, Bracken met with Miller and succeeded in persuading him to stay until the next election. For him to resign then would seem like an open criticism of the party. Bracken was by now very tired and severely depressed by the obvious unrest and breakdown around him.

It was in this mood that Bracken travelled out to Kelowna, British Columbia, to speak on behalf of W.A.C. Bennett, the Progressive Conservative candidate in the Yale by-election to be held on 31 May. The riding had been held by party stalwart Grote Stirling who in 1945 had beaten the CCF candidate, O.L. Jones, by 1912 votes. In the interim several thousand new residents had come into the riding and advance forecasts suggested the CCF would be difficult to beat.[43] All three federal parties saw the election as a key barometer to current political fortunes and all sent leading party members into the riding. Jimmy Gardiner, J.L. Ilsley, and C.D. Howe spoke for the Liberals; Coldwell, Angus McInnis, and a number of others for the CCF; and Bracken, Green, Fulton, and Diefenbaker for the Conservatives. An interested observer was Bracken's former colleague R.W. Craig. Unfortunately, he felt Bracken was 'an outstanding disappointment – and a vote loser for his candidate.'[44] In the event, Jones won handily with Bennett a distant second.

Although Bennett wrote reassuringly to Bracken in June about the forces in the constituency that no one could have controlled,[45] Bracken's poor performance in the by-election was the last straw. Fulton was particularly distressed and on the last evening of the session had to be restrained from denouncing his leader from the floor of the House.[46] By early July the move was well advanced to get rid of him. The problem was how to present the ultimatum so that Bracken would accept. A very stubborn man, he did not like to walk away from problems.[47]

Ray Milner, Macdonnell, and Bell, his closest friends in the party, met to discuss what should be done. It was decided that Milner should travel to Brandon where Bracken was going to speak and tell him that the situation was critical. Bracken returned immediately to Ottawa where Bell sat down with him and reviewed what he had gleaned from telegrams and letters from across the country. Bell put his conclusion as plainly as he could. He told Bracken that 'no longer could he hold the party together.' Calls for his resignation were going up everywhere. He stated 'with absolute bluntness,' but in friendship, that he should resign for his own good and the welfare of the party. According to Bell, Bracken took it very well. It was as if he had prepared himself for that moment. He showed absolutely no sign of resentment then or later.

Bell later summarized the reasons for wanting Bracken out: lack of public appeal, lack of parliamentary ability, and the feeling in the party that 'we can't win with him.' All this had been crystallized and brought into focus as a result of his poor showing during the Yale by-election. Bell added that he, Milner, and Macdonnell had all reached similar conclusions about the necessity for Bracken to resign. Both Milner and Macdonnell had believed Bracken would listen to Bell, a man he had always liked and whose judgment he respected. Bell thought the whole business a tragedy. He was convinced that Bracken would have made a good prime minister. He had found him a man of unquestioned integrity, but stubborn. As he put it, 'he didn't shove very readily.' And that, to a degree, was his failing.

As it happened, Hanson had just died on 14 July, so both Bell and Bracken had to leave immediately to attend the funeral in Fredericton. While on the train Bracken finally told Bell that he would resign. He and Bell then sat up and drafted Bracken's resignation letter. By the time they arrived in Fredericton it was more or less finished.[48]

The letter of resignation was dated 17 July and was addressed to Jim Macdonnell as president of the Progressive Conservative Association of Canada. Bracken pointed out that as a result of a widespread desire for a restatement of the principles of the party a number of informal committees had been appointed after the 1947 session to study various aspects of policy. Prior to the opening of parliament in January 1948 Bracken had spent several days with the chairmen of caucus committees discussing policy. Subsequently a number of interim-policy statements had been presented to the Resolutions Committee at the party's annual meeting in April. It had then been recommended that Bracken establish a Policy and Publicity Committee whose task would be to consider the resolutions and other matters of policy and that a restatement of the party's policy should be made before August 1st. The report of the committee had been completed and Bracken was passing it on to Macdonnell. Bracken recommended that a convention be called as soon as possible to discuss the statement. Since the weight of responsibility for vigorously expounding the new principles would primarily fall on the party leader, Bracken felt it best in view of his age and his relatively poor health that the task be assumed by a younger man. He therefore intended to resign at the convention to be called by the president.[49] This letter was released to the press on Monday, 19 July.

Later that day Macdonnell wrote Bracken a letter full of thanks, of relief, and of regret:

I cannot let the day end without writing you a line to say how very deeply I respected and admired the way in which you conducted yourself today. Your courage and magnanimity were beyond praise. That you should be able to allow this to make no difference whatever in our relationship is something that I thought almost impossible.

It has been a tremendous relief to me more particularly as it means that our friendship remains unchanged.

I shall look forward to many happy associations in days to come.[50]

The next day he wrote again, ' ... never in my life have I seen anyone behave in difficult circumstances with more courage and magnanimity. I shall never cease to be grateful to you.'[51]

Bracken gave up the leadership with mixed emotions. He felt relief at the removal of the enormous burden of responsibility and the day-to-day tension that the job had always meant for him. But he regretted the loss of the Port Hope programme and the unfulfilled dreams of the Winnipeg Convention. Although he did not show it then and was not to later, he was more than a little bitter at how the 'Old Guard' in Toronto had never really accepted him on his own terms and had complicated his passage. The press reaction to Bracken's announcement was fairly uniform. Most suggested that his five years of agony were over; that he had been in the wrong party and that he had quickly realized it; while others, as usual, thought that Bracken had not been sufficiently aggressive in the Tory leadership.[52]

The Progressive Conservative convention was held in Ottawa from 30 September to 2 October. Bracken spoke briefly on 'the nation's need and the party's opportunity' and then wished his successor well.[53] The convention chose George Drew, the premier of Ontario, to succeed Bracken, thus realigning the leadership with the traditional base of the party. Drew won a by-election in Carleton County on 20 December and shortly afterwards Bracken removed his effects from the opposition leader's office in the Centre Block.

Bracken had one more session in the House but he played little part in it. He spoke only twice in any substantive manner and on both occasions on agricultural subjects.[54] One thing he had agreed to do, albeit reluctantly, was to run in the Brandon constituency in the next federal election. Although anxious not to be involved for much longer in politics, he was as good as his word and in June 1949 campaigned in Brandon. He lost by over 4000 votes to James Matthews, a Liberal. Bracken was neither surprised nor hurt by the result. He had expected it to happen and was rather relieved that it had.[55] Having done his duty to his Brandon supporters and to the party, he could now retire with a clear conscience.

15

Retirement

One afternoon in the autumn of 1943 John and Alice decided to get out of their apartment in the Chateau and go for a drive. It was a beautiful day and as they drove along the Prescott Highway the land looked soft and inviting in the golden September haze. After half-an-hour they reached Manotick about fourteen miles south of Ottawa where Bracken turned the car off the highway over the swing bridge and down the road that hugged the bank of the Rideau River. They had hardly made the turn when they suddenly came upon the abandoned remains of an old farmhouse and outbuildings standing at rakish angles and beaten by storms to a dilapidated paintless condition. Curious, they turned the car in the gate and tramped up the gentle knoll to where the house stood overlooking the Rideau. Reaching the door John and Alice turned and were struck immediately by the beauty of the spot. From where they were standing the land sloped gently down to the river bank. On the other side of the Rideau lay beautiful Long Island while around and behind to the east stretched 200 acres of gently rolling farm land. Captivated by the beauty of the setting, drawn to its potentially rich earth, and intrigued by its derelict condition, Bracken discovered that the farm belonged to an elderly man who had found it too much to handle alone.

Since the farm was available at a reasonable price, Bracken decided to buy it with the intention of knocking down the old buildings and developing a modern farm on the site. Closer inspection, however, revealed that beneath the discouraging exterior lay an impressive structure built some 125 years earlier by pioneer settlers. The house and farm buildings had stone foundations some three feet thick, in perfect condition, mounted by sturdy ash logs sixteen inches deep and eight inches across. The logs had been trimmed and smoothed with a hand axe and joined by dovetailing and were unmarred by nails. When the old ceilings were pulled down they also discovered white pine log beams in perfect condition. The Brackens decided to preserve all they could and renovate where necessary.

They kept everything that was sound and destroyed none of the simplicity of line of the original structure. A few extra windows were added; the floor space was increased by adding a 30' × 12' sun room; a closed porch at the back of the house was unboarded; the roof was raised in a couple of places to give additional bedroom space; the stairs were slanted a little more; and a few confining interior walls were removed. The roof was reshingled in soft dark red, and white clapboard covered the logs. The windows were reframed in ash, the house was insulated, and a hot air furnace installed. The house and barn were completely wired, water pipes were laid, and a refrigeration system installed in the barn. Bracken, with the help of local gardeners, landscaped the land around the house. Lawns were sown, flower beds dug, trees trimmed, fences rebuilt, and shrubs planted. By the autumn of 1944 the remodelling and the landscaping of Rideau Bend Farm were virtually complete, and Bracken had already begun to build up the nucleus of a herd of Jersey cows. Initially, John and Alice used the farm only at weekends and for a few weeks each summer, but shortly after he relinquished the leadership they moved permanently out to Manotick.[1]

It was to Rideau Bend Farm that Bracken retired after the election of 1949. For the remainder of his life he devoted most of his energies to his farm activities. They were happy years for Bracken, who had never really enjoyed the political game. Not that he ever spoke bitterly of his political experiences. Quite the contrary. He was always generous in his remarks and often spoke of the loyalty of the men who had worked with him. But he was glad to be free of the strain and the constant attention to detail that political life had demanded of him. His regimen of hard work and long hours had taken its toll over the years and when he retired in 1949 he was not in good health. He found himself 'played out physically' and more tired than he realized. The first two years after his withdrawal to the farm were spent quietly regaining his health and rebuilding his strength. He dropped all his public responsibilities and, as he put it, tried 'to get back to normal.' Pictures taken in the early fifties reveal a much more relaxed, less gaunt, and less haggard man than those taken in the late forties. The fresh air, good and regular food, limited travelling, and the sheer pleasure of working once more with cattle, horses, and the land had revitalized him.[2]

By 1949 Rideau Bend Farm had become a beautiful and well-known showplace in eastern Ontario. Bracken had not only enlarged his herd of Jerseys and sown fields of alfalfa but had also built up a herd of palominos with the intention of breeding 'the most beautiful horse in the world.' But breeding two palominos did not always produce a creamy beige or golden horse and often foals were of a different colour. Bracken hoped to eliminate the chance elements and produce the prized golden colour every time. By the early fifties he had built up a sizable herd and had one of the few palomino breeding farms in Canada. The horses were a magnificent sight as their golden coats glistened against the backdrop of green pastures and hardly a car passed that did not stop and the passenger get out to admire the beautiful animals. Bracken's pride and joy was his first stallion foal, Bourbon Pot O'Gold, whose golden coat, white mane and tail, and majestic appearance brought the grand championship of the Toronto Winter Fair to Rideau Bend Farm for three straight years in the late forties. Bracken also won the Reserve Grand Champion Mare Award in the palomino class at Toronto in 1951 and in the same year swept the saddle class.

In addition to his interest in horses and Jersey cattle Bracken also continued to experiment with alfalfa, and in 1953 won the reserve championship in alfalfa at the Chicago Winter Fair with Ladak, a hardy disease-resistant variety that he had grown in Manitoba for twenty years. He was justifiably proud of his achievement and took great pleasure in describing his experiments on the CBC farm broadcast of 9 December.[3]

During these early years the farm was run by Clarke Mansfield, a neighbour, who leased land and cattle from Bracken, but this arrangement came to an end in 1952 and Bracken and his youngest son George then ran the farm together.[4] Bracken settled easily and contentedly into the gentle rhythm of life at Rideau Bend. He was never happier than when old friends from the West or from his political days dropped in for a visit. Invariably, he would serve them ice-cold milk and fresh baked cakes and tarts and would delight in showing them around his farm and displaying his beloved Jerseys and palominos. Many a pleasant Sunday afternoon was passed in this fashion.

Bracken also welcomed the local chapters of the Alumni Associations of the Ontario Agricultural College and the University of Saskatchewan to his farm for their annual picnics, and happily allowed local organizations to use his grounds for their yearly teas. As his strength returned he played a more active part in the local community, joining the local agricultural societies, judging at the Ottawa Winter Fair, and making speeches to farm and community groups as well as to local schools and, on occasion, to the Rotary Club. He got great pleasure from advising young local debaters about their briefs and was always available to the competitors in the local agricultural shows. When written to for advice, as he often was, he tried to help where he could or referred the writer to someone better informed than himself, but he rarely became too deeply involved and tried to avoid overtaxing his energy and strength.

For the most part Bracken disassociated himself from main-line politics during his retirement years. He did remain an executive member of the Progressive Conservative Association and he usually attended conventions but he no longer spoke at Progressive Conservative meetings. He maintained an interest in Carleton County political activities and was prepared to support certain candidates but he did not take an active part. And he shunned the role of a backstage political manager. After the Diefenbaker victory of 1957 he was often approached and asked to lobby on behalf of prospective Senate appointees, but he usually refused. He did not think it appropriate to offer gratuitous advice to the prime minister. Such advice, he believed, was rarely welcomed. Earlier he had watched the 1953 federal election results with considerable interest. He was pleased, he told Graydon, to see many of the old boys survive, but he shared their disappointment at the prospect of more long years in opposition. 'Democracy,' he wrote, 'demands a big price from some of its devotees. Its incidence of sacrifice is often far from fair in our man-made and far from perfect "system" of party Government.'[5] Bracken had not changed his opinions much in thirty years. The party system still did not sit well with him.

It was during these years that Bracken began to experience personal loss. His sister Gertie died in 1954 and his brother Manfred in 1955 and he lost a grandson, Christopher, in 1959. Although always subject to fatigue and thus constantly reminded of his age, Bracken never appears to have worried unduly about death. There is evidence in his papers that he was particularly careful to ensure that all his business arrangements and records were in order, but then he had always been fastidious about personal business matters. In his rare comments upon advancing age he usually spoke or wrote of 'those of us who have little time left' but in a matter-of-fact rather than a maudlin way. He simply accepted death as an inevitability. There was not much point in worrying about it. In the same way that he rarely looked back, and almost never with regret, so he seldom philosophized about human existence. Always the pragmatist, he simply accepted that the older he became the closer to death he was. His only concern was that his affairs were in order.

One scheme that Bracken did become involved in, and within a year or so of his retirement, was the formation of a small insurance company called Professional and Industrial Pensions Ltd. The brain-child of E.L.R. (Landon) Williamson, who had served as an economic adviser to the Conservatives during Bracken's leadership, it was designed to offer coverage to professional groups, such as dentists, lawyers, and nurses, that had skills not necessarily protected by conventional insurance and pension schemes. By the end of 1951 Professional Pensions had been taken under the wing of the Beacon Insurance Company of Birmingham, England, working through the National and Colonial Insurance Company of London, and Bracken was listed as chairman of the board. Despite Williamson's initiative and hard work over the next four years the company had little success, owing primarily to under-capitalization, and by mid-1956 it was dead and Bracken was out of pocket.[6]

Bracken's involvement with Williamson did not mean that he was a rich man with large sums of money to invest. In fact, for most of his life he had lived very frugally on his salaries from the University of Saskatchewan and the Manitoba government. In 1934 and 1942 he had borrowed $11,000 and $15,842, respectively, from the Royal Bank, backed by Max Steinkopf of Winnipeg, in order to purchase land and farm machinery. By the time he left Winnipeg he owned land at Great Falls, Hudson Bay Junction, Tessier, Marchand, St Vital, and Le Ross. He leased all the land except for the Marchand farm which was run by Manfred until the latter's move to the old Crerar farm at Selkirk in 1944. None of these properties was bringing in much money by the early forties, so that although Bracken was prosperous in that he owned land – purchased on borrowed money – he had little ready cash. His cash situation was so grave when he left for Ottawa in 1943 that he had to sell his house at 604 Stradbrooke quickly. One source suggests that, unknown to Bracken, a friend bought the house in order to provide him with cash with which to go to Ottawa. Bracken realized a profit of $2281.86 from the sale. He had borrowed a further $8000.00 from Fred K. Morrow of Toronto in 1943–4 to help pay for the renovations and landscaping at Manotick.[7]

It is evident that Bracken was not wealthy when he retired from the leadership of the Progressive Conservative party. Contrary to rumour he did not receive a large sum from the party, only a new automobile.[8] But during 1948–50 Bracken sold most of his properties in Saskatchewan and Manitoba and transferred the title of the Great Falls farm to his nephew John Bracken, Junior. By 1950 both the Tessier property and the Marchand farm had been sold. The various sales brought Bracken almost $30,000 and he used most of it to build up his herds of Jerseys and palominos and to continue renovations. Some did find its way into Professional Pensions but Bracken's overall financial commitment to the company was never great in capital terms and most of the loans he had made had been repaid. Despite the additional flexibility that the sales of his farms gave him, Bracken in the early fifties was still heavily dependent for cash on his share of the profits from the Great Falls farm. In a letter to Williamson in November 1952 he explained that the revenues from the West were badly delayed and that heavy demands for building additions had left him short of funds.[9] Bracken was by no means poor, in fact he was a prosperous man, but in the early fifties his money was tied up in property, horses, and cattle. Only later in the decade, with the sale of land at a handsome profit to construction companies seeking to appease the Ottawa civil service demand for attractively located housing, did Bracken finally become truly well-off; even so he was far removed from the millionaire or magnate status.

One day in April 1954 Bracken received a surprise visit from Douglas Campbell, the premier of Manitoba. The two friends enjoyed a brief chat about old times before Campbell revealed the true purpose of his visit. The Manitoba government had decided to establish a commission to enquire into the sale of liquor in the province and the cabinet wanted Bracken to be the chairman. The last major changes in liquor legislation had been made almost thirty years before by Bracken's own administration. The Government Liquor Control Act of 1928 had provided for the sale of liquor by liquor stores on a cash and carry basis, as well as by home delivery, but had restricted public consumption to beer sold in rigidly segregated and aridly functional beer parlors. The legislation had been favourably received at the time and, in the main, had proven acceptable through to the end of the war. But, as Campbell now explained, higher incomes, the greater availability of cars, and a change in social mores had meant that by the fifties the legislation was being acknowledged more in the breach than in the observance. Campbell and his colleagues thought it was time for a full-scale enquiry. Since the topic was bound to be controversial, they wanted a prominent and well-respected man to head the commission. Bracken's name had logically come up. He was flattered to be asked and though he knew it would severely tax his health, he readily agreed to chair the enquiry. He saw it as an act of public service for a province that in his ten-year absence had never been far from his heart or his thoughts.[10]

For the next eighteen months Bracken was preoccupied with the work of the commission. Organizational meetings were held with the other four members of the enquiry in May, staff was hired, and the services of experts on economics and the problems of alcoholism were secured. The formal proceedings opened with public hearings in Winnipeg in July and concluded with the submission of the final segment of the report in November 1955.[11]

Although himself a virtual teetotaller, Bracken was well aware that it was the responsibility of government to respect the wishes of the majority as long as these preserved the public welfare. He realized from the beginning of the enquiry that a liberalization of the liquor legislation in Manitoba was desirable, but that made him determined to provide Manitoba with a comprehensive examination of legislation elsewhere and a review of alcohol education and rehabilitation practices that could be adopted in the province. In pursuit of these aims Bracken and his fellow commissioners visited nine provinces, six states in the United States, held twelve hearings throughout Manitoba, heard 140 briefs, received more than 100 private communications, and, in January 1955, interviewed a number of noted experts including the internationally reknowned Dr E.M. Jellinek, the consultant on alcoholism for the World Health Organization. All this information, coupled with the special studies prepared by their staff and advisers, presented the commissioners with a daunting mound of paper to wade through and the completion of the report was delayed beyond the original May deadline.

The final report of the Bracken Commission was the most thorough study ever made in Canada of what a government's role should be in the field of liquor control. It was a tribute to Bracken's drive, willpower, and concern for the public welfare. Throughout their deliberations the commissioners had kept constantly in mind that the state had two responsibilities: to provide effective control over the actions of individuals or groups when such actions were or might become anti-social, and to respect and protect the freedom of action of individuals or groups when such action was not contrary to the public welfare. The state therefore had an obligation to promulgate laws which would promote temperance in the use of alcoholic beverages since abuse in any form was against the common good. The state should also provide for the adoption and strict enforcement of such laws, should adhere to the practice of local option in municipalities and respect the stated wishes of the majority, should promote by all possible means a sound and thorough alcohol education programme, and, finally, should provide the best possible facilities for the prevention of alcoholism and the rehabilitation of alcoholics.

With this code in mind the Bracken Commission recommended that the permit system be abolished and that mixed drinking be allowed in cocktail rooms, cabarets, dining rooms, in beverage rooms attached to restaurants, and with meals in restaurants. The commissioners advised the retention of beer parlours, as long as they offered light foods, soft drinks, fruit juice, and drinking water in addition to beer, and the abolition of the old 'resident' requirement, so that a purchaser would be able to take liquor to any bona fide residence. There were also detailed suggestions about hours of opening and the provisions of outlets in rural areas. The commissioner urged strict enforcement of the new legislation, including a stiff scientific test for persons suspected of driving while intoxicated, and a vigorous government-sponsored alcohol education programme. Bracken and his colleagues were emphatic that new outlets should only be provided if the majority in a municipality decided it wanted them. For Bracken, it was crucial to the success of the new programme that democratic procedures be ensured and that local option be preserved. Finally, the report recommended that all beer, wine, and liquor sales in Manitoba were to remain under the control of a liquor commission.[12]

The Bracken Report was received favourably by the government and in 1956 its recommendations were implemented. In local plebiscites most Manitobans opted for some or all of the expanded facilities for the sale of beer, wine, and liquor. But the old values and mores had not entirely disappeared, and the government maintained the ban on the sale of alcohol on Sundays.

At the end of the eighteen months Bracken was exhausted, and on the day when the final segment of the report was handed to the government he was admitted to the hospital for a checkup and a much needed rest. His doctors had urged him to enter the hospital in the summer of 1955 but he had resolutely refused to do so until the report was finished. As a result Bracken was haggard and drained when he returned to Manotick. His life over the next year-and-a-half was spent peacefully at Rideau Bend Farm tending to his Jerseys and palominos.

He interrupted this quiet routine only twice. He went to England in March 1956 to attempt to save the failing professional pensions scheme and later in the year he attended the Progressive Conservative convention in Ottawa that finally selected John Diefenbaker as leader of the party. Although Bracken took no active part, he remained an interested observer of the back-stage manoeuvring, and shortly afterwards passed on his musings to R.D. 'Doc' Guy, an old Manitoba friend:

I gather that the 'inner circle' did not like the way things were shaping up – and are no more happy over the outcome. Let us hope their disappointment will not have any serious consequences in the days ahead.

As political conventions go, this could very well be regarded as successful. Enthusiasm was above average – George was let out of harness in a wave of glory – John ushered in with noisy and widespread acclaim – the speeches and debates were above average – and the resolutions about what you would expect.

'Duff' Roblin made a good impression as a 'futurity' candidate; Bob Stanfield made one of the best addresses of the convention and Fleming (N.B.) measured up quite well.

The young people were in evidence more than usual, and it seemed to me the gray-heads were fewer in number. The die-hards got a spanking in their 'change the name' resolution. Many Quebecers were disappointed with the leadership vote – and some did not hide their feelings.

On the whole I think the outcome is as good as could have been expected under all the circumstances. It will be interesting to see what the years will bring ... The leadership was perhaps coming to John if persistence hard work and speaking ability deserve a reward – but his organisation would have given him the edge in any event ... [13]

The formation of the Diefenbaker administration after the federal election of 1957 brought Bracken his last government job. Early in 1958 he was appointed to inquire about box-car distribution for the movement of grain amongst country elevators in western Canada and asked to recommend improved procedures and methods to relieve congestion. It was a perennial problem and considered by many to be impossible of solution since it involved the warring interests of the grain trade. Bracken was, as usual, optimistic. He believed the problem could be solved if all concerned were willing to do two things: 'get together on the essential facts ... look them straight in the face, and then sit around a table ... as reasonable and intelligent men, and say we are going to find the best way through.'[14]

Bracken's approach to his last major task was in complete keeping with his approach to all problems throughout his agricultural and political career – cautious, pragmatic, and rational, refusing to give undue recognition to the special demands of economic or political interest groups. He looked upon the inquiry and all who participated in it 'as a team seeking a means to find a better way.'[15]

The difficulties were inordinately complex. The box cars, some 50,000 of them, were owned by the two major railway companies, the CPR and the CNR; there were twenty-three different elevator companies and they owned over 5000 elevators in three provinces; and there were some 230,000 farmers with approximately 600 million bushels of grain to be shipped each year. Faced with these competing interests, Bracken tried to persuade them to see the problem in a wider context. 'We are fighting an economic war – not between ourselves. We could straighten that out, but the challenge faces us to work out a solution to a problem in a type of economy that we have not known before. I do not think any of you want to slip back into the reactionary period of fifty years ago and I do not think any of you want to slip forward into a communistic dictatorship. We are trying to live in an economy between these two extremes and, gentlemen, we have to feel our way through that situation ... If we succeed in our present undertaking we will be helping win a war for the type of economy we stand for and if we fail we will just be another step nearer to a more extreme type of social economy.'[16]

In his report of December 1958 Bracken praised the Wheat Board for its outstanding service in marketing the western grain crop in the previous seven years of massive yields. He then made a number of detailed recommendations about the relationship of the elevator companies to the farmer but essentially he simply advised a more fully competitive system between the various companies as a means of improving efficiency. The government did introduce certain detailed changes but the core problems of shipping grain out of the West were not entirely resolved, despite Bracken's optimism.[17]

After completing the inquiry Bracken returned to Rideau Bend Farm and the last nine years of his life were spent primarily in gentle retirement far from the political stage. He did serve on the National Capital Commission from 1959 to 1962 but this was not an overly onerous task and he appears to have played no vital role in its proceedings.[18] He continued to make occasional speeches about the rapidly mushrooming world population and the danger of insufficient food production as he had done since his days in Saskatchewan. The problem seemed particularly urgent in the sixties and when, at the age of eighty-four, after attending the opening of the Glenlea Research Station in Manitoba in 1967, Bracken wrote to L.H. Shebiski, the dean of agriculture at the University of Manitoba, congratulating him on his experimental work, he commented that: 'You and others like you must find the way to maximum production – 3,000,000,000 others must find their way to population control.'[19]

Later that year he sat on the platform at the Progressive Conservative convention that chose Bob Stanfield to succeed Diefenbaker. The political blood that flowed on that occasion probably did nothing to endear the party to Bracken's heart, and the following year he apparently considered coming out in support of Pierre Trudeau and the Liberals but finally decided such an action would be too disloyal.

In these later years he and Alice made a number of trips during the Canadian winter to California where they enjoyed the sunshine and freedom from all responsibilities. While there they made friends in San Diego with Art and Nancy Baker and for the first time it was suggested that Bracken should write about his political career. Since Bracken had made no effort to keep any truly private papers from his political days and had neither examined the surviving public material in Winnipeg and Ottawa nor made any attempt to write about his own career, this was a daunting task for someone in his mid-eighties and Bracken refused to think about it. With that, Art Baker, elderly and partially crippled, began to put material together himself and tried his hand at the early chapters. Untrained as an historian and severely handicapped by his distance from relevant documents, Baker had not proceeded very far by early 1969.

Other than their trips to California John and Alice stayed close to Rideau Bend Farm where they happily received a continual flow of friends and were frequently visited by their sons and grandchildren. Bracken enjoyed walking across the fields to his palominos or sitting quietly on the stoop gazing contentedly at the beauty of the Rideau. It was a serene and peaceful twilight to a long and arduous career. It was here at Manotick, close to the river and canal that linked him with his boyhood home in Seeley's Bay, that Bracken died on 18 March 1969, three months short of his eighty-sixth birthday. He was buried in the Rideauvale Cemetary at Kars, Ontario. Alice survived him for only two years and on her death in March 1971 she was buried beside her husband.

Epilogue

John Bracken was not by nature a politician. He had no deep ideological conviction and no deep respect for the narrow exactitudes of party politics. He had no compelling vision and no commitment to a restructuring or remodelling of society. He saw the role of the politician as primarily administrative. Problems had to be handled with care and caution and advice sought from experts before a solution could be tried. He thought that party politics wasted energy and emotion and often distracted attention into frivolous and egotistical pathways. He believed one should draw on the talent and wisdom available in a society no matter who the individual concerned happened to be, what his background was, or what his political, economic, or social attitudes were. Not to make use of all the available talent in an effort to resolve society's problems was to squander the obvious.

Bracken's pragmatic, non-partisan, administrative approach to government was in keeping with similar attitudes in various parts of the English-speaking world in the early twentieth century and certainly was not without support in Manitoba during the inter-war years. It was unadventurous and no doubt unimaginative but it is difficult to see what else would have worked given Manitoba's small population and its political and economic circumstances. In the twenties none of Bracken's political opponents had any workable alternatives to offer and the straitened financial conditions of the thirties underlined that Bracken's low-key, frugal approach to the province's difficulties was acceptable to most Manitobans. His was an honest and businesslike administration, unspectacular, and in hind-sight frustrating to the impatient intellectual or ideologue, but in its day workable. That this style of politics and of government could prove stultifying in a more prosperous and hopeful time was dramatically demonstrated in the 1950s but for Manitobans during the inter-war period it was quite in keeping with their mood and circumstance.

Cautious, conservative, but with a puritan sense of duty, Bracken twice in his life responded to a request to assume added burdens. The first time proved appropriate, the second not. It was clear by late 1943 that he would have been well-advised to stay in the provincial arena. His low-key style, his quiet unflamboyant personal qualities, and his eclectic, anti-party approach to government that had served him well in Manitoba were totally unsuited for the narrowly focused, factionally intense, party warfare of Ottawa. Had he been blessed with personal charisma, an eloquent speaking style, and a quicker more adaptive mind he might have been more successful. But it is doubtful, for those attributes could not have hidden for long his lack of deep commitment to party. Thus Bracken's years as leader of the Progressive Conservatives were a personally difficult and eventually painful period in his life.

Although Bracken was not a success on the federal stage the disappointments of his last years in public office should not cloud his achievement in Manitoba. During his years as premier Bracken developed into a strong advocate of a readjustment of federal-provincial constitutional and financial powers. The problems confronting both Manitoba particularly and the West generally led him eventually to argue both a strong regionalist and a strong centralist position. On the face of it these stances seem antithetical or at best paradoxical. But such was not the case. Bracken believed that the West had been ill-served by the legislation of 1867 and by the so-called 'national,' but really central Canadian, policies that the various federal governments had promoted since the late 1870s. He considered that the West's problems and the problems of all the peripheral regions should be given due attention by the central government but that the latter should also be given the power to assume responsibilities that were country-wide in nature. He did not want to splinter the country into regions nor did he wish to create an omnipotent and unresponsive federal authority. He believed that Canada would be strongest and most unified if regional difficulties were handled with sensitivity and if the central government had the authority to grapple with problems that were national in scope. This was Bracken's most important contribution to the debate about the future of the Canadian state. In essence, his ideas were upheld by the Rowell-Sirois Commission. By the late thirties he had emerged as an important and forceful figure on the national stage, representing as he did a strong regionalist / centralist viewpoint. Not only had he provided stable, efficient, and honest government in Manitoba but he had become the recognized voice of the West and had made a considerable contribution to a searching examination of Canadian federalism.

Notes

CHAPTER 1: EARLY YEARS

1 The above information on the Bracken family is drawn from interviews with George Bracken (John's first cousin), Ellisville, 1 Aug. 1972; Dr Frank Bracken (John's first cousin), Winnipeg, 19 Aug. 1973; and Mrs Gladys Wilson (John's sister), Portland, Oregon, 18 Feb. 1974; and from a family tree compiled by Dr Frank Bracken and Susan Bracken (John's grand-daughter).

2 See interviews with Gladys Wilson, 18 Feb. 1974, and with George Bracken, 1 Aug. 1972. In 1946 Austin Cross wrote a series of articles entitled 'Plow to Parliament' for the *Ottawa Citizen* tracing Bracken's life up to his acceptance of the leadership of the Progressive Conservative party. In gathering his material Cross interviewed many of Bracken's relatives and friends. Bracken kept these articles in a small scribbler that is now in MG 13 I 4, BP, PAM. In the above two paragraphs I have drawn on the introduction and chapter 2 which were based on an interview with Alberta Bracken in the early 1940s.

3 Interview with Gladys Wilson, 18 Feb. 1974, and with Dr Frank Bracken, 19 Aug. 1973

4 Cross, 'Plow to Parliament,' chap. 2, and interview with Gladys Wilson, 18 Feb. 1974. Ephraim and Alberta had two other children neither of whom survived childhood. Mary Blanche died on 18 May 1899 aged 5 years 9 months, and William died on 9 December 1903 aged 9 months 5 days.

5 Information supplied by Don Ferguson, records clerk, the Leeds and Grenville County Board of Education, in letters to the author, 11 and 22 Jan. 1973.

6 *Brockville Times*, 15 July 1897

7 All the records of the Brockville Collegiate prior to 1929 were destroyed in a fire that year. See Don Ferguson to author, 11 Jan. 1973.

8 *Brockville Times*, 21 Dec. 1897

9 For information about the examination system in use in Ontario schools in 1898 I am grateful to Mr G.E. Mills, information officer, Ontario Ministry of Education. See G.E. Mills to author, 22 April 1977. Also *Brockville Times*, 15 and 18 Aug. 1898

10 For John's and his parents' reaction see interview with Gladys Wilson, 18 Feb. 1974.

11 Interview with George Bracken, 1 Aug. 1972

12 W.J. Rutherford to Walter Murray [nd], file Rutherford, W.J. (1909-30), series I, B99, Presidential Papers, U Sask A (S)

13 *Brockville Times*, 20 June 1901

14 Interview with Gladys Wilson, 18 Feb. 1974

15 John Bracken's registration card is filed in the Records of the Registrar, University of Guelph.

16 For the early years of the OAC see C.A. Zavitz, 'History and Development of the Ontario Agricultural College,' *Scientific Agriculture*, March 1921, 101-5. Also *The O.A.C. Calendar*, 1902-7

17 See *Guelph Daily Mercury*, 4 and 13 Oct. 1902, and *The O.A.C. Review*, Jan. and March 1903. Also interview with Bruce and Doug Bracken, 22 Jan. 1973

18 Professor J.B. Reynolds who Bracken was to succeed as principal of the Manitoba Agricultural College in 1920 later described Bracken, the student, as 'a most competent man and a possessor of a methodical, orderly mind ... able to meet all emergencies.' *Manitoba Free Press*, 25 July 1922

19 For a detailed breakdown of his standing see *Guelph Daily Mercury*, 4 Feb. 1903.

20 For the final results see ibid., 20 May 1903.

21 See *The O.A.C. Review*, Dec. 1905, 144, and April 1906, 365.

22 For the above see interview with Gladys Wilson, 18 Feb. 1974, and with George Bracken, 1 Aug. 1972; and Austin Cross, 'Plow to Parliament,' chap. 4. Bracken's copy of the latter has been ticked and acknowledged by Bracken.

23 *The O.A.C. Review*, May 1904, 70; and *Guelph Daily Mercury*, 2 and 3 June 1904

24 The team was composed of Bracken, W.A. Munro, H.A. Craig, G.G. White, and H.B. Smith. They were first in cattle, sheep, and swine, and second in horses. See *Guelph Daily Mercury*, 14 Nov. and 18 Dec. 1905; and *The O.A.C. Review*, Dec. 1905, 194, and Jan. 1908, 179-83.

25 *The O.A.C. Review*, Dec. 1905, 144

26 *Guelph Daily Mercury*, 3 April 1906

27 *The O.A.C. Review*, April 1906, 365

28 J. Bracken, 'Retrospectus,' *The O.A.C. Review*, Feb. 1907, 213-18

CHAPTER 2: THE WEST AND AGRICULTURE

1 Bracken had also been offered a job in South Africa as superintendent of both a farm and Christian and agricultural education work, and one as assistant in Animal Husbandry at the Ohio Agricultural College. See W.J. Rutherford to Walter Murray [nd], file Rutherford, W.J. (1909-30), Series I, B 99, Presidential Papers, U Sask A (S) [hereafter Rutherford file].

2 For the above information see 'Report of the Seed Commissioner for the period from January 1905 to March 1911,' Department of Agriculture (Ottawa 1911), 1-9.

3 In 1906-7 seed fairs were held at Carman, Gilbert Plains, Swan River, Dauphin, Virden, Deloraine, Morden, Hamiota, Manitou, Hartney, Portage la Prairie, Killarney, Brandon, and Neepawa. See 'Report of the Minister of Agriculture 1906-7,' *Sessional Papers*, XLII, 7, 1907-8, xxxiii. Also 'Report of the Seed Commissioner for the period from January 1905 to March 1911,' Department of Agriculture (Ottawa 1911), 94

4 Bracken's activities that winter can be followed in the following Manitoba newspapers: *Western Canadian – Manitou*, 13 Dec. 1906; *Virden Advance*, 7 Feb. 1907; *Morden Chronicle*, 14 Feb. 1907; *Hamiota Echo*, 14 Feb. 1907; *Weekly Review, Portage la Prairie*, 21 Feb. 1907; *Neepawa Register*, 28 Feb. 1907; *Killarney Guide*, 1 March 1907; *Dauphin Press*, 7 March 1907; *Dauphin Herald*, 8 March 1907; and *Manitoba Free Press* [hereafter *Free Press*], 14 Dec. 1906, 4, 12, 20, 21, 27 and 28 Feb. 1907.

5 *Annual Report of the Saskatchewan Department of Agriculture*, 1907, 247

6 'A Good Record,' Special to The Leader, *Morning Leader* (Regina), 17 May 1907

7 For a detailed look at Motherwell's ideas and activities see A.R. Turner, 'W.R. Motherwell and Agricultural Education, 1905-18,' *Saskatchewan History*, autumn 1959, 81-96. For parallel American experiences see Roy V. Scott, *The Reluctant Farmer: The Rise of Agricultural Extension to 1914* (Urbana 1970).

8 I have depended heavily in the above paragraph on Turner, 'W.R. Motherwell and Agricultural Education,' 81-2. To a degree Motherwell's programme was a continuation and expansion of policies initiated in territorial days. See F.H. Auld, 'Farmers' Institutes in the North-West Territories,' *Saskatchewan History*, spring 1957, 41-54.

9 See 'Report of the Superintendent of Fairs and Institutes' and 'Report of the Saskatchewan Stock Breeder's Association' in *Annual Report of the Saskatchewan Department of Agriculture*, 1907-9.

10 Much of his work can be followed in 'Farmers Institutes 1908-10,' file I.135, Agricultural Society Papers, SAB (R); see also Bracken to Walter Scott, 30 Aug. 1907 and 27 May 1908, file M 1 IV.4, 23124 and 23126-7, Walter Scott Papers, SAB(S); and Bracken to E.W. Early, 28 Jan. 1908, file I.196, 'Organization of Agricultural Societies,' Agricultural Society Papers, SAB(R).

11 'Institute Meetings, 1906-09,' file I.134, Agricultural Society Papers SAB(R)

12 See Austin Cross, 'Plow to Parliament,' chap. 8, BP, PAM, MG 13 I 4.

13 Reprinted in Nor-West Farmer, 20 Dec. 1907, 1124-5

14 See Jean E. Murray, 'The Contest for the University of Saskatchewan,' Saskatchewan History, winter 1959, 1-22; also W.P. Thompson, The University of Saskatchewan: A Personal History (Toronto 1970).

15 For Rutherford's letter of reference see W.J. Rutherford to Walter Murray [nd], Rutherford file.

16 Morning Leader, 12 April 1909

17 Minutes of a meeting held in City Hall, Regina, 5 April 1909, Governors' Minutes, series I, B 55, Presidential Papers, U Sask A (S)

18 Walter Murray to D.P. McColl (registrar), 24 Nov. 1909, file McColl, D.P., 1909, series I, B 67, ibid.

19 The above paragraph is based on the following material: Bracken to Walter Murray, 23 and 28 Nov. 1909 and 13 March 1910, file Gen. Corresp. (Bra-Bre), series I, A-9, ibid., and Austin Cross, 'Plow to Parliament,' chaps. 9 and 10, based on interviews done in the 1940s.

20 See interview with Dr Jean Murray, 18 Dec. 1972.

21 For the details of the homesteads see N.O. Coté to Ephraim Bracken, 21 April 1915, file no 1320332; and M.A. MacInnes to John Bracken, 25 Aug. 1913, file no 1187353, Homestead Records, Department of Interior, Land Patents Office, SAB(S); also Austin Cross, 'Plow to Parliament,' chap. 11; and interview with Gladys Wilson, 18 Feb. 1974.

22 Interview with Dr Jean Murray, 18 Dec. 1972

23 Faculty discussions and Bracken's involvement can be followed in 'Minutes of a meeting of the Faculty of the College of Agriculture,' file 40/1/1, Agricultural Minutes 1911-28, U Sask A(S).

24 For Bracken's activities during the period 1912-20 see: Presidential Papers, series I, B 38/28, Departmental Reports, Field Husbandry, 1918-26, U Sask A (S); and Reports to the President 1912-28, Dean's Correspondence A, College of Agriculture I, ibid; also President's Report, University of Saskatchewan, 1912-21.

25 J. Bracken, The Management of Saskatchewan Soils, Department of Agriculture, Province of Saskatchewan [nd], 1

26 J. Bracken, Wheat Growing in Saskatchewan, Field Husbandry Bulletin no 1 [nd], U Sask A (S)

27 See Thompson, *The University of Saskatchewan*, 88; L.E. Kirk, 'Early Years in the College of Agriculture,' *Saskatchewan History*, winter 1959, 25-7; and particularly Bracken's annual reports on his experiments in Presidential Papers, series I, B38/28, Departmental Reports, Field Husbandry, 1918-26; and Reports to the President 1912-28, Dean's Correspondence A, College of Agriculture I, U Sask A (S).
28 See A.F. Mantle to Bracken, 8, 16 and 17 June 1915, and Bracken to Mantle, 2 July 1915, file I.296, General Correspondence 1909-37, Agricultural Societies Papers, SAB (R).
29 For various opinions of Bracken's work see L.C. Paul, 'History of Extension, University of Saskatchewan 1910-70' (draft only), 701, in box Extension: L.C. Paul, History and Tapes, U Sask A (S); L.C. Paul interview with W.P. Thompson, 9 Oct. 1968, ibid.; also interview with Dean L.H. Shebiski, 2 Feb. 1973.
30 Interview with Dr Jean Murray, 18 Dec. 1972
31 See *The Sheaf*, Dec. 1916, 33, 50-1; Dec. 1917, 73-4.
32 W. Murray to W.M. Martin, 6 May 1920, 23386-7, file M 4.I.69, W.M. Martin Papers, SAB(S)
33 See *President's Report*, University of Saskatchewan, 1920-1, 10 and 20.
34 For Bracken's initial progress report see Bracken to G.G. Malcolm (Minutes of Agriculture, Manitoba) [nd], and 'Maps and Charts,' both in file Economic Survey, box 109, series MG 13 I 2, BP, PAM.
35 For impressions of Bracken during those years see interviews with two former colleagues, Professor L.H. Ellis, 5 March 1973, and Professor Shanks, 7 March 1973.

CHAPTER 3: PREMIER OF MANITOBA

1 For the Progressive Association and UFM platforms see *Free Press*, 31 May 1922. Also the Winnipeg Progressive Association Minute Book May 10, 1922-July 15, 1922, box 21, UFM Papers. For further information on the UFM see W.L. Morton, *The Progressive Party in Canada* (Toronto 1950), and Gerald E. Panting, 'A Study of the United Farmers of Manitoba to 1928' (unpublished MA thesis, University of Manitoba, 1954).
2 See interview with Bracken on his 76th birthday and 50th wedding anniversary. *Tribune*, 22 June 1959
3 The account of the meeting on Kennedy Street and of Bracken's decision is based on interviews of 4 Feb. 1973 and 5 Dec. 1977 with Douglas Campbell, former premier of Manitoba and a participant in the discussions. See also Dafoe to Sifton, 25 July 1922, reel M 74, Dafoe Papers, University of Manitoba Library (microfilm).

4 *Free Press*, 22 July 1922
5 *Tribune*, 22 July 1922. For opinions of other Canadian newspapers see the compilation in the *Free Press*, 28 July 1922.
6 See particularly Craig's speech of 30 May 1922, *Free Press* 31 May 1922.
7 *Tribune*, 1 and 2 Aug. 1922
8 The *Canadian Parliamentary Guide* (1922-8) lists Bracken as a Presbyterian. It is difficult to know why this is so. It is clear that Bracken was raised a Methodist and he made a point of mentioning that in his first political speech in The Pas in September 1922. Since coming West Bracken had not attended church on a regular basis and had left the religious upbringing of the boys to Alice, a Presbyterian. Thus when he did attend church he tended to go with the family to the Presbyterian service. This may account for the entry in the *Guide*. By 1929 he was listed as a member of the United Church. See interview with Gladys Wilson, 18 Feb. 1974, and Dr Frank Bracken to the author, 21 March 1977.
9 *Free Press*, 8 Aug. 1922
10 For full coverage of Bracken's first visit to The Pas see *The Pas Herald and Mining News*, 1 Sept. 1922.
11 For Bracken's speech see ibid.
12 For the local political manoeuvrings see ibid., 8 and 15 Sept.
13 For Finger's opening speech and for profiles of all the candidates see ibid., 22 Sept. 1922.
14 For Sullivan's speech see report in *Free Press*, 30 Sept. 1922.
15 For Bracken's final speech in The Pas see *The Pas Herald and Mining News*, 6 Oct. 1922, and *Free Press*, 2 Oct. 1922.
16 For the election result and subsequent comments see *The Pas Herald and Mining News*, 6 Oct. 1922; and 'Political Scrapbook Aug. 1922-Feb. 1924,' 20, Manitoba Legislative Library.

CHAPTER 4: BRACKENISM

1 For general reflections upon Bracken's years as premier of Manitoba see W.L. Morton, *Manitoba: A History* (Toronto 1957), 380-450; Tom Peterson, 'Ethnic and Class Politics in Manitoba,' in Martin Robin, ed., *Canadian Provincial Politics* (Scarborough 1972), 69-115; and Murray Donnelly, *The Government of Manitoba* (Toronto 1963).
2 One can follow the dismissals and the concern in the local newspapers. See *Free Press*, 20, 22, and 23 Dec. 1922 and 4 Jan. 1923; and *Tribune*, 23 and 26 Dec. 1922.
3 *Tribune*, 20 Feb. 1923
4 Ibid.

5 Ibid., 21 Feb. 1923
6 For Haig's legislative speech see ibid., 24 Feb. 1923.
7 *Free Press*, 21 Feb. 1923
8 See particularly Bracken's speech to a UFM district convention at Portage la Prairie, *Free Press* and *Tribune*, 10 Nov. 1923.
9 *A Few of the Achievements of the Bracken Government: Summary of Addresses by Premier Bracken on the Record of the Government* (Winnipeg 1927)
10 Ibid.
11 At the end of 1924 Black resigned to accept the vice-presidency of the Winnipeg Electric Company. Bracken took over the portfolio and remained provincial treasurer until 1932.
12 See particularly *Free Press* and *Tribune*, 20 Nov. 1923.
13 For Bracken's speech see *Free Press*, 23 Jan. 1923.
14 See interview with Douglas Campbell, 5 Dec. 1977.
15 Ibid.
16 See Panting, 'A Study of the United Farmers of Manitoba,' chapter V.
17 For a full report of the 'secret meeting' see *Tribune*, 4 Dec. 1923.
18 *Free Press*, 27 Oct. 1922
19 See *Report of the Educational (Murray) Commission* (Winnipeg 1924) and *Report of the Commission on the Re-adjusting of the Relations of the Higher Institutions of Learning* (1924).
20 For a valuable breakdown of costs and the hardships they reaped see *Free Press*, 1 Aug. 1924, 'Secondary Education in Manitoba.' Also *Free Press* and *Tribune*, 19 Feb. 1925.
21 See Greenfield to Dunning, 27 Dec. 1922; Greenfield to Bracken, 27 Dec. 1922; and Dunning to Greenfield, 2 Jan. 1923, file Corresp. Wheat Marketing 1922, box 11, C.A. Dunning Papers, SAB (S).
22 See Bracken's speech to annual UFM convention in Brandon, 9-12 Jan. 1923, reported in *Tribune*, 13 Jan. 1923. Also Bracken to Dunning, 23 Jan. and 5 Feb. 1923; and Dunning to Bracken, 30 Jan. and 7 Feb. 1923, file Wheat Marketing 1923 A-B, box 12, Dunning Papers. Also Greenfield to Dunning, 26 Jan. 1923; and Dunning to Greenfield, 29 Jan. and 7 Feb. 1923, file Wheat Marketing 1923 G-I, ibid.
23 *Tribune*, 19 Jan. 1923
24 *Free Press*, 7 March 1923
25 *Tribune*, 15 March 1923
26 *Free Press*, 17 March 1923
27 Ibid., 13 April 1923
28 For complete coverage of Bracken's lengthy speech see *Free Press*, 14 April 1923.

29 'Under the Dome,' *Free Press*, 15 April 1923
30 *Free Press*, 28 April 1923
31 Ibid., 1 May 1923
32 Ibid., 21 Jan. 1923
33 For Bracken's initial announcement see *Tribune*, 29 Jan. 1923. For subsequent discussion in and out of the legislature see ibid., 31 Jan., 3 and 6 Feb. 1923; and *Free Press*, 3 and 6 Feb. and 14 and 27 March 1923.
34 For the Walker Theatre meeting see both *Tribune* and *Free Press*, 15 May 1923.
35 For the complete results of the referenda see *Free Press* and *Tribune*, 23 and 25 June 1923 and 12 and 13 July 1923. For Bracken's comment see record of interview in *Tribune*, 8 Oct. 1927.
36 See the summary in the *Canadian Annual Review*, 1923, 708-9.
37 For the results of the referendum and subsequent government activity see *Tribune* and *Free Press*, 30 June, 13 Aug., and 16 and 18 Nov. 1927.
38 *Free Press*, 4 Dec. 1923
39 Ibid., 12 Dec. 1923
40 Ibid., 18 Dec. 1923
41 For the final results see ibid., 25 Dec. 1923.
42 *Tribune*, 8 March 1924
43 Interview with Bruce and Doug Bracken, 22 Jan. 1973
44 Interview with Douglas Campbell, 4 Feb. 1973
45 See *Deloraine Times*, 8 Dec. 1926

CHAPTER 5: WOOD, MINERALS, AND LIBERALS

1 See particularly undated draft speech to Board of Trade, box 3, series MG 13 I 1, BP, PAM. See also draft speech to UFM in Brandon, 15 Jan. 1926, ibid.
2 See *Free Press*, 18 Sept. 1925; *The Monetary Times*, 30 Oct. 1925; and Bracken's speech at the first annual meeting of the IDB, 2 June 1926, file IDB, box 12, series MG 13 I 2, BP, PAM. Unless otherwise indicated all further references to BP, PAM, will be to this series.
3 See Bracken's speech at the IDB dinner, 2 June 1926, ibid.
4 The scale was: pop. 250,000-400,000, subsidy $375,000; pop. 400,000-800,000, subsidy $562,000; pop. 800,000-1,200,000, subsidy $750,000; pop. 1,200,000 and over, subsidy $1,125,000.
5 Chester Martin, *Dominion Lands' Policy* (Toronto 1938), 483
6 See John Ingram, 'Manitoba and the Natural Resources Question 1870-1930' (unpublished graduate research paper, University of Manitoba, 1974).
7 For a copy of the 1922 agreement see file Natural Resources, box 20, BP, PAM. See also King Diary, 20 and 21 April 1922, King Papers, PAC.

8 Fiduciary: holding, held, or founded in trust
9 For the November 1922 meetings see *Tribune*, 15 and 20 Nov. 1922, and *Free Press*, 20 Nov. 1922. Also King Diary, 14-17 Nov. 1922; and Bracken to King, Nov. 1922, 59842-4, box 70, series J1, King Papers. For attempts during 1923-7 see Bracken-King correspondence in boxes 84, 97, 128, and 141, ibid.
10 Quoted in a summary of the negotiations supplied to the *Tribune* by A.M. McFadyn, 2 June 1925
11 Ibid.
12 For the details see *Free Press*, 21 Oct. 1924.
13 For the reaction in the city see the *Free Press* and the *Tribune*, Oct. and Nov. 1924, particularly *Free Press*, 12-15 Nov. 1924.
14 *Free Press*, 14 and 15 Nov. 1924
15 Ibid., 25 Nov. 1924
16 Ibid., 8 and 10 Dec. 1924
17 For a full account of the negotiations and the auction described in the previous two paragraphs see *Tribune*, 19 Dec. 1924, and *Free Press*, 17 and 20 Dec. 1924. See particularly Dafoe to Clifford Sifton, 31 March 1925, reel M 74, Dafoe Papers, University of Manitoba Library (microfilm).
18 *Free Press*, 20 Dec. 1924
19 See *Tribune* editorial, 22 Dec. 1924.
20 Dafoe to Sifton, 23 April 1925, reel M 74, Dafoe Papers
21 Bracken to Craig, 6 May 1925, tel., box 1, BP, PAM. Also Travers Sweatman to W.J. Healy, 10 June 1925, box 2, Healy Papers, PAM
22 See *Free Press*, 16, 19, and 20 May 1925.
23 Dafoe to Sifton, 27 May 1925, reel M 74, Dafoe Papers
24 *Free Press*, 29 May 1925
25 See *Tribune*, 'Raw Deal for Winnipeg,' 29 May 1925.
26 See ibid., 16 July 1925, for a map and the degree of monopoly.
27 For an analysis of the Flin Flon deposit and the problems facing its owners see B.F.C. Hunter, 'The Development of New Manitoba 1912-1930' (unpublished MA thesis, University of Western Ontario, 1973), 89-114.
28 Ibid., 110
29 *Free Press*, 13 Dec. 1925
30 Bracken to Coleman, 2 Dec. 1925, and Coleman to Bracken, 3 Dec. 1925, tels., file Mining, box 19, BP, PAM. Also Bracken to Graham, 1 Dec. 1925, and Graham to Bracken, 12 Dec. 1925, file Mineral Development, box 13, ibid.
31 See H.H. Elliott to Bracken, 20 Nov. 1925; W.E. Davis to Bracken, 14 Dec. 1925; and Bracken to Davis, 15 Dec. 1925, ibid. See also William Burt (president of The Pas Board of Trade) to Ralph Webb (mayor of Winnipeg),

2 Dec. 1925; Webb to Bracken, 14 Dec. 1925; and Bracken to Webb, 16
Dec. 1925, ibid. See also Bracken's speech in the Manitoba legislature on 28
Jan. 1926, *Free Press*, 29 Jan. 1926.

32 Thornton to Bracken, 5 March 1926, file Mineral Development, box 13, BP,
PAM. Also see H.H. Elliott to Bracken, 18 Jan. 1926, and G.A. Bell to
Elliott, 11 Jan. 1926, enclosing 'Report on Proposed Line to Flin Flon Mine'
dated 23 December 1925. Bracken to Channing, 29 Dec. 1925, and Channing
to Bracken, 5 Jan. 1926, ibid.

33 See Ed. Brown, 'Memorandum for Council re Flin Flon Mine No. 2. Private
and Confidential,' March 1926, ibid.

34 For Bracken's thoughts at this time see undated notes in Bracken's hand and
undated and unsigned memorandum, ibid.

35 Parker, Clark, and Hart to Bracken, 18 March 1926, ibid.

36 For the legislative debates see *Tribune*, 31 March, 10, 15, 16, 20, 21, 24
April 1926; and *Free Press*, 2, 9, 15, 16, 20, 21, 24 April 1926.

37 See R.E. Phelan to Bracken, 1 Sept. 1926 and [March] 1927; and Bracken to
Phelan, 22 March 1927, file Mining, box 19, BP, PAM.

38 H.J. Symington to Bracken, 4 Nov. [1927], and Bracken's notes at foot of
letter dated Saturday, 5 Nov., ibid.

39 See undated Bracken statement [probably 17 Nov. 1927], ibid.

40 Phelan to Bracken, 12 Nov. 1927, ibid.

41 Phelan to Bracken, 12 Nov. 1927, ibid. Phelan restated the position again on
16 November at Bracken's request. See Bracken to Phelan, 16 Nov. 1927,
and Phelan to Bracken, 16 Nov. 1927, ibid.

42 Bracken to Dunning, 17 Nov. 1927, ibid.

43 For further details of the above negotiations see undated Bracken statement
[probably 17 Nov. 1927], ibid.

44 Parker to Bracken, 30 Nov. 1927, and Bracken to Parker, 30 Nov. 1927, ibid.

45 For Bracken's early thoughts see Dafoe to Sifton, 27 Dec. 1923, in R. Cook,
ed., *The Dafoe-Sifton Correspondence* (Winnipeg 1966), 174-5.

46 F.C. Hamilton to King, 12 Feb. 1926, 112140-1, box 132, series J 1, King
Papers

47 The following account of the activities of Maybank and the Young Liberals
is taken from R. Maybank, 'Political Memos of 1926-27,' folder 'Letters
Political 1926-27,' file 138, box 5, R. Maybank Papers, PAM. For the initial
interview see entry for 26 March 1926.

48 Ibid.; entry for 8 April 1926

49 For a synopsis of the discussion at the Liberal convention of 23 Nov. 1926
see ibid., 76-84.

50 Ibid.; entry for 11 April 1927

51 Ibid.
52 Gardiner to King, 11 April 1927, 121702-3, box 143, series J 1, King Papers.
   The connection between the two men was clearly acknowledged in a letter
   written by Robson to Gardiner three days after the convention: 'I do not
   want the slightest slip in our connection ... We understand each other and
   know the situation ... please don't hesitate to do or suggest anything you see
   fit and *don't wait for us*.' Robson to Gardiner, 2 April 1927, 8291-2,
   Gardiner Papers, quoted in Gordon Unger, 'James G. Gardiner: The Premier
   as a Pragmatic Politician 1926-1929' (unpublished MA thesis, University of
   Saskatchewan, 1967), 51
53 Crerar to A.K. Cameron, 1 April 1927, box 97, Crerar Papers, Queen's
   University Archives
54 Crerar to Cameron, 18 May 1927, ibid.
55 *Free Press*, 18 April 1927
56 Robson to King, 5 April 1927, 125552, box 147, series J 1, King Papers
57 Interview with Douglas Campbell, 19 Oct. 1976
58 Maybank, 'Political Memos,' 83
59 For an excellent analysis of the 1927 election see Richard Grover, 'The 1927
   Manitoba Provincial Election' (unpublished Honours research paper,
   University of Manitoba, 1970).

CHAPTER 6: THE SEVEN SISTERS SITE

1 Bracken's undated notes (probably May / June 1928), file Personal, box 28,
  series MG 13 I 2, BP, PAM. Unless otherwise indicated all further references to
  BP, PAM, will be to this series.
2 R. Maybank, 'Political Memos of 1926-27,' folder 'Letters Political 1926-27,'
  file 138, box 5, R. Maybank Papers, PAM, entry for 1 Aug. 1927
3 Ibid., entries for 1, 17, and 18 Aug., 8 Oct., and 8 Dec. 1927
4 Crerar to A.K. Cameron, 12 Aug. 1927, box 97, Crerar Papers, Queen's
  University Archives; also Robb to King, 4 Nov. 1927, 125468-9, box 147,
  series J 1, King Papers, PAC
5 Taylor's account of his visit is in his 'Memo to Senator Haydon. Report on
  Manitoba. 15 December 1927,' c84459-64, box 72, series J 4, ibid.
6 Robson to King, 2 Dec. 1927, 125586-7, box 147, series J 1, ibid.
7 Robson to King, 4 Jan. 1928, 133117-8, box 156, ibid.
8 King to Robson, 7 Jan. 1928, 133119-20, ibid.
9 Gardiner to King, 17 Jan. 1928, 129730-36, box 152, ibid.
10 See King to Gardiner, 3 March 1928, 129737-41, ibid.
11 Bracken to King, 10 Jan. 1928, 128324-5, box 150, ibid.

12 Robson to Stewart, 9 Feb. 1928, 133126-7, box 156, ibid.

13 Robson to King, 25 Feb. 1928, 133130-3, ibid.

14 King to Bracken, 28 Feb. 1928, 128326-7, box 150, ibid. Also King Diary, 28 Feb. 1928, ibid.

15 See Bracken to King, 5 March 1928, 128336, and King to Bracken, 17 March 1928, 128337; also 128345-57, box 150, ibid.

16 Bracken had initially been drawn to problems associated with water resources in late 1924 by the efforts of E.W. Backus to control both the water level of the Lake of the Woods and the flow on the Winnipeg River with his Norman Dam which spanned the river just below its outlet from the Lake. The Manitoba power companies, the City of Winnipeg, and Bracken had put pressure on Stewart not to comply with Backus. In the end full ownership of the dam remained with Backus but sufficient protection of Manitoba interests had been guaranteed by the federal government to satisfy Bracken, the city, and the Manitoba power companies. The issue was extensively covered in the *Tribune* and the *Manitoba Free Press*, Oct.-Dec. 1924. See also C. Sifton to Dafoe, 3 Oct. 1924, reel C735, Sifton Papers, University of Manitoba Library (microfilm).

17 This information is taken from Bracken's speech to the Young Men's Section, Winnipeg Board of Trade, 16 July 1928, box 3, series MG 13 I 1, BP, PAM.

18 For the policy of the Waterpowers Branch see H.V. Nelles, 'Public Ownership of Electrical Utilities in Manitoba and Ontario, 1906-30,' *Canadian Historical Review* LVII, 4, Dec. 1976, 461-84.

19 See A.M. McLimont (vice-president of the WEC) to Charles Stewart, 21 Aug. 1925; Charles Stewart to McLimont, 27 Aug. 1925; Bracken to Stewart, 1 Sept. 1925; Stewart to Bracken, 1 Sept. 1925; Bracken to Stewart, 12 Jan. and 19 March 1927; Stewart to Bracken, 16 Feb. 1927, file Seven Sisters-Fed. Govt. Return, box 28, BP, PAM. Also Clubb to Bracken, 31 Aug. 1925, folder Dept'l. Corresp., box 2, ibid.

20 See *Report of the Royal Commission re Seven Sisters Falls Agreement. Evidence and Proceedings* (1929) [hereafter *Proceedings*], I, 877 (Clubb).

21 Bracken to McLimont, 13 Dec. 1927, file Seven Sisters-Corresp., box 29, BP, PAM. It is clear that Bracken was not aware at this time that the WEC had reapplied for a lease in June 1927. See *Proceedings*, V, 3844 (Bracken).

22 *Proceedings*, II, 1633-4, 1654, and 1659 (Anderson)

23 See ibid., V, 3849-50 (Bracken); also McLimont to Bracken, 10 Jan. 1928, and Bracken to McLimont, 26 Jan. 1928, file Seven Sisters-Corresp., box 29, BP, PAM.

24 Bracken to J.T. Johnston, 26 Jan. 1928, tel.; F.A. Gaby to Bracken, 27 Jan. 1928, tel.; Bracken to Hogg, 27 Jan. 1928, tel.; Hogg to Bracken, 28 Jan.

1928, tel.; Johnston to Bracken, 2 Feb. 1928, tel., file Seven Sisters-Fed. Govt. Return, box 28, ibid.; and Bracken to C.A. Magrath, 26 Jan. 1928, file Seven Sisters Corresp., box 29, ibid.

25 *Proceedings*, V, 3861 and 3863 (Bracken)

26 Ibid., 4069-70 (Hogg)

27 Ibid., 4070-1 (Hogg), and 3871 and 3881 (Bracken). Also Bracken to Hogg, 6 Feb. 1928, file Seven Sisters-Corresp., box 29; and Bracken to Johnston, 6 Feb. 1928, file Seven Sisters-Fed. Govt. Return, box 28, BP, PAM

28 *Proceedings*, I, 584 and 601 (Clubb) and 2404 (Major); and V, 5011 (Hogg)

29 Bracken to Allen, 6 Feb. 1928, file Seven Sisters-Corresp., box 29, BP, PAM

30 Allen to Bracken, 15 Feb. 1928; Bracken to Hudson, 17 Feb. 1928; and Hudson to Bracken, 21 Feb. 1928, ibid.

31 For the letter, dated 7 Feb. 1928, see file Seven Sisters-Fed. Govt. Return, box 28, ibid.

32 See *Proceedings*, V, 3906, 27 (Bracken); 5012-22 (Hogg); III, 2418 (Major); and I, 604 (Clubb). No minutes of the cabinet meetings or copies of the various memoranda, including Hogg's draft report, exist because there was no formal secretariat. The ministers were usually informed of cabinet meetings by telephone from the premier's office, ibid., I, 606-7 (Clubb). By the time he saw Hogg's draft report Bracken had also received the material from Johnston which reaffirmed the need to concentrate development of hydro-electric power at the Seven Sisters site. The material forwarded by Johnston is printed in *Reports Relating to Development of Seven Sisters Power Site on the Winnipeg River and Agreement for Supply of Power to Provincial Hydro Electric System* (Winnipeg 1928), file Seven Sisters-Personal, box 28, BP, PAM.

33 Bracken to McLimont, 5 March 1928, file Seven Sisters-Corresp., box 29, ibid.

34 McLimont to Bracken, 7 March 1928, ibid.

35 See *Proceedings*, VI, 5208-20 (Bracken).

36 See ibid., V, 3906-27 and 3941 (Bracken).

37 Hogg Report in *Reports Relating to Development of Seven Sisters ...* file Seven Sisters-Personal, box 28, BP, PAM

38 The above account is based on *Proceedings*, II, 1712-14 (Anderson); I, 613, 624, 646, 935 (Clubb); III, 2433-4 and 2463-5 (Major); VI, 5211-19 (Bracken).

39 Bracken to McLimont, 17 March 1928, file Seven Sisters-Corresp., box 29, BP, PAM, and Hogg Report

40 *Proceedings*, II, 1734 (Anderson)

41 Ibid., 1735 (Anderson)

42 McLimont to Bracken, 19 March 1928, file Seven Sisters-Corresp., box 29, BP, PAM. See also *Proceedings*, II, 1734 (Anderson); and IV, 2980 (McLimont).

43 For this account see ibid., I, 937-8 (Clubb).

44 Bracken to McLimont, 20 March 1928; and McLimont (per E.A.) to Bracken, 20 March 1928, file Seven Sisters-Corresp., box 29, BP, PAM. Also Anderson to Major, 20 April 1928; and McLimont to Bracken, 25 April 1928, file Seven Sisters (extra copies), box 30, ibid.

45 *Proceedings*, III, 2528 (Major)

46 For the federal reaction see unsigned memorandum on Seven Sisters prepared for Mackenzie King, 26 June 1928, copy, file Seven Sisters-Personal, box 28, BP, PAM.

47 *Proceedings*, II, 1741-6 (Anderson); also I, 662-3 (Clubb); and IV, 3067 (McLimont)

48 Ibid., IV, 2985 (McLimont)

49 Bracken to Stewart, 22 March 1928, file Seven Sisters-Fed. Govt. Return, box 28, BP, PAM

50 Debates on power development had taken place on 2 and 21 Feb. and 9 March 1928.

51 See *Tribune*, 29 and 30 March; 4, 6, 7, 9, and 10 April 1928; and *Free Press*, 24 and 27 March; 3, 4, 5, and 6 April 1928. For Taylor's views see his speeches to the Conservative Club in Winnipeg, 23 March 1928, and to the Young Men's Conservative Club at Brandon, 4 May 1928; also his letter to Stewart of 25 June 1928, file Seven Sisters-Fed. Govt. Return, box 28, BP, PAM.

52 See unsigned report of the Public Utilities Committee, 9 April 1928, file Seven Sisters-Fed. Govt. Return, box 28, and for a complete list of resolutions, petitions, and letters see unsigned memorandum dated 26 June 1928, prepared for Mackenzie King by the Waterpowers Branch, file Seven Sisters-Personal, ibid. For the City Council votes see *Winnipeg Council Minutes*, 12 April and 14 May 1928. Also *Free Press*, 6, 9, 13 April and 15 May 1928.

53 See his letter to the *Tribune*, 19 May 1928. Also *Tribune*, 1 June 1928; *Free Press*, 3, 4, and 5 June 1928; and Taylor to Stewart, 25 June 1928, file Seven Sisters-Fed. Govt. Return, box 28, BP, PAM.

54 See Bracken to Stewart, 25 April 1928; McLimont to Stewart, 5 May 1928; Stewart to McLimont, 10 May 1928; and J. Allison Glen to Stewart, 15 May 1928, ibid.

55 *Free Press*, 7 June 1928

56 Robson to King, 18 May 1928, 133146-51, box 156, series J 1, King Papers. Also Robson to King, 21 April and 1 May 1928, 133139-42, and King to Robson, 19 May 1928, 133143-5, ibid. On 17 May Robson issued a public statement supporting the Seven Sisters deal. See *Free Press*, 18 May 1928.

57 Undated notes [probably May / June 1928] by Bracken, file Personal, box 28, BP, PAM

58 Bracken to King, 15 June 1928, personal and confidential, 128340-2, vol. 150, series J 1, King Papers

59 King Diary, 28 June 1928

60 There is a digest of the discussion in the King Papers. See 'Natural Resources Conference with Province of Manitoba July 3, 1928,' confidential, c88408-14, vol. 121, series J 4, King Papers. For additional background see Blair Neatby, *William Lyon Mackenzie King, 1924-1932: The Lonely Heights* (Toronto 1963), 251-5 and 299.

61 King Diary, 3 July 1928

62 For an account of this meeting see ibid. A copy of Skelton's original memorandum prepared that night at Laurier House is in file Natural Resources, box 20, BP, PAM. The revisions made to it during the evening's discussion can be found in 'Draft No. 1,' c88415, file 901, box 121, series J 4, King Papers. A clear copy of the revised draft is at c88406, ibid.

63 The nature of the changes made as a result of the discussion on Wednesday, 4 July, can be followed on c88419 and c88420, ibid., and in King Diary, 4 and 5 July 1928.

64 See King to Robert Forke, 19 July 1928, 129576-9, box 152, series J 1, King Papers.

65 King Diary, 7 July 1928

66 See King Diary, 5-10 July 1928. The last-minute revisions, the long-range negotiations, and King's activities can all be followed in file 901, box 121, series J 4, King Papers; on 128360-71, box 150, series J 1, ibid., on 128376-81 and 134748-53, box 158, ibid., and in file Natural Resources, box 20, BP, PAM.

67 A copy of the text is at c88401, file 901, box 121, series J 4, King Papers. See also *Free Press*, 12 July 1928.

68 Bracken to King, 13 July 1928, 128385, box 150, series J 1, King Papers

69 King to Bracken, 16 July 1928, 128389, ibid.

70 For Bracken's speech see box 3, series MG 13 I 1, BP, PAM.

71 Dafoe to Sifton, 17 July 1928, reel M 75, Dafoe Papers, University of Manitoba Library (microfilm)

72 Robson to King, 17 July 1928, 133164-5, box 156, series J 1, King Papers

73 See Stewart to Bracken, 18 Aug. 1928; and Bracken to Stewart, 21 Aug. 1928, file Seven Sisters-Fed. Govt. Return, box 28, BP, PAM.

74 For the final stages of the negotiations see file Seven Sisters-Fed. Govt. Return, ibid.

CHAPTER 7: SCANDAL

1 Aunt Sarah to Howard Winkler, 25 Feb. 1929, file Correspondence 1921-34, box 1, Winkler Papers, PAM

2 See report of Robson's speech at Griswold of 21 Oct. 1928 in *Free Press*, 22 Oct. 1928.

3 There had been tension from the beginning over McKenzie's nomination. See *Tribune*, 11, 12, and 22 Oct. 1928, and *Free Press*, 22 and 23 Oct. 1928. For dissentient Liberal opinions see J. MacLean to Norris, 17 Oct. 1928, and Norris to MacLean, 22 Oct. 1928 and 2 and 13 Nov. 1928, box 4, Norris Papers, PAM.

4 See *Tribune*, 4 Oct. 1928, for full coverage of Taylor's nominating speech, the bulk of which is devoted to the Seven Sisters lease.

5 In a speech at Harding on 30 October 1928 Taylor pointed out that the treasurer of the committee was Allan S. Bond, manager of the National Trust Company, transfer agents for the WEC. The chairman of the committee had been J.B. Coyne, KC, a director of the WEC. An active worker had been W.H. Carter, a director of the WEC and head of the contracting firm of Carter, Halls, Aldinger, Ltd which had the construction contract on a percentage basis for the railway to Seven Sisters Falls and such part of the power plant as the company proposed to build. Taylor declared the latter contract had been signed before the Seven Sisters agreement was announced. He also pointed out that Carter's firm had drainage contracts from the Bracken government. *Tribune*, 29 Oct. 1929

6 Taylor repeated his charges on numerous occasions, and in many places, throughout the campaign, but see particularly his speeches at Oak Lake on 4 and 29 October and at Harding on 30 October reported in the *Free Press* and *Tribune*.

7 *Free Press*, 31 Oct. 1928

8 McKenzie also received considerable assistance from A.L. Beaubien, the federal MP for Provencher who spent two weeks in the constituency talking with the approximately fifty resident French-speaking families. The subsequent results revealed that these votes had gone almost solidly for McKenzie.

9 *Free Press*, 8 Nov. 1928

10 Bracken's books are in the PAM. One can follow his routine, check his dates of departure and return, and estimate his bills from his entries in his diary of 1928 which under the 31 December entry has his January 1929 entries through to his departure from Battle Creek on 19 January. The diary is in box 1, series MG 13 I 1, BP, PAM. See also Bracken's speech to the Union of Municipalities, 4 Dec. 1929, box 3, ibid.

11 *Tribune*, 20 and 21 Dec. 1928

12 Ibid., 8 and 9 Jan. 1929

13 For the full text of the order-in-council see *Manitoba Gazette*, vol. 58, no 5, 2 Feb. 1929, 70-4.

14 See A. Sullivan, 12 Feb. 1929, file Royal Commission, box 31, series MG 13
   I 2, BP, PAM. Unless otherwise indicated all further references to BP, PAM,
   will be to this series.
15 Benjy Levin, 'The Seven Sisters Affair' (unpublished Honours research paper,
   University of Manitoba, 1972)
16 Dysart later submitted a minority report that made this point. See also
   *Report of the Royal Commission re Seven Sisters Falls Agreement. Evidence
   and Proceedings* (1929) [hereafter *Proceedings*], IV, 2999-3020 (McLimont),
   and V, 3526-7, 3538 (Blodgett).
17 A reading of the commission evidence leaves one unimpressed with the WEC's
   general accounting procedures, its mechanisms for personal accountability,
   and the capacities of many of its senior officials.
18 *Free Press*, 13 Feb. 1929
19 *Tribune*, 14 Feb. 1929
20 This account has been drawn from 'Under the Dome' by G.V.F., *Free Press*,
   16 Feb. 1929, and the regular news story in the *Free Press*, 16 Feb. 1929.
21 *Proceedings*, VI, 5241 (Bracken)
22 For full coverage of that remarkable week see *Free Press* and *Tribune*, 19-23
   Feb. 1929.
23 See *Free Press* and *Tribune*, 2 March 1929. Crerar thought the whole affair
   rather funny: 'The Seven Sisters are having a merry time. The situation in
   Manitoba has much in it that is quite comical. There is no one who knows
   either Clubb or Major that thinks for a second that their purchase of a few
   shares of stock, on which they lost quite heavily, had the slightest thing to
   do with their judgment in making the contract with the Street Railway. But
   there was, of course, nothing for them to do but to hand in their resignations,
   and Bracken should have accepted them PDQ. He is cautious, however, and
   has to weigh everything, and I believe finally it was something in the way of
   an ultimatum delivered to him by Donald McKenzie that brought action.'
   Crerar to Cameron, 4 March 1929, box 98, Crerar Papers, Queen's University
   Archives
24 For Clubb's evidence on this point see *Proceedings*, I, 651-787; and II, 1374
   and 1775.
25 Ibid., II, 1788 and 1829 (Haig)
26 Ibid., III, 2451-3 (Major) and 2462-3 (Major)
27 Ibid., II, 1791 (Haig)
28 *Tribune*, 20 Feb. 1929
29 This paragraph is based on Dafoe to King, 24 Feb. 1929, reel M 75, Dafoe
   Papers, University of Manitoba Library, and Dafoe to King, 2 March 1929,
   136837-8, box 161, series J 1, King Papers, PAC. Dafoe referred to the

'stupidity and folly' of Major and Clubb in a letter to Harry Sifton. Dafoe to
H. Sifton, 19 Feb. 1929, reel M 75, Dafoe Papers. Clifford Sifton shared
Dafoe's opinion about coalition. He wanted Bracken and Robson 'to join
hands and fight it through.' C. Sifton to Dafoe, 2 March 1929, ibid.

30 King to E. Brown, 11 March 1929, 136084, box 160, series J 1, King Papers
31 For King's ideas see King to Robson, 4 March 1929, personal and confidential, 142074-80, box 167, ibid.
32 See King to Dafoe, 11 March 1929, reel M 75, Dafoe Papers; and Haydon to
King, 8 March 1929, 138005, box 162, series J 1, King Papers.
33 Dafoe to King, 9 March 1929, 136839-42, box 161, ibid.
34 Bracken to Robson, 6 March 1929, file Coalition 1929-36, folder 1929, box
4, MG 13 I 1, BP, PAM
35 Much of the following account of Taylor's activities in Winnipeg and Regina
is taken from a series of lengthy memoranda written by Taylor to Senator
Haydon, 7-15 March 1929 [Taylor memoranda], 138016-36, box 162, series
J 1, King Papers. See also Taylor to King, 8 March 1929, 144205-8, box 169,
ibid.; 'Longbury' to Haydon, 8 March 1929, 138006, box 162, ibid.; and
Dafoe to King, 9 March 1929, 136839-42, box 161, ibid.
36 See Haydon to King, 11 March 1929, 138009, box 162, ibid.
37 Taylor to King, 11 March 1929, 144209-12, box 169, ibid.; and Haydon to
King, 12 March 1929, 138010, box 162, ibid.
38 See Robson to King, 8 March 1929, 132081-2, box 167, ibid.
39 J.F. Fisher to Haydon, 17 March 1929, 138013-5, box 162, ibid.
40 See King to Taylor, 15 March 1929, 144217, box 169, ibid.; and Haydon to
King, 14 March 1929, 138011, box 162, ibid.
41 King to E.D.R. Bissett, 16 March 1929, 135822, box 159, ibid.; and Bissett
to King, 23 March 1929, 135823-5, ibid.
42 These letters were sent in the form of telegrams to Taylor who hand-
delivered them. King to Taylor, 11 March 1929, 144213-14, box 169, ibid.;
and WLMK, 'Message to be sent today to Mr. Taylor in Winnipeg,' 13 March
1929, 144215-16, ibid.
43 King to Dafoe, 13 March 1929, reel M 75, Dafoe Papers, and King to Taylor,
15 March 1929, 144217, box 169, series J 1, King Papers. Also W.R. Motherwell to Gardiner, 15 March 1929, 141275, box 166, ibid., and King Diary,
15 March 1929. Also the entry in the Taylor memoranda for 15 March
(Saturday, 4:30 AM)
44 Bracken had met with Jack Davis and W.J. Lindal, the president and secretary, respectively, of the Manitoba Liberal Association, on Monday, 18
March, and had given them a copy of his letter to Robson of 6 March. He
had indicated that if the Liberal convention decided upon the principle of

coalition his government was ready to consider details immediately. See Bracken to Davis, 18 March 1929, file Coalition 1929-36, box 4, series MG 13 I 1, BP, PAM. Also *Tribune*, 19 March 1929
45 For the convention see *Tribune*, 19 and 20 March 1929; and *Free Press*, 20 March 1929.
46 King Diary, 19 March 1929
47 *Tribune*, 21 March 1929
48 Robson to King, 22 March 1929, 142085-6, also Robson to King, 21 March 1929, 142083-4, box 167, series J 1, King Papers
49 See Bissett to King, 23 March 1929, 135823-5, box 159, ibid.
50 *Tribune*, 21 March 1929
51 For Bracken's evidence see *Proceedings*, V, 3799-946; VI, 5208-311, 5546-606, and 5917-6052.
52 See *Report of the Royal Commission re Seven Sisters Falls Agreement* (Winnipeg 1929), 14, and *Minority Report of Mr Justice Dysart re Seven Sisters Falls Agreement* (Winnipeg 1929).
53 *Proceedings*, II, 1884-5 (Taylor)
54 Ibid., III, 2201 (Taylor)
55 Ibid., II, 1291-2; also III, 2554-5 (Coyne)
56 'Memorandum re R.K. Elliott,' file 112, box 3, Maybank Papers, PAM
57 *Proceedings*, VI, 5747-852 (Elliott)
58 Ibid., II, 1872-99; and III, 1956-2258 (Taylor)
59 Ibid., IV, 2987-90 (McLimont); II, 1219 (Coyne); 1608-11 (Anderson); and 1776 (Haig)
60 *Free Press*, 4 May 1929
61 See 'Transcript of Proceedings on the transfer of natural resources to Manitoba', files 902-4, box 122, and file 905, box 123, series J 4, King Papers. Also *Free Press*, 16 Feb. and 10 April 1929
62 See Turgeon to King, 3 May 1929, 144569-76, box 169, series J 1, King Papers. Also King Diary, 17 April 1929. Until Manitoba's population reached 800,000 the subsidy would be $562,500. While the population was between 800,000 and 1,200,000 it would be $750,000. Above a population of 1,200,000 the subsidy would be $1,125,000 and would remain unchangeable thereafter.
63 See memorandum of discussion 26 June 1929, 'Transfer of Natural Resources of Manitoba,' by O.D. Skelton, dated 28 June 1929, c88477-83, vol. 121, series J 4, King Papers.
64 King Diary, 14 Dec. 1929
65 *Tribune*, 16 July 1930
66 *Canadian Annual Review*, 461

67 Bracken's activities can be followed in 'John Bracken. Diary of Trip Overseas, September 1929,' box 1, series MG 13 I 1, BP, PAM, and in 'Bracken Pocket Journal 1929,' ibid.

CHAPTER 8: 'WORK, ECONOMY, PATIENCE'

1 H.A. Robson to Bracken, 23 Nov. 1929, file Coalition 1929-40, box 4, series MG 13 I 1, BP, PAM

2 E. Brown to King, 29 June 1929, 136085-6, box 160, series J 1, King Papers, PAC

3 Andrew Haydon was one who felt both should depart. See 'Memorandum,' Andrew Haydon to King, 4 Sept. 1929, 138075-6, box 162, ibid.

4 E. Brown to King, 16 Sept. 1929, 136093-5, box 160, ibid.; and King to Brown, 19 Sept. 1929, 136096, ibid.

5 He admitted, however, that McPherson was not enthusiastic about the idea. Howden to King, 28 Nov. 1929, 138333-7, box 162, ibid.

6 Bissett to King, 6 Dec. 1929, copy, file 1929, box 80, Crerar Papers, Queen's University Library

7 King to Howden, 7 Dec. 1929, 138338-9, box 162, series J 1, King Papers

8 King Diary, 13 Dec. 1929

9 See King to Bissett, 15 Jan. 1930, 135837, box 159, series J 1, King Papers. Also *Free Press*, 4, 16, 17, and 30 Jan. 1930; *Tribune*, 10 Jan. 1930.

10 Undated rough notes by Bracken, file Livestock Conference, box 37, series MG 13 I 2, BP, PAM. Unless otherwise indicated all further references to BP, PAM, will be to this series. For full-scale analyses of the impact of the depression on Canada see A.E. Safarian, *The Canadian Economy in the Great Depression* (Toronto 1959), and George Britnell, *The Wheat Economy* (Toronto 1939).

11 Bracken's rough notes of speech at Reston, 10 Dec. 1930, file Livestock Conference, box 37, BP, PAM; and Bracken's addendum to a memorandum by his economic adviser, Professor Hank Grant of the University of Manitoba Economics Department, on the 'Changing World Wheat Situation,' file Wheat Pool, box 42, ibid.

12 Bracken's draft address at the Royal Winter Fair, 25 Nov. 1930, ibid.

13 The rigid attitude of the banks on the necessity of meeting the 15 per cent margin had prompted the Manitoba Wheat Pool to approach the provincial government. See P.F. Bredt to Bracken, 8 Feb. 1930, ibid.

14 For the details see file Wheat Pool Corresp., box 41, ibid.

15 See Bracken's rough speech notes, 'Pool Guarantee Bill 27 February 1930,' file Wheat Pool, box 42, ibid. Also *Tribune*, 28 Feb. 1930

16 When explaining this to the House on 4 February, Bracken said: 'It should be clearly understood that the financial responsibility the Government is assuming is almost negligible as before the Government would be in any way involved all the Pool's wheat would have to be sold on an average of below $1.00 per bushel basis No. 1 Northern Wheat at Fort William, which, of course, there is not the least likelihood of happening.' *Free Press*, 5 Feb. 1930

17 In Manitoba not only the wheat pool disappeared but in 1931 revelation of mismanagement in the pool elevator operations resulted in the Bracken government reorganizing the system into the Manitoba Pool Elevators Ltd, although still as a co-operative organization. The details of negotiations over the pools in 1930 and 1931 can be followed in the wheat pool files in boxes 41, 42, 52, and 53, BP, PAM. For the pool elevator investigation see file Williams Report, box 52, ibid.

18 Similar meetings had been held in 1923 and 1924 between the government and all the credit corporations of the province. The government had pointed out the necessity of no action being taken that would cripple the production of the farmer. A voluntary debt-adjustment board had been set up under the supervision of D.L. McLeod, minister of municipal affairs, and it had worked effectively. Bracken to H. McConnell (minister of municipal affairs, Sask.), 18 Sept. 1930, file Creditors Conference, box 34, ibid.

19 See both Bracken's rough notes and the typed version of his speech of 22 Sept. 1930, ibid.

20 See Bracken's rough notes for the speech of 17 Oct. 1930, ibid.

21 See 'Press Release,' 14 Aug. 1931, file Creditors Conference, box 44, ibid.

22 Since 1922 the policy had been to assist the municipalities in bearing the cost of direct relief to the extent of paying one-third, and in some cases, one-quarter, of the money expended for the purpose. The cost to the province had varied each year. During the winter of 1929-30 the provincial government had paid out over $60,000 as its share of direct relief. See unsigned memorandum probably written in August 1931, 'Re Participation of Provincial Government in Assisting To Relieve the Unemployment Problem,' file Unemployment-Ottawa, box 40, ibid.

23 *Tribune*, 20 Dec. 1929; and *Free Press*, 21 Dec. 1929

24 See Bracken to King, 7 and 14 Jan. 1930, 146023-8, and 146032-4; and King to Bracken, 8 Jan. 1930, 146026-8, box 171, series J1, King Papers. A resolution supporting Bracken's position was unanimously passed by the Manitoba legislature on 3 February 1930.

25 For a detailed list of projects see memorandum 'Re Participation of Provincial Government in Assisting to Relieve the Unemployment Problem,' file

Unemployment-Ottawa, box 40, BP, PAM; also Mr Peterson (Winnipeg city clerk) to Bracken, 24 June 1930, and Bracken to Peterson, 9 July 1930, file Unemployment (Old File), ibid.

26 For Bracken's speech see 'Remarks on Unemployment Conference,' 17 Sept. 1930, file Unemployment Conference, ibid.

27 On this see G. Robertson to Bracken, 26 Sept. 1930, ibid.

28 For Bracken's statement see 'Press statement 24 September 1930,' file Press, box 38, ibid.

29 For the details of Manitoba's submission see file Unemployment Conference 1930, box 40, ibid.; and for a breakdown of federal, provincial, and municipal commitments see file Unemployment, box 51, ibid. For a detailed outline of the projects in progress by early 1931 see 'Summary,' 5 Jan. 1931, ibid.

30 Bracken to Bennett, 13 Jan. 1931, ibid.

31 Bracken to Bennett, 23 April 1931, ibid.

32 Bracken to Mayors of Cities, Reeves of Towns and Municipalities, 4 June 1931, file Unemployment Conference 1931, ibid.

33 For Bracken's remarks to both the 17 June conference and the meeting with Robertson on 25 June see 'Unemployment Conference,' 17 June 1931, ibid., and 'The Need for Markets,' 25 June 1931, file Unemployment, ibid. The various briefs presented to Robertson are in file Unemployment Conference 1931, ibid.

34 For a full outline of the programme see an interview with Bracken, *Free Press*, 23 Aug. 1931. Also 'A Suggested Policy for the Relief of Unemployment in Manitoba,' included in Clubb to Robertson, 6 Aug. 1931, file Agricultural Relief, box 54; and Clubb to Robertson, 14 Aug. 1931; Robertson to Bracken, 19 Aug. 1931; and Bracken to Robertson, 20 Aug. 1931, file Unemployment, box 51, BP, PAM.

35 Sweatman to Bennett, 25 Aug. 1931, 487279-81, series F, box 791, Bennett Papers, PAC

36 For Bracken's rough notes of the interview with Bennett, Weir, and Murphy on 29 August see file Unemployment, box 51, BP, PAM. See also 'Matters to be Taken Up With ... Bennett August 30,' ibid.

37 See Bracken's statement, *Free Press*, 31 Aug. 1931, and Bracken to Bennett, 19 Aug. 1931, file Unemployment, box 51, BP, PAM.

38 Bennett to S.F. Tolmie, J.E. Brownlee, J.T.M. Anderson, and John Bracken, 4 Sept. 1931, 350152-3, vol. 565, Bennett Papers

39 For the details of the salary cuts see Bracken to Robert Drummond (comptroller general), 31 Aug. 1931, file Civil Service Salary Reductions and Economy Studies, box 55, BP, PAM.

40 Memo: 'Suggestions for Economy and Reduced Expenditures,' Sept. 1931, ibid.
41 Bracken to all ministers and A. Prefontaine, 30 Oct. 1931, ibid.
42 Crerar to King, 29 June 1931, 157351-3, and King to Crerar, 2 July 1931, 157354-6, box 184, series J 1, King Papers. For the convention and earlier Liberal meetings see *Free Press*, 3 Dec. 1930, and 27 June 1931; and *Tribune*, 2 and 3 Dec. 1930, and 25 and 27 June 1931.
43 See Crerar to King, 7 Oct. 1931, 157363-6, box 184, King Papers.
44 For a synopsis of the plan see *Tribune*, 6 Oct. 1931, and *Free Press*, 7 Oct. 1931.
45 See Bracken speech at Killarney on 7 Oct., *Tribune*, 7 Oct. 1931, and *Free Press*, 8 Oct. 1931.
46 *Tribune*, 6 Oct. 1931; and *Free Press*, 7 Oct. 1931
47 *Tribune*, 7 Oct. 1931
48 See *Free Press*, 10 and 21 Oct. 1931; and *Tribune*, 10 Oct. 1931.
49 For Bracken's speech see *Tribune* and *Free Press*, 17 Oct. 1931.
50 Bracken to E.N. Rhodes (minister of finance), 18 Nov. 1931, file Treasury-Financing, box 71, BP, PAM
51 See Bracken to Bennett, 14 Oct. 1931, 350160-1, and Bennett to Bracken, 16 Oct. 1931, 350162, vol. 565, Bennett Papers; Bracken to Bennett, 17 Oct. 1931, file Unemployment Relief Financing, box 62, BP, PAM; and Bracken to Bennett, 23 Oct. 1931, file Treasury-Financing, box 71, ibid. Also Bracken to Rhodes, 17 Nov. 1931, and Rhodes to Bracken, 30 Nov. 1931, ibid.; Bracken to Rhodes, 1 and 4 Dec. 1931, and Rhodes to Bracken, 1 and 4 Dec. 1931, file Unemployment Relief Financing, box 62, ibid.
52 See Bracken to Rhodes, 16 Nov. 1931, ibid.
53 For an outline of Manitoba's financial situation in late 1931 see unsigned and undated memorandum, 'Matters for Urgent Consideration,' file Treasury-Financing, box 71, ibid.; also Bracken to Rhodes, 11 Dec. 1931, confidential, file Savings Office, box 60, ibid.
54 Bracken Diary, Dec. 1931
55 Bracken to Rhodes, 11 Dec. 1931, file Savings office, box 60, BP, PAM
56 Bracken to Bennett, 18 Dec. 1931, 350166, vol. 565, Bennett Papers
57 Bracken to Bennett, 30 Dec. 1931, file Unemployment Relief Financing, box 62, BP, PAM
58 Webb to Bennett, 7 Jan. 1932, 350171, vol. 565, Bennett Papers
59 Bennett to Webb, 7 Jan. 1932, 350172, ibid.
60 See H. Sifton to Dafoe, 8 Jan. 1932, and Dafoe to Sifton, 6 and 11 Jan. 1932, reel M 75, Dafoe Papers, University of Manitoba Library (microfilm).

61 In an interview in June 1973 Thorson claimed that he was the unofficial head of the Manitoba Liberals and that Mackay was 'a nobody.' Thorson interview, Ottawa, 21 June 1973

62 The early drafts and the final form of the letter to Mackay of 6 January 1932 are in file Coalition 1932-6, box 4, series MG 13 I 1, BP, PAM.

63 *Tribune*, 6 Jan. 1932

64 See Crerar to Cameron, 18 Jan. 1932, vol. 34, Cameron Papers, PAC, and *Free Press*, 11 Jan., 28 May, and 1 June 1932. Also Bracken to Bennett, 10 Jan. 1932, and Bennett to Bracken, 11 Jan. 1932, file Unemployment Relief Financing, box 62, and Bracken to Bennett, 23 Jan. 1932, file Treasury-Financing, box 71, BP, PAM.

65 For full coverage of the Liberal meeting see *Tribune*, 12 and 13 Jan. 1932, and *Free Press*, 13 Jan. 1932.

66 For King's activities in Winnipeg see the King Diary, 12, 13, and 14 Jan. 1932.

67 Ibid., 14 Jan. 1932

68 For Bracken's statement see *Tribune* and *Free Press*, 13 Jan. 1932.

69 For Bracken's proposal and its reception see *Tribune*, 14 and 15 Jan. 1932; and *Free Press*, 15 Jan. 1932.

70 See particularly John Haig to Bracken, 15 Jan. 1932, and Bracken to Haig, 18 Jan. 1932, file Savings Office, box 60, BP, PAM. Also Bennett to Bracken, 18 Jan. 1932, and Bracken to Bennett, 21 Jan. 1932, ibid.; and Bracken Diary 1932.

71 Bracken to Rhodes, 30 Jan. 1932, 350206-9, vol. 565, Bennett Papers

72 See particularly the evidence of E.K. Williams and Bracken to the special investigative committee: 'Report of Special Committee on Closing of the Provincial Savings Office,' *Votes and Proceedings of the Legislative Assembly of Manitoba*, no 46, Fifth Session, Eighteenth Legislature, 5 May 1932, 20-3. For Bennett's views see *Free Press*, 21 April 1932.

73 For the details of the transfer see Bracken to S.H. Logan (representing all the chartered banks in Winnipeg), 16 Feb. 1932, 350200, vol. 565, Bennett Papers; and Bennett to General Managers of Chartered Banks doing business in Winnipeg, 17 Feb. 1932, 350201, ibid. The banks even stated the date when the legislature should convene so that the transaction could be effected. See 'Report of Special Committee ... '

74 Ibid.

75 *Tribune* and *Free Press*, 22 March 1932

76 *Free Press*, 22 and 23 March 1932

77 See F.G. Tipping to E.W. Montgomery, 2 Feb. 1932, file Health Department-Mothers' Allowance, box 57, BP, PAM.

78 Thorson to King, 19 Feb. 1932, 164845, box 194, series J1, King Papers; also Crerar to King, 8 March 1932, 161954-5, box 190, ibid.; also *Tribune*, 15 Feb. 1932
79 Thorson interview, 21 June 1973
80 *Free Press*, 28 May 1932
81 Ibid., 31 May 1932
82 *Tribune*, 9 June 1932
83 *Free Press*, 28 May 1932
84 Ibid., 30 May and 16 June 1932
85 Thorson interview, 21 June 1973
86 The provincial Conservatives offered this explanation themselves.

CHAPTER 9: HANGING ON

1 For the above analysis see G.F. Towers, 'Report on the Financial Position of the Province of Manitoba,' 11 Feb. 1937, 10-13, file Debt Refunding, box 101, series MG 13 I 2, BP, PAM. Unless otherwise indicated all further references to BP, PAM, will be to this series.
2 'Report of the Royal Commission on the Impairment of University of Manitoba Trust Funds, 1932-1933'
3 Bracken to all cabinet ministers, 28 June 1932, file Civil Service Salary Reductions and Economy Studies, box 55, BP, PAM. Also *Tribune* and *Free Press*, 24 Aug. 1932
4 McPherson to Rhodes, 2 Aug. 1932, file Unemployment Relief Financing, box 62, BP, PAM. See also Bracken to Rhodes, 15 June, 6, 15, and 22 July 1932, ibid. For an outline of Manitoba's financial commitments through to 31 December 1932 see 'Memo' prepared by the provincial Treasury Department, 21 July 1932, file Treasury-Financing, box 71, ibid.
5 See Rhodes to Bracken, 15 and 25 July 1932, file Unemployment Relief Financing, box 62, ibid.; also Rhodes to McPherson, 5 and 16 Aug. 1932, ibid.
6 McPherson to Rhodes, 13 Aug. 1932, ibid.
7 For the above see 'Memo: Re: Financing' [nd], and Royal Bank 'Memorandum,' 26 Aug. 1932, copy, in file Treasury-Financing, box 71, ibid. See also 'Memo' by Clarence Jackson to McPherson, 3 Sept. 1932, file Treasury Minister, box 62, ibid. See McPherson to Bennett, 9 Sept. 1932, file Unemployment Relief Financing, ibid.; and Bennett to Wilson, 22 Sept. 1932, 350261, vol. 565, Bennett Papers, PAC.
8 Manitoba had to make available on 15 December at the Royal Bank of Canada in New York a sum of $6,158,000.00 *'in New York funds'* to cover

the principal amount of maturing debentures. The province marketed an issue of $4,000,000 face value of debentures dated 1 October 1932 in the Canadian market for which it received at 94.50 per cent a total of $3,780,000 in Canadian funds. With these proceeds the province had purchased New York funds totalling $3,352,617.36. It was the balance – $2,805,382.64 – that Bennett loaned Manitoba. See Bracken to Bennett, 30 Nov. 1932, 350264-6; Bennett to Bracken, 5 Dec. 1932, 350267-8; Bennett to Wilson, 5 Dec. 1932, 350269-70; and Bracken to Rhodes, 6 Dec. 1932, 350273, vol. 565, Bennett Papers.

9 See a letter from the provincial treasurers, Ewen McPherson, M.A. Macpherson, and R.G. Reid to Bennett, 21 Jan. 1933, 350299-302, ibid. W.C. Clark, the deputy-minister of finance, while disliking 'the united front' of the West, did realize that the prairies faced a crisis and that a major change in policy might have to be considered. See W.C. Clark to R.K. Finlayson, 7 Jan. 1933, 487589-90, vol. 791, ibid. The mayors of Winnipeg and St Boniface, Ralph Webb and F.R. Dowse, respectively, wrote at this time of their financial difficulties. Both were under pressure from the banks, merchants were refusing to advance credit, and wholesalers were refusing city vouchers. Both hinted at default. F.R. Dowse to Bracken, 16 Jan. 1933, file Unemployment Relief Financing, box 72, BP, PAM; and Ralph Webb to Bennett, 19 Jan. 1933, 350296-8, vol. 565, Bennett Papers

10 Bennett to Bracken, 9 March 1933, file Treasury-Financing, box 71, BP, PAM

11 Dafoe thought Bennett's letter reflected his 'peculiar mentality.' Dafoe to H. Sifton, 17 March 1933, reel M76, Dafoe Papers, University of Manitoba Library (microfilm)

12 See draft letter McPherson to Bennett, 25 Feb. 1933, file Treasury-Financing, box 71, BP, PAM.

13 Bracken to Bennett, 18 March 1933, 350318-23, vol. 565, Bennett Papers

14 *Free Press*, 29 April 1933. The 2 per cent tax did not affect those whose total annual income when married was less than $960.00 or when unmarried was less than $480.00. See also undated memorandum on 'Taxation,' file Wage and Income Tax, box 71, BP, PAM.

15 Towers, 'Report,' 12

16 See particularly in this connection the results of a conference in Ottawa in June 1933: 'Notes taken at an interview between Hon. Mr. Bracken and Sir George Perley, June 12, 1933,' 350714-19; also 'Memo for Sir George Perley 12 June 1933,' 350711-13; and Perley to Bennett, 16 June 1933, 350725-6, vol. 566, Bennett Papers.

17 See Bracken to Gordon, 23 Feb. 1934, file Unemployment, box 82, BP, PAM. Also 'Minutes of Meeting Held at Victoria, B.C.,' box 72, ibid.

18 See 'Memorandum of Agreement entered into this thirty-first day of July A.D.

1934 ... ' file Unemployment Relief Financing, box 81, ibid.

19 Clubb to Gordon, 11 Oct. 1934, ibid.

20 MacNamara to Bracken, 28 Dec. 1935, file Unemployment Relief Financing, box 90, ibid.; also Bracken to King, 4 Nov. 1935, file Unemployment, ibid.

21 See 'Memorandum of Agreement'; Norman Rogers (minister of labour) to Bracken, 14 and 24 July 1936; and Bracken to Rogers, 17 and 29 July 1936, file Unemployment Relief Financing, box 98, ibid.

22 See S.P. Greaves to Bracken, 18 March 1932, file Unemployment, box 62, ibid.; also A.H. Atwater to Bracken, 14 Jan. 1933, file Dominion-Inter-Provincial Conference 1933, box 67, ibid. For the general atmosphere and tensions in Winnipeg see James Gray's readable memoir *The Winter Years* (Toronto 1966).

23 *Free Press*, 15 and 19 Oct. 1932

24 See file Communists, box 85, BP, PAM.

25 See particularly, file Unemployment, box 72, ibid.

26 See *Free Press* and *Tribune*, 1 Dec. 1932.

27 Unsigned memorandum dated 9 June 1934, file Flin Flon Strike, box 78, ibid. For a detailed outline of conditions in Flin Flon, conditions in the market, the relation of wages to costs, and a background of trade union action, particularly of the WUL, see two unpublished graduate papers: D.J. de Beer, 'The Flin Flon Strike 1934' (unpublished graduate research paper, University of Manitoba, 1973), and S. Rosenstock, 'The 1934 Flin Flon Strike' (unpublished graduate research paper, University of Manitoba, 1974). Also Stuart Jamieson, *Times of Trouble* (Ottawa 1971); H.A. Logan, *Trade Unions in Canada: Their Development and Functioning* (Toronto 1948); Ivan Avakumovic, *The Communist Party in Canada: A History* (Toronto 1975); and the *Free Press, Tribune*, and *Flin Flon Miner*, June-July 1934.

28 For Bracken's statement see *Tribune*, 11 June 1934, and *Free Press*, 12 June 1934.

29 *Free Press*, 23 June 1934. For background on the three-week hiatus see de Beer, 'Flin Flon Strike,' and Rosenstock, 'Flin Flon Strike'; also J.O. Stevens and Wm. McFadden, 'Anti-Communist League of Flin Flon Constitution,' June 1934; E.E. Foster (mayor) to Bracken, 9 and 12 June 1934; Bracken to Foster, 11, 13, and 18 June 1934; and 'Statement by R.H. Channing Jr.,' 23 June 1934, file Flin Flon Strike, box 78, BP, PAM.

30 Foster to Bracken, 1 July 1934; and Bracken to Foster, 1 July 1934; and Major to Hugh Guthrie (minister of justice), 2 July 1934, ibid.

31 *Free Press*, 3 and 4 July 1934

32 'Statement made by Mr. R.H. Channing Jr., July 3rd 1934,' file Flin Flon Strike, box 78, BP, PAM

33 See Bracken's rough notes on back of envelope dated 2 July [1934], ibid.

34 Rough notes on #10 envelope, ibid.

35 See Bracken's rough notes of interviews, 7-8 July 1934, ibid.

36 See Arthur Bennett to Bracken, 8 July 1934; and Bracken's rough notes of interviews, 7-8 July 1934, ibid.

37 *Tribune*, 10 July 1934

38 See Bracken's various rough drafts of this statement prepared on Sunday, 8 July, and issued late on 8 July 1934, file Flin Flon Strike, box 78, BP, PAM. Also *Tribune*, 9 July 1934

39 See *Tribune* and *Free Press*, 9 and 10 July 1934, for coverage of the weekend events in Flin Flon.

40 For post-strike reactions see R.E. Phelan to Bracken, 14 and 18 July 1934; and C.C. Sparling to Bracken, 17 July 1934; also a letter enclosing a view from the miner's side, J.S. Taylor to Bracken, 8 Aug. 1934, file Flin Flon Strike, box 78, BP, PAM.

41 T.R. Deacon to Bracken, 9 Aug. 1934; and Bracken to Deacon, 13 Aug. 1934, ibid.

42 Bracken to General Strike Committee, 20 July 1935, file Unemployed Single Men, box 91, ibid.

43 *Free Press*, 26 July 1935

44 *Tribune*, 23 June 1936

45 The legislative reporters for the two Winnipeg newspapers often commented in the thirties on the dreariness of the Manitoba legislature and on the length and dullness of Bracken's speeches. See particularly *Tribune*, 'Mr. Speaker,' 9 Feb. and 15 March 1934, and 15, 16, and 26 Feb. and 8 March 1935; and *Free Press*, 'Under the Dome,' 14 Feb. 1934, 13 March 1935, and 22 Feb. 1936.

46 See interviews with Locksley McNeill, 1 March 1973 and 29 May 1975. For Bracken's full speech see *Tribune*, 4 July 1936.

47 *Free Press* and *Tribune*, 30 June 1936; and *Free Press*, 3 and 25 July 1936

48 *Tribune*, 4 July 1936

49 For the full Conservative platform see *Free Press* and *Tribune*, 24 June 1936; also Willis' main speech, *Free Press*, 19 June 1936.

50 See *Tribune* and *Free Press*, 27 June 1936.

51 See *Tribune*, 24 June 1936, and *Free Press*, 25 June 1936.

52 For the full CCF platform see *Free Press*, 30 June 1936.

53 See *Tribune*, 9 July 1936, for a speech by S.J. Farmer criticizing the 2 per cent 'wage tax.' As the *Free Press* pointed out, the 2 per cent tax was not a wage tax *per se*, it was an income tax. It was also collected on profits, dividens, fees, and rents. It did not fall exclusively on the workers, although it would naturally have a greater impact on them because it was not graduated. *Free Press*, 13 Aug. 1936

54 *Tribune*, 25 July 1936
55 *Free Press*, 31 July 1936
56 For an excellent analysis of the 1936 election see Lyle Dick, 'The 1936 Provincial Election in Manitoba: An Analysis' (unpublished graduate research paper, University of Manitoba, 1975).
57 *Free Press*, 30 July 1936
58 Bracken to Willis, 4 Aug. 1936, printed in *Tribune*, 5 Aug. 1936
59 Willis to Bracken, 4 Aug. 1936, ibid.
60 *Tribune*, 14 Aug. 1936
61 *Free Press* and *Tribune*, 2 Sept. 1936
62 *Free Press*, 23 Sept. 1936

CHAPTER 10: MANITOBA'S CASE

1 See Bracken to Dunning, 14 Oct. 1936, file Dominion Government, box 93, series MG 13 I 2, BP, PAM. Unless otherwise indicated all further references to BP, PAM, will be to this series. Also *Tribune*, 5 Dec. 1936, and *Free Press*, 8 Dec. 1936
2 Dunning to Bracken, 25 June and 29 Sept. 1936, file Dominion Government, box 93, BP, PAM
3 See 'Proceedings of the Permanent Committee on Financial Questions,' Dominion-Provincial Conference, 20 Dec. 1936, file Debt Refunding, box 101, ibid.
4 King Diary, 16 Nov. 1936, King Papers, PAC
5 See 'Proceedings of the Permanent Committee ... ' Also Bracken to Dunning, 5 Jan. 1937, and Bracken to Floyd Chalmers, 5 Jan. 1937, file Debt Refunding, box 101, BP, PAM, and Bracken to John Imrie (*Edmonton Journal*), 18 Dec. 1936, box 113, ibid.
6 *Free Press*, 30 Dec. 1936
7 Ibid., 9 Dec. 1936
8 King Diary, 18 Dec. 1936
9 See *Free Press*, 31 Dec. 1936 and 5 and 14 Jan. 1937.
10 *Free Press*, 5 Jan. 1937
11 *Tribune*, 8 Jan. 1937
12 Ibid., 9 and 20 Jan. 1937
13 King Diary, 8 Jan. 1937
14 *Free Press*, 21 Jan. 1937
15 Ibid. and *Tribune*, 21 Jan. 1937
16 *Tribune*, 21 Jan. 1937
17 King Diary, 21 Jan. 1937
18 Ibid., 23 Jan. 1937

19 *Free Press*, 5 Feb. 1937
20 See *Tribune*, 2 Feb. 1937, and *Free Press*, 3 Feb. 1937.
21 *Free Press*, 8 and 9 Feb. 1937, and *Tribune*, 8 and 9 Feb. 1937. For an excellent summary of Manitoba's financial position see Bracken to Dunning, 8 Feb. 1937, file Debt Refunding, box 101, BP, PAM.
22 For a copy of the report see ibid.; also G.F. Towers to Bracken, 11 and 12 Feb. 1937, ibid. For the cabinet discussion see King Diary, 15 Feb. 1937.
23 King Diary, 15 Feb. 1937, H of C *Debates*, 1937, 921-2; *Tribune*, 17 Feb. 1937
24 *Canadian Annual Review*, 1937-8, 431
25 The above correspondence and negotiations can be followed in file Royal Commission on Dominion-Provincial Relations, box 113, BP, PAM. See also Bracken to Dunning, 11 March 1937, file Debt Refunding, box 101, ibid. It is evident from Garson's working-files in RG 20 A 7 (Royal Commission on Dominion-Provincial Relations) at the PAM that Garson and Bracken relied heavily on the outside economic advisers in the preparation of the Manitoba brief.
26 For Manitoba's preliminary ideas and the co-operative plans see Bracken to Viner, 15 May 1937, file Royal Commission on Dominion-Provincial Relations, box 113, BP, PAM.
27 For the role and attitudes of Dafoe and Rowell during their association with the Royal Commission see Ramsay Cook, *The Politics of John W. Dafoe and the Free Press* (Toronto 1963), 214-34; and Margaret Prang, *N.W. Rowell: Ontario Nationalist* (Toronto 1975), 488-97.
28 The Manitoba submission was in nine parts. For Bracken's remarks see *Manitoba's Case: A Submission presented to The Royal Commission on Dominion-Provincial Relations by The Government of Manitoba* (Winnipeg 1937), part I, Introduction, 4-5.
29 *Manitoba's Case*, part VII, 69-73
30 *Manitoba's Case*, 'Summary and Recommendations,' part VIII, 58
31 The correspondence on this issue is bulky but can be followed in file Unemployment Relief-City of Winnipeg, box 115; and file Unemployment Relief-City of Winnipeg, box 106; and file Unemployment Relief Financing-Material for Hon. Mr. Bracken to take to Ottawa Conference,' 17 July 1937, box 105, BP, PAM. Both the *Free Press* and the *Tribune* followed the issue with great interest in June and July 1937.
32 See *Report of the Royal Commission on the Municipal Finances and Administration of the City of Winnipeg* (Winnipeg 1939). In the 1938 spring session Bracken also cut the special income tax by 1 per cent with a subsequent loss in revenue of $850,000. This was partly offset by further taxes on banks, corporations, and grain elevators.

33 See *Free Press* and *Tribune*, 3 May 1938. For background on Hepburn's position see Neil McKenty, *Mitch Hepburn* (Toronto 1967), 156-62.

34 *Free Press*, 3 and 4 May 1938

35 *Tribune*, 21 July 1938

36 Ibid., 19 Oct. 1938

37 Ibid., 28 Nov. 1938

38 *Free Press*, 30 Nov. 1938

39 See *Financial Post*, 3 Dec. 1938

40 *Financial Times*, 7 Dec. 1934. See 'Some Problems of Western Agriculture,' a speech delivered at the Annual Convention of the United Farmers and United Farm Women of Manitoba at Portage la Prairie, 1 Nov. 1933, file UFM, box 63, BP, PAM; also Bracken's rough undated notes, file Agricultural Drought, box 75, ibid.; and 'The Rehabilitation of the Drought Area,' a speech to the Canadian Club of Winnipeg, 25 Oct. 1934, file 9, F.H. Auld Papers, SAB (R). See also two important files: 'Wheat Correspondence' and 'Wheat' in boxes 82 and 83, BP, PAM.

41 Blair Neatby, *William Lyon Mackenzie King*, III: *1932-1939. The Prism of Unity* (Toronto 1976), 305-6

42 *Free Press*, 6 Aug. 1938. See also two lengthy memoranda prepared by Clive Davidson: 'Review of Economic Conditions in Canada' and 'The Canadian Wheat Situation' both dated August 1938, file Davidson & Co., box 108, BP, PAM.

43 *Tribune*, 13 Oct. 1938

44 Ibid., 1 Nov. 1938, and *Free Press*, 2 Nov. 1938

45 For coverage of the conference and the establishment of the Wheat Committee see *Free Press* and *Tribune*, 10-17 Dec. 1938.

46 *Financial Post*, 24 Dec. 1938

47 This analysis and prediction was made by Chester Bloom in *Free Press*, 21 Dec. 1938.

48 *Edmonton Journal*, 17 Jan. 1939

49 For the personnel see *Tribune*, 21 Jan. 1939.

50 See 'Minutes of meeting of Western Committee on Markets and Agricultural Readjustment,' 31 Jan. 1939, file Wheat Committee-Correspondence with Members, box 126, BP, PAM; also file Wheat Committee-C.B. Davidson, ibid.; and file Wheat Committee-Ottawa Meeting, box 125, ibid.

51 For a report on the meeting see *Tribune*, 15 Feb. 1939, and *Free Press*, 17 Feb. 1939.

52 *Free Press* and *Tribune*, 16 Feb. 1939

53 For an outline see *Free Press*, 17 Feb. 1939.

54 For a comment see *Tribune*, 17 Feb. 1939, and *Free Press*, 18 Feb. 1939.

55 Bracken went East with the unanimous support of the Manitoba legislature

for the proposals of the Wheat Committee. Endorsation had been given on 24 February 1939.

56 Bracken's rough speech notes, 1 March 1939, file Wheat Committee-Ottawa Meeting, box 125, BP, PAM. For a copy of the submission see ibid.

57 King Diary, 1 March 1939

58 For Gardiner's early statements in the House of Commons see *Free Press* and *Tribune*, 28 Feb. 1939.

59 See Bracken speech of 24 March 1939 to Canadian Club in Winnipeg, *Free Press*, 25 March 1939. Previously he had spoken in Brandon on 23 March, and on 31 March he spoke in Montreal.

60 See 'Canadian Agriculture from a Western Viewpoint,' 28 March 1939, file Marketing Conference-Eastern Canada, box 112, BP, PAM.

61 See *Free Press* and *Tribune*, 28 March 1939.

62 See Bracken's statement, originating in Montreal, in *Tribune*, 29 March 1939.

63 King Diary, 31 March 1939

64 See *The Western Farm Leader*, 21 April 1939. Bracken and the committee were guided to their conclusions by memoranda by Davidson; see particularly file Wheat Committee-C.B. Davidson, box 126, BP, PAM. See Bracken to King, 14 April 1939, file Wheat Committee-Ottawa Meeting, box 125, ibid.

65 *The Financial Post*, 22 April 1939

66 For the text of the submission see file Wheat Committee-Ottawa Meeting, box 125, BP, PAM.

67 King Diary, 24 April 1939

68 Ibid., 25 April 1939

69 *Tribune*, 2 and 4 May 1939, and *Free Press*, 4 May 1939

70 See also W.R. Motherwell to Bracken, 26 May 1939, file Wheat Committee-Ottawa Meeting, box 125, BP, PAM.

CHAPTER 11: WAR

1 *Tribune*, 8 Sept. 1939

2 *Free Press*, 9 Sept. 1939; and *Tribune*, 18 Sept. 1939. See also file Wheat Committee Correspondence with Members, box 126, series MG 13 I 2, BP, PAM. Unless otherwise indicated all further references to BP, PAM, will be to this series.

3 For some of Bracken's arguments see his speech to the Manitoba Winter Fair, *Free Press*, 19 March 1940.

4 Heenan to King, 27 Jan. 1940, pc227169, file F 3494, box 329, King Papers, PAC

5 See *Tribune*, 6 April 1940, and *Free Press*, 8 April 1940.

6 *Tribune*, 7 June 1940
7 King Diary, PAC, 27 May 1940
8 See Willis to Bracken, 25 June 1940, file Coalition 1929-36, box 4, MG 13
    I 1, BP, PAM. Also *Tribune* and *Free Press*, 9 July 1940.
9 See Crerar to G. Dexter, 4 July 1940, and Dexter to Crerar, [nd] box 105,
    Crerar Papers, Queen's University Library.
10 Dexter to Crerar, [nd] ibid.
11 *Tribune* and *Free Press*, 10 Aug. 1940, and *Tribune*, 13 Aug. 1940
12 One can follow this issue in the *Free Press* and *Tribune* for August and
    September 1940.
13 King Diary, 22 Oct. 1940
14 See Bracken to Willis, Farmer, and Rogers, 25 Oct. 1940, file Coalition
    1929-36, box 4, MG 13 I 1, BP, PAM.
15 See Willis to Bracken, 26 Oct. 1940; Farmer to Bracken, 29 Oct. 1940; and
    Rogers to Bracken, 30 Oct. 1940, ibid. The CCF reaction can be followed in
    vols. 8 and 51, CCF Records, PAC. See also Stanley Knowles interview, 15
    Dec. 1974, and interview with Lloyd Stinson, 19 Feb. 1974. The CCF side of
    the negotiation has been well covered by Nelson Wiseman, 'The C.C.F. and
    the Manitoba Non-Partisan Government of 1940,' *Canadian Historical
    Review*, LIV, 2, June 1973, 175-93.
16 See interview with Stanley Knowles, 15 Dec. 1974.
17 *Free Press*, 4 Nov. 1940
18 Crerar to Dafoe, 16 Jan. 1941, reel M 79, Dafoe Papers. Also J.L. Granat-
    stein, *Canada's War* (Toronto 1975), 159-66
19 The proceedings of the conference are reprinted in *Dominion Provincial
    Conferences 1927-1941* (King's Printer, Ottawa, 1951) and all references to
    speeches are taken from it. The press also provided extensive coverage. For
    Hepburn's role see Neil McKenty, *Mitch Hepburn* (Toronto 1967), 225-30.
20 *Dominion Provincial Conferences*, 20-37
21 Ibid., 85-7
22 Ibid., 103-8
23 For a full inside look at the conference see Crerar to Dafoe, 16 Jan. 1941,
    reel M 79, Dafoe Papers, University of Manitoba Library (microfilm). Crerar
    thought Bracken's speech the best. For King's attitudes see King Diary, 14
    and 15 Jan. 1941.
24 *Tribune*, 22 Jan. 1941
25 For the full Bracken speech see *Free Press* and *Tribune*, 28 Jan. 1941.
26 *Tribune*, 29 Jan. 1941
27 See his speech of 6 Feb. 1941 to the Young Men's Section of the Board of
    Trade. *Tribune* and *Free Press*, 7 Feb. 1941

28 *Tribune*, 21 April 1941
29 For a breakdown of the Winnipeg vote see K.W. Taylor and N. Wiseman, 'Class and Ethnic Voting in Winnipeg: The Case of 1941,' *Canadian Review of Sociology and Anthropology*, May 1977, 174-87.
30 For details see *Free Press* and *Tribune*, 16 Jan. 1942.
31 *Tribune*, 16 Jan. 1942

CHAPTER 12: LEADER OF THE PC PARTY

1 This account is taken from a memorandum prepared by Meighen for his biographer Roger Graham. See 149367-9 in vol. 226A, Meighen Papers, PAC, also quoted at length in R. Graham, *Arthur Meighen* (Toronto 1965), III, 98-9.
2 *Tribune*, 7 Nov. 1941
3 Meighen memorandum
4 There is no mention of contact between Bracken and Meighen between Tuesday and Friday in Meighen's memorandum and no evidence in either the Meighen or Bracken Papers of any correspondence, telegrams, or phone calls between the two men.
5 Meighen memorandum. For local coverage and speculation see *Free Press* and *Tribune*, 6 and 7 Nov. 1941.
6 See the accounts in Graham, *Meighen*, III, 100-7, and J. Granatstein, *The Politics of Survival: The Conservative Party of Canada, 1939-1945* (Toronto 1967), 89-94.
7 *Tribune*, 19 Nov. 1941
8 The vote took place on 16 December 1941. See *Free Press*, 17 Dec. 1941.
9 H of C, *Debates*, 10 June 1942, 3236. For extensive coverage of York South and the impact on the Conservatives see Granatstein, *Survival*, chap. 5, and Graham, *Meighen*, III, chap. 4.
10 See Hanson to H.H. Stevens, 20 Feb. 1942, 36115-6; J.M. Macdonnell to Hanson, 24 March 1942, and Hanson to Macdonnell, 26 March 1942, 36218-9; Hanson to D.C. Coleman, 11 June 1942, 36170-1; Meighen to Hanson, 15 July 1942, and Hanson to Meighen, 16 July 1942, 35235-7; and Macdonnell to Hanson, 15 July 1942, 36238-9, reel C3104, Hanson Papers, PAC.
11 Meighen to Bracken, 19 Aug. 1942, file Correspondence Personal 1942-6, box 139, BP, PAC
12 Bracken to Meighen, 1 Sept. 1942, private, ibid.
13 Meighen to Bracken, 4, 16, and 19 Sept. 1942, and Bracken to Meighen, 12 and 17 Sept. 1942, ibid.; and Bracken's 1942 Diary, vol. 142, ibid.
14 For the Port Hope programme see *Report of the Round Table on Canadian*

Policy, 36225-34, reel C3104, Hanson Papers. For the conference see Granatstein, *Survival*, 129-34.

15 Hanson to Dick Bell, 9 Sept. 1942, 37677, reel C3106, Hanson Papers

16 For Meighen's reaction see Meighen to Ray Milner, 17 Oct. 1942, copy. Notable Persons files, Bennett Papers, PAC; also Bell to Hanson, 11 Sept. 1942, 37931, reel C3106, Hanson Papers

17 Bell to Donald Fleming, 24 Sept. 1942, copy, private and confidential, box 1, Bell Papers, PAC. See also Bell to Grote Stirling, 16 Sept. 1942, 36490-1, reel C3105; Hanson to Meighen, 9 Oct. 1942, 46542-3, reel C3123; and Hanson to Bell, 20 Nov. 1942, 325, reel C3076, Hanson Papers. Also Bell to Milner, 12 Nov. 1942, box 1, Bell Papers; and Graham, *Meighen*, III, 138-44; and Granatstein, *Survival*, 137-45

18 Bennett to Meighen, Nov. 1942, 136407-8, vol. 214, Meighen Papers

19 Meighen to Bracken, 17 Nov. 1942, quoted in Graham, *Meighen*, III, 142-3

20 For the details of Bracken's 'people's charter' see *Free Press* and *Tribune*, 7 Nov. 1942.

21 *Free Press* and *Tribune*, 17 Nov. 1942. On reading this speech King commented: 'I see Bracken attacking our manpower problem as having no plan ... all this leading up to the Winnipeg Convention makes sure that there is more behind what is going on, than we see on the surface. It will be the conscription issue over again but directed at the National Selective Service.' King Diary, 18 Nov. 1942. There is evidence that Meighen did in fact prompt Bracken's speech. See Meighen to Bracken, 12 Nov. 1942, file Correspondence Personal and Confidential 1942-8, box 141, BP, PAC.

22 *Free Press*, 30 Nov. 1942

23 See Grant Dexter, 'Way Paved for Call to Bracken,' *Free Press*, 30 Nov. 1942. See also Crerar to Dafoe, 1 Dec. 1942, reel M80, Dafoe Papers, University of Manitoba Library (microfilm); *Tribune*, 23, 26, and 30 Nov. 1942; *Free Press*, 27 Nov. 1942; also Mrs Bracken to her sons, 17 Dec. 1942, series MG 13 I 4, BP, PAM.

24 Interview with Doug Campbell, Winnipeg, 19 Oct. 1976

25 This paragraph is based on Granatstein, *Survival*, 144, which in turn is based on (1) an interview with F.G. Gardiner, one of those present, and on (2) the following newspaper reports: Toronto *Globe and Mail*, 10 and 12 Dec. 1942, and *Montreal Gazette*, 9 and 15 Dec. 1942.

26 See Mrs Bracken to her sons, 17 Dec. 1942, MG 13 I 4, BP, PAM.

27 Ibid.

28 *Tribune*, 9 Dec. 1942

29 See 'Official Report National Conservative Convention (1942) Winnipeg, Manitoba 9, 10, 11 December 1942,' 59-61, 77, 147-53, 155-82, 182-3, 187.

Also Granatstein, *Survival*, 145-6; and *Free Press* and *Tribune*, 9, 10, and 11 Dec. 1942.

30 Garson advised Bracken to have no further dealings with the Conservatives if they would not consider changing the name. According to Alice Bracken, her husband seemed to agree. See Mrs Bracken to her sons, 17 Dec. 1942, MG 13 I 4, BP, PAM.

31 Meighen to Bennett, 16 Dec. 1942, copy, 136409-10, vol. 214, Meighen Papers

32 Mrs Bracken to her sons, 17 Dec. 1942, MG 13 I 4, BP, PAM

33 Ibid., and interview with Doug Campbell, 5 Dec. 1977

34 [A.R.M. Lower], 'Lohengrin and the Conservative Party,' *Canadian Forum*, Feb. 1943, 327-8

35 *Free Press*, 11 Dec. 1942

36 Ibid., 12 Dec. 1942

37 John Bracken, 'Acceptance address,' 11 Dec. 1942, vol. 87, BP, PAC

38 For various comments see A.K. Cameron to Crerar, 3, 12, 16 Dec. 1942, and Crerar to Cameron, 14 Dec. 1942, box 98, Crerar Papers, Queen's University Library. Bernard Warkentine to Howard Winkler, 13 Dec. 1942, file Correspondence 1942-4, box 2, Winkler Papers, PAM. Hanson to Bell, 17 Dec. 1942, 45333-4, reel C3122, Hanson Papers. Dafoe to C. Sifton, 19 Dec. 1942, and B.K. Sandwell to Dafoe, 28 Dec. 1942, reel M80, Dafoe Papers. Dafoe to Cameron, 24 Dec. [1942], vol. 30, A.K. Cameron Papers, PAC

39 King Diary, PAC, 9 Dec. 1942

40 Ibid., 10 and 11 Dec. 1942

41 'Address of the Honourable John Bracken, Leader of the Progressive Conservative Party,' 21 Dec. 1942, vol. 87, BP, PAC

42 Cameron to Dafoe, 28 Dec. 1942, copy, vol. 30, A.K. Cameron Papers

43 Ibid., and Meighen to Bennett, 16 Dec. 1942, copy, 136409-10, vol. 214, Meighen Papers

CHAPTER 13: OUT OF THE HOUSE

1 John Bracken on the CBC, 26 July 1944, vol. 89, BP, PAC

2 For the secret arrival see Bell to Bracken, 11 Jan. 1943, file Correspondence Personal Dec. 1942-Jan. 1943, box 142, ibid.; and Bell to Hanson, 11 Jan. 1943, 36520-1, reel C3105, Hanson Papers, PAC.

3 All the letters are in file Correspondence Personal, Dec. 1942-Jan. 1943, box 142, BP, PAC.

4 Adamson to Bracken, 27 Dec. 1942, ibid.; and Hanson to Bell, 17 Dec. 1942, reel C3122, 45333-4, Hanson Papers

5 Macdonnell to Colonel Lionel Baxter, 28 Dec. 1942, box 1, Bell Papers, PAC; also Bell interview, 13 Dec. 1974

6 Bell interview

7 King Diary, PAC; 30 June 1943

8 Ray Milner supported Bracken's decision, but then he believed 'Bracken ... would not be an effective opposition leader.' Milner to Macdonnell, 28 Dec. 1942, box 1, Bell Papers. Also Milner to Bracken, 15 Dec. 1942, file Correspondence Personal Dec. 1942-Jan. 1943, box 142, BP, PAC

9 Milner to Bracken, 15 Dec. 1942, box 142, BP, PAC; and Macdonnell to Baxter, 28 Dec. 1942, box 1, Bell Papers

10 Bell to Graydon, 30 Dec. 1942, copy, private, box 1, Bell Papers

11 Bell to Milner, 30 Dec. 1942, reel C3105, 36493-8, Hanson Papers; and Bell to Bracken, 6 Jan. 1943, file Correspondence Personal Dec. 1942-Jan. 1943, box 142, BP, PAC

12 Macdonnell to Milner, 30 Jan. 1943, copy, box 1, Bell Papers

13 King Diary, 19 Jan. 1943

14 See box 44, BP, PAC, for this type of material.

15 For an elaboration of these remarks see his speeches of 3 February 1943 to the Holstein-Friesian Breeders Association, and of 13 March 1943 to the Annual Meeting of the Dominion Progressive Conservative Association, box 87, ibid. Also his speech of 6 June 1943 at the Sir John A. Macdonald Memorial Service, reprinted in [John Bracken] *John Bracken Says* (Toronto 1944), 9-19. Bracken's tours and speeches during 1943 can be followed in both the 'Speeches' boxes and the 'Clippings' boxes in BP, PAC.

16 See two letters from Macdonnell to Bell, 28 June 1943, file J.M. Macdonnell,, box 62, ibid.

17 For the speech see *John Bracken Says*, 20-38; also box 87, BP, PAC.

18 H of C, *Debates*, 5 July 1943, 4330. Also *Toronto Star*, 6 July 1943; and J. Pickersgill, ed., *The Mackenzie King Record* (Toronto 1960), I, 567

19 See Toronto *Globe and Mail*, 7 July 1943. Meighen was very happy with the speech and he haw-hawed over King's response. Meighen to Bracken, 7 July July 1943, file Correspondence Personal and Confidential 1942-8, box 141, BP, PAC

20 J. Granatstein, *The Politics of Survival: The Conservative Party of Canada, 1939-1945* (Toronto 1967), 160; and Meighen to Bracken, 29 July 1943, 137479, vol. 215, Meighen Papers, PAC

21 See *Edmonton Journal*, 14 Aug. 1943, on Bracken's attitudes to his task.

22 Granatstein, *Survival*, 162

23 Bird to Ross Brown, 15 Sept. 1943, file P-20-G, reel M1149, PC Party Headquarters Papers, PAC

24 Adamson Diary, 30 June 1943, quoted in Granatstein, *Survival*, 170
25 Adamson to Graydon, 23 Sept. 1943, box 18, Graydon Papers, PAC
26 Grote Stirling to Graydon, 27 Sept. 1943, and George Tuston to Graydon, 24 Sept. 1943, ibid. Also Macdonnell to Bracken, 18 Nov. 1943, file C.P. McTague, box 62, BP, PAC
27 See Pickersgill, ed., *Mackenzie King Record*, I, 582-5.
28 See *Calgary Herald*, 1 Oct. 1943.
29 Meighen to Bracken, 8 Oct. 1943, copy, 137484, vol. 215, Meighen Papers
30 For the speech see *John Bracken Says*, 39-53.
31 Interview with Victor Mackie, 24 April 1975
32 For Bracken's style and the tour itself see interviews with Mel Jack and Victor Mackie, 24 April 1975, and an excellent series of articles by Mackie in the *Regina Leader Post*, 9, 12, 15, 24-26 Nov. 1943. Also Bell to Bracken, 9 Nov. 1943, file Correspondence Personal 1942-4, box 139, BP, PAC.
33 John Bird said party members were yearning to fight for a leader and a movement, but they had 'very little to go on.' Bird to Ross Brown, 15 Sept. 1943, file P-20-G, reel M 1149, PC Party Headquarters Papers
34 A Progressive Conservative Association had been formed in Quebec in early 1943 with Bona Arsenault as president, but when Bracken visited the province in the spring he attracted only faithful supporters of the party. He led a party with traditions that French Canadians were not prepared to support. See Bell to Bracken, 20 Jan. 1943, file speech material (S-800M), box 71, BP, PAC; and Roger Duhamel, 'En Compagnie de M. Bracken,' *Le Devoir*, 3 avril 1943. Also Bona Arsenault, *Malgré les Obstacles* (Québec nd), 78-81; and Marc La Terreur, *Les Tribulations des conservateurs au Québec de Bennett à Diefenbaker* (Québec 1973), chap. 5
35 For a more extensive discussion of the party's organizational difficulties see Granatstein, *Survival*, chap. 7.
36 Bell to Bracken, 24 Nov. 1943, private and confidential, copy, file Correspondence, Memoranda, etc. 1942-4, box 1, Bell Papers
37 By the end of 1943 Meighen was referring to Bracken as 'super cautious,' and he told Henry Borden that Borden had been right to suspect in December 1942 that Bracken would prove inadequate to the task of leadership. See Meighen to Bennett, 30 Dec. 1943, copy, 136442-4, vol. 214, Meighen Papers; and Borden interview, 22 April 1975.
38 For a trenchant analysis of Bracken's leadership and the dismal state of party organization see two undated and unsigned memoranda in box 136, BP, PAC.
39 For Halifax's speech see *Globe and Mail*, 25 Jan. 1944.
40 Quoted in Granatstein, *Survival*, 171
41 M.A. MacPherson to Bracken, 27 Jan. 1944, box 117, BP, PAC

42 Granatstein, *Survival*, 171
43 Meighen to Bracken, 17 Feb. 1944, and enclosure entitled 'Lord Halifax's Speech,' box 117, BP, PAC
44 Macdonnell to Bracken, 14 March 1944, file J.M. Macdonnell 1945-8, box 38, ibid.
45 Ibid.
46 See copy of press release, 18 April 1944, box 89, BP, PAC.
47 See Meighen to L. Hunt, 25 April 1944, quoted in Granatstein, *Survival*, 172. For press comment see *Toronto Star*, 18 and 19 April 1944; Toronto *Telegram* and the *Globe and Mail*, 18 April 1944.
48 Herridge sent Bracken many pamphlets and other material. See file W.D. Herridge, box 135, BP, PAC.
49 See 'A New National Policy,' 3 March 1944, in *John Bracken Says*, 90-107. Also 'Partnership for Labour and Teamwork in Industry,' 12 Feb. 1944, and 'A Charter of Rights for Youth,' 23 April 1944, ibid., 73-89 and 108-26. It was in his Ottawa speech that Bracken said he found 'a kernel of truth in Social Credit.' Their mistake had been to implement their policies in the wrong way.
50 Granatstein, *Survival*, 175
51 *Ottawa Journal*, 20 June 1944. There is a copy of McTague's speech in box 83, BP, PAC.
52 See a copy of this speech of 28 Feb. 1944 in box 67, ibid.
53 See 'Remarks by Hon. John Bracken at Guelph, June 19, 1944,' file Charles McTague, box 34, ibid.
54 See Granatstein, *Survival*, 178. Grant Dexter and Dick Bell both say that the pressure for acceptance of conscription as an issue came from Drew and his supporters and that Bracken was not convinced it was a good idea. See Bell interview, 13 Dec. 1974, and memorandum by Grant Dexter on 'Tory Party and Conscription,' 24 June 1944, file Conscription 1941-4, box 13, Grant Dexter Papers, Queen's University Archives.
55 Bell interview, 13 Dec. 1974
56 On 1 August Bracken and McTague met and drew up and signed a document that formally demarcated their policy and administrative responsibilities. With respect to overseas reinforcements the agreement read: 'Both understand that this policy is unpopular in the Province of Quebec but that in the interests of national unity it must be pushed energetically without regard to political consequences in Quebec.' See 'Memo of understanding made this 1st day of August 1944,' file Correspondence Personal and Confidential, 1942-8, box 141, BP, PAC. Granatstein and Hitsman suggest Bracken was responsible for the shift in policy. See J.L. Granatstein and J.M. Hitsman, *Broken*

Promises: A History of Conscription in Canada (Toronto 1977), 209

57 Copy of press release, 24 June 1944, box 89, BP, PAC. Bracken here seems dependent on Charlotte Whitton's ideas. See Whitton to Graydon, 15 June 1944, box 136, ibid.

58 Bruce's words. Bruce to Graydon, 20 July 1944, quoted in Granatstein, *Survival*, 169

59 For this crucial incident see Granatstein, *Survival*, 168-70; Henry Borden interview, 22 April 1975; Diefenbaker interview, 18 Feb. 1975; and Charlotte Whitton to Gordon Graydon, 16 June 1944, vol. 136, BP, PAC. Graydon was concerned by Whitton's ideas and Bracken's support of them. He asked H.H. Stevens to comment on a memorandum by her entitled 'Progressive Conservatives and the Public Welfare' that Bracken wanted the party to adopt. Stevens was critical. See vol. 162, H.H. Stevens Papers, PAC. It is possible Stevens' criticisms helped swing Bracken from his anti-position. See also Whitton's various memoranda, and Macdonnell to Bracken, 18 Dec. 1943, files Social Security and S-452, box 65, BP, PAC.

60 See particularly a column by H.R. Armstrong, 'Rebels May Not Provide Safe Seat for Bracken,' *Toronto Star*, 17 July 1944.

61 A copy of this speech is in box 89, BP, PAC. For the initial draft by John Collingwood Reade and Bracken's revisions see box 136, ibid.

62 The telegram was widely reprinted. See *Quebec Chronicle Telegraph*, 24 July 1944. For Arsenault's version of the incident see Bona Arsenault, *Malgré les Obstacles*, 82-94.

63 *Telegram*, 29 July 1944

64 In four articles in the *Winnipeg Free Press* in April Dexter had accused Bracken and the Progressive Conservative party of conspiracy with Duplessis' nationalistes to upset the Liberals in Quebec. He had little hard evidence except that the majority of the platform party at Bracken's February speech in Quebec City were known to be important supporters of Duplessis. See *Free Press*, 17-20 April 1944. The articles were reprinted by the *Toronto Star*, 29 April 1944.

65 For the problem of organization see undated memorandum, [R. Bell] 'Problem of Organization,' vol. I, Bell Papers.

66 See Colonel L. Baxter to McTague, 25 Sept. 1944, box 39, BP, PAC.

67 Hugh Mackay to Bracken, 21 Sept. 1944, box 44, ibid.

68 Stevens to Bell, 19 Oct. 1944, file S-7-G, reel M 1152, PC Party Headquarters Papers

69 For Bracken's 14 October speech see *Globe and Mail*, 16 Oct. 1944. For his 28 October speech at Ormstown, Quebec, see *Toronto Star*, 30 Oct. 1944. There is also a copy in box 89, BP, PAC.

70 Quoted in Granatstein, *Survival*, 179
71 See J.L. Granatstein, *Canada's War* (Toronto 1975), 352, fn 69.
72 For a full-scale treatment of the crisis see ibid., 338-74.
73 M.J. Coldwell was the federal leader of the CCF. See statements made by
   Bracken on 2, 6, and 9 November 1944, vol. 34, BP, PAC, and *Telegram*, 14
   Nov. 1944. Also Stevens to Bracken, 6 Nov. 1944, file Manpower 1944-5
   (Conscription), box 34, BP, PAC; 'Memorandum-Honourable Mr. Bracken' by
   Macdonnell, 7 Nov. 1944, vol. 49, ibid.; undated speech called 'Roots of
   National Disunity,' vol. 87, ibid.; and Earl Rowe to Bracken, 14 Nov. 1944,
   file Earl Rowe, box 37, ibid.
74 For Graydon see H of C, *Debates*, 27 Nov. 1944, 6622, and 7 Dec. 1944,
   6890; for Bracken see speech in Ottawa, 27 Nov. 1944, box 89, BP, PAC, and
   CBC address of 6 Dec. 1944, box 90, ibid.
75 Bell to Hanson, 27 Dec. 1944, 388-9, reel C3076, Hanson Papers. Also
   Hanson to Bell, 18 Dec. 1944, 387, ibid.
76 For Bracken's activities and summaries of his interviews see 'Diary-Overseas
   Tour' covering the period 25 Dec. 1944-28 Jan. 1945 kept by Mel Jack, box
   124, BP, PAC.
77 Earl Rowe interview, 23 Feb. 1975
78 See Ross Brown to Bell, 19 Jan. 1945, file Elections-Grey North, box 17,
   BP, PAC.
79 For the preparatory work and the various memoranda and drafts see ibid.
80 For Bracken's Owen Sound speech of 31 Jan. 1945 see box 90, ibid. Also
   Undated memoranda entitled 'Excerpts from Drew's Memorandum' and 'The
   plan suggested by Mr. C.P. McTague,' box 34, ibid.
81 See McNaughton's press statement of 31 Jan. 1945, copy, box 17, ibid.
82 See Geo. D., undated draft memorandum, box 66, ibid.
83 See press release of Bracken's Meaford speech, 1 Feb. 1945, ibid.
84 In his 2 March speech Bracken also called for a royal commission to investigate the incident, see press release of speech, box 90, ibid. See also Ray
   Milner to Bracken, 5 March 1945, and Bracken to Milner, 10 March 1945,
   file R. Milner, vol. 62, ibid.; Earl Rowe to Mel Jack, [nd], file Earl Rowe,
   vol. 37, ibid.; and Mel Jack to Earl Rowe, 10 April 1945, box 34, ibid. The
   Conservatives employed a man in Halifax to investigate the rifle incident.
   For his report see Bell to Bracken, 12 April 1945, ibid.
85 Rowe interview, 23 Feb. 1975
86 Mel Jack interview, 24 April 1975
87 Bracken spoke on the radio in Owen Sound on 2 February and at Clarksburg
   on 4 February. See box 66, BP, PAC, and the Toronto *Telegram*, 5 Feb. 1945.
88 See *Globe and Mail*, 4 Feb. 1945.
89 Granatstein, *Survival*, 190

90 H. Borden interview, 22 April 1975
91 For an analysis of the Progressive Conservative organization during the election see R. Bell, 'Memorandum for Mr. Bracken,' private and confidential, 9 June 1945, vol. 6, BP, PAC. For an excellent survey of the Progressive Conservative party's handling of the 1945 election and an analysis of its lack of success see chap. 8 in Granatstein's *Survival*.

CHAPTER 14: IN THE HOUSE

1 Bell elaborated on his difficulties and on the organizational changes that had been made in the party structure since the election in the draft of his 1946 speech to the annual party meeting, box 1, Bell Papers, PAC.
2 R.A. Bell, 'Memorandum for the Honourable John Bracken regarding the future of the Progressive Conservative Organization,' private and confidential, July 1945, ibid.
3 See Bracken to all members, 20 July 1945, vol. 83, BP, PAC. The committees were War, External Affairs, Dominion-Provincial Relations, Veterans' Affairs including Rehabilitation, Agriculture, Labour, Fiscal Policy including Taxation, Employment, Business, Development of Natural Resources, and Social Security. See also a memorandum, probably prepared in 1946, outlining the system and stating its value: 'Official Opposition Organization in House of Commons,' box 52, BP, PAC. See also Bell to Bracken, 23 July 1945, box 124, ibid., re private members bills.
4 Rowe to Jack, 23 July 1945, file Earl Rowe, box 37, BP, PAC
5 H of C, *Debates*, 10 Sept. 1945, 33
6 Ibid., 28
7 Ibid., 27 Sept. 1945, 521-8
8 Ibid., 13 Nov. 1945, 2072-7, and 5 Dec. 1945, 2986-9
9 See Bracken to Meighen, 15 Oct. 1945, personal, 137542, and Meighen to Bracken, 17 Oct. 1945, 137549-50, vol. 215, Meighen Papers, PAC.
10 J.M. Macdonnell to Bracken, 2 Jan. 1946, file Personal 1942-6, box 139, BP, PAC
11 See Dr J.W. Macleod to Bracken, 21 Jan. 1946, ibid.
12 Bell to Bracken, 26 Jan. 1946, private and confidential, enclosing 'Memorandum for Mr. Bracken,' ibid.
13 For advice and criticisms re Bracken's speaking see Ross Cameron to Dick Bell, Oct. 1945, file Parliamentary, box 124, ibid. In a supportive way, Dick Bell was one of Bracken's strongest critics. Some of his comments on Bracken speeches cut very close to the bone: 'too verbose,' 'too many admissions favourable to government,' 'not a sufficiently thorough going attack on gov-

ernment's past failures ... the denunciation should be sweeping and blunt.' Of
Bracken's speech on price control in the autumn of 1945 Bell commented:
'This may be alright for an Economics Journal – but too academic and theoretical – not to say verbose – for a political leader. When I finished reading
it, I had no idea where we stood on the subject. It seemed to me we had been
at both extremes and were trying to wriggle back into an uncomfortable
middle position. I see nothing in it that will gain us political support; I see
much that might lose us considerable support.' As for another proposed
speech on trade: 'I see no health in it. If it had been conceived with the idea
of antagonizing almost every section of our population, this document could
not have been more skillfully drafted. The historical introduction is futile ...
The balance is a tilting at explosive windmills.' For these comments see file
Speeches 1945, box 90, BP, PAC.

14 See undated 'notes to self re broadcasting technique' and [J.B.] 'Broadcasting,' 5 Dec. [nd], ibid.
15 Jack to Bracken, 28 Feb. 1946, box 51, ibid.
16 H of C, *Debates*, 15 March 1946, 24-40
17 H of C, *Debates* (1946) 3598-604, 3738-45, 3961ff, 4076-84, 4227-9,
4811-15, and 4821-5
18 Ibid., 1244-6, 1843-7, and 1852-5.
19 See Bell's draft of the 1946 speech to the party's annual meeting, box 1, Bell
Papers.
20 Macdonnell to Bracken, 14 Jan. 1946, file Personal 1942-6, box 139, BP, PAC
21 Bracken to J.O. Lateur, 6 March 1946, and Lateur to Bracken, 9 Feb. 1946,
file PC Party Quebec 1945-6, box 44, ibid.; also unsigned 'Memorandum for
Mr. Bell,' ibid.
22 Bracken to Sabourin, 16 April, 1946, ibid.
23 J.H. Bender to Macdonnell, 21 Nov. 1946, box 1, Macdonnell Papers, Queen's
University Archives
24 Bell to Bracken, 25 Nov. 1946, file Personal 1942-6, box 139, BP, PAC
25 See Bracken scrapbook, MG 13 I 4, BP, PAM; also Bracken to Macdonnell,
25 Nov. 1946, file Personal 1942-6, box 139, BP, PAC.
26 For his speech on the Address see H of C, *Debates*, 3 Feb. 1947, 36-55; for
the Wheat Board debate see 575-9; for old-age pensions, 4290-6 and 4702-
4718; and for tax agreements with the provinces 5319-23 and 5368-71. For
a typical Bracken speech on wheat see his radio speech of 11 March 1947
over CKRC, copy in box 95, BP, PAC.
27 See R.K. Finlayson, 'Memorandum for Mr. Bracken re Caucus Committees,'
20 Jan. 1947, file Caucus, box 83, ibid.
28 Hees to Bracken, 8 April 1947, file George Hees, box 135, BP, PAC

29 For reactions to and descriptions of Bracken's leadership see interviews with R.A. Bell, 13 Dec. 1974; Earl Rowe, 23 Feb. 1975; Stanley Knowles, 15 Dec. 1974; John Diefenbaker, 18 Feb. 1975; Henry Borden, 22 April 1975; Mel Jack, 24 April 1975; John Charlton, 19 April 1975; Douglas Harkness, 7 June 1975; H.O. White, 18 April 1975; H.R. Jackman, 22 April 1975; and L.W. Skey, 22 April 1975. Also Donald Fleming to author, 24 Sept. 1975

30 Bracken had been provided with a background memorandum by Donald Fleming. See Fleming to Bracken, 'Re Halifax By-election' [nd], box 44, BP, PAC.

31 On the latter see particularly D.M. Hogarth to Bracken, 6 Aug. 1947, and Bracken to Hogarth, 7 Aug. 1947, box 135, ibid.

32 Rowe to Bracken, 2 Sept. 1947, box 124, ibid.

33 Fulton to Bracken, 15 Oct. 1947, ibid.

34 R.A.B., 'Confidential Memorandum' [nd], file Correspondence Personal and Confidential 1942-8, box 141, ibid.

35 See *Free Press*, 27 Nov. 1947.

36 *Printed Word*, Dec. 1947, No 157

37 See statement by Bracken issued 5 Dec. 1947, box 97, BP, PAC. For *Free Press* comment see issue of 12 December 1947.

38 Fulton to Bracken, 19 Dec. 1947, box 37, BP, PAC

39 See a speech on CBC, 22 Jan. 1948, vol. 97, BP, PAC. For Bracken's reply to the Address see H of C, *Debates*, 1948, vol. I, 47-60. For his comments on the cost of living see vol. I, 751-61. For his comments on communism see vol. III, 2303-7, also Bracken to Major T.A. Aisthorpe, 20 Feb. 1948, file Miscellaneous 'A,' box 25, BP, PAC. Also 'Today's Challenge' by Bracken, 20 April 1948, his speech to the PC Assoc. annual dinner, copy, vol. 98, BP, PAC. In the latter he does attempt to be specific on policy. Also Bracken, 'Report from Parliament Hill,' 3 May 1948, CKRC broadcast, ibid.

40 See Maybank Diary, 19 March 1948, file 138 Politics and Correspondence 1948, Maybank Papers, PAM.

41 See R.A. Bell, 'Report of National Director to the Annual Meeting of P.C. Assoc. of Canada – April 19, 1948,' box 1, Bell Papers. Apparently there was a move at the annual association meeting to have the leadership changed but this did not become well organized. See H.O. Wright to Bracken, 19 May 1948, box 127, BP, PAC.

42 Miller to Bracken, 7 May 1948, file Correspondence Personal and Confidential 1942-8, box 141, ibid. Also R.D. Guy to Bracken, 14 May 1948, ibid.

43 J.P. Wadge to Bracken, 26 Oct. 1947, file BC, box 110, ibid.

44 See R.W. Craig to Stuart Garson, 15 Aug. 1948, series MG 13 J 1, Garson Papers, PAM. For a typical Bracken speech see the script of his radio broadcast of 26 May 1948, box 98, BP, PAC.

45 Bennett to Bracken, 12 June 1948, and Bracken to Bennett, 21 June 1948, box 48, ibid.
46 Bell interview, 13 Dec. 1974
47 See Maybank Diary, 2 July 1948, file 138, Maybank Papers
48 For the information in the previous three paragraphs see Bell Interview, 13 Dec. 1974.
49 Bracken to Macdonnell, 17 July 1948, file Correspondence Personal, Sept.-Dec. 1948, box 139, BP, PAC
50 Macdonnell to Bracken, 19 July [1948], Scrapbook 1947-62, MG 13 I 4, BP, PAM
51 Macdonnell to Bracken, 20 July [1948], file Correspondence Personal 1948-52, box 140, BP, PAC
52 Box 104, BP, PAC, contains most of the newspaper articles written after Bracken's resignation.
53 See Bracken's speech, 30 Sept. 1948, box 98, ibid.
54 See H of C, *Debates*, 1949, vol. III, 1963-5, 1993-2003, and 2781-4.
55 Bracken to Graydon, 20 July 1949, file Correspondence Personal 1948-9, box 140, BP, PAC. Also Bracken to Douglas Campbell, 20 Aug. 1949, and Campbell to Bracken, 28 June 1949, ibid.

CHAPTER 15: RETIREMENT

1 For the purchase and renovations see G.B. Curran, 'John Bracken Buys a Farm,' *Canadian Countryman* (March 1946), and Mary Jukes, 'Renovation turned THAT into THIS,' *Canadian Homes and Gardens* (Dec. 1946). Also Gwen Herbst, 'Progressive Conservative Party Leader Takes Over 200 acres at Manotick,' *Ottawa Journal*, 13 Sept. 1944; and an article by Helen Allen in the *Evening Telegram* (Toronto), 28 Aug. 1948, on Bracken's move to Manotick.
2 See Bracken to Art Pearson, 3 Sept. 1950, file Irrigation, box 119, BP, PAC.
3 See also Bracken to George, 6 Feb. 1954, file Correspondence Personal and Confidential 1952-4, box 141, BP, PAC.
4 See 'Memorandum of Agreement between John Bracken and Clarke Mansfield,' box 142, ibid. In 1952 Mansfield terminated the agreement. See above file for the relevant correspondence; also interview with Clarke Mansfield, 12 June 1976.
5 Bracken to Graydon, 28 Aug. 1953, file Correspondence Personal and Confidential 1952-4, box 141, BP, PAC
6 For the gradual demise of the company see the correspondence in the three E.L.R.W. files in box 144, BP, PAC.
7 For the details of Bracken's land-holding, his loans, and his personal assets

see the following files: Correspondence Personal; Finance-Personal 1944-8; Income tax 1948; and L.D. McNeill, all in box 142; and file LD. McNeill, box 143, ibid. Locksley McNeill, Bracken's secretary from 1935-43, looked after Bracken's farm and financial interests in Manitoba after Bracken's departure for Ottawa.

8 See interviews with Locksley McNeill, Dick Bell, Mel Jack, and Earl Rowe.
9 Bracken to Williamson, 29 Nov. 1952, file E.L.R.W., Personal, box 144, BP, PAC
10 Interview with Douglas Campbell, 19 Oct. 1976
11 The other members of the commission were Maj.-Gen. Harold Riley, Dr Paul L'Heureux, Mrs Jean Whiteford, and Mr Clifford McCrae. Two valuable advisers were Professor Ruben Bellan of the University of Manitoba and Professor R.N. Hallstead of United College, Winnipeg.
12 See *Report of the Liquor Enquiry Commission* (Winnipeg 1955). For the commission's working files see MG 20 B 5, PAM.
13 Bracken to R.D. Guy, 17 Dec. 1956, file Correspondence Personal 1950-60, box 140, BP, PAC
14 *Report on Box Car Distribution*, vol. I, *Proceedings*, 9, box 145, BP, PAC
15 Ibid., 12
16 Ibid., 15
17 The draft report is in box 148, ibid.
18 See box 143, ibid.
19 Bracken to Shebiski, 18 April 1967, file Correspondence Personal 1964-8, box 141, ibid.

A note on sources

The framework for this biography has been provided by the Bracken Papers housed in the Provincial Archives of Manitoba and the Public Archives of Canada. Although they contain little personal material and a disappointingly small number of politically related letters and memoranda by Bracken, the two collections do give an insight into Bracken's major preoccupations and his style of government, and the book could not have been written without reference to them.

There are four series in the Bracken material at the Provincial Archives of Manitoba. Series MG 13 I 1 (4 boxes) contains Bracken's small pocket diaries for the years 1924-33 and 1937-40, drafts of many of his speeches, and correspondence related to coalition negotiations. Series MG 13 I 2 (160 boxes) contains the Premier's Office Papers for the period 1924-39 and has been extensively used for the chapters on resource development and financial negotiations. Series MG 13 I 3 contains a two-page transcript of an interview with Bracken conducted by Hartwell Bowsfield on 21 October 1966. Series MG 13 I 4 (8 boxes) has a number of valuable clipping books covering various facets of Bracken's career at Guelph, Winnipeg, and Ottawa. There are also copies of speeches from throughout his career and a copy of a revealing letter written by Mrs Bracken to her sons shortly after John had accepted the leadership of the Progressive Conservative party in December 1942.

The Bracken collection at the Public Archives of Canada (MG 27 III C 16) contains over 160 boxes of material related to Bracken's years as leader of the Progressive Conservative party and to his activities in retirement. Although there is some valuable and informative incoming correspondence and revealing internal party memoranda, the collection is essentially disappointing because it contains very little by Bracken himself. One can get a general sense of Bracken's style and of his major interests but the existing evidence makes it impossible to establish clearly either the degree of Bracken's involvement in certain critical policy decisions or the nature of his thoughts throughout that difficult period in his and the Progressive Conservative party's life.

This biography would have been difficult to complete if one had had to rely solely on the Bracken Papers and evidence gleaned from the *Winnipeg Free Press* and the Winnipeg *Tribune*. Fortunately, historians of twentieth-century Canada can turn to a wide range of private and public sources. In particular, no adequate account of the protracted coalition negotiations in Manitoba of 1926-32 or of the complex financial problems facing the province during the thirties could have been provided without heavy dependence on the King and Bennett Papers. These two collections, the former already much used and the latter surprisingly rich although badly organized, have been indispensable in the preparation of this book. Similarly, the chapter dealing with Bracken's years in scientific agriculture depends heavily on the excellent private and government material in the Saskatchewan Provincial Archives and in the Archives of the University of Saskatchewan. As the biographer of a Manitoba politician, I can only envy the extensive collection of private papers available to the historian of Saskatchewan. I have also used or consulted a number of other collections and, although not all of them are extensively cited, each one has provided background material and a general 'feel' for an issue that would otherwise have been missed.

A complete list of the collections, interviews, research papers, theses, newspapers, and periodicals used in preparing this book follows. Relevant books and articles are referred to in footnotes.

MANUSCRIPTS

PUBLIC ARCHIVES OF CANADA

Bell, R.A.
Bennett, Richard Bedford
Bracken, John
Cameron, A.K.
CCF Papers
Finlayson, R.K.
Graydon, Gordon
Hanson, Richard B.
Hudson, A.B.
King, William Lyon Mackenzie
Meighen, Arthur
Progressive Conservative Party Headquarters Papers
Stevens, H.H.

PROVINCIAL ARCHIVES OF MANITOBA

Bracken, John
Clubb, William
Garson, Stuart
Healy, W.J.
Historical and Scientific Society of Manitoba (interviews by Lionel Orlikow in
    1961)
Manning, R.A.C.
Maybank, Ralph
Norris, T.C.
Poole, A.J.M.
United Farmers of Manitoba
Winkler, Howard

SASKATCHEWAN ARCHIVES BOARD (SASKATOON)

Auld, F.A.
Calder, J.A.
Dunning, C.A.
Martin, W.M.
Motherwell, W.R.
Scott, Walter

QUEEN'S UNIVERSITY ARCHIVES

Chipman, George
Crerar, T.A.
Dexter, Grant
Dunning, C.A.
Lambert, Norman
Macdonnell, J.M.
Mackintosh, W.A.
Power, C.G.

UNIVERSITY OF MANITOBA LIBRARY

Dafoe, John (microfilm)
Sifton, Clifford (microfilm)

UNIVERSITY OF SASKATCHEWAN ARCHIVES

Agenda for Governors' Meetings
Agricultural Minutes
College of Agriculture Correspondence
General Correspondence
Minutes of the Board of Governors
Minutes of Council
Murray, W.C.
Presidential Papers

GOVERNMENT RECORDS

PROVINCIAL ARCHIVES OF MANITOBA

Manitoba Liquor Enquiry Commission (RG 20 B 5)

SASKATCHEWAN ARCHIVES BOARD (REGINA)

Agricultural Societies Papers
Deputy Ministers (Agriculture)
Department of Agriculture

SASKATCHEWAN ARCHIVES BOARD (SASKATOON)

Department of Education
Department of Agriculture
Homestead Records, Department of the Interior, Land Patents Office

PUBLISHED RECORDS

Annual Report of the Department of Agriculture of Ontario (1903-6)
Annual Report of the Saskatchewan Department of Agriculture (1906-20)
Canada, Parliament, *Sessional Papers*
Canada, House of Commons, *Debates*
Report of the Seed Commissioner for the period from January 1905 to March 1911. Department of Agriculture (Ottawa 1911)

INTERVIEWS AND LETTERS

Bona Arsenault (letter to the author, 8 April 1977)
Dick Bell (Ottawa, 13 Dec. 1974)
Henry Borden (Toronto, 22 April 1975)
Bruce and Doug Bracken (Winnipeg, 22 Jan. 1973)
Dr Frank Bracken (Winnipeg, 19 Aug. 1973)
George Bracken – cousin (Ellisville, 1 Aug. 1972)
George M. Bracken – son (Manotick, 23 June 1973)
Bill Buchanan (Ottawa, 24 April 1975)
Douglas Campbell (Winnipeg, 4 Feb. 1973, 19 Oct. 1976, and 5 Dec. 1977)
John Charlton (Paris, Ontario, 19 April 1975)
Jean Curtis (Winnipeg, 27 Feb. 1973)
John Diefenbaker (Ottawa, 18 Feb. 1975)
Professor L.H. Ellis (Winnipeg, 5 March 1973)
Donald Fleming (letter to the author, 24 Sept. 1975)
Douglas Harkness (Calgary, 7 June 1975)
Mel Jack (Ottawa, 24 April 1975)
H.R. Jackman (Toronto, 22 April 1975)
Stanley Knowles (Ottawa, 15 Dec. 1974)
Miss E. Lasiuk (Winnipeg, 18 Jan. 1975)
Victor Mackie (Ottawa, 24 April 1975)
Clarke Mansfield (Ottawa, 12 June 1976)
Locksley McNeill (Winnipeg, 1 March 1973, 29 May 1975, and 28 May 1977)
Dr Jean Murray (Saskatoon, 18 Dec. 1972)
J.W. Pickersgill (Ottawa, 20 June 1973, interviewer: Don A. Wicks)
Earl Rowe (Newton Robinson, 23 Feb. 1975)
Professor Shanks (Winnipeg, 7 March 1973)
Professor L.H. Shebiski (Winnipeg, 2 Feb. 1973)
L.W. Skey (Toronto, 22 April 1975)
Ralph Stanton (Seeley's Bay, 3 June 1973)
Lloyd Stinson (Victoria, 19 Feb. 1974)
Judge Roy St George Stubbs (Winnipeg, 28 Oct. 1976)
J.T. Thorson (Ottawa, 21 June 1973)
H.O. White (Glanworth, 18 April 1975)
Gladys Wilson (Portland, Oregon, 18 Feb. 1974)

NEWSPAPERS AND PERIODICALS

The Brockville Times

The Canadian Annual Review
The Financial Post
The Grain Growers' Guide
The Guelph Daily Mercury
The Guelph Weekly Mercury
Manitoba/Winnipeg Free Press
The Monetary Times
The Morning Leader (Regina)
The Northern Mail
The O.A.C. Review
The Pas Herald and Mining News
The Public Service Monthly (Regina)
The Saskatoon Star Phoenix
The Sheaf (University of Saskatchewan)
Tribune (Winnipeg)

UNPUBLISHED THESES AND RESEARCH PAPERS

Dick, Lyle, 'The 1936 Provincial Election in Manitoba. An Analysis' (Honours research paper, University of Manitoba, 1975)

de Beer, Dan, 'The Flin Flon Strike 1934' (Graduate research paper, University of Manitoba, 1973)

Grover, Richard, 'The 1927 Manitoba Provincial Election' (Honours research paper, University of Manitoba, 1970)

Hunter, B.F.C., 'The Development of New Manitoba 1912-1930' (MA thesis, University of Western Ontario, 1973)

Ingram, John D., 'Manitoba and the "Natural Resources Question" 1870-1930' (Graduate research paper, University of Manitoba, 1974)

Levin, Benjy, 'The Seven Sisters Affair' (Honours research paper, University of Manitoba, 1972)

McKillop, A. Brian, 'Citizen and Socialist: The Ethos of Political Winnipeg, 1919-1935' (MA thesis, University of Manitoba, 1970)

Panting, Gerald E., 'A Study of the United Farmers of Manitoba to 1928' (MA thesis, University of Manitoba, 1954)

Rosenstock, S., 'The 1934 Flin Flon Strike' (Graduate research paper, University of Manitoba, 1974)

Thompson, John, 'The Prohibition Question in Manitoba 1892-1928' (MA thesis, University of Manitoba, 1969)

Thompson, John, 'The Harvests of War: The Prairie West 1914-1918' (PHD thesis, Queen's University, 1975)

Turenne, Roger E., 'The Minority and the Ballot Box: A Study of the Voting Behaviour of the French Canadians of Manitoba 1888-1967' (MA thesis, University of Manitoba, 1969)

Unger, Gordon, 'James G. Gardiner: The Premier as a Pragmatic Politician 1926-1929' (MA thesis, University of Saskatchewan, 1967)

Wiseman, Nelson, 'A Political History of the Manitoba CCF-NDP' (PHD thesis, University of Toronto, 1975)

Index